THE
SONGS AND SONETS
OF
JOHN DONNE

SONGS AND SONETS
OF
JOHN DONNE

SECOND EDITION

EDITED BY
THEODORE REDPATH

ST. MARTIN'S PRESS · NEW YORK

First published in 1956 by
Methuen and Co. Ltd
11 New Fetter Lane, London EC4P 4EE

Second Edition 1983

ISBN 0–312–74490–0

Library of Congress Cataloging in Publication Data

Donne, John, 1572–1631.
The songs and sonets of John Donne.

Bibliography: p.

Includes index.
I. Redpath, Theodore.   II. Title.
PR2246.   R32   1982   821.' 3   82–10612
ISBN 0–312–74490–0

CONTENTS

v

Contents

Contents

LIST OF ABBREVIATIONS

Editions

EARLY EDITIONS

1633, 1635, 1639, 1650, 1654, 1669, 1719.
Contractions: 1633–69 = all editions from *1633* to *1669* inclusive, and so
for other such cases, whilst *1633–1719* = all early editions.

MODERN EDITIONS

Chambers	*The Poems of John Donne*, ed. E. K. Chambers, 2 vols, London, 1896.
Gardner (cited in textual apparatus as *Gar* and in commentary as *ESS*)	*John Donne: The Elegies and the Songs and Sonnets*, ed. Helen Gardner, Oxford, 1965.
Grierson (cited as *Gr*)	*The Poems of John Donne*, ed. H. J. C. Grierson, 2 vols, Oxford, 1912.
Hayward (cited in textual apparatus as *Hayward* and in commentary as Nonesuch Donne)	*John Donne: Complete Poetry and Selected Prose*, ed. John Hayward, London, 1929.
Norton	*The Poems of John Donne*, ed. C. E. Norton, New York, 1895.
Redpath (cited as *Ed. (1956)*)	*The Songs and Sonets of John Donne*, ed. Theodore Redpath, London, 1956.
Smith	*John Donne: The Complete English Poems*, ed. A. J. Smith, Harmondsworth, 1971.

MS sigla

(a) MSS CONTAINING COLLECTIONS OF DONNE'S POEMS

GROUP I

H49	British Library, Harleian MS 4955
D	Dowden MS, Bodleian Library, MS Eng.Poet. e 99
SP	St Paul's Cathedral Library, MS 49 B 43
Lec	Leconfield MS (in the library of Sir Geoffrey Keynes)
C57	Cambridge University Library, Add. MS 5778

Closely associated with Group I

H40	British Library, Harleian MS 4064

GROUP II

TCC[1]	Trinity College, Cambridge, MS R 3 12
A18	British Library, Add. MS 18647
TCD[1]	Trinity College, Dublin, MS G 2 21
N	Norton MS, Harvard College Library, MS Eng. 966/3

Closely associated with Group II

L74	British Library, Lansdowne MS 740

Manuscripts generally associated with Groups I and II

Wed	Wedderburn MS, National Library of Scotland, MS 6504
DC	Dolau Cothi MS, National Library of Wales (closer to Group II than to Group I)

GROUP III

S96	British Library, Stowe, MS 961
Dob	Dobell MS, Harvard College Library, MS Eng.966/4
Lut	Luttrell MS (in the library of Sir Geoffrey Keynes)
O'F	O'Flaherty MS, Harvard College Library, MS Eng.966/5

GROUP IV

W	Westmoreland MS, Berg Collection, New York Public Library

[1] *TC*. Grierson used the siglum *TC* for *TCC* and *TCD* reading together. I follow his practice.

CATEGORY V

HK2	Haslewood-Kingsborough MS (2nd part), Huntington Library, MS HM198
Cy	Carnaby MS, Harvard College Library, MS Eng.966/1
P	Phillipps MS, Bodleian Library, MS Eng.Poet. f 9
A25	British Library, Add. MS 25707
D17	Victoria and Albert Museum, Dyce Collection, MS D25 F17
B	Bridgewater MS, Huntington Library, MS EL 6893
S	Stephens MS, Harvard College Library, MS Eng.966/6

(b) MS MISCELLANIES CONTAINING POEMS BY DONNE

H40[1]	British Library, Harleian MS 4064
RP31	Rawlinson Poetical MS 31, Bodleian Library
S962	British Library, Stowe MS 962

Note: I have not collated for this edition the following manuscripts collated by Professor Gardner for *ESS*:

O	Osborn MS (in the library of Mr James Osborn, Yale University);
JC	John Cave MS, George Arents Tobacco Collection, New York Public Library (*D17*, which I have collated, is, however, a duplicate of *JC*);
K	King MS (in the library of Mr James Osborn, Yale University). This MS is described by Professor Gardner as having the worst text which she had encountered.

I have, on the other hand, collated one of the most important of the miscellanies, *S962* (see above), which contains 49 of the *Songs and Sonets*.

In the critical apparatus the original spellings of MSS are indicated in all cases where they could possibly be of editorial significance; otherwise the modern spelling is given. To indicate all MS spellings would not only have expanded the already ample apparatus to gigantic proportions, but also have choked it into utter confusion.

Periodicals

Crit.Q.	*Critical Quarterly*
EC	*Essays in Criticism*

---

[1] I follow Professor Gardner in adopting this siglum for the miscellany, and *H40* for the collection of Donne's poems.

List of abbreviations

ELH	*Journal of English Literary History*
ES	*Essays and Studies by Members of* (later 'collected for') *The English Association*
Et.Angl.	*Études Anglaises*
JEGP	*Journal of English and Germanic Philology*
JHI	*Journal of the History of Ideas*
Ken.R.	*Kenyon Review*
MLN	*Modern Language Notes*
MLR	*Modern Language Review*
MP	*Modern Philology*
N&Q	*Notes and Queries*
Part.R.	*Partisan Review*
PMLA	*Publications of the Modern Language Association of America*
PQ	*Philological Quarterly*
REL	*Review of English Literature*
RES	*Review of English Studies*
RLC	*Revue de Littérature Comparée*
RLMC	*Rivista di Letterature Moderne e Comparate*
Sew.R.	*Sewanee Review*
SP	*Studies in Philology*
TLS	*The Times Literary Supplement*

PREFACE TO THE
FIRST EDITION

The present volume has a twofold origin. It arises partly out of my academic work and partly out of a personal experience.

In the course of supervising Cambridge undergraduates for honours degrees in English, I have become convinced that they require an edition of Donne's *Songs and Sonets*, containing notes on every point likely to cause difficulty to a reader of reasonable intelligence. Such an edition has not previously appeared, nor do the notes in any edition of the Poetical Works, or in any selection, hitherto published, fulfil this requirement. Even the notes in Professor Grierson's epoch-making edition of Donne's Poetical Works do not meet the precise case, quite apart from the bulk of those volumes, and the expense of purchasing them. Professor Grierson's purpose was clearly quite different from the present purpose, for which a far greater *number* of notes are required than appear in his edition; but for which, on the other hand, many of his notes are fuller than is necessary.

The other source of the present volume was the visit to Cambridge a few winters ago of a friend of the family, to whom Donne was hitherto entirely unknown, and to whom I read some of the *Songs and Sonets*, by way of a friendly exchange for having some Spanish and German poems read to me. Our friend was enchanted with the *Songs and Sonets*, but often only after considerable explanation. This made me think that there was probably a place for an edition for the general reader, which would bring these remarkable poems to readers both in England and abroad, neither merely as a sometimes exasperatingly obscure plain text, nor as part of a bulky specialist volume or series of volumes.

It seemed to me on further consideration that my university purpose and this more general purpose could be combined, at the comparatively small cost of probably irritating some readers by including notes on points which they might regard as obvious, and of perplexing others (and perhaps some of the same readers) by including certain references to variant readings, which might at first sight be thought to be of interest only to scholars. On the former point I have been considerably influenced by the revelations of that unique book, *Practical Criticism* by Professor I. A. Richards, which makes it amply clear that even considerable numbers of English students of poetry, at universities where the standard of education is certainly high, make elementary blunders in disentangling even the literal sense of poetry less elusive than much to be found in the *Songs and Sonets*. With regard to variants, I have found, in the course of reading Donne with students, that, in many cases, a consideration of variants has strikingly sharpened our impression of the passages concerned.

A great problem for me has been to what lengths I should go in interpretation; what amount of interpretation I should, in this particular case, take editing to involve. In the end I have adhered to the practice of not attempting full interpretations of the poems, and contented myself with hinting, in a few particularly interesting cases, at a full realization of the poems concerned. The edition therefore leaves readers plenty of scope for interpretation of the poems, though, on the other hand, I should hold that interpretations which contradict undoubted meanings, such as many of those to which attention has been drawn in these notes, must of necessity be wrong. Again, even on particular points, I have preferred to err, if at all, by not indulging in a chase for ambiguities and recherché interpretations; not because I dislike ingenuity, but because I have here set myself only the more modest task of clearing the ground.

In compiling the notes I have drawn, where I thought it advisable, on the work of previous editors, my obligations to whom are acknowledged in the appropriate places. My greatest debt is to the work of Professor Sir Herbert Grierson, without which so many of us might well have known little of Donne. Professor Grierson's notes, which have thrown light on so many dark places, need no praise of mine: but, as a subsequent editor, I owe my gratitude to them. Where I have differed from Grierson, either on interpretation or on the text, it has always been with a sense of respect.

In addition to writing the notes, I have also completely revised the text, largely on the basis of the variants noted by Grierson,[1] but also taking account of certain of the manuscript evidence which has come to light since his great edition was published. My revision of the text has

---

[1] The present edition therefore makes no pretensions to being textually an *editio major*; though I have re-examined a number of the MSS.

not resulted in much departure from Grierson's. With respect to the canon I have followed him completely. With regard to the text of individual poems I have departed from him on occasion. Wherever I have done so, on any point of sufficient importance, I have explained my reasons for doing so, in the notes. I had originally intended adding textual notes, to cover *all* my departures from Grierson's text, but after taking Sir Herbert's own opinion on the point, I have decided not to burden the work with a large critical apparatus.

Except where there was some very special reason for not doing so, I have everywhere modernized the spelling. To the bibliopurist this may appear a retrograde step, but for my present purpose, where an understanding of the poems is the paramount object, any quaintness of impression, so easily produced by the sight of Elizabethan or Jacobean spelling, is to be carefully avoided. A minor problem arising from this, has been whether to retain initial capitals. I have decided only to retain these where to do so seems to contribute to an understanding of the poem, despite the somewhat unfamiliar impression they are likely to make.

The matter of punctuation has been fascinating, but at times almost unendurably teasing. Professor Grierson's purpose and my own are quite distinct on this point. Grierson was concerned to establish an accurate text, in the old spelling, and in a punctuation which would probably have been Donne's, had the poet himself revised the text of his poems for the press. My own purpose, on the other hand, has been to produce a text in modern spelling, and in a punctuation designed to aid in bringing out to a modern reader (whether a silent reader or a reader reading aloud), the full meaning of the poem concerned. I have found, as I have gone through the poems, that the Elizabethan, Jacobean or Caroline punctuation often does this, but sometimes has the opposite effect. I have in every case tested the point by my general principle, and adopted the punctuation which passed the test. The variations of punctuation from Grierson's text, with a defence of my departures where these seemed of sufficient importance, would have appeared in the textual notes, but since I have decided to dispense with textual notes, I have included the most important cases in the general notes. With regard to the old editions, one common case of difference between my text and that of the 1633 edition (to take the most important edition) is in the matter of commas. Very often, admittedly, the comma at the end of a line in the 1633 edition, where we might expect a semicolon, is correct, even according to my principle, since it expresses a hurrying-on of the sense, which is typical of Donne. Sometimes, on the other hand, no such hurrying-on seems to occur, and yet there is a mere comma in the 1633 edition. In such cases, it has seemed to me, the explanation is probably that the comma had different limits of value in sixteenth- and seventeenth-century English from those which it has today, and I have therefore often used a semicolon in such cases, or even, where a still longer stop seemed to be required, a full colon. I hope that those who, in my view, are too puristically inclined on this point, will give due weight to the consideration that a poem does not maintain its life constantly in any one set of marks on paper, but that at different periods the same poem, with all its subtlety of intonation, may be correctly represented by different sets of signs, and, in particular, by different marks of punctuation: that, in the present case, what one must try to be faithful to, when producing a modern text, is Donne's finesse, passion, argumentary evolution, and rhythmic spirit, and that, *where one has to choose*, it is far worse to be unfaithful to these than to a mere system of signs, which often exhibits nothing but a creaking antiquity without any of its original functional life. Those who may feel inclined to object to the policy I have adopted may cease to do so if they bear in mind the ascertainable fact that the punctuation of even the best extant manuscripts is often very different from that of the early printed editions, and so realize the possibility that those editions may often owe their punctuation to editors or printers and not to Donne's own intentions.

It is appropriate to end this Preface by expressing acknowledgement for help received. My first debt of gratitude is to Professor Sir Herbert Grierson himself, who very kindly read through most of my typescript at an early stage, and discussed doubtful points with me at some length on several occasions. On points of detail he has made a number of highly useful suggestions, and he has also given me the benefit of his wise advice on matters of policy. I was indeed fortunate to have guidance from one who is, in this realm, so obviously *facile princeps*. My second obligation is to Professor Basil Willey, Fellow of Pembroke College, and King Edward VII Professor of English Literature in the University of Cambridge, for his encouragement, advice and help to me soon after I had set out on this project. Two of my most recent debts are to Mr F. L. Lucas, Fellow of King's College, and Reader in English in the University of Cambridge, and Mr T. R. Henn, Fellow and Senior Tutor of St Catharine's College, and Lecturer in English in the University of Cambridge, who have given their valuable time in reading through my typescript in its almost final form, and made most useful criticisms and suggestions. I owe thanks also to Sir Geoffrey Keynes for kindly letting me work on the Leconfield and Luttrell manuscripts: and similar thanks to the Rev. W. M. Atkins, Librarian of St Paul's Cathedral Library, for permission to work on the St Paul's manuscript. Finally, I wish to say how grateful I am to Mr W. G. Ingram, Lecturer in Education in the University of Cambridge, whose immense help, throughout the period of proof-reading and final revision, has greatly benefited the edition, and has made this last stage not only bearable but enjoyable.

Trinity College
Cambridge
June 1955

THEODORE REDPATH

NOTE ON THE
SECOND IMPRESSION

I have been asked to confine changes to a minimum, and those made are
therefore mainly verbal. There are, however, a few alterations and
additions of substance. I have benefited from the recent publication of
Sir Geoffrey Keynes's *Bibliography of Dr John Donne*, Cambridge, 1958.
A few changes are also due to a reading of Professor Pierre Legouis's
edition of Selected Poems of Donne (*Poèmes choisis*, Traduction, intro-
duction et notes par P. Legouis, Paris, n.d [1955]), and of his article
'Donne, l'amour et les critiques', *Études anglaises*, avril-juin, 1957.
Some interesting textual suggestions by Mr John Sparrow (*TLS*, 21
December 1956) have prompted two notes. I also am indebted to Mr
G. P. Simons, of the University College of North Staffordshire, for
drawing my attention to a possible biblical reference in l. 24 of *The
Curse*.

In the above-mentioned letter Mr Sparrow also urges that the canon
of the *Songs and Sonets* should include *Elegy X: The Dream*. He rightly
indicates that this poem has a quite different rhyme-scheme from all the
other Elegies, which are in rhymed couplets. He also points out that the
transfer would have the authority of one group of MSS. Mr Sparrow's
case seems to me strong; and had I not to restrict changes to a minimum
I should have printed the poem with notes. This would, however, have
involved many consequential changes, and I must therefore postpone
doing so.

January 1959   T.R.

PREFACE TO THE
SECOND EDITION

This edition is more ambitious than my edition of 1956. I have consulted far more manuscripts, and am offering a fairly full, though perforce selective, *apparatus criticus*. I am therefore dropping the technical term *Editio minor* from the description of the book. The variants I have recorded are most often such as have some claims to be considered reasonable readings; but I have also at times recorded readings which may be of interest to specialists curious about relations between manuscripts. I have also, while recognizing the superior authority of the 1633 edition over all other early editions, often recorded their readings also.

With regard to the text itself, I have made a number of revisions. The text presented is, however, still a text in modern spelling, and punctuated in a way designed to bring out the full meanings of the poems to a modern reader. I hold by the principles stated in the Preface to my first edition (1956). In that Preface I indicated that the punctuation of even the best extant manuscripts of the *Songs and Sonets* (none of which is an autograph manuscript) is often very different from that of any of the early editions, so that the punctuation in those editions may well owe more to editors or printers than to Donne's own intentions. The unique discovery in 1970, by Mr P. J. Croft of Sotheby's, of Donne's own draft of one of his English poems (a verse-letter) affords further interesting evidence. As Professor A. J. Smith pointed out (*TLS*, 7 January 1972, p. 19), the 1633 edition differs in over forty instances from Donne's own punctuation of the poem. The same discovery, however, also encourages a certain scepticism in regard to the extant manuscripts which have been used to correct in certain instances the text of the 1633 edition of Donne's poems. As Professor Smith also indicated, none of the early manuscripts or editions offers the same text of the poem concerned as Donne's own manuscript, and some of the most highly regarded manuscripts contain the least accurate texts.

This should not, however, cause us to lose all faith in the manuscripts, or, indeed, in the early editions. Those manuscripts and editions are, after all, all we have at present for establishing a text of any of Donne's English poems except that particular verse-letter. Moreover, the policy adopted by Grierson of using the 1633 edition as the basis of the text, and correcting it where advisable from the manuscripts, is still clearly the best we can follow. If further autograph manuscripts of the poems should come to light, we would need to think again. In the meanwhile, with regard to the particular matter of punctuation, we do not need to nurse a reverence for the punctuation of any of the early editions or of the copied manuscripts as if it were Donne's own. I would, however, go further. Even Donne's own punctuation would not, in certain instances, be the best punctuation to adopt in a modern edition, since it is evident that the system of punctuation has changed since his day and that his poem might often come out more effectively to a modern reader if punctuated in a modern way.

To turn to the matter of canon. In my 1956 edition I included all the poems which Grierson printed among the *Songs and Sonets* in his 1912 edition, and none which he did not. In the present edition I have omitted two poems not certainly by Donne, *Sonnet: The Token* and [*Self-Love*]; but I have included the poem which Grierson, following the early editions, printed among the *Elegies*, as *Elegy X: The Dream*. Mr John Sparrow (as he then was) suggested in a letter to the *TLS*, 21 December 1956, that this poem belongs rather to the *Songs and Sonets*, and Professor Gardner has since included it among them with the suggested title [*Image and Dream*]. Since I tentatively favour a different interpretation of the poem I have equally tentatively suggested the title [*Picture and Dream*].

The order of the poems in this edition differs from that I adopted in 1956. Then I followed the order adopted by Grierson, which was that of the editions of 1635 onwards with certain modifications. Modern readers often find that order rather bewildering. In the present edition I have, in general, adopted an order corresponding to the moods of the poems. Roughly speaking it starts with bitter and cynical poems, moves through courting poems, to poems expressing greater and greater satisfaction in a love relationship, and then on to poems of parting and of illness and death. I have, however, sandwiched in between the poems of parting and those of illness and death, a few poems expressing a certain serious frustration which may or may not be resolved in the poem concerned (*The Funeral, Love's Deity, Twickenham Garden* and *The Primrose*), and two expressing 'Platonic' love, in the modern sense of the term (*The Relic* and *The Undertaking*). I do not hold firmly by the order in detail, and can think of plenty of arguments for changing poems round; but I believe that the general plan is fairly reasonable; and I hope it may have some appeal. To obviate difficulty in finding particular poems, I have adopted a suggestion by Dr John Butcher and provided an alphabetical Index of Titles besides the list of poems in the Table of Contents and the Index of First Lines.

I have made no general attempt at dating the poems. I suspect that many of the more cynical or bitter poems were probably written before Donne met and fell in love with Ann More in 1598. Professor Gardner has suggested that 'the earlier *Songs and Sonnets*' were written before 1600, and the 'majority' of the 'later' ones between 1602 and 1605. I do not feel really happy about the suggested gap between 1600 and 1602, nor do I see why, as Professor Gardner suggests, it is hard to believe that while Donne was reading authors alluded to in *The Progress of the Soul*, and writing that ambitious poem, whose dedication is dated August 1601, he would also have been writing love-lyrics. I would have thought rather that the whole period between 1598 and 1605, when he could well have been experiencing very strong feelings with regard to the woman he loved and married, could easily have been fertile in love poetry. It is sometimes held, indeed, that there is no good reason to suppose that Donne's love poems correspond at all closely to specific experiences in the poet's own life: and even that more than a few of these poems may simply have been 'exercises' in wit. Such contentions are hard to refute; but it would be at least as hard to establish lack of correspondence, or the 'exercise' theory as more than a bare possibility. Personally I am much attracted by a reply which Pietro Bembo made to Niccolò Astemio in the spring of 1529 about Petrarch. Niccolò Astemio had written to Bembo saying that Petrarch had not succeeded in persuading him of the sincerity of his love for Madonna Laura. Bembo replied that if Petrarch had not been able to do so by his own writings, he, Bembo, would not presume to persuade him himself.[1] Now, Petrarch's love poems show as great a quantum of wit as the love-lyrics of Donne, and I suggest that there is no more reason to suppose that Donne's poems are mere 'exercises' or detached from personal experience than that Petrarch's were.

Professor Gardner associates the *Songs and Sonets* which she thinks

[1] P. Bembo, *Opere*, Milano, 1810, vol. VII, p. 255, quoted L. Baldacci, *Lirici del Cinquecento*, Firenze, 1957, p.v.

were written in the period 1602–5 with Donne's reading of neo-Platonic love theory, which has been much discussed in the light of modern scholarly research.[1] It may, indeed, be that, as she suggests (*ESS*, pp. lviii–lix), such reading as Donne did of Italian love-treatises of the late fifteenth and the sixteenth centuries occurred largely during the years 1602–5. Yet he could easily have become acquainted with such work a good deal sooner, even, indeed, well before he met Ann More. He could have done so in the course of earlier desultory reading, or perhaps through conversation with friends. Sir Richard Baker tells us that when Donne was a law student (1591–4) he was 'a great visitor of ladies';[2] and a man of his intellectual curiosity would, one might think, very probably have looked into the work of philosophers of love, and discussed love theory, well before the age of twenty-six, when he first met Ann. The presence in any of the lyrics of neo-Platonic elements does not, therefore, in my submission, make it at all highly probable that the poems concerned were written after 1601. There are, indeed, plausible reasons for dating some of the lyrics after 1601. Professor Praz long ago argued that *The Sun Rising* (l. 7) refers to James I's early rising to go hunting, and that l. 7 of *The Canonization* implies that a king was reigning. Both these poems also refer scornfully to worldly activities in comparison with the love of the lovers, and *The Canonization* mentions the poet's 'ruin'd fortune' (l. 3). This would, as Professor Gardner suggests, fit well with Donne's situation from 1602 to 1605. With regard to *The Anniversary*, however, which Professor Gardner also places after 1601, if we are to be even-handed in the matter of biographical reference, we may well (in virtue of l. 4) feel inclined to date it 1599, in the reasonable belief that it probably alludes to the poet's first meeting with Ann in 1598. Professor Gardner argues that the lovers of *The Anniversary* must be unmarried (*ESS*, p. xxix); but that is precisely what John and Ann were in 1599. Again, I see no cogent reason for dating *Air and Angels*, *Love's Growth*, *Lovers' Infiniteness*, *The Dream*, *The Ecstasy*, or *A Lecture upon the Shadow* after 1601; nor do I see any good ground for believing that any of these poems was not written to Ann during a period of courting from 1598 onwards. Furthermore, we have no knowledge of whether or not Ann was Donne's mistress before she

---

[1] The extensive literature includes M. Y. Hughes, 'The lineage of "The Extasie"', *MLR* 27 (1932); A. J. Smith, 'The metaphysic of love', *RES* n.s. 9 (1958); H. Gardner, 'The argument about "The Ecstasy"', in H. Davis and H. Gardner (eds), *Elizabethan and Jacobean Studies*, Oxford, 1959; M. Y. Hughes, 'Some of Donne's "Ecstasies"', *PMLA* 75 (1960).

[2] *A Chronicle of the Kings of England (1643)*, 1684, p. 427.

became his wife, and, if she was, even *The Good-morrow* could have been written before 1601; though it could equally well have been written after marriage, which clearly need not always correspond to Sidney Webb's joking description of it as 'the wastepaper-basket of the emotions'. The sexual joy implied in *The Sun Rising* and the deeper spiritual satisfactions expressed in *The Canonization* are surely far from unknown in fortunate marriages? With regard to *A Valediction: forbidding mourning* Professor Gardner argues that the poet's appeal to the woman in stanza 2 not to indulge in tears and sighs at their parting would not be appropriately addressed to a wife, 'who has no need to hide her grief at her husband's absence' (*ESS*, p. xxix). With respect, I would urge that this is by no means evident. The poet could, one would suppose, have held such a spiritually aristocratic view of the love between himself and his wife that he did not wish them to indulge publicly in scenes more characteristic of the general run of couples. There is, however, also the possibility that the poem refers to a parting between the poet and Ann before their marriage. Professor Gardner herself is justifiably unconvinced by Walton's statement, first made in 1675, that the poem was written in 1611, on the occasion of Donne's parting from his wife to go with Lord Hay's embassy to France.

Without further argument, then, I hope I have said enough to cast substantial doubt on Professor Gardner's scheme of dating the lyrics. On the other hand, there seems little doubt that Donne had some acquaintance with Italian love theory, and Professor Gardner may well be right to lay stress on Leone Ebreo's *Dialoghi d'amore* (Rome, 1535, but probably written 1501–2),[1] and to believe that Donne knew that work well. There are, however, passages in other love treatises, e.g. Mario Equicola's *Libro di natura d'amore*, Venice, 1536, and Sperone Speroni's *Dialogo d'amore*, Venice, 1543, which have close affinity with Donne in places,[2] and the general views of Flaminio Nobili in his *Trattato dell' amore humano*, Lucca, 1567,[3] are very close to Donne's reiterated insistence in some of the lyrics that the love of man and woman should be just as full in a bodily as in a spiritual sense. In the considerable array of Italian literature on love theory, however, one

---

[1] There is a modern edition by S. Caramella, Bari, 1929; and an English translation, *The Philosophy of Love*, by F. Friedeberg-Seeley and Jean H. Barnes, London, 1937.

[2] e.g., as Professor Donald Guss has pointed out, fols. 206^r–207^r of Equicola's book, and fols. a5^r–a7^r of Speroni's afford close analogues to the general position of *The Ecstasy* (*John Donne, Petrarchist*, Detroit, 1966, pp. 142–4).

[3] Republished Rome, 1895.

finds a great deal of repetition both of general propositions and of specific points, so that it would be hard confidently to pin down definite sources for all the passages in Donne's lyrics probably influenced by such works. Moreover, in the case of such a voracious reader as Donne, it could be especially difficult, since the literature of love philosophy up to his time included not only the prose treatises but the vast corpus of love poetry stretching back through the many varieties of Petrarchism in England, France and Italy in the fifteenth and sixteenth centuries, through the poetry of Petrarch, then of Dante, of the poets of the *dolce stil nuovo* and of the court of Frederick II in Sicily, right back to the Provençal troubadours. It would take more than a lifetime to read all that material and come to justifiably confident conclusions. In any case, however, such an investigation would be almost exclusively of historical interest, since Donne's own views about love are usually fairly clear after a bit of thought without the need to trace the specific ideas to precise sources in the work of other writers of whom Donne is, in any case, not likely to have been a slavish imitator. I have, at all events, not attempted any such extensive historical investigation for this edition, whose Introduction and Commentary are concerned mainly with interpretation and description.

On the other hand, I have considerably revised my Introduction. In point of biography I have derived much help from the works of the late Professor R. C. Bald, especially from his admirable *Life of John Donne*, completed by Professor Milgate, Oxford, 1970. I have also reconsidered the poems themselves, and made more extensive critical comments than before, within the limited space available. I have added a sketch of the relations between the *Songs and Sonets* and the Petrarchan tradition; and I have expanded discussion of the text and canon of the poems. In a number of appendices there will be found discussions of matters of specific interest which it would have been disproportionate to treat in the Introduction or the body of the Commentary. I am fully aware that the book, as revised over the years, could be further greatly improved; but I have come to feel that it is probably more useful to publish it now than never to publish it at all.

In preparing this second edition for the press I owe a special debt of gratitude to my friend and colleague Dr Paul Hammond, Fellow of Trinity College, Cambridge, both for his valuable suggestions and for his help in proof-reading. I have also gained from discussion and/or correspondence with Dr Robert Arnold, Dr John Butcher, Dr Lynne Lawner, Professor John Parish, Mr Leo Salingar, the late Sir Charles

Tennyson, Mr James Winny and Dr Keith Walker. I am also grateful for valuable secretarial assistance from Miss Clare Russell, Miss Diana Piggott, Miss Ruth Webb and Mrs K. N. Serby. Finally, I cannot say how much I owe to the encouragement and help of my wife.

Sir Geoffrey Keynes has again generously allowed me to examine the Leconfield and Luttrell manuscripts, and, as always, I have benefited from his deep knowledge of Donne. The late Mr A. R. B. Fuller, Librarian of St Paul's Cathedral Library, kindly deposited the St Paul's Manuscript in the Cambridge University Library for my use. I wish he were alive to read my thanks.

Trinity College   THEODORE REDPATH
Cambridge
November 1981

INTRODUCTION

The status of the 'Songs and Sonets' in English poetry

Donne's *Songs and Sonets* are far more widely read and appreciated now than they were, say, twenty-five years ago. Then it still seemed necessary to insist on claiming them to be among the three or four finest collections of love-lyrics in the English language. Too many readers of poetry, even in this country, would have omitted Donne's name from such a short list of the supreme love-lyrists of England, while readily including the names of Herrick, Shelley, Keats, Tennyson, Browning and Swinburne. Probably this was partly because the *Songs and Sonets*, despite Grierson's great edition of the Poetical Works in 1912, and some subsequent notable critical studies of Donne, still remained for many general readers of poetry comparatively little known. This was in part due to the sparse representation of his work in some widely circulated anthologies.[1] Yet there were other reasons. One was the lingering prejudice that love-lyrics should be expressions of feeling unalloyed with any marked degree of cerebration. This prejudice has recently shown signs of weakening, at least among serious readers of poetry. Another reason was that many people were still deterred by the sheer difficulty of

[1] In the old *Oxford Book of English Verse* only four of the *Songs and Sonets* were included, and Donne's work as a whole was allotted only 7 pages (as compared with 21 to Herrick, 19 to Shelley, 24 to Keats, 23 to Tennyson, 20 to Browning and 12 to Swinburne). In the new *Oxford Book* (1972) Helen Gardner has remedied this, allotting over 18 pages to Donne, and including about a dozen of the *Songs and Sonets*. In the last edition of Palgrave's *Golden Treasury* (1964), however, not a single poem by Donne is included. It was Palgrave's deliberate policy to omit Donne from his anthology, first published in 1861. For information on his criteria, and further references, see the valuable study by Raoul Granqvist, *The Reputation of John Donne, 1779–1873*, Uppsala, 1975, pp. 134–7. Cf. also A. J. Smith (ed.), *John Donne: The Critical Heritage*, London, 1975, pp. 432–5.

1

seizing the sense of many passages. Ben Jonson prophesied that Donne's poetry would perish for lack of being understood. It has not perished yet, and I believe that, barring a cosmic cataclysm, it is unlikely to do so; but its survival as work whose meaning is reasonably well understood has had to depend in considerable measure on the elucidation of difficulties. A good deal of effort has been directed during the last quarter-of-a-century or so towards such elucidation, and the sense of many passages has become far clearer; though a plain text of some of the poems is often hard to understand for an unprepared reader. A further obstacle to a just appreciation of the love poems in particular has been a fairly widespread impression that Donne as a love poet was dominantly flippant and cynical. This impression probably arose from the choice for anthologies of such cynical poems as 'Go and catch a falling star', the cumulative impression of the often cynical *Elegies* and some of the *Songs and Sonets*, and the influence of certain outstanding critical studies, such as the late Professor Pierre Legouis's pioneering work, *Donne the Craftsman* (Paris, 1928). In actual fact, one of the many remarkable features of the *Songs and Sonets* is the wide range of feelings and attitudes expressed in them, from contemptuous loathing and buoyant promiscuity to the most tender and even idealistic love. Then again, although some discerning critics, Coleridge, for instance, had long ago realized that in Donne's work, as in much other work before Dryden, rhythm was dependent upon sense, including emotion, many people have continued to feel an absence in Donne's love-lyrics of the kinds of music they demand from such poems. This dissatisfaction may also have become less widespread in recent years; but it is still rare to find people who read Donne's lyrics aloud convincingly. What is quite certain is that in the *Songs and Sonets* there is great variety and subtlety of music, and that, once it is properly sensed, it can be felt to have attractions at least equal to, and sometimes transcending, those of poetic music of a more obvious character.

All in all I hope, and indeed believe, that it is not necessary now to argue for the view which I baldly expressed in the first edition of this book about twenty-five years ago, that the *Songs and Sonets* are superior as a body of love-lyrics to any equivalent number of poems by the poets mentioned above; and that, if we survey English poetry from end to end, we are unlikely to find any serious rivals to the *Songs and Sonets* as love-lyrics, except the sonnets of Sidney and Shakespeare, and the love poems of Yeats and, possibly, of Hardy.

The place of the 'Songs and Sonets' within Donne's work

The *Songs and Sonets* were not all written within one short period, but at various times over probably more than twenty years. We do not know when Donne wrote the first of them, whichever that was; but it may even have been before 1590. Some evidence supports the view that he may have written practically all these poems before the middle of 1614; and there is no positive evidence that he wrote any of them after 1611, when he was nearly forty.[1]

According to Drummond of Hawthornden, Ben Jonson told him that Donne had written all his best pieces before he was twenty-five, i.e. by some time early in 1597. We must not, however, allow Jonson's statement to mislead us. It was made in 1618, and so, at all events, could not apply to such poems as the great *Hymns*, written after Jonson's pronouncement. Moreover, it is hardly likely that Jonson was taking into account such outstanding love-lyrics as *Twickenham Garden* or *A Nocturnal upon St Lucy's Day*. *Twickenham Garden* is unlikely to have been written before 1608, when Lady Bedford began to occupy Twickenham Park. The *Nocturnal* may have been written as late as 1612, or even 1617 (if it refers to the death of Donne's wife). In any case, Jonson's statement could at most be evidence that the best poems of Donne which had been seen by Jonson were written before Donne was twenty-five. Furthermore, which of the *Songs and Sonets* Jonson had seen by that date is quite uncertain. Only two of them are known to have been printed in whole or in part by 1618, and no more before Donne's death in 1631.[2] Like many of the poems of his contemporaries, there was some circulation of them in manuscript. Probably, however, only his particular friends had collections of any size; and it is quite impossible to say which poems came to Jonson's notice. Besides, there are definite indications that some of the best *Songs and Sonets* were written well after 1597. *The Canonization* and *The Sun Rising*, for instance, were probably written after the accession of James I (1603).

On the other hand, it is extremely probable from external evidence that forty-five out of the fifty-four poems here printed were written

[1] The date of Donne's birth has been subject to controversy. Scholarly opinion now favours early in 1572.
[2] For details see Sir Geoffrey Keynes's *Bibliography of Dr John Donne*, 4th edn, Oxford, 1973, pp. 161–8.

before mid-1614, and of the remaining eight[1] only the *Nocturnal* (and perhaps *The Dissolution*) could possibly have been written after that date. Donne took holy orders at the beginning of 1615, and he was already preparing for this in the latter half of 1614. He took the step extremely seriously, and it is out of the question that he should have written any of the other six poems after he made his final decision.

We may, indeed, say with a high degree of confidence that all Donne's love-lyrics, with the possible exceptions of the *Nocturnal* and *The Dissolution*, were written before the middle of 1614, when Donne was probably forty-two.

In our present state of knowledge it is impossible to date the individual love-lyrics precisely; but it is possible to assign a number of them with reasonable certainty to earlier or later parts of the period in which they were all written. Capital dates are 1598, when Donne first met Ann More, his future wife, and December 1601 (or January 1602), when he married her.[2] It would seem likely that a fair number of the poems, including some of the more flippantly cynical ones, such as *The Indifferent*, *Community*, the *Song* 'Go and catch a falling star', and *Love's Usury*, were written before Donne met Ann More in 1598, and were therefore contemporary with Donne's *Elegies* and *Satires*. Other poems express such deep satisfaction that it seems reasonable to suppose that they arose out of Donne's marriage or the relationship which led up to it. Such poems, then, were probably written between 1598 and 1614. They include, for instance, *The Anniversary*, *The Good-morrow*, *A Valediction: of weeping* and *A Valediction: forbidding mourning*. Of these, on the credible assumption that they all spring from real occasions, the first would seem to accord with the pre-marital period 1598–1601. *The Anniversary* marks the first anniversary of the lovers' *meeting* (see ll. 4–5), and might well therefore have been written in 1599. *The Good-morrow* could belong either to a liaison or to the early years of a marriage. The two *Valedictions* could hardly have been written before 1605[3] when Donne went abroad for the first time during his married life. A good many of the poems, however, it seems hard to assign with confidence to one of the two periods rather

---

[1] *Witchcraft by a Picture, The Expiration, The Computation, The Paradox, Negative Love, Farewell to Love, A Nocturnal upon St Lucy's Day* and *The Dissolution*.

[2] There is some interesting evidence concerning the precise date of Donne's marriage. See Edward Le Comte, 'Jack Donne: From Rake to Husband', in P. A. Fiore (ed.), *Just So Much Honor*, University Park, Pa., 1972, pp. 9–32.

[3] Walton says *A Valediction: forbidding mourning* was written by Donne for his wife when he left her to go with Sir Robert Drury to France in 1611. Walton's dates, however, are frequently in need of confirmation.

than the other. I should *guess* that *The Dream* might well belong to the period when he was courting Ann, and that *Air and Angels*, which touches that poem at one or two points, springs from the same time. *Lovers' Infiniteness* and *Love's Growth* might well also belong to that period; but these poems, like 'Sweetest love, I do not go' and *A Lecture upon the Shadow*, could easily belong to some earlier serious relationship. Two poems present a special difficulty, *The Canonization* and *The Sun Rising*. Both of these refer to a king as if he were on the throne, and so look as if they were written after James I's accession in 1603. On the other hand, if they do refer to a real love relationship, they somewhat suggest that this relationship is an extra-marital rather than a marital one. A husband does not usually fulminate at people for gossiping about the fact that he loves his own wife; nor does a husband scold the sun for calling him and his wife from their bed of love. The solution, however, I believe, may be that Donne is wishing to emphasize that romantic love is not the exclusive property of unauthorized liaisons: and also that this marriage for which he was in disgrace and which for some people savoured of the extra-marital, was an assertion of the value of love against all competing worldly values. For two other poems Professor Gardner suggests[1] that dates can be inferred from allusions: *The Undertaking* alluding to Guido Panciroli's *Rerum Memorabilium Libri Duo*, Hamburg, 1599; and *A Valediction: of the book* to Lipsius's *De Bibliothecis Syntagma*, Antwerp, 1602. *The Undertaking* has the air of a poem referring to some secret Platonic attachment, and if we date it 1599 or after, the natural inference will be that it was a Platonic attachment by the poet either in the early stages of courtship, or during marriage, to some woman other than his wife. A further alternative, as always, is to suppose that the poem had no specific biographical basis. If a real situation lies behind *A Valediction: of the book*, and we date that poem after 1602, we shall again need to refer it to a period of prolonged absence, which would date the poem either in 1605 or 1611 or after. The absence, moreover, would be from a woman with whom Donne had already exchanged a vast number of letters (ll. 10–11), but of whose love (or of his love for whom) in absence he did not feel completely confident (ll. 55–63). Whether the woman was his wife or someone else would need to be regarded as uncertain. In any case, as already mentioned, *wickenham Garden* was most probably written after 1607, and the *Nocturnal* even later. *Twickenham Garden* was evidently written at least *for*, if not *to*, the Countess of Bedford; and the *Nocturnal* may

<hr>

[1] *ESS*, p. lx.

possibly be connected with her. *The Dissolution*, moreover, not only occurs in much the same extant manuscripts as the *Nocturnal*, but is also close in subject and may well, therefore, be also a late poem.

It may be possible to make more extensive assignments to the two periods (before 1598 and between 1598 and 1614) on the basis of the kind of reading reflected in the poems; though this is somewhat hazardous in the absence of firmer indications of what books Donne was reading at various periods. It is, however, important to bear in mind that during the earlier period he is known to have read avidly in the Roman poets; and that during the second period he read very widely in theological and philosophical works, including not only works by the Christian Fathers and the Scholastics, but also works by Jewish, neo-Platonic, and neo-Aristotelian writers. It is also vital to remember that the second period largely coincides with that in which he wrote the earlier and larger part of his religious poetry. The date of that curious and ambitious poem, *The Progress of the Soul*, which, though a satire, is also a religious work, is 1601; and reliable authorities hold that the majority of the other religious poems were written between 1607 and 1614. It is therefore a complete mistake to think of Donne's poetry as falling into two quite distinct phases, the first secular and the second religious. To realize the true situation helps one to understand why a number of the love-lyrics (those probably written in the second period) are shot through with religious references and suggestions.

After his ordination in 1615 Donne wrote little poetry of any sort. Apart from his letters, in which he appears, from time to time, as a shrewd observer of political events, Donne's later writings consist almost entirely of prayers, religious meditations and sermons, those remarkable sermons which some discriminating critics have rated as highly as his poetry.

Let us now look a little more closely at Donne's activities during the two periods in which his love-lyrics (with the possible exceptions of the *Nocturnal* and *The Dissolution*) were written.

Just before the first period (*c.* 1590–8) Donne was at Cambridge (1588–9), where he had come after a period at Oxford. He was unable to take his BA degree at either University, for that would have meant taking the Oath of Supremacy, and also subscribing to the Thirty-Nine Articles, neither of which the son of a staunch Catholic family could have been expected to do. Since, however, the Oath of Supremacy was not demanded of freshmen under sixteen, Donne was, by starting at Oxford at the age of twelve, and at Cambridge at fifteen, able to get three years at each University. After Cambridge he may have travelled abroad (1589–91), and from 1591 to 1594 he was in London as a law student, first at Thavie's Inn (1591), and then at Lincoln's Inn (1592–4), where he was Master of the Revels in 1593. During that period he was remembered as a 'great visitor of ladies' and 'frequenter' of the theatre. He seems also to have become keen on acquiring modern languages, and reading French, Spanish and Italian literature, while continuing to delve into Roman poetry. At some time (probably within the period 1594–6) he appears to have travelled in France, Italy and Spain; and we find him on board one of Essex's men-of-war in the expeditions against Cadiz (1596) and to the Azores (1597). There is also some evidence that early in 1598 he may have been employed by Cecil as a confidential messenger to and from France during Cecil's negotiations with Henry IV.

Donne's poetic output during this first period included his first four *Satires* (*c*. 1593–7) – lively and pioneering work in English satire, plentiful in ripe speech about the life and abuses of the London of the day, and plentiful also in marks of study and learning. These satires bear strong traces of the influence of Horace and of Persius; but Donne's eyes and ears were alive to his contemporary world, and his specific impressions and turns of wit are generally his own, as is also his racy language, though at times it bears a striking resemblance to that of Nashe. Donne made a considerable reputation for himself as a satirist. His *Epigrams*, most of which belong to the same period, and his *Elegies*, all of which seem to do so, were evidently held in high repute by those who did not find the hyper-Ovidianism of the *Elegies* shocking. The surviving epigrams are moderately dexterous imitations of Martial and of the Greek Anthology. Besides Ovidian influence on the *Elegies*, the impact of Italian poetry (particularly of Tasso) shows itself. Again, however, Donne always strikes out for himself. Towards the end of the same period, he began writing verse-letters to his contemporaries. Among the first are the two remarkably fine poems probably written to his close friend from Cambridge days, Christopher Brooke. The first, called *The Storm*, describes the great storm in July 1597 which harassed the large fleet which Elizabeth had fitted out to destroy a second armada which was being prepared by the King of Spain. The second, *The Calm*, gives a vivid impression of the becalming aftermath. These poems show that Donne had an outstanding talent for descriptive poetry. Among the output of this first period, it is possibly these two poems, a few of the *Elegies*, and the great bulk of the love-lyrics, that most deserve the attention of modern readers.

As to prose, all we have of Donne from this period are most of the *Paradoxes and Problems*, a few miscellaneous essays, and the early letters. The *Paradoxes and Problems* and the essays are written in a tone of flippancy, and they are full of ingenious sallies and striking comparisons. The letters are also alert and witty. Donne was clearly intent on entertaining and astonishing his friends by his clever and often paradoxical 'evaporations'.

At the beginning of the second period (1598–1614), Donne was appointed private secretary to Sir Thomas Egerton, Lord Keeper of the Great Seal and a member and benefactor of Lincoln's Inn. Donne had become friendly with Egerton's elder son Thomas and with his stepson Francis Wolley, while they were all serving in Essex's fleet. Egerton *père* was evidently much struck with Donne's 'learning, languages and other ability'. Donne seems to have worked hard and well for him until the beginning of 1602,[1] when he was dismissed for having secretly married, allegedly in December 1601, Ann More, niece of Egerton's second wife. At the instigation of Ann's father, Sir George More, Donne was even (February 1602) imprisoned in the Fleet, where he languished for some days, till Egerton allowed him to return to his lodgings and remain there under house arrest. After his final release later in the year, Donne, whose promising career was now blasted, lived for some years on charity and patronage. He was, however, by no means idle. Walton tells us that while Donne and his wife were enjoying the kind and welcome hospitality of Francis (by now Sir Francis) Wolley at Pyrford (1602-end 1604), Donne made himself expert in civil and canon law. In 1605 he went abroad with Sir Walter Chute, and may have continued legal study in France; but after returning to England in April 1606 he moved to Mitcham, and started to act as a consultant (possibly a legal expert), and apparently also helped Thomas Morton (later Dean of Gloucester and Bishop of Durham) in anti-Catholic polemic. Donne had lost enthusiasm for Catholicism in the 1590s, and seems to have passed through a period of religious indifference; but, possibly under the influence of Ann, who was a pious girl, he had now begun to find satisfaction in the Anglican Church, and to interest himself in its medial position between Romanism and Calvinistic Puritanism. In 1607 Morton actually offered Donne a living; but Donne declined. How strongly he was motivated in so doing by a sense of what Walton

---

[1] Donne sat as one of the members for Brackley during a short period late in 1601. Egerton evidently used his interest to get him returned. (See I. A. Shapiro in *TLS*, 10 March 1932, p. 172, 'Was Donne a member of the 1601 and 1614 Parliaments?')

reports as Donne's reason, namely, 'irregularities' in his past life, is hard to estimate. At all events, Donne still had political ambitions. In 1608 he applied for a political post in Ireland, and in 1609 he tried hard to obtain the appointment of Secretary in Virginia. He was financially in a poor way, and his family was rapidly expanding. The next year, however, Sir George More at last, through Sir Francis Wolley's intercession, made a handsome settlement on the Donnes. Donne was also presented at about this time to James I, who enjoyed his learned conversation, and especially his participation in theological discussions. Donne dedicated to the King the *Pseudo-Martyr* (published 1610), which argues the case that Roman Catholics resident in the kingdom might and indeed ought to take the oath of allegiance.

Donne, who for some time had taken lodgings in the Strand, continued to be employed as an adviser by important people, but made no headway towards obtaining the kind of post he wanted. At the end of 1610 he wrote, possibly at the suggestion of his sister Ann, a funeral elegy on Elizabeth Drury, fifteen-year-old only daughter of Sir Robert Drury, a rich Suffolk landowner, whom he may have known at Cambridge, and possibly also on the Cadiz Expedition. Friendship with the Drurys soon ripened, and Sir Robert, three years younger than Donne and like him nursing hitherto frustrated political and diplomatic ambitions, invited Donne in 1611 to go abroad with him and his wife for three years. According to Walton, Donne's wife, who was pregnant, begged Donne not to go, and only finally consented with great reluctance. Donne gave up the house at Mitcham, and arranged for Ann and the children to stay with her sister in the Isle of Wight. The Drurys and Donne spent the winter at Amiens. Drury probably hunted with his friend the Comte de St Paul. Donne seems to have read law books. Both made contact with important people passing through the town on their way to and from Paris. In March the party moved to Paris, and there and in their subsequent travels to Frankfurt for the Imperial Election, and to Heidelberg and Brussels, they seem to have been cultivating important acquaintances and aiming at ultimate employment in diplomatic posts. They returned to London at the end of the summer of 1612, and Drury put paid to his own ambitions by some tactless language about the Elector Palatine. Drury evidently much valued having Donne near him, and arranged for Donne and his family to occupy a house next to Drury House. Walton says that this was rent-free; but there is some evidence that Donne may have paid Drury a substantial rent. Both Drury and Donne soon set about angling for political employment or a diplomatic post abroad. Drury unsuccessfully attempted to get appointed Ambassador to France. Donne received a seat, this time for Taunton, in the ineffectual Addled Parliament (April–June 1614); but he aimed higher. At one point he petitioned James I's favourite at the time, Robert Ker,[1] Earl of Somerset, to obtain for him the Embassy at Venice, and, subsequently, the corresponding post at The Hague, either of which Drury himself would have been glad to hold. But neither Donne nor Drury was successful in obtaining high secular preferment. According to Walton, Somerset also asked the King to appoint Donne to a vacant Clerkship of the Council; but James declined to do so, saying that Donne was well suited to be a 'learned Divine' and a 'powerful Preacher', and that he wished to promote him that way. Donne had already, in 1612–13, considered again the possibility of taking Orders, but still hankered after a secular career. Now, however, he decided to enter the Church, and was ordained in January 1615. Early in the same year James appointed him a royal Chaplain, and made an amply fulfilled promise to pay particular attention to his preferment.

We may now briefly consider Donne's writings (other than the love-lyrics) during this second period (1598–1614). The verse includes the fifth Satire (against the bribing of judges) (*c*. 1599) and *The Autumnal*, a very fine Platonic love poem, probably written about Mrs Herbert, mother of the poet George Herbert. Donne also wrote many verse-letters, some in a tone of equality to intimate friends like Rowland Woodward and the Brookes, and some in a vein of hyperbolical compliment to socially elevated individuals, especially women, such as the Countesses of Bedford and Huntingdon. It is more than likely that some of these were intended, even if only indirectly, to advance his career and improve his social position in the lean years. Donne also wrote a number of *Epicedes* and *Obsequies*, mainly on socially distinguished people; and in 1611–12, followed up his funeral elegy on Elizabeth Drury by penning the two *Anniversaries*. These contained such high-flown tributes that Ben Jonson dubbed them 'blasphemous'. Donne then explained that he had been describing 'the idea of a Woman', not an individual. The *Epithalamion* for Princess Elizabeth's marriage with the Elector Palatine, and the *Epithalamion* for the marriage of the Earl of Somerset with the

---

[1] Not to be confused with the far more attractive character, Sir Robert Ker, subsequently Earl of Ancrum, a close friend of Donne's, and legatee of the admirable Lothian Portrait of Donne as a young man, discovered by Mr John Bryson in 1959 (see *The Times*, 13 October 1959).

ultimately notorious Frances Howard, Countess of Essex (both written in 1613) are occasional poems of no great merit. A good deal earlier in the period (in 1601) Donne had completed *The Progress of the Soul*, an extraordinary satirical poem tracing the progress of the soul of heresy from its origin in the apple of Eden, through many animal forms, to its final human state in a female arch-heretic, who has been variously identified – for instance, as Queen Elizabeth, and as the Roman Catholic Church! In this poem Donne reaches the most exaggerated heights of his 'metaphysical' style, putting his learning to the most bizarre purposes, while maintaining a general tone of absurdity in keeping with his satiric intention. Finally, many of the *Divine Poems* probably belong to the latter part of this period (1607–14). These include *La Corona* (*c.* 1607), almost all the *Holy Sonnets* (*c.* 1609), *A Litany* (*c.* 1608), and a number of short poems, among which *Good-friday, 1613. Riding Westward* is particularly noteworthy as showing Donne's state of mind at a point not long before his ordination. These religious poems are no less imbued with passion, imagery, learning, intellectual agility and subtlety than the secular poems of the same period.

The chief prose works of the period 1598–1614 are the curious *Biathanatos* (written after 1605 and before 1610 – possibly in 1607 or 1608 – but not printed during his lifetime), *Pseudo-Martyr* (1610), already mentioned, *Ignatius his Conclave* (written 1610–11; published 1611) and the *Essays in Divinity* (completed in 1614, but partly written some years earlier). *Biathanatos* is 'a declaration of that paradox or thesis, that self-homicide is not so naturally sin, that it may never be otherwise'. It is ingeniously argued, and also throws light on Donne's inner life.[1] *Pseudo-Martyr*, for which Donne was awarded an Honorary MA at Oxford in 1610, must be regarded as an occasional work, and now makes tedious reading; and *Ignatius his Conclave*, in which Donne attacks the Jesuits in a scurrilous manner characteristic of much of the polemic of the time, though containing some clever strokes of wit, is not a work of much substance. The *Essays in Divinity* are learned, and of great interest as showing Donne's theological difficulties before ordination, but, save in the prayers, they lack both personal urgency and literary value. It is only in *Biathanatos* and in his letters that we find writing that is likely to prove perennially attractive.

With these exceptions it is only in the last period of Donne's life

---

[1] For an interesting modern discussion of Donne's 'attraction to death' see D. R. Roberts, 'The death-wish of John Donne', *PMLA* 62 (1947) pp. 958–76.

(1615–31), in his period as a priest, that Donne's prose writings attain a quality comparable with that of his best poetry. It is in the *Devotions* and the *Sermons* that we find the blend of intellectual ingenuity and subtlety with strong and urgent feeling that marks his best writing in both prose and verse. Here they vivify the ramifications of his prose, just as they have formerly sustained the complex stanza forms of some of the *Songs and Sonets*. In the *Sermons*, too, we find elaborated in a masterly way a systematic Anglican theology. The *Sermons* follow a general pattern, rising from exact and forceful exposition to sublime flights of religious prose poetry. Learning, logic and rhetoric and imaginatively conceived imagery combine here with the forward drive of a relentless energy to produce some of the most remarkable passages in English prose. These passages, however, often depend for their full effect on what, in the particular sermon, has led up to it. Yet even now that the great modern edition of the *Sermons*[1] is complete, it is doubtful whether they will become general reading for the literary public of modern times. Splendid as they are, and overwhelming as was often their effect when Donne delivered them, they contain too much outmoded seventeenth-century theology, and they are too long for any but devotees to be expected to read more than a few of them. It is probably as a poet, and especially as a love-lyrist, that Donne is likely to have widespread appeal.

Some approaches to the poems

What makes the *Songs and Sonets* so remarkable? Naturally enough, many things. One unexpected answer could be: their titles. This is meant, of course, as a kind of joke; but I hope it would appeal to Donne, especially if, as is possible, he did not invent any of the titles! Joke or no joke, however, it would not be without point as a serious, though admittedly only partial answer. If we were to consider some of the titles – *The Canonization*, *The Legacy*, *Air and Angels*, *The Relic*, *The Computation*, *The Prohibition*, *A Fever*, *The Flea* – without know-ing the poems, we might well ask: what have these to do with love? And we would be quite right to answer that they have not necessarily anything to do with it at all. Yet, if we know the poems, we shall also know that each of the titles expresses the guiding idea or image round which the whole poem revolves. It is the powerful polarity of Donne's

---

[1] G. R. Potter and E. M. Simpson (eds), *The Sermons of John Donne*, 10 vols, Berkeley and Los Angeles, 1953–62.

love impulses which transmutes all these seemingly neutral or alien spheres of experience, which the titles may suggest, into love poetry. This is not the yoking of heterogeneous ideas by violence together. It is the electro-magnetizing of whole fields of experience in their subtle details. Now, for there to be (as there is) a fair number and variety of examples of this process presupposes at least four things in Donne as a poet: (1) a considerable range of knowledge and experience; (2) an intellectual and a perceptive sharpness and accuracy of knowledge and observation; (3) powerful love-impulses capable of making these neutral or alien fields of knowledge and experience relevant; (4) the poetic ability, emotional and intellectual, to draw these into order, so as to make firm and well-articulated poems.

I have insisted on the titles in order to concentrate attention on the *guiding* ideas of the poems, for it is these, as a general rule, that go far towards constituting their unity. In *The Canonization*, for instance, the unity depends on the fact that Donne and his mistress are not merely harmless (as the second stanza maintains), but will be *saints*; and that they will then be prayed to by lovers who wish to achieve passions of a high spiritual order. In *The Anniversary* the unity depends on the central fact that this is an *anniversary* of the meeting of the poet and his beloved, and so a time for looking back, and also a time for looking forward – the idea being rounded off by the dream of the possible diamond jubilee of their love. This use of neutral or alien *guiding* ideas as the material for love poetry seems to be worth emphasizing because it does not usually appear in commentary on Donne's love poems. It is a very different thing from the drafts which Donne draws on even more various fields of knowledge and experience *within the course* of the individual poems. That is, of course, an important characteristic of Donne's poetry, and it has been commented upon again and again; but over and above all that we have, I am suggesting, this polarization of the actual guiding ideas of the poems.

It could well have been enough to make Donne a great love poet if he had simply done these two things very effectively: that is, polarized the guiding ideas, and drawn in the mass of ancillary thoughts and images from still more diverse fields of knowledge and experience in the course of the poems. Yet he did a great deal more than this. Taking the whole body of the *Songs and Sonets* we find, for instance, that they cover a fair array of love situations: more than is normal in the love poetry of a single poet – more, for example, than in the love poetry of those great love poets Catullus, Ovid, Propertius, Dante, Petrarch and Ronsard.

There is the complete freedom from any serious commitment, as in *The Indifferent*, *Community* and *Confined Love*. There is frustrated passion, of varying degrees and kinds, as in *The Apparition*, *Love's Deity* and *Twickenham Garden*. There is the situation of courting, as in *Lovers' Infiniteness*, *Air and Angels*, *The Primrose* and, I believe, *The Ecstasy*. There are satisfying love relationships, of different kinds, as in *The Sun Rising*, *The Canonization*, *The Undertaking* and probably *The Relic*. There is the more or less apprehensive situation of parting, as in 'Sweetest love, I do not go', the four Valedictions, and *The Expiration*. There is the terrible threat of illness or the grim actuality of death, as in *A Fever*, *A Nocturnal upon St Lucy's Day* and *The Dissolution*. And even within these general categories there are fairly wide differences of situation. The strong sexuality of *The Apparition* marks off its situation quite sharply from the 'higher' frustration of *Twickenham Garden*, where the mention of beds and midnight tapers would have been wholly out of key. In *Air and Angels* the poet is asking his mistress to love him: in *The Ecstasy* he knows she loves him, but possibly wants her to give the love physical fruition.

The range of situations is noteworthy; but perhaps still more remarkable are the moods in which Donne faces them in the poems. These moods are generally strong, whether discontented or satisfied. In a number of the *Songs and Sonets* Eros speaks out quite unashamedly. There is a frank and uncompromising egoism which is determined to make its demands heard. If frustrated it will not whine but curse (as in *The Apparition*), or cynically shrug its shoulders (as in *The Blossom*), or, in a manly fashion, request to be put to death (as in *Love's Exchange*), where there is probably also some degree of ironical exaggeration, or at least saving humour. If it is being satisfied it will protest at disturbance:

> Busy old fool, unruly sun. . . .

or

> For God's sake hold your tongue and let me love. . . .

When roused to fury it does not pull its punches. Wyatt sometimes gets angry with a woman who frustrates him, but there is nothing so 'ungentlemanly' in his poems as Donne's outpourings in *The Apparition*. The egoism also disdains to flatter. The *Songs and Sonets* generally dispense with poetic gallantries. This does not mean to say that there is not occasionally hyperbolical praise; but where it does occur it is certainly highly unconventional, and may even be so obviously exaggerated as to be intended to appear so:

> This face, by which he [Love] could command
> And change the idolatry of any land;
> This face, which, wheresoe'r it comes,
> Can call vow'd men from cloisters, dead from tombs,
> And melt both poles at once, and store
> Deserts with cities, and make more
> Mines in the earth, than quarries were before.
>
> (*Love's Exchange*, ll. 29–35)

When Donne is satisfied it is more typical for him to recognize the situation as a mutual one: either in very plain language without honours and decorations, as in:

> My face in thine eye, thine in mine appears,
> And true plain hearts do in the faces rest; . . .
>
> (*The Good-morrow*, ll. 15–16)

or, where there *are* honours and decorations, with fairly equal distribution to his beloved and himself; though sometimes with male dominance:

> She is all States, and all Princes I,
>   Nothing else is: . . .
>
> (*The Sun Rising*, ll. 21–2)

or

> The Phoenix riddle hath more wit
> By us; we two being one, are it.
>
> (*The Canonization*, ll. 23–4)

or

> Here upon earth, we are Kings, and none but we
> Can be such Kings, nor of such subjects be.
>
> (*The Anniversary*, ll. 23–4)

In some of what are almost certainly the earlier *Songs and Sonets* we find a high-spirited animal promiscuity: a refusal to be bound down to one person, as in *The Indifferent, Community, Confined Love*. Variety is seen as the natural course; monogamy as the creation of human laws.

We also find bitter disillusion with sexual activity, as in *Love's Alchemy* and *Farewell to Love*. The plain-speaking in these poems is uncommon enough. Again, in a few places there is another mood, similar to one found in a number of other poets, e.g. Petrarch and Shakespeare, and yet not precisely the same. I mean the mood in which falling in love is regarded as a weakness and even danger. For Donne this does not mean having a pretty arrow shot through his heart by some 'dimpled smiling Cupid'. It means the peril of real torture. Varieties of this mood are expressed in *Love's Usury*, *The Broken Heart*, *Love's Exchange*, and, somewhat more lightly, in *The Triple Fool* and *The Paradox*.

What is still further removed from the ordinary, at least in English love-lyrics, is Donne's enthusiastic expression of satisfaction in a love relationship. Sometimes this is quite frankly physical – at least in part – as in *The Good-morrow*, *The Sun Rising* and *The Canonization*. Sometimes there is no direct physical implication, as in *The Anniversary* and *Love's Growth*. Sometimes the whole point is that the satisfying love is Platonic, as in *The Undertaking* and *The Relic*.

To find all these moods in the work of one love-lyrist is more than striking; but perhaps even more remarkable is that there should also be lines like the opening lines of *A Fever*, and poems like 'Sweetest love, I do not go', *A Valediction: of weeping*, *A Valediction: forbidding mourning* and *A Nocturnal upon St Lucy's Day*, each expressing or implying the greatest tenderness, and the sense of a deep and (save in the case of the *Nocturnal*) stable mutual love. Probably some of these poems were written by Donne to his wife or wife-to-be, and there may be among them, in this case, exceptions to the general rule which I once heard propounded by a Chinese poet, that men do not write love poems to or about their wives after they have got married.

So much, for the moment, for the kinds of basic moods we encounter in the *Songs and Sonets*. I have only mentioned a fair selection of characteristic ones. I want now to comment on another aspect of the moods of the poems: namely, that it is fairly typical for them to be fluid and shifting; and, what is more, that the fluid and shifting character of the moods is one of the features that contribute to the distinction of the poems in which it occurs. A very simple instance is *The Indifferent*, in which, though there is certainly an overall binding connexion, the moods of each of the three stanzas are sharply different from one another. The shifts of mood are, however, not so evenly distributed in general as in that poem. Let us follow through a case, still comparatively simple, in *The Triple Fool*. We start with a half-serious, half-ironical admission:

> I am two fools, I know,
> For loving, and for saying so
> In whining poetry;. . . .

But then comes the hard-headed self-justifying question, which implies that this mug's game of loving and writing poems about it, has, after all, a real chance of achieving signal satisfaction:

> But where's that wiseman, that would not be I,
> If she would not deny?

Then the mood, despite the connecting word implying continuity ('Then'), abruptly shifts. Donne reveals the fierce and destructive passion behind it all, the real tears and sharp suffering; and propounds his deliberate attempt to control them by packing them into lines of verse:

> Then, as the earth's inward narrow crooked lanes
> Do purge sea-water's fretful salt away,
>   I thought, if I could draw my pains
> Through rhyme's vexation, I should them allay:
> Grief brought to numbers cannot be so fierce;
> For he tames it, that fetters it in verse.

But his resolve was brought to nothing by the vanity of some musical composer who turned his lines into a song. How far Donne's expression of disappointment is serious, and how far affected, is left tantalizingly uncertain. It is probably at first only half-serious at most, because of its dependence on the conceit that by pleasing listeners the grief which was tied up in the poetry will once again be at large. Yet a bitter note comes in, I think, in the lines:

> To love and grief tribute of verse belongs,
> But not of such as pleases when 'tis read;
>   Both are increasèd by such songs:
> For both their triumphs so are publishèd,. . . .

the implication being that 'love and grief' are wretched nuisances that only deserve to be paid off by the tribute-money of painful poems, and kept quiet. If the poetry is made to please people, the love and grief, and

17

so the poet's shame, will be published to the world. He will have loved, written about it, *and* everyone will know about it:

> And I, which was two fools, do so grow three;
> Who are a little wise, the best fools be.

Here we have the thrill of the neat conceit or 'evaporation of wit', intermingled with the mock sense of injury in the penultimate line, and with the complex poise of mood in the last line of all.

In this comparatively simple poem the basic mood has shifted several times. And a fair number of the *Songs and Sonets* are mercurial poems in this way. Yet some of the best are not mercurial at all. The steadiness of comfort and faith in mutual constancy of *A Valediction: forbidding mourning*, with its rather slow, firm movement, is of itself enough to disprove any generalization that the *Songs and Sonets* are 'mercurial poems'. 'Sweetest love, I do not go', another of the best of the poems, is also fundamentally stable in mood. At the other end of the positive-negative spectrum, the poems of predominantly negative emotion also vary in stability of mood. *The Apparition* and *The Curse* are single-mooded, whereas in *The Message* the moods shift according to a fairly regular pattern, and in *The Blossom* the shifts are more irregular and subtle.

Whether the moods are shifting or stable, however, one feature is always in evidence: the appearance of an intellectual force capable of thinking very precise thoughts, and alert to seize any opportunity, and to effect a rapid transition from one relevant thought to another. Donne does not waste words by spinning out his thoughts. He packs many thoughts into few lines. The tendency, if anything, is rather towards excessive compression: packing thoughts into lines so that the thoughts bulge out a bit, as in the lines in stanza 2 of *The Curse*:

> Madness his sorrow, gout his cramp, may he
> Make, by but thinking who hath made him such: . . .

or in ll. 7–8 of *The Paradox*:

> Love, with excess of heat, more young than old
> Death kills with too much cold; . . .

But to return to the precision of the thinking. I believe that it is significant that Donne was trained as a lawyer. Some of the precise trains of thought are of the kind we might expect in a brilliant advocate; though, of course, the counters used are quite often rather diverse from any likely to be current in a law court. Especially among the apparently earlier poems there are plenty of instances of arguing a case, and brilliant forensic points are made from time to time. As a simple instance we may take the point made in l. 4 of *Break of Day*. *Break of Day* is an *aube* (dawn-song) put into the mouth of the woman; and she is trying to persuade her lover not to get up in the early morning and leave her:

> 'Tis true, 'tis day, − what though it be?
> Oh, wilt thou therefore rise from me?
> Why should we rise? because 'tis light?
> Did we lie down because 'twas night?

An admirable point, just as a point, and made with humour. It is, of course, also reinforced by the very thinly veiled indication of the reason why they *did* 'lie down'. An excellent example of intricate advocacy is *The Prohibition*, whose third stanza may well, however, not be by Donne, but by his friend Thomas Roe, whom he had known already in his early days of association with the law. The sort of preposterous and ingenious argumentation exemplified in that poem may well have delighted young men trained in the Inns of Court. Other good examples are *The Sun Rising*, *Love's Usury*, *The Canonization*, *Community*, *Confined Love*, *The Flea*, *A Lecture upon the Shadow* and *The Damp*, among which, however, *The Sun Rising* and *The Canonization* may well have been written after James I's accession in 1603. All these poems are, at least ostensibly, attempting to persuade by argument, with varying degrees of seriousness. Obviously Donne does not imagine that in *The Sun Rising* he is really going to persuade the sun to do anything; but in *The Flea* he seems to want very much to persuade the lady to yield to him; and in *A Lecture upon the Shadow* he wishes to make her alert to the wonder and precariousness of their present love. These poems are not simply attempts to express feelings, or attitudes to life or even to the present situations. They are attempts to persuade, and not to persuade by merely showy rhetoric, but, as with the best advocates, by at least the appearance, and often the reality, of sound arguments. And this necessarily involves precise thinking. I do not wish, however, to push the lawyerly element in the thought of the *Songs and Sonets* too far. There is plenty of precise thinking in poems not endeavouring to persuade by argument, for instance in the analytical poems *Love's Diet* and *The Broken Heart*, or in poems which are primarily expressing a complex of feeling or an attitude to a specific situation, such as *A Nocturnal upon St Lucy's Day*, and *Twickenham Garden*. Yet in a good many of the *Songs and Sonets*, even including a few probably belonging to the later period 1598–1614, we do find characteristically lawyerly argument.

Both in argumentative poems and in poems which are dominantly analytical or even narrative, the *Songs and Sonets* abound in unexpected references, richness and rapidity of invention, and sheer ingenuity. These features are clearly meant to astonish. Yet the poems work in different ways. In *A Lecture upon the Shadow* one is astonished by the ingenuity of the point-by-point exploration of the concrete symbols of sun and shadows – all in service of the argument, which rests in turn upon passionate feeling. In *The Will*, on the other hand, what astonishes is the persistent invention of rich and apt references which follow one another like dazzling fireworks in a well-arranged display, where a fresh thrill comes before we have had time to tire of the old one. Dr Johnson's pronouncement that the metaphysical poets were men of learning, and that to show their learning was their whole endeavour, goes too far. Donne was, indeed, a 'man of learning', even by the time he came to write the *Songs and Sonets*, but it was not his 'whole endeavour' to show that learning. It would be truer to say that in some (though not all) of the *Songs and Sonets* there is an attempt to astonish, not so much by a display of learning (though this sometimes comes in), but by a grasp of the experience of various spheres, and by an insight into analogies between them, and relevancies in them to love situations. This is not as exciting a generalization as Dr Johnson's; but at least it has the advantage of being true. Now, if this grasp of various spheres of experience were very widespread, so that any fool could have thought up the analogies which Donne presents us with, the factor of astonishment would disappear. The truth is, however, that Donne had become familiar, through living and through reading, with an unusual range of realms of experience, such as law, war, medicine, science, philosophy and theology, as well as with a considerable array of the facts of everyday life; and had, moreover, cultivated and used a remarkable gift for seizing analogies and relevancies within the scope of love situations. Donne's range of realms of knowledge and experience was a singular one, and his gift for seizing significant analogies and relevancies was perhaps only rivalled by Shakespeare's. It is therefore understandable that there are many splendid instances in the *Songs and Sonets* of poetry surprising *not* 'by a fine excess' but by 'singularity': a conclusive proof that Keats's generalization, like so many generalizations, will not stand the test of facts.

The evident intention to astonish, which bulks so large in the

Songs and Sonets, naturally raises the whole question of 'sincerity'. Grierson himself, admirer of Donne's work as he was, nevertheless expressed a doubt whether it matched Shakespeare's in 'artistic sincerity'.[1] The wish to astonish is clearly not confined to obvious cases like 'Go and catch a falling star' or *The Will* or *The Flea*. It is also present where the feelings expressed are passionately positive, as in *A Valediction: forbidding mourning* and *Air and Angels*, and the element of display where strong positive feeling also appears to be present might seem to cast doubt on the ultimate authenticity of the feelings. One of my colleagues once said of *Air and Angels* that it seemed to him 'one of the inanest pieces of intellectual frippery that ever noodle tortured himself to contrive'. Now this opinion is a very honest and independent one, and represents a point of view which deserves a serious answer. My own answer, in the case of *Air and Angels*, would be that the central spring of the poem is a real passion, in a specific situation, and that it carries the ingenuity, which, in its turn, reflects some kind of credit on the feelings from which it springs. The feelings, one might say, deserved the display of pyrotechnics. I would say the same of *The Canonization*. I would, however, want to go further, and to maintain that, in general, a pyrotechnician would often fail to be sincere if he did not allow his basic emotions to stir him to pyrotechnical creation. Now Donne was an engrained, perhaps even a born, pyrotechnician. His sermons, and even his letters, are full of pyrotechnical writing. We must not consider such writing, either there, or in the *Songs and Sonets*, as inconsistent with or derogating from the strength of genuine impulses. Nor (and this is a distinct point) must we be dazzled like Dr Johnson was, and allow the display to obscure the central structure, attitudes and feelings of the poems. The *Songs and Sonets*, are, in general, fusions of (at least apparent) genuineness with display. Without the genuineness they would, indeed, often be frippery: without the display they would not be Donne; and we might well not be reading them today.

Some 'psychological' features of the poems

Here I want to consider briefly some characteristic (and uncharacteristic) attitudes, thoughts, feelings and sensations in the *Songs and Sonets*.

[1] *Metaphysical Lyrics and Poems of the Seventeenth Century: Donne to Butler*, Oxford, 1921, p. xx.

One characteristic attitude found in what may well be the earlier poems in the collection is that of more or less buoyant inconstancy, and a reluctance or a refusal to be bound down to any one individual:

> Let me, and do you, twenty know,
> Rob me, but bind me not, and let me go.
>
> (*The Indifferent*, ll. 15–16)

The buoyancy is particularly evident in *Confined Love* and *Community*, which becomes even brutal in its final stanza. In *Love's Usury* the poet begs the God of Love to spare him from loving until late middle age, when he will be willing to love *even* a woman who loves him. Here the reluctance to be tied down is evident enough; but the self-propelling buoyancy has gone. Help is needed to stave off the evil day when he must give himself to a more than superficial relationship. In *Love's Diet* he manages, without external help, to curb an aggravating impulse to love one woman, but he needs to be constantly vigilant, and use a great deal of cunning and resource to achieve the longed-for freedom expressed in the final stanza:

> Thus I reclaim'd my buzzard love, to fly
> At what, and when, and how, and where I choose;
>   Now negligent of sport I lie,
>   And now, as other falconers use,
> I spring a mistress, swear, write, sigh and weep:
> And the game kill'd, or lost, go talk, and sleep.

In one or two of these poems the principle of reciprocity is expressed: 'Let us both feel quite free'. In four out of the five poems mentioned, however, the inconstancy and reluctance to be bound down is expressed in general terms. It is only in *Love's Diet* that we feel the definite presence of a particular woman within the situation.

In a good half-dozen other poems, however, again probably among the earlier in the collection, we find resentment expressed at the scorn, falseness or inconstancy of some particular woman or of women in general. The most violent reaction is poured out in *The Apparition*, where the whole poem of seventeen lines consists of one sentence of concentrated ironic loathing and threatened vengeance fired off at some woman who has evidently rebuffed the poet's advances. *The Message* is also a poem of indignation and also of revenge, directed at a particular woman, for her apparently real, rather than simply imagined, infidelity. Dissatisfaction at a woman's infidelity is also the drive of *The Legacy*, though here there is a sense of tenderness and regret that the woman seems to be naturally fickle, just as the poet of *The Indifferent* thought *himself* to be. An attitude of regret, though not of tenderness, again seems to be present in the slighter poem *A Jet Ring Sent*. In *Woman's Constancy*, on the other hand, where again a particular woman is involved, though there is clearly some demur at the imagined infidelity of the woman the very next day, the poet adopts an attitude of hypothetical reciprocity, which places this poem close to those expressing an attitude of inconstancy. In all these five poems the poet is addressing a particular woman, not simply talking generally. Even in the case of the much more elaborate composition, *The Will*, though a woman is not directly addressed, she is clearly referred to in the third person in every stanza. The poet is in love with the woman, who is promiscuous, incapable of really receiving love, scornful of the poet's love and finds him too old (or too young – see my note on l. 45). Once again the poet feels vengeful; but his resolve, declared in the witty final stanza of this especially witty poem, is to take a general revenge, not only on the woman, but also on the world in general, and particularly on Love, who made him fall for a woman who was so unsatisfactory. The only other poem in the collection primarily concerned with female infidelity is the song 'Go and catch'. There the sceptical thought that there is no such being as a woman both faithful and beautiful is, perforce, offered in general terms. It is the only expression in the *Songs and Sonets* of that wide generalization.

There is, however, one other poem involving a broad and critical generalization about women: *Mummy* or *Love's Alchemy*. Here we encounter an attitude not at all characteristic in the *Songs and Sonets*: complete disillusion with love, which promises to realize dreams like those of alchemists for the philosopher's stone, but proves to be nothing but 'imposture'. The poem has, moreover, more to say: that women are mentally negligible. At their best they are merely sweet and lively, but once a man has sexually enjoyed them they are mere lumps of dead flesh. The nausea in this poem is, I think, more pervasive than the negative attitude to love in *Farewell to Love*. There also love is no longer considered worthy of attachment, but there is no reflection on women's mental endowments. The rejection of love is based on the evanescence of sexual enjoyment, and on the thought that, in any case, it shortens life.

In some other poems the poet seems to have fallen in love, but so far has not received from the woman either physical satisfaction or any satisfaction at all. In *The Broken Heart* the poet expresses the *coup de foudre* which has struck him, and, whatever the precise situation implied at the end of the poem, it is at least obvious that he has not yet been given satisfaction by the woman either spiritually or physically. The poem could, however, be an oblique courting poem. So could *The Paradox*, which is a slighter, more wire-drawn account of such a blow, resulting in this case in a Petrarchan death. *The Bait* represents a some- what similar situation; but here the courting is explicit. In *The Prohibi- tion*, again, the poet is already clearly committed, and here he seems to be asking more plainly for physical satisfaction. In *Love's Exchange* one has once more the sense of a *coup de foudre*, but the poem is more complex. It seems as if the lover himself had shown some reluctance to give way to his feelings, and as if the *coup* is thought of by him as a punishment for that. He is now in a state of acute torture, and says that he wishes neither himself nor the woman to know that this is love. The poem is, however, one suspects, primarily intended to let her know just that, and the poet himself, of course, knows it full well already. The strong military and medical references in this poem, incidentally, like the images of the pike and the chained shot in *The Broken Heart*, help to give the poem a masculine force, which, though in varying degrees, is, I think, characteristic of Donne's love-lyrics.

In *The Damp* the poet has evidently been rebuffed in attempting a sexual move. The woman has been disdainful, and concerned to protect her honour, and the poet argues for his aim by promising constancy and secrecy. In *The Flea* and *The Dream*, on the other hand, the lover seems to have already achieved a close and happy relationship, but his hope to sexualize it is balked by the woman's fear of sin or shame. In each poem the lover attempts to overcome the woman's resistance by argument. *The Funeral* and *The Blossom* also seem to refer to a rebuff. *The Funeral* leaves it slightly unclear whether it was a total rebuff, or a refusal of sexuality; but, since body is central in the poem, I am inclined to think it refers to a refusal of sexuality. Here the lover takes 'revenge' by having a 'wreath' of the woman's hair round his arm buried with his body. In *The Blossom* he detaches himself from the woman in a pique, and blazons that in London there will be a woman as glad to have his body as his mind. In all these five cases the lover takes some positive action in response to the rebuff. Lovers in the *Songs and Sonets* are, indeed, characteristically active lovers. The action in face of a rebuff may, however, only take the form of a strong protest, as in *Twickenham Garden*. In one case, *Love's Deity*, the lover actually says that he prefers that his love should not be reciprocated, since that would make the woman unfaithful to someone else. This attitude, which, if genuine, is also generous, is resolutely expressed – just as resolutely, indeed, as the opposite attitude is expressed in the last two lines of *Twickenham Garden*.

In *A Valediction: of my name, in the window* and *A Lecture upon the Shadow* the lover's attitude is one of firm commitment, and there is mutuality between the lovers, but the lover has some fear lest his beloved should be unfaithful to him (the *Valediction*) or that their love might decline (*A Lecture*). Both may represent an early stage in a deep and reciprocal love. So may *Air and Angels*, in which, indeed, it is clear that the woman has not yet given the poet her love, but only dazzled him by her beauty, and evoked his passionate attachment.

We now come to some fifteen poems or more which seem to express or imply great or complete satisfaction for the lover, and considerable or total mutuality: *The Expiration, The Computation, The Ecstasy, The Good-morrow, The Sun Rising, Break of Day, The Canonization, The Curse, Lovers' Infiniteness, The Anniversary, Love's Growth, A Valediction: of the book, A Valediction: of weeping, 'Sweetest love'* and *A Valediction: forbidding mourning*. Among these, *Break of Day* is the slightest, and is spoken by the woman. In *The Computation* and *A Valediction: of the book* there is some anxiety that the love may last, and this is so even in *The Good-morrow*. Donne seems there, as elsewhere (e.g. in *A Lecture*), to tend to be temperate in his forecasts of the future of a love already in existence. We do not find him saying that it will last for ever, or even for a long time. He does express hope that a love will continue, but when he expresses a *faith* that it will, the faith is only a hypothetical one, of the form 'If you and I love equally, our love (*or* we ourselves) will never die'. This is what Donne says in several places. Statements of this sort are, indeed, almost tautologous; but these near-tautologies seem much more satisfyingly near the truth than rash categorical faith in eternal constancy. Another, rather subtle, way in which Donne's thought about love distinguishes itself from more commonplace views, is in its uncertainty as to how far lovers are really united by their love (see *A Valediction: forbidding mourning* and *The Ecstasy*, ll. 41–56, as well as *The Good-morrow*, ll. 20–1). This uncertainty should, I believe, be regarded as the sign of an honest attempt not to exaggerate about the relationship of love, while at the same time recognizing its unifying force. It may well be, as some scholars believe, that Donne was influenced in his thinking about such problems by reading Italian love treatises, such as those by

Leone Ebreo, Mario Equicola, Pietro Bembo and Sperone Speroni; and he must have known Castiglione's *Cortegiano*.[1]

In *The Ecstasy* it is plain that the lovers have not yet slept with each other. In *The Sun Rising* it is amply evident that they have. In *The Good-morrow* it seems probable. In some of these poems of mutual love (e.g. *The Ecstasy*, *The Canonization*, *A Valediction: of the book* and *A Valediction: forbidding mourning*) there occurs the thought that the lovers are adepts in a mystery whose secrets are unknown to the common run of humanity. (The thought that there might, for a discerning lover, be no special relationship inaccessible to all and sundry, was, incidentally, one of the dissatisfactions felt about love in *Mummy* or *Love's Alchemy*.) In some poems great pride in the relationship is, in any case, expressed, e.g. in *The Good-morrow*, *The Sun Rising*, *The Anniversary*, and also the other four poems just mentioned; and other things and activities are hyperbolically considered insignificant in comparison with their love. In *Lovers' Infiniteness* the shared feeling is great but not complete, and Donne's fascinating logic is exercised in pointing the way to making it so. Resentment at anything interfering with the great love prompts the violent outbursts of *The Curse* and the early part of *The Canonization*.

Probably to be reckoned as belonging to the group of poems registering great or complete satisfaction for the lover, and considerable or total mutuality, are *The Undertaking* and *The Relic*, though in the former the shared feeling is not explicit. In both cases the love expressed is 'Platonic' (in the common modern sense), and it is regarded as a great achievement. It is interesting that these seem to be the only poems in the *Songs and Sonets* where the lover finds satisfaction in a purely 'Platonic' love. Indeed, there runs through the collection, taken as a whole, the belief that physical passion is a good thing. Sometimes, especially in the apparently earlier poems, it is seen as good in itself; even, at times, as preferable to the perils of love. Sometimes it is seen as a necessary and valuable element in a full and satisfying mutual attachment. In general, however, we are not in the realm of *amour physique*. We are most often in the realm of *amour-passion*; and we are never in that of *amour-goût*, to

---

[1] For the treatises by Leone Ebreo, Equicola and Speroni see the references on p. xxii above. Bembo's views are contained in *Gli Asolani* (1505). There is a modern edition edited by C. Dionisotti, with the *Rime*, Torino, n.d. [1929]. The *Cortegiano* was started in 1508 and revised over many years. It was printed at Venice in 1528. The best known modern edition is by V. Cian, Florence, 1894 (4th edn 1947). It was translated into English by Sir Thomas Hoby in 1561.

make use of Stendhal's illuminating distinctions.[1] Passionate feeling is paramount; even passionate sensuality is secondary; mere elegant gallantry (so frequent both in Elizabethan and seventeenth-century love-lyrics) is completely absent.

Finally, in the poems dealing with the illness or death of the beloved, Donne expresses grief and desolation, but in each case intellectual ingenuity and agility are evident. Here as elsewhere Donne's love-lyrics are not mere outpourings of feeling. They seldom escape from the poet's firm cerebral control. This is even so, perhaps especially so, in the magnificently desolate *Nocturnal*. It is important to realize, however, that in that poem, and in *The Dissolution*, we find a belief in personal immortality.

In a number of the *Songs and Sonets*, e.g. *Air and Angels*, *The Relic* and *A Nocturnal*, the poet credits his beloved with religious significance. In *The Dream* he even goes so far as to maintain that his lady possesses some of the divine attributes. Another typical thought is that the two lovers are self-sufficient. Donne sometimes extends this idea, and asserts that together they are the whole world. In this way the poems concerned become, in a certain respect, more than love poems: they become glorifications of love.

Besides the overall variety of attitudes and feelings about love in the *Songs and Sonets* as a whole, there is also often (though not always) considerable variety of attitudes and/or feelings within individual poems. One especially interesting type of case is where negative attitudes and feelings, such as petulance, bitterness, cynicism, irritation or contempt, arise in the course of poems which are predominantly positive. *The Sun Rising* is a happy poem of consummated love; but it is strewn with insults and scornful references. *The Canonization* is a vigorous glorification of love, but it begins with a voluminous outpouring of exasperation and contempt. Even in *Lovers' Infiniteness*, where the wooing is conducted in a tone of gentle reasonableness, there are overtones of petulance in places, for example in the use of such words as 'bargain' (l. 8), 'stocks' (l. 16), and 'outbid' (l. 17), which introduce the bitter suggestion of a love market. If the matter is looked into it will be found that there is scarcely a single positive poem in which some such feeling as cynicism, bitterness or contempt does not to some degree intrude. This strengthens the poems. It gives a sense of a fully ranging sensibility behind them, and it even adds to the wonder of the love. For just as

---

[1] *De l'amour*, Paris, 1822, bk I, ch. 1 and *passim* (1959 edn, pp. 5–7 and *passim*), where the distinctions are fully discussed.

when a hard man weeps it is impressive, so it is when a sceptical or cynical man loves.

It is time to pass on now to consider the rather peculiar sensory atmosphere of the *Songs and Sonets*. They contain very little colour. (With one exception, we do not know the colour of the hair or the eyes of any of the women involved in any of the poems, in contrast with those of Sidney's Stella and Shakespeare's Dark Woman. The exception is the 'bracelet of bright hair' in *The Relic*, l. 6, and even that is vague.) There are, on the other hand, from time to time, remarkably sharp, colourless visual impressions. Even these are, however, exceptional, and the focus of attention is very rarely the visual aspect of experience. The rarity of auditory sensations is even more marked. There is nothing in the whole of the *Songs and Sonets* like Wordsworth's 'casual shout that broke the silent air', or Vigny's

> J'aime le son du cor, le soir, au fond des bois.

There is, indeed, scarcely any reference to sounds at all. (The verse itself, on the other hand, provides interesting sound-effects; but that is quite a different matter, which will be considered in the following section of the Introduction.) Again, sense impressions of smell, as distinct from taste, do not seem to occur in the *Songs and Sonets*. There are, however, a few references to sensations of taste, and a fair number to the motor sensations involved in sucking, feeding, drinking and swallowing. This strain of often rather coarse physicality gives its definite tang to the poems in which it occurs, and sometimes contrasts strangely with the intellectual and spiritual interests which lie beside it. Other motor sensations are frequently referred to, such as the sensations involved in running, walking, snatching, winking and leaning; so also are organic sensations, such as the sense of inflammation of the veins which love may cause, or the sense of 'sorrowing dulness' after sexuality. In point of fact, in the *Songs and Sonets* motor and organic sensations definitely predominate over sensations of sight, sound, smell, taste, and even touch, and this is so even if we include in 'touch' cutaneous sensations of temperature as well as those of pressure. This may help to account for a feeling of *physical inwardness* that one often senses in the poems, despite all their references to the outside world.

With regard to what psychologists would call 'feeling-tone', painful sensations are quite often stimulated in the course of poems which are dominantly pleasurable. This is a parallel feature to that already noted in the case of feelings.

Some 'literary' features
of the poems

One of the most striking features of the *Songs and Sonets*, well enough known in general terms, is undoubtedly the pressure of the most diverse thoughts, images and allusions into the service of love poetry. References are made to astronomy, law, religion, war and military affairs, medicine, physics, metallurgy, meteorology, scholastic philosophy, politics, alchemy, astrology, botany, commerce, literary scholarship, hawking, angling, and the world of exploration, as well as to details of city life, and of the life of the home, and to such everyday activities as eating and drinking. Very often there is an astonishing difference between the field to which reference is made and the context in which the reference appears in the poem. A celebrated instance is Donne's comparison of himself and his beloved to a pair of compasses. Another remarkable instance occurs in *A Fever*, which deals with the illness of some woman to whom the poet seems deeply attached. The Stoics had disputed among themselves as to what sort of fire would consume the world at the end of each cycle of existence; and a similar controversy had arisen in the early Christian era centred on the reference in 2 Peter, iii. 7 to the final fire which would destroy the world. This was continued and elaborated by the Scholastics, and lasted until Donne's own time. Donne deliberately makes a preposterously witty use of that old dispute:

> O wrangling schools, that search what fire
> > Shall burn this world, had none the wit
> Unto this knowledge to aspire,
> > That this her fever might be it?

The turn of wit actually strengthens the poignancy of the poem. Indeed, even the most far-fetched references generally seem compellingly apt within their contexts in the poems. The combination of surprise and aptness is, moreover, certainly one of the chief merits of the imagery and allusion in the *Songs and Sonets*.

Possibly it was more especially Donne's references to scholastic philosophy that led Dryden to censure him for affecting metaphysics even 'in his amorous verses, where nature only should reign'. It was probably this criticism that brought into currency the application of the term 'metaphysical' to the poetry of Donne and his followers. But the term 'metaphysical' soon acquired a more general sense than Dryden probably intended, and came to connote the employment of learning as the stuff of poetry. Later still the term, owing to its traditional association with the work of particular poets, such as Donne, Crashaw, and Cowley, acquired a still broader connotation, namely the body of characteristics common and peculiar to the work of those English poets whom tradition has called 'metaphysical'. Thus the term 'metaphysical imagery' would now be quite commonly understood to refer to imagery which was *inter alia* both far-fetched and apt, like much of that of such poets as Donne, Crashaw, Cowley and Cleveland.

Another characteristic of the imagery and allusion in the *Songs and Sonets* is the near absence of mythological and pastoral reference. This was early recognized as a general characteristic of Donne's poetry. It was, no doubt, partly to this feature that Carew was referring in the following lines from his admirable *Elegy* on Donne's death:

> The Muses' garden with pedantic weeds
> O'erspread, was purg'd by thee; the lazy seeds
> Of servile imitation thrown away,
> And fresh invention planted.

(ll. 25–8)

This near absence of mythological and pastoral reference is closely bound up with the absence of conventional remoteness and gallantry from the *Songs and Sonets*. In their place a firm and even stern realism is often imparted to the poems by the references to war and military affairs, anatomy, politics, torture, commerce, and coarse details of day-to-day life; while, on the other hand, a certain lofty, recherché strain is often provided by the references to Scholastic doctrine, astronomy, religion, and learning; and a less lofty strangeness is injected by the references to alchemy, astrology and superstition.

The provenance of the imagery and of the allusions is much the same. Yet a distinction needs to be made between allusion and 'imagery' in the strict sense of simile and metaphor. The rich range of reference in that astonishing *tour de force*, *The Will*, consists almost entirely of allusion. It is only in the final stanza that we come upon imagery, in the comparisons of the woman's 'beauties' to unmined gold, and of her 'graces' to 'a sun-dial in a grave'. There is plenty of both allusion and imagery in the *Songs and Sonets*. Yet diverse allusions are seldom, if ever, packed so tightly as in *The Will*. *A Valediction: of the book* is also pretty closely filled with references, but in this case we have a mixture of allusions and imagery, and the images are mainly metaphors, though there are also similes, e.g. in ll. 54 and 56. (It is a mistake to think that similes are absent from the *Songs and Sonets*, though metaphors do predominate over them.)

Imagery is used very differently in different poems. Occasionally a single image is developed strictly throughout a poem, as with the simile of the sun for the love of the lovers in *A Lecture upon the Shadow*, and the fantastic metaphor of 2400 years for a 24-hour day in *The Computation*. Far more often Donne changes his images in the course of a poem, sometimes switching rapidly, as in *The Broken Heart*, sometimes in a more leisurely way, as in *A Valediction: forbidding mourning*. On the other hand, we do not find the running of one image into another, as so often happens in Shakespeare, both in the later plays and in the later *Sonnets*. Sometimes, in any case, imagery is only fitful, as in *A Nocturnal*, or even introduced at the start of a poem, and soon dispensed with, as in *The Blossom*. Conversely, there may be no imagery at the start, but a strong use of it at the end, as in the cynical last stanza of *Community*. There is no one pattern of the use of imagery in the *Songs and Sonets*.

Much of the vocabulary of the *Songs and Sonets* is surprisingly simple for a poet with such a reputation for obscurity as Donne. For a modern editor, glossing individual words is in fair measure a matter of metaphrasing or paraphrasing from the usage of Donne's time to that of the present day. It is generally Donne's uncommon turns of thought, tortuous syntax, subtle allusions, or obscurely working images, rather than his individual choice of words, that cause difficulty to a modern reader.

Let us look for a short while at some of Donne's diction. I have the impression that Donne uses a higher proportion of verbs in these poems than most love-lyrists do. There is, indeed, seldom such a helter-skelter of verbs as in ll. 5–8 of *Love's Usury*, but there is many a poem in which the quantity of verbs is conspicuous. Consider the first two stanzas of *The Canonization*:

> For God's sake hold your tongue, and let me love,
>   Or chide my palsy, or my gout,
> My five gray hairs, or ruin'd fortune flout,
>   With wealth your state, your mind with arts improve,
>   Take you a course, get you a place,
>   Observe his Honour, or his Grace,
> And the King's real, or his stampèd face
>   Contémplate; what you will approve,
>   So you will let me love.

31

> Alas, alas, who's injured by my love?
>> What merchant's ships have my sighs drown'd?
> Who says my tears have overflow'd his ground?
>> When did my colds a forward spring remove?
>>> When did those heats which my veins fill
>>> Add one man to the plaguy bill?
> Soldiers find wars, and lawyers find out still
>> Litigious men, which quarrels move,
>>> Though she and I do love.

or the first stanza of *The Curse*:

> Whoever guesses, thinks, or dreams he knows
> Who is my mistress, wither by this curse;
>> His only and only his purse
>> May some dull heart to love dispose,
> And she yield then to all that are his foes;
>> May he be scorn'd by one, whom all else scorn,
>> Forswear to others, what to her he hath sworn,
>> With fear of missing, shame of getting, torn: . . .

There are, indeed, stanzas and whole poems with a less high proportion of verbs; but there are quite a number of cases where the frequency of verbs runs not all that far short of this level. There is little doubt that this goes some way towards accounting for the active, lively impact of the poems.

Nouns there are also in plenty; and Donne seems to have a fondness for piling them one upon another as closely as he often does his verbs. This is true, for instance, of the first two stanzas of *The Canonization* quoted above, and of the last stanza of *The Curse*:

> The venom of all stepdames, gamesters' gall,
> What tyrants, and their subjects, interwish,
>> What plants, mines, beasts, fowl, fish
>> Can cóntribute; all ill which all
> Prophets, or poets, spake; And all which shall
>> Be annex'd in schedules unto this by me,
>> Fall on that man; for if it be a she,
>> Nature beforehand hath out-cursèd me.

and also of the first stanza of *The Anniversary*:

> All Kings, and all their favourites,
> All glory of honours, beauties, wits,

> The Sun itself, which makes times, as they pass,
> Is elder by a year now, than it was
> When thou and I first one another saw:
> All other things to their destruction draw,
>   Only our love hath no decay;
> This, no tomorrow hath nor yesterday;
> Running it never runs from us away,
> But truly keeps his first, last, everlasting day.

In the case of the last stanza of *The Curse* the effect is one of acceleration before the dead stop and unexpected side-sweep. In that of the first stanza of *The Anniversary* the effect is rather one of cumulative weight, making the contrast with the ever-fresh and buoyant love of the lovers all the more impressive.

There is also great use of personal pronouns in the *Songs and Sonets*, 'I', 'thou', 'me', 'thee', 'her', and, very notably, 'we', especially in the poems of satisfying love; and with these we may also mention such possessive adjectives as 'my', 'thy', 'our'. This helps to give to the poems a concentratedly and intensely personal character. Donne is especially skilful at juggling with these personal pronouns and possessive adjectives, as in:

> Coming and staying show'd thee, thee,
> But rising makes me doubt, that now
>   Thou art not thou.
> > > > (*The Dream*, ll. 21–3)

> To me thou, falsely, thine,
> And I to thee mine actions shall disguise.
> > > > (*A Lecture upon the Shadow*, ll. 20–1)

and in the clever play on personal identity in stanza 2 of *The Legacy*:

> I heard me say: 'Tell her anon,
>   That my self' (that is you, not I)
>   'Did kill me'; and when I felt me die,
> I bid me send my heart when I was gone;
> But I alas could there find none,
>   When I had ripp'd me, and search'd where hearts should lie;
> It kill'd me again, that I who still was true
> In life, in my last will should cozen you.

The brilliance of such play is a delight in itself; and it never detracts from the strength of the poems in which it occurs. Donne's overall alertness and control guarantee that such dazzling displays seem to have their natural place in the lively, personal wholes of which they form part.

Before leaving parts of speech I do want to mention one set of words of very frequent occurrence in these poems: the conjunctions 'if', 'but', 'yet', 'and', 'or' and, somewhat less often used, 'though'. All are of interest, but I have only space to say a little about 'if', 'but' and 'yet'. There is scarcely a poem that does not contain the word 'if'. Most often it is used to present a hypothetical possibility or possibilities occurring to the poet, as in *Lovers' Infiniteness* (ll. 1 and 12), 'Go and catch' (ll. 10 and 19), *Community* (ll. 7 and 13), *The Relic* (l. 12), and a host of other cases. It is one of the many signs of the fertility of Donne's imagination. 'But' and 'yet' are often used to slew a poem round in its course, and pursue another line of thought, as with 'but' in *Twickenham Garden* (l. 14), *The Ecstasy* (l. 49), *A Valediction: forbidding mourning* (l. 17), *The Will* (l. 46), *The Anniversary* (l. 22), *The Triple Fool* (l. 12), and in many other instances; and as with 'yet' in *The Legacy* (l. 17), *Lovers' Infiniteness* (l. 23), *The Message* (l. 17), *The Broken Heart* (l. 25), *A Jet Ring Sent* (l. 9), and some other cases. Both 'yet' and 'but' have in most of these cases a dynamic function, indicating a change of feeling or of mind on the part of the poet. In others they are used to present a contrast, clearly felt by the poet, between two states of affairs, for instance the love of 'dull sublunary lovers' and that of himself and his beloved.

A really detailed study of all the parts of speech in these poems could be rewarding, but I can only offer a few impressions for consideration. I must now mention a few other features of vocabulary that have struck me, then move on to some observations about combinations of words and typical structures of sentences, and next on to rhythm and metre and speed of movement, and finally to stanza forms and the formal structure of whole poems.

What sorts of verbs and nouns does Donne use in these lyrics? The verbs are for the most part very ordinary, for example, 'come', 'go', 'think', 'know', 'see', 'tell', 'love', 'give', 'say', 'make', 'get', 'live', 'die', 'kill,' 'send', 'find', and, naturally, the verb 'to be' in many of its forms. Just occasionally one encounters a verb of some sophistication, such as 'antedate' (*Woman's Constancy*, l. 3), 'emparadis'd' (*A Valediction: of my name, in the window*, l. 26), 'transubstantiates' (*Twickenham Garden*, l. 6), 'interinanimates' (*The Ecstasy*, l. 42). On a liberal rough count I have found about 50 such verbs, an average of less than one per poem (or one in every 32 lines of the 1600 lines of the whole corpus of the *Songs and Sonets* as printed in this edition). On the other hand, there are also, from time to time, among the simple verbs, some which are not just ordinary. There are a number of violent verbs, e.g. 'cut up', 'torn' (*Love's Exchange*, l. 39), 'shiver' (= 'smash into smithereens') (*The Broken Heart*, l. 24), 'smother' (*The Dissolution*, l. 8), 'ripp'd' (*The Legacy*, l. 14), 'bind' (*The Indifferent*, l. 16), while 'break' and 'kill' occur a number of times. Then there are particularly homely words, such as 'thread' (*The Ecstasy*, l. 7), 'knit' (ibid., l. 63), 'blew out' (*The Computation*, l. 5), 'feed' (*Love's Diet*, l. 5), 'nestle' (*The Blossom*, l. 10), 'kindle' (*The Dream*, l. 19); and some of the homely words are even more or less coarse: 'suck'd', 'snorted' (= 'snored') (*The Good-morrow*, ll. 3–4), 'brin'd' (*Love's Diet*, l. 13), 'sweat' (ibid., l. 18), 'pinch' (in bed) (*The Apparition*, l. 8), 'chaws' (*The Broken Heart*, l. 14). The homely verbs are somewhat more frequent than the sophisticated verbs. As can be seen, the range from the learned to the physically basic is therefore considerable. Yet the vast majority of the verbs Donne uses in these poems (over 1500 out of some 1700, including duplicates, but not including 'to be' or auxiliaries) are, as I have said, quite ordinary verbs, such as those indicated.

The case of the nouns is somewhat different. There are, on a rough count, about 200 nouns (including duplicates) of some sophistication in the 54 poems here printed, that is, nearly 4 per poem (or one per 8 lines), and so they are about four times as numerous as the sophisticated verbs. Yet these nouns seem to be carried by the simple verbs, so that there is no effect of stodginess or undue heaviness. An unusual number of such nouns occur in some poems – the largest number, and the highest proportion, in that elaborate poem *A Valediction: of the book*. A stanza from that poem may help to indicate how Donne succeeds in making the verse weighty with impressive nouns without making it halt, or clogging it:

> Study our manuscripts, those myriads
>   Of letters, which have past 'twixt thee and me,
>   Thence write our Annals, and in them will be,
> To all whom love's subliming fire invades,
>   Rule and example found;
>   There, the faith of any ground
>   No schísmatic will dare to wound,
>   That sees, how Love this grace to us affords,
> To make, to keep, to use, to be, these his Recórds.

Here there are 13 verbs, all but 4 of which are of the simplest kind, and only one of which is to any substantial degree elaborate. These simple verbs keep the verse moving, and in the last line they impart to it an added impetus, leading up to the final, sophisticated noun.

Though there are this quite large number of sophisticated nouns in the collection as a whole, a few poems have none, e.g. *Lovers' Infiniteness, The Broken Heart* and *The Expiration*; or hardly any, e.g. *The Anniversary, Community*, 'Sweetest love' and *The Prohibition*. *Lovers' Infiniteness* is wholly concerned with following through a complicated set of changing thoughts, feelings and arguments; *The Broken Heart* is an explosive expression of a *coup de foudre*; and *The Expiration* of a highly emotional parting. In none of these poems would elaborate language be in place. *Community* is simply an evaporation of wit with a coarse sting at its close, whilst 'Sweetest love' is a limpid, tender lyric; and in such poems we can see that elaboration would be equally inappropriate. *The Anniversary* is, indeed, metrically elaborate, and it is interesting that its nouns are almost all simple. Yet if we contrast it with the monumental *Valediction: of the book* we can clearly see that it is preoccupied with the love rather than with the splendours of magniloquence. It is also progressive, whereas the *Valediction* is comparatively static. As for *The Prohibition*, that is a poem of as nimble a wit as *Community*, and it is in keeping that elaborate nouns should not impede its brisk forward thrust.

Homely nouns are, nevertheless, even more frequent in the *Songs and Sonets* than their sophisticated brethren – on a rough count I should say there are about 300 including duplicates (slightly less than six per poem, or slightly less than one per five lines); and in some poems their proportion is very high, e.g. in *The Canonization*, which, however, also contains a few more elaborate nouns like 'legend', 'chronicle', 'hermitage' and 'pattern'. This combination of the down-to-earth and the learned corresponds to the evolution of that astonishing poem, which proceeds so remarkably from the mundane to the 'mysterious'. It is notable that the more elaborate nouns mainly occur late in the poem. In contrast, in *The Broken Heart* there are no elaborate nouns, but a high proportion of homely ones, some of which are violent ('plague', 'pike', 'blow') or coarse ('rags') in implication or tone. This goes a fair way towards producing the impact of explosive destructiveness which is of the essence of that poem.

Once again, however, it is nouns that are neither particularly elaborate nor particularly homely that form the staple of Donne's vocabulary of substantives: about 1500 out of about 2000 nouns (including duplicates) in the whole collection. I mean nouns like 'love', 'lover', 'eye', 'heart', 'thought', 'word', 'tears', 'name', 'thing', 'hour', 'year', 'day', 'life', 'death', 'part', 'man', 'woman', 'mind', 'soul', 'truth', 'world', 'hope', 'fear', 'pain', 'shame', 'fire', 'heat', 'cold', 'sun', 'moon'.

With regard to other parts of speech I have only space to add something brief about the adjectives. Adjectives are, perhaps naturally, less numerous than nouns and verbs. On an average there are rather less than one in every two lines. Some poems have scarcely any. The impetuous rush of the 32 lines of *The Curse* only allows three. The intensity of the passion and the swift ingenuity of the conceits in *A Valediction: of weeping* has only room for the same number. On the other hand, occasionally, there are many adjectives in a poem, as in that richly and curiously sensuous poem *The Bait* (25 in its 28 lines). In the whole collection more or less sophisticated adjectives are pretty evenly matched with those which are homely, coarse, or violent. There are some 80–90 in each of the two opposing camps. In between there is a large contingent of quite ordinary adjectives, e.g. 'little', 'great', 'new', 'old', 'true', 'false', 'good', 'bad', 'weak', 'strong', 'short', 'long', 'dear', 'poor', 'cheap', 'young', 'more', 'less', 'first', 'last'. Once again, as we would expect, the elaborate *Valediction: of the book*, in so far as it contains adjectives at all, tends towards the sophisticated, with such instances as 'subliming', 'all-gravèd', 'new-made', 'ravenous', 'abstract', 'spiritual', 'convenient', and affords no instances of adjectives of the homely type, for 'lame' in l. 8 is used in a highly sophisticated sense. On the other hand, in *The Bait* there is an uncanny *mélange* of the sophisticated and the coarse, which probably serves well Donne's parodic intention.

In respect, therefore, of three of the most noteworthy verbal units, verbs, nouns and adjectives, Donne uses a wide range from the elaborate to the homely and even coarse, with a broad band, between these minorities, of quite ordinary words, which do journeymen's work in carrying the sense along. As to the provenance of elaborate words, they almost all come from the areas from which the particular images or allusions they express are drawn.

With regard to the phonal aspect of Donne's use of these parts of speech, and, indeed, of his diction in general, we need to bear in mind his own statement:

> I sing not siren-like to tempt; for I
> Am harsh.
> (*To Mr S.B.* [Samuel Brooke], ll. 9–10)

With regard to the *Songs and Sonets*, in which, as love-lyrics, one might expect to find many instances of a 'dying fall' (to borrow Shakespeare's phrase), there is seldom, if ever, to be found a word chosen simply for its mellifluousness. Even in the poems lending themselves to musical setting, the semantic aspect of words is dominant in Donne's art. This is not to say, however, that the sound of words is unimportant for Donne. Indeed, sometimes the sound affords signal reinforcement to the sense. This is especially so, though, where the effect achieved is astringent, as where a stanza ends with a laconic snap, such as we find at the ends of stanzas 1 and 2 of *A Nocturnal*:

> . . . yet all these seem to laugh,
> Compar'd with me, who am their epitaph.

and

> He ruin'd me, and I am re-begot
> Of absence, darkness, death; things which are not.

and stanza 1 of *The Sun Rising*:

> Love, all alike, no season knows, nor clime,
> Nor hours, days, months, which are the rags of time.

and stanza 3 of [*Picture and Dream*]:

> Though you stay here, you pass too fast away;
> For, even at first, life's taper is a snuff.

An especially fine use is made in *The Expiration* of the explosive word: 'Go'. The final line of that poem is, indeed, altogether a masterpiece of phonal expression of the heaviness of the lovers' parting:

> Being double dead, going, and bidding go.
> [Possibly 'bidding: "Go!"']

It is high time that I moved on to discuss syntax, a few points concerning which I have, indeed, already touched upon. Although the basic units of Donne's language in these poems are, in the vast majority of cases, simple, he achieves with them effects of considerable complexity. His art in the *Songs and Sonets* is, in a stronger sense than with most poets, essentially a combinatory art. At the most elementary level we find him using simple units to form unusual compounds or short phrases (my italics):

> And makes one little room, an *everywhere*.
>
> (*The Good-morrow*, l. 11)

A *she-sigh* from my mistress' heart, . . .
> *(Love's Diet,* l. 10)

And if some lover, such as we,
  Have heard this *dialogue of one,* . . .
> *(The Ecstasy,* ll. 73–4)

No *tear-floods,* nor *sigh-tempests* move; . . .
> *(A Valediction: forbidding mourning,* l. 6)

I have already mentioned Donne's lively play with personal pronouns and possessive adjectives. A closely related phenomenon is the repetition of key words within a short space. A simple case is the logically alert play with 'give' in stanza 3 of *Lovers' Infiniteness,* a poem which I shall be discussing in more detail presently:

> Thou canst not every day give me thy heart;
> If thou canst give it, then thou never gav'st it: . . .

A more complex instance is the serpentine convolution produced by the repetition of 'love' and 'know' in stanza 3 of *Love's Exchange*:

> Love, let me never know that this
> Is love, or that love childish is;
> Let me not know that others know
> That she knows my pains, lest that so
> A tender shame make me mine own new woe.

Sometimes, on the other hand, the key word is not only repeated within a short space, but also features as central to a whole poem; as does the word 'love', and, to a lesser extent, the word 'god' in *Love's Deity*; the word 'all' in *Lovers' Infiniteness*; and the two words 'love' and 'hate' in *The Prohibition*. Sometimes, again, a key word simply runs through a poem, helping to bind it together, as 'give' does in *The Will*; and the negatives 'not', 'none', 'nothing' and 'nothingness' do in *A Nocturnal*. In that poem, however, the desolate impression of the whole owes much to a number of other privative words, especially nouns and verbs, but also adjectives.

In a few cases Donne achieves a very subtle effect by giving to a word through its context a strong sense which it would not have without that specific environment. A striking instance occurs in stanza 1 of *Love's Usury*, where the abstract word 'relict' (l. 7) is made by its context to take on with sublime contempt the sense 'cast-off mistress'.

A further case occurs in stanza 2 of the same poem, where 'místake' in l. 11, while retaining its usual sense, is made by the context to take on the further sense 'seduce' (and sleep with). Again, in ll. 8–9 of *The Apparition*, the word 'more' in 'think thou call'st for more' is conditioned by its context to mean 'more sexual play', and with highly telling effect.

It is well known that in the *Songs and Sonets* the tone is almost always that of a speaking voice. It does not follow, however, that the word order is almost always that of normal speech. It very often is; yet there are countless instances of inversion, such as:

> 'Twas so; but this, all pleasures fancies be:
> If ever any beauty I did see, . . .
>> (*The Good-morrow*, ll. 5–6)

> Must to thy motions lovers' seasons run?
>> (*The Sun Rising*, l. 4)

> My five gray hairs, or ruin'd fortune flout,
>   With wealth your state, your mind with arts improve, . . .
>> (*The Canonization*, ll. 3–4)

Sometimes the cause of the inversion may simply be that it was easier to keep metre by rhyming with the verb. Occasionally, indeed, such a consideration seems to have forced Donne into some very tortuous syntax, as in ll. 14–15 of *Lovers' Infiniteness*, where 'shall' in l. 14 rhymes with 'all' in l. 12:

> But if in thy heart, since, there be or shall
> New love created be, by other men, . . .

and possibly in ll. 7–8 of *The Paradox*:

> Love with excess of heat, more young than old
>   Death kills with too much cold; . . .

Generally, however, the syntax is either that of the spoken language, or very close to it. Sometimes Donne is able to construct passages of some length with very little departure from the word order of talk. *The Apparition* is a splendid example, the only palpable deviations being the position of the verbs at the ends of ll. 5 and 10. It is to be noted, however, that in that poem, as, indeed, often in the *Songs and Sonets*, a large syntactical whole is built up out of a number of short *co-ordinate* units. In this case the hypothetical narrative is conducted by the use of the connectives 'and' and 'then'. Donne uses various methods of linking the shorter units to form wholes of some size. The long first stanza of *A Lecture upon the Shadow* is an interesting case. The initial couplet announces the lecture, which starts at l. 3. Lines 3–5 form one unit, 6–8 a second one, 9 to 'care' in l. 11 a third, and the rest of l. 11 a fourth. There is only slight deviation from the word order of speech. The contrast within the allegory of ll. 3–8 is signalled by 'But' at the start of l. 6; and the corresponding contrast within the situation of the lovers is likewise signalled by the 'but' in l. 11; while the relation between allegory and 'reality' is indicated by 'So'. Sometimes, on the other hand, no connectives are used, but short statements follow one another in ordered sequence, as in stanza 2 of *The Broken Heart*. This comparatively informal method is probably more in keeping with the speed and violent emotion of this poem, whereas the more formal use of connectives in the *Lecture* is appropriate to the deliberateness of the lesson it is concerned to teach.

Lovers' Infiniteness is an especially remarkable instance of the construction of large wholes out of shorter units, and I want to discuss it at some length. As I hope to show, it is not without what seem to be defects, but it is an astonishing performance all the same. Each long stanza is a single sentence, and the whole poem (save ll. 29–30) is a tightly connected argument of considerable intricacy, with an admirably satisfying resolution in its last three lines. The poem starts off with a hypothetical assumption, and an inference from it. Then follows (ll. 2–6) a statement of exhaustion, and inability to woo any further. Next, however, there comes a change of direction, with the chilling thought that perhaps all his beloved had contracted to give her lover was part of her love (ll. 7–10), in which case the inference stated in l. 2 would be valid: he would never have all her love. The whole of the stanza is thus constructed out of four units, which together form a complete sentence. Moreover, the units, and, furthermore, the transitions between them, give an impression of intimate speech; and there is, indeed, only one deviation from conversational word order (the inversion of 'fall' in l. 10). At the start of stanza 2 we find Donne's argumentative invention bubbling up yet again, with the thought of another upsetting possibility: that if the beloved had given her lover all her love, it could be held that this was, indeed, the gift of all she had at the time, but that if other lovers were to come along and make her love them by shedding more tears, sighing more sighs, swearing more oaths, or writing more letters than the poet, that would cause him more anxiety, since any such love was not part of the original bargain with him. All this forms the first unit of stanza 2 (ll. 11–19). Then, however, Donne swiftly swivels round, preposterously invoking the legal image of a gift of land, carrying with it the gift of whatever may grow on it (ll. 20–2). This involves ingeniously springing upon the beloved the assumption that she had given the poet her *heart* (Donne is cheating here, and almost certainly knows that quite well). The transition is effected without infringing the normal syntax of prose. On the other hand, earlier in the stanza (in ll. 14–15) there occurs, as already mentioned (on p. 40), a violent syntactical deviation and contortion. Is this to be regarded as a defect? I doubt it. The lines evoke a certain delight by their tortuous ingenuity, and the cunning with which they are fitted into the stanza. With regard to connectives, so far Donne has only used them to mark changes of direction ('yet' in l. 7; 'Or' in l. 11; 'but' in l. 14; 'And yet' in l. 20). Otherwise the argument has proceeded by straight statements, hypotheses, and inferences, each unit lasting for several lines. The resolution at the end of stanza 2 could mark the end of the poem; but Donne's invention is far from exhausted. Stanza 3 starts with a further change of direction, introduced by the connective 'Yet'. The lover does not want all the beloved's love at once: otherwise he could not have more, and he deserves always more and more, to match the daily growth of his own love (which the poet is here able to mention for the first time, and so to woo further, though in stanza 1 he had said that such a thing was impossible!). This brings us to l. 26. In l. 27 Donne plays another clever trick. He no longer talks in terms of the mistress giving him further *love*, but in terms of her giving her *heart* all over again each day. He wants to argue convincingly that any further gift by her would be impossible, so that he may offer his own solution, with which the poem is to end. Therefore, instead of suggesting that she match the daily increases in his love by daily increases in her love for him, which would seem the natural quid pro quo, he argues in terms of her heart, and concludes in l. 28 with the required impossibility (since l. 20 has already indicated that she has given her heart before). This trick (in ll. 27–8) is played without using any connective with the preceding lines, thus giving the impression that the sequence is wholly natural, which it most certainly is not. But what are we to say of ll. 29–30, which have the air of being some kind of explanatory comment on ll. 27–8? Actually they cut right across the reason already given for the impossibility of her going on giving her heart every day, namely, that she had already given it. What the poet is now saying is that by giving away her heart she actually keeps it – from which the natural inference would be, however, that she *could* go on giving it every day (contrary to ll. 27–8). The new idea is brilliant in itself, and draws strength from biblical authority, but it does not seem to fit satisfactorily into the poem. There is, however, textual difficulty here (see my note on the lines), and the true reading could easily be:

> Except mine come when thine doth part,
> And so in giving it thou savest it.

which might just make sense with what has gone before (though far from perfect sense), and would certainly fit in well with l. 32, which suggests that ll. 29–30 are meant to refer to an exchange of hearts. In view of this textual difficulty we can probably at most say that Donne definitely overreached himself if and when he wrote the version printed in the 1633 edition; though it must be admitted that the alternative reading is not wholly satisfactory either, since the beloved would not actually be saving *her* heart, and certainly not *by* receiving his instead, which the lines seem most naturally to imply. There seems, then, on either reading, to be some blemish here in an otherwise admirable poem. A connective such as 'except' is, in any case, needed if the lines are to offer some sensible idea, and not to indicate simply a matter of hocus-pocus. The final resolution, on the other hand, contained in ll. 31–3, and introduced by the connective 'But', is entirely satisfying. Moreover, stanza 3, though suffering from the blemish in ll. 29–30, never departs, even in those two lines, from the word order of spoken prose. Structurally, it falls into four parts (ll. 23–6, 27–8, the weak 29–30 and the excellent 31–3), and, like the other two stanzas, it consists of a single sentence. The poem as a whole is totally bare of allusion, utterly concentrated on the highly inventive and intricate argument; and written in the simplest words, seldom ordered differently from the language of spoken prose, and permeated with a steady tenderness of feeling. It is a *tour de force* of texture and structure; and all the more human for the slight blemish towards its close.

The fact that in these lyrics the word order is normally that of spoken prose naturally raises the question how Donne manages to combine the rhythms of speech with the exigences of metrical form. He does almost always succeed in doing so; though not always in the same way. In a few instances it is at least questionable whether he does succeed. Drummond tells us that Ben Jonson declared that 'for not keeping of accent' Donne 'deserved hanging'. In making such a general observation Jonson only revealed one of his own limitations. Remarkable literary man though Jonson was, the validity of Donne's 'unmetrical' use of speech rhythms, springing straight from strong feeling or brilliant wit, or a combination of both, was beyond him. Actually, Donne's verse is generally more regular than Jonson's statement would suggest. Consider stanza 1 of *The Good-morrow*, with its lively questions and statements, all in the word order, and bearing the rhythms, of spoken prose:

> I wonder, by my troth, what thou and I
> Did, till we lov'd; were we not wean'd till then?
> But suck'd on country pleasures, childishly?
> Or snorted we in the Seven Sleepers' den?
> 'Twas so; but this, all pleasures fancies be:
> If ever any beauty I did see,
> Which I desir'd, and got, 'twas but a dream of thee.

Here the only metrical irregularities are in ll. 2 and 4, and the irregularity of l. 4 is merely the substitution of an anapaest for an iambus in the third foot. Sometimes, indeed, it is the metre itself which guides us how to read lines which could be stressed in more than one way with normal speech-rhythms. A good example is ll. 23–4 of 'Go and catch a falling star':

> Though she were true, when you met her,
> And last, till you write your letter, . . .

It is the metre, on the pattern of the preceding stanzas, which tells us to put the stresses on 'Though', 'were', and 'And' and 'till', rather than on other words. Again, in l. 5 of *Woman's Constancy*:

> We are not just those persons which we were?

it is metre that indicates that we must stress 'are' and 'just'. The same kind of thing happens in a number of cases. There are even a few whole poems in which there is very little metrical irregularity indeed, e.g. *The Undertaking*, *The Bait*, *The Broken Heart*, *The Ecstasy*. It is, indeed, probably significant that three of these four poems are in quatrains. We generally find somewhat more metrical irregularity in poems written in longer stanzas. There are, indeed, extreme cases, such as the third stanza of *Farewell to Love*, in which the irregularity borders on metrical breakdown; but generally, even in poems with complex stanza forms, the quantum of irregular lines is not all that high, e.g. *A Nocturnal* and *A Valediction: of the book*. Moreover, the occurrence of occasional irregular lines is welcome both as bearing the life of speech-rhythms and as affording variety. In sum, then, Donne sometimes succeeds in combining speech-rhythms with the demands of metre by writing lines which, though in spoken language, are also metrically regular; at other times by writing metrically irregular lines among regular lines in such a small proportion that one is not disturbed by their irregularity, but more often than not exhilarated by it. Very occasionally he makes a serious sacrifice either of metrical regularity for the sake of the speech-rhythms, or of the order and rhythms of spoken language for the sake of metrical regularity. In some of these cases the sacrifice seems worthwhile, in others not.

The speed of the poems varies according to their overall mood. The savage comminations of *The Curse* boil forth like a torrent of lava. The peremptory injunctions and the pseudo-petulant questions in *The Canonization* are snapped out briskly. In contrast, the formal pronouncements of *The Will* and the detailed instructions of *A Valediction: of the book* proceed at a leisurely pace; while the sombre *Nocturnal* moves with all the heaviness of deep despondency. These slow poems, moreover, do not all move in the same way. The *Nocturnal* is more involuted than the other two, with its heavy caesurae, which bring the movement in places to a dead stop. Between the extremes of *The Curse* and the *Nocturnal* there are a host of poems which move at all manner of speeds. Within single poems the overall speed is for the most part fairly constant, though in the stanzaic poems it must perforce always come to a stop at the end of each stanza. However, there are exceptions to overall constancy, as, clearly, in the last stanza of *The Curse*, which accelerates until the middle of l. 31, and then pivots deftly for the delivery of the final joke. Donne is a master of speed, as of so much else. He is also a master of weight, with a great range from the buoyancy of 'Go and catch a falling star' and *Community* and *The Indifferent*, through the ruminatory *Love's Growth* and *Love's Alchemy* to, once again, the *Nocturnal*, which is the weightiest as well as the slowest of the *Songs and Sonets*.

The cohesion of stanzas, and, indeed, of whole poems, is often achieved partly by the skilful use of rhymes. Twenty of the poems start with a couplet, and the opening rhyme-scheme *aabb* is very common. Donne is fond of reiterated rhymes. Eighteen of the poems end in triplets or quadruplets. The use of reiterated rhymes, whether in the openings or endings or in the body of poems, acts as a strong counter-force to any tendency for the distortion of metre by speech-rhythms to result in a stanza or passage breaking into disorder. The triplets in ll. 5–7 of each stanza of *A Nocturnal* afford an instance of this effect.

The forms of the *Songs and Sonets* are almost all stanzaic. The stanzas are exceedingly various, and many of them very complex. Donne only uses one stanza more than once: the simple octosyllabic quatrain with alternate rhymes, which he uses in three poems. Seemingly, over forty of the stanza forms were invented by him. The vast majority of the poems are in stanzas of six to eleven lines. Eight- and nine-line stanzas occur most frequently. Occasionally two or three poems have the same rhyme-scheme; but where that is so, they differ in line lengths. It is as if Donne proudly scorned to repeat the same stanza form. Some of the stanza forms are very attractive in themselves. Much play is made with variations of line length. Stanzas of more than six lines seem to give Donne the scope he so often needs to develop the complex interplay of thought and feeling which is so typical of him. In some cases the stanza forms seem especially appropriate to their respective poems. This is so, for instance, with the *Song*, 'Go and catch a falling star', where the piquant slightness of the short lines prepares by contrast the elongated sting in the tail of each stanza. A similar effect is achieved in *The Blossom*, where the short sixth line of each stanza sets off the epigrammatic couplet which follows. Again, the sharp changes of line length in *A Valediction: of weeping* accord magnificently with the turbulent passion underlying the conceits; while the steady fixity of the lines of *A Valediction: forbidding mourning* is at one with the firm, substantial love in which the poem shows such settled confidence. The stanza forms do not always seem so peculiarly appropriate as in these cases; but they frequently delight by their intricacy: and the fact that the rich texture of feeling, thought, and imagery, and the odd quirks and ironies, could be made to take on shapes of such fairly strict complexity is often a subject for astonishment.

The overall forms of the poems are sometimes very clearly patterned. Twenty-two of the poems are substantially ternary in form, and eight binary. The rest have, at all events, more than three stanzas, if they are stanzaic; though five of the poems are in single stanzas. (It is a curious fact – which may have some significance for the superstitious – that the poems in quatrains have 7, 9 or 17 stanzas, and that the long poem *A Valediction: of my name, in the window* has 11!). Among the poems in binary or ternary form the formal pattern can almost always be seen to fit the general drift of the poem with great appropriateness. Particularly clear instances are the binary poems *Witchcraft by a Picture*, *The Triple Fool*, *Air and Angels*, and *A Lecture upon the Shadow*, which is also substantially binary; and the ternary poems *The Message*, 'Go and catch a falling star', *Lovers' Infiniteness*, *A Valediction: of weeping*, and *The Prohibition*, whose last stanza, even if not by Donne, is brilliantly successful. In the case of the more extended poems, there is often no apparent relation between the number of stanzas and the substance of the poem. Yet, even in such cases, the poems give one the impression of possessing firm shape. Sometimes, indeed, as in the device of the 'dialogue of one' in *The Ecstasy*, and the wonderful thematic modification of the opening line of *A Nocturnal* at the end of the poem, we come across especially satisfying examples of formal beauty.

The 'Songs and Sonets' and Petrarchism

The *Songs and Sonets* are, in many ways, unlike the *Canzoniere* of Petrarch. The *Canzoniere* represents the continuous love-relationship of one man to one girl (later woman) over many years, and even beyond her death. The *Songs and Sonets* most probably refer to a number of women, where they refer to particular women at all, though a number of them may well be concerned with the girl who became Donne's wife. Again, in so far as the poems grew out of personal experiences (and I find it hard to believe that the great majority of them did not), they have the appearance of representing discontinuous, mostly momentary, reactions to specific love-situations, 'spots of time', over a number of years. Another plain point of difference from the *Canzoniere* is that none of the clearly authentic poems is a sonnet, whereas the immense majority of the poems in the *Canzoniere* are sonnets. This is quite important, since one of the dominant traditions in English love poetry from Wyatt till Donne's own time had adopted the sonnet form. I cannot help believing that Donne regarded it as important to show his independence of the sonnet craze in his love poetry. The *Canzoniere*, however, contains a fair number of songs (*canzoni*), and some of these are written in complex stanza forms not unlike some of Donne's lyrics. It seems to me quite possible that Donne was deliberately choosing the 'song' as the type of poem in the Petrarchan tradition which had not been overworked in recent years. Donne certainly can be taken to have known his Petrarch. He chose as one of his mottoes 'Per Rachel ho servito e non per Lea' (*Canz.* 206.55),[1] where Petrarch is, of course, referring to the story in Genesis 29. Donne inscribed this motto in the books in his

[1] In Petrarch the form is actually 'Lia'.

library. As indicated, the line comes from one of the *canzoni*, and its bearing in Petrarch is possibly that he is not using his love for one woman as a screen for his love for another, or, more probably, that he is not 'serving' Love for any woman but the best. It is tantalizing to wonder when Donne first thought of using the motto, and what special significance it had for him. In any case, his use of it suggests a strong attachment at least to that particular line, which seems to have a key role in the *canzone* from which it comes. Yet Donne's lyrics are, in many cases, in varying degrees, out of keeping with anything in the *Canzoniere*. One has only to think of 'Go and catch', *Woman's Constancy*, *The Sun Rising* (where the lovers are in bed together), *The Indifferent*, *Love's Usury*, *The Legacy*, *Love's Alchemy*, *The Flea*, or *Love's Diet*, to realize how sharply different Donne can be from Petrarch; and, indeed, the majority of the collection is quite divergent from Petrarch in spirit. Some of the poems are out of keeping with the *Canzoniere* because they are too cynical or flippant, others because they express or imply satisfaction in a physical relationship, or clearly invite one, yet others because they evidently spring from a mutual love of great depth and possible permanence. Conversely there are many poems in the *Canzoniere* which cannot be matched by attitudes in the *Songs and Sonets*: poems where Petrarch is struggling against his love for Laura on religious grounds; or such a poem as his Sonnet 12 ('Se la mia vita da l'aspro tormento') in which the poet imagines himself many years later revealing the long sufferings he will have gone through for his love; or poems which express Petrarch's timidity in Laura's presence (e.g. 49: 'Perch'io t'abbia guardato di menzogna'); or, naturally, on a more commonplace level, all the poems in which Petrarch plays, in one way or another, on Laura's name. These are only a few of the cases. There are a number of other kinds of poem in the *Canzoniere* which have no correlatives in the *Songs and Sonets*. The poems in which Petrarch expresses the obsessional torture of not being able to forget the eyes which had enslaved him to love (85), or in which he compares himself to a ship swept away by love on to the fury of a stormy sea (239), have no parallels in the *Songs and Sonets*. Moreover, many of the day-to-day incidents and changes represented in the *Canzoniere* have nothing to correspond to them in Donne's lyrics. (Shakespeare's *Sonnets* are closer to Petrarch in this last respect.) It is, in any case, not really surprising that the riches of Petrarch's collection of well over 300 poems should not be matched point for point in Donne's fifty-four.

Yet there are certain Petrarchan features in some of Donne's lyrics, and I shall discuss them presently. Meanwhile, however, let us consider briefly some anti-Petrarchan features in the *Songs and Sonets*. There is rather little of the kind of anti-Petrarchism found in the burlesque poems of Burchiello (1404–48), Berni (1498–1535) and Aretino (1492–1556). One form of burlesque was the so-called 'Contre-blason', in which laudatory poems on the physical 'points' of women were satirized. Such poems were written in the sixteenth century both in Italy and in France. The 'Contre-blasons' were directed rather against the exaggerations of 'Petrarchists' than against the work of Petrarch himself. Yet some of the master's own poems, though chiefly restricting physical reference to the beauty of Laura's eyes and hair, the power of her quick glances and longer looks, and the fascination of her movements and gestures, were so magniloquent in their praises that it is not surprising that more sensually-minded (or more *openly* sensually-minded) followers should have expanded the field of physical specification. There are no instances of 'Blasons' in the *Songs and Sonets*; but there are no instances of 'Contre-blasons' either (in contrast there are striking examples of 'Contre-blasons' in some of Donne's *Elegies*, e.g. *Elegy 2: The Anagram*, and *Elegy 8: The Comparison*). There are, however, occasionally burlesque elements of other kinds in the *Songs and Sonets*. I suppose one could say that *The Flea* is a burlesque form of wooing, and that the intended result is far from what any of the poems of Petrarch seem to be aiming at. There may also be some burlesque of Petrarchan hyperbole in places, e.g. in *The Bait*. Anti-Petrarchism in Donne's lyrics mostly, however, takes other forms. One is the cynical advocacy of male promiscuousness in *Community*, with the 'low' comparisons in its final stanza. Another is the buoyant endorsement in *The Indifferent* of unfaithfulness as a mode of life for both sexes. Yet another is the generalized depreciation of love and women displayed in *Mummy* or *Love's Alchemy*. Again, so sharply contrasting with the special attitudes of Petrarch as to deserve being called 'anti-Petrarchan', there are poems accusing the woman concerned of fickleness or falseness, such as *The Legacy*, *The Message* and *The Apparition*; and the Song 'Go and catch', with its disbelief in the existence of any woman who is both beautiful and faithful.

Other poems in Donne's collection, without being positively 'anti-Petrarchan', clearly belong to the larger class of poems 'in varying degrees out of keeping' with those of the *Canzoniere*. Such a poem as *The Expiration*, for instance, implying a number of passionate kisses between the lovers, is remote from Petrarch. Equally remote are the injunctions to the woman addressed in *The Prohibition* to beware of loving or hating the poet, and then both to love and to hate him (the incidental *double entendre* of 'dying the gentler way' being also alien to the spirit of Petrarch's poetry). As to the blatant sexual realism of *Farewell to Love*, though it does involve the Petrarchan element of a belief in the dangerousness of sexual love, the reasons given for the lover's dissatisfaction are wholly diverse from those adduced from time to time by Petrarch.

On the other hand, there is much use in the *Songs and Sonets* of themes typical of Petrarch. It has been rightly pointed out,[1] for instance, that complaint against rejection of love is a thematic element in over a quarter of the *Songs and Sonets*; and generally in conjunction with some ancillary theme of the Petrarchan tradition. It is, however, characteristic of Donne that in the poems concerned the complaint takes a broad variety of forms. In *Twickenham Garden*, for example, after two stanzas in which Donne pours out his sense of frustration, he turns, in a manner quite divergent from Petrarch, to the generality of lovers, sarcastically suggesting the grotesque experiment of taking lachrymatories and assessing the genuineness of their mistresses' tears by comparing their taste with that of his. Then, after slipping in the highly original comparison 'thoughts: tears :: clothes: shadow', he comes to a semi-Petrarchan close, in which a Petrarchan expression of impending death from exasperated love is combined with the un-Petrarchan suggestion that it is the woman's fidelity to another which is the cause, and that literally no other woman whatever is faithful. In contrast, in *Love's Deity*, not only are the complaints against love more generalized, even savouring of Scholasticism, but in the closing stanza the poet turns about and reproaches himself for his discontent, on the grounds that it would be worse if he were made to cease loving, and even worse if the beloved were to return his love, since this would involve her in infidelity (the very thing which the poet of *Twickenham Garden* would apparently have welcomed). In *Love's Deity*, then, we have in much of the poem an attitude of complaint very similar to attitudes typical of Petrarch, though expressed in more abstract argumentation than usual in the *Canzoniere*; and then a surprising reversal in which the poet appears, after all, to prefer the *status quo* to possible alternatives. It is, of course, not impossible that this reversal is only ostensible, and that the final stanza is ironical. If so, however, it would be even more alien from

[1] By Werner von Koppenfels in *Das Petrarkistische Element in der Dichtung von John Donne*, Munich, 1967, p. 83.

Petrarch. *Love's Diet* is yet more tenuously connected to attitudes characteristic of the *Canzoniere*. It is, indeed, in some sense a love complaint. The mistress is shown as disinclined to return the poet's love. Yet the imagery is of a 'low', physical kind, which brings the poem close to the burlesque tradition of Burchiello, Berni and Aretino. The mock-precision of the measures taken by the poet to keep his love within bounds seems to be Donne's original contribution, as does the nonchalant impertinence of the ending, with its satisfaction in the sense of freedom from amorous constraint. In this poem the Petrarchan complaint is, indeed, used, but to burlesque and strongly anti-Petrarchan ends. *The Funeral* is much closer to Petrarch in spirit. The use of a scene imagined as after the poet's death is quite typical of Donne, though such uses are found in Classical poetry, and in Petrarch himself. Yet the images from politics, physiology, and even war, are more characteristic of Donne than of Petrarch. On the other hand, the general attitude of resentment against the woman who refuses to return the poet's love is quite Petrarchan, and it is basic to the poem. So also is the attribution of superior powers even to the woman's 'wreath of hair', capable of preserving the poet's body from dissolution. In contrast, the sense of uncertainty about the true situation, the shifting awareness of alternative possibilities, seems more typical of Donne than of the *Canzoniere*; and the open defiance in the concluding lines is a good instance of the 'toughness' of Donne's amatory temperament.

Another central feature in the *Canzoniere* is, of course, high praise and even worship of Laura. Interestingly enough, the praise is more often physical in Petrarch than in Donne's lyrics. Moreover, when Donne does indulge in hyperbolical wonder at the mistress's earthly attractions, he may do so with some indirectness (as in *The Bait*), and there is sometimes even a sense that he may to some degree be mocking the very convention that he is exploiting (as both in that poem and in *Love's Exchange*). On the other hand, in *The Dream*, *The Canonization* and *The Relic* the sanctification expressed in their respective ways does not seem to involve any element of parody. With *Air and Angels* the case is somewhat different. Here there seems to be a balance between laudatory hyperbole and various eroding touches and associations, culminating in the reversal of the status of the sexes declared in the final lines. This poem is, however, a *tour de force* of *wit*; and the apparently un-Petrarchan or anti-Petrarchan elements (e.g. the 'low' associations of 'ballast') should not, I think, be given excessive weight. Here again, though, in any case, Donne exploits the Petrarchan features in a thoroughly original way.

The same is true of the subordinate themes, and the equipment, including the recurrent conceits, in the *Canzoniere*. Such commonplaces in Petrarch as the equation of absence with death occur repeatedly in the *Songs and Sonets*, but with far greater tonal diversity than in the *Canzoniere*. The conceit is sometimes largely an occasion for an evaporation of wit, as at the conclusion of the brilliant pyrotechnics (matched, however, by strong underlying feeling) in *The Computation*. In contrast, in *The Legacy* it both affords an apparently tender parenthesis, and generates the recital of a series of preposterous pseudo-events, ending in the accusation of promiscuity. Donne's exploitation of subordinate themes found in Petrarch is generally equally lively and original, as in his expression of a *coup de foudre* in *The Broken Heart*, with its most un-Petrarchan images of artillery and of the predatory pike. The same is true of his treatment in *The Anniversary* of the theme which Petrarch dwells upon at several points in the *Canzoniere*, the anniversary of his first sight of the beloved. The three stanzas of Donne's poem range far beyond the scope of any of the treatments of the theme in the *Canzoniere*. As for the dream-fulfilment of love, that idea goes back well beyond Petrarch, whose own use of it is limited to the fantasy of Laura appearing to him after death, and looking upon him with pity, further expressed in sighs and tears (*Canz.* 356). Donne, in *The Dream*, and also in [*Picture and Dream*], has clearly in mind a physical satisfaction. With regard to the situation of parting, which occurs at a number of points in Petrarch, Donne's treatment is far more various than Petrarch's. All the four Valedictions are different in tone and in detailed development, and they are not the only poems of parting in the *Songs and Sonets*. Among the others there is equal variety, for instance, in 'Sweetest love' and *The Expiration*.

So far we have only considered the *Songs and Sonets* in direct comparison with Petrarch's *Canzoniere*, and briefly at that. Yet, if we ask how far the *Songs and Sonets* are 'Petrarchan', to compare the poems to Petrarch's lyrics is only one kind of answer, albeit an important kind. The term 'Petrarchan' is somewhat slippery. Clearly, poems can be like those of Petrarch in various ways, and in varying degrees, and the term 'Petrarchan' therefore covers a wide spectrum of work. Now, it is probably fair to say that for love-lyrics the central tradition in Europe from Petrarch's day (1304–74) at least till the time when Donne had written his love-lyrics – say, at all events, up till 1617 – was 'Petrarchan'. That field is, moreover, vast. Hundreds of thousands of love-lyrics were written and printed in Italy, France, England and Spain during that time. (Hugues Vaganay estimated[1] that in Italy and France alone over 300,000 sonnets – many of which were love sonnets – were printed in the sixteenth century, that is, during only half the period covered.) To determine the precise relations of the *Songs and Sonets* to the Petrarchan tradition, or to Petrarchism, would therefore be a gigantic task. All I can claim to offer here are a few comparisons between the characteristics of Donne's love-lyrics, and those of a few other love poets who had written since Petrarch's day, whose work I have come across in nosing round in Italian, French, English and Spanish poetry written in the period indicated. In Germany the phenomena, both of Petrarchism and of anti-Petrarchism, were of a far later growth than in the other four countries.[2]

The first Petrarchans with whom it seems interesting to compare Donne are the *quattrocentisti* Benedetto Cariteo (*c.* 1450–1514), Antonio Tebaldeo (1463–1537) and Serafino Ciminelli dall'Aquila (1466–1500). Cariteo's *Canzoniere* celebrates a certain Luna, whom he seems to have wooed for twelve years without success, and who then died, and was celebrated by him in a fashion somewhat similar to Petrarch's celebration of Laura. Cariteo's poems, often sonnets, more often eight-lined *strambotti*, are packed with conceits and hyperboles. His 'model', in a formal sense, was evidently Petrarch, but he clearly intended to outdo Petrarch in the boldness and extravagance of his images. On the other hand, the literary inspiration of his poetry was very different from that of his literary model, being often drawn from Roman poets, or popular songs, or his own original resources. He is frequently openly sensual, and indulges in obscene ambiguities. Compared with Donne the range of his images is very restricted, and the spirit of the poems is fairly uniformly gentle and courtly. In his most famous sonnet, which was several times imitated both in France and in Italy ('Voi, Donna, e io per segni manifesti'), Cariteo imagines his beloved and himself both being sent to hell, he for having dared to love her and she for her cruel disdain, but he says that her fate will be worse than his, since he will be able to see and enjoy her beauty, whereas she may well be tortured by the sight of him. The idea is quite striking, and the turn of thought ingenious and witty; but the spirit is clearly quite different from that of any of the *Songs and Sonets*, the range of references is very limited, and

---

[1] *Le Sonnet en Italie et en France au XVIe siècle*, Lyons, 1903.

[2] See Hans Pyritz, *Paul Flemings Liebeslyrik. Zur Geschichte des Petrarkismus*, Göttingen, 1963; J.-U. Fechner, *Der Antipetrarkismus*, Heidelberg, 1966; L. W. Forster, *The Icy Fire*, Cambridge, 1969.

the wit rather elementary when compared with Donne's. Cariteo was, in any case, a somewhat less extravagant poet than Tebaldeo. Tebaldeo's love sonnets, printed in 1499 without his knowledge, had an enormous success. Stylistically they are a mélange of a popular style with more learned strains possibly derived from Roman poetry, and from a personal taste for ingenious inventions and ornate expressions. His sonnets are frequently contrived to lead to an epigrammatic close. The particular mixture of styles and the ingenuity of his inventions could have attracted Donne to some extent had he known of his work, which is as yet uncertain. Tebaldeo's choice of the sonnet as his primary form, his adoption of the attitude of wooer, and his development of characteristically Petrarchan imagery to even more extravagant lengths than those achieved by Cariteo, make Tebaldeo a love poet in the Petrarchan tradition, though a highly original one. Among many examples of fantastic ingenuities the following must suffice. The house of his lady having caught fire, he carefully avoids going near it − the flame of his love would have made the fire rage more vigorously. The people who did try to put it out failed, because, set on fire themselves by the lady's eyes, they were obliged to throw the water they had brought on to their own bodies. These fancies naturally evoked enthusiasm in the courtiers and their ladies. Like Donne's sallies they are ingenious, but they are far more limited, and they do not pass beyond the bounds of mere entertainment. There is nothing particularly personal about this kind of compliment. Its limitations are its own impersonal extravagance. Serafino even outdid his two masters in this kind of art. He was essentially a court entertainer. He was a fine singer and instrumentalist, and during his short life he performed at a number of Italian courts with immense success, at first singing his own settings of Petrarch, and later his own songs. He himself said that he set more store by immediate applause than by a posthumous fame equal to that of Dante and Petrarch. He snapped up ideas and images from other poets, and inflated them into fantastic hyperboles whose main object was to astonish and delight his hearers. On one occasion Charles VIII of France was present at one of his performances, and loaded him with praises and gifts. This seems to have encouraged young French poets to imitate the Italian virtuoso. Serafino circumspectly did not publish any of his work; but his admirers began doing so in 1502, mainly sonnets and *strambotti*, and nearly thirty editions were published before 1550. Serafino's poems, besides being ingenious, were also often frankly epicurean and sensual. He did not sing of long years of fidelity, or of the worship of moral qualities. Typical of his attitudes is the following instance of *carpe diem*: 'See, lady, how time flies, how everything runs to its end. In a short while every violet fades, roses fall, and only thorns remain. The same with your beauty. Do not imagine that, like gold, it will refine in the fire. So be aware of your season of happiness: and do not hope to be born again like the phoenix.' The germ here of later refinements will be clear enough to readers of later poets including Ronsard and Góngora. As for ingenuities the poems swarm with them, whether the subject is the lady's dog, falcon, gloves, girdle, bracelet, fan, blouse, mirror, or what you will. There is a whole series on the lady's mirror, one of which (Stramb. 122) calls to mind stanza 4 of *The Broken Heart*. Serafino expresses astonishment that the fragile glass does not break when it receives the lady's image; for the day he saw her for the first time his heart was shattered into a thousand pieces. Donald Guss (op. cit., chs IV and V) has compared several poems of Serafino with some of Donne's lyrics, and made some comparative generalizations. These comparisons are valuable, and Guss is right to direct attention to the *quattrocentisti* in relation to the *Songs and Sonets*. More generally, indeed, Guss is right to emphasize that those poets whom he calls 'the witty Petrarchists', starting with Cariteo, Tebaldeo, Serafino, and their followers, offered 'a tradition characterised by peregrine comparisons, extravagant hyperboles, and epigrammatic statement' (p. 63), and that Donne probably knew their work, and made use of what it had to offer, including taking literally typical Petrarchan metaphors (fire, ice, stone, sigh-tempests, tear-floods, and so on), expanding them, and using them as material for elaborate argument resulting in surprising turns of wit. Indeed, Donne often does something similar in the *Songs and Sonets*; but it is frequently still more elaborate, the mixture of imagery is thicker, the passage from image to image is nimbler, and the density of concrete reference greater. Donne's whole achievement is also immeasurably more individual.

Serafino had a host of imitators, both in Italy and in France. François I held Serafino and his imitators in high regard, but it was Serafino himself who was most enthusiastically imitated by the French love-lyrists of the early sixteenth century, including Clément Marot (1496–1544). Donne's lyrics share the high spirits of Marot's attractive lyrics, and also sometimes there is a certain dramatic development within Marot's poems which resembles that in Donne. The range of feeling in the *Songs and Sonets* is, on the other hand, far greater than that in Marot, and the imagery far more various. The central ideas of Donne's poems are also often well beyond Marot's range. The most interesting of the early sixteenth-century French poets to compare with Donne as a love poet is Maurice Scève (1510–52). Scève is a very fine, subtle, and somewhat arcane poet. His kinds of conceit and themes basically derive from the Italian *quattrocentisti*, and many of his specific images are actually borrowed. Yet Scève often elaborates them, and he also invents even more extravagant turns, as when he defies the furnace of a factory in Lyons to raise its breath higher than the smoke of his sighs, and a cannon to make a more terrifying noise than his sobs (*Délie*, dizain 360); or, as when one day Délie hears her mirror begging her to lower her eyes because her divine image is both burning and freezing it, as it does men (*Délie*, dizain 230). On the other hand, Scève is far less sensual and far more concerned with the moral virtues and the soul of his idol than most of his Italian masters were. The full title of his long and fascinating poem, *Délie ou l'object de la plus haulte vertu*, has some significance. Scève was evidently influenced by some of the early sixteenth-century Platonists. He knew Bembo's *Asolani*, Leone Ebreo's three dialogues on Love, and eventually *La Parfaite Amye* of Antoine Héroët. Yet there are passages in Scève showing strong physical desire also. *Délie* is, in any case, 'Petrarchan' in a deeper sense than the work of Serafino, though at least as extravagant. To compare *Délie* with the *Songs and Sonets* is to compare a long poem of over 4000 lines with 54 lyrics. Moreover, the situation behind *Délie* is that of a poet deeply in love with a married woman who eventually returns his love, though the poet suffers greatly from the natural changes and counter-changes in the course of the relationship. There is little to correspond to the cynicism of some of Donne's lyrics, or to the joyous fulfilment of a few of them. Nor is there anything to correspond in *Délie* to the nauseated aversion from love in such a poem as *Love's Alchemy*. The great point of similarity lies in the ingenuity, and often unexpectedness, of the images. Scève is, however, far more purely Petrarchan than Donne. His language is also often premeditatedly literary, and the thoughts in some of the dizains are frequently very difficult to seize. Neither of these features is typical of Donne. Fundamentally, Scève's attitude towards his Délie is one of more or less sublimated adoration. Virtue bulks large in his conception of the beloved, as it does in Petrarch. In some of Donne's lyrics there is also a tendency towards glorification of the beloved, but often the emphasis is on the mutuality of the love between the poet and the beloved, who is seen as an equal partner.

The Lyonnaise School, of which Scève was the chief poet, were writing in a way no longer fashionable in Italy. Bembo had not only tried to restore a Petrarchism closer to Petrarch. He had also tightened up style and form, to achieve a total effect rather than local successes, cut out banalities, facile repetitions, extravagances and indecencies. Bembo dominated Italian poetry by theory and practice in the second quarter of the sixteenth century. His many followers included some poets of distinction. The apogee of the movement was the publication at Venice in 1545 of the first book of an anthology, *Rime diverse di molti eccellentissimi auttori nuovamente raccolte*. Another 'Bembist' anthology came out at Venice in 1547, and others in the next twenty years. The first two greatly influenced the Pléiade.

In 1548 Du Bellay let loose his famous *Deffence et Illustration de la langue française*, urging poets to follow Classical and Italian models instead of staying in the rut of indigenous poetry. He himself certainly followed Italian models in his collection of love sonnets, *L'Olive* (1549), whose success was immediate. He took very little from Classical sources, and he did not reveal his Italian borrowings. Yet he contrived to impress his own manner on most of the poems. The subject matter was, however, staple Petrarchan material: protestations of fidelity through all trials, indifference, ingratitude, absence, death; descriptions of the poet's sufferings, and the joy nevertheless drawn from them, invocations to nature, sometimes thought of as indifferent, sometimes as benevolent; and so on. Generally, the poems evince little depth or passion. Their strength lies in their admirable structure and texture, and the lively and original use of language. Many of the poems have considerable charm, but they seldom surprise with ingenious conceits, and there is little of the argumentative or dramatic development found in so. many of the *Songs and Sonets*.

The *Erreurs amoureuses* of Pontus de Tyard (1521–1605), also published in 1549, were closer to Scève and the Italian *quattrocentisti*. 'Tear-floods' and 'sigh-tempests' attack the ship on which the poet has loaded his desire. We can see here just the sort of extravagance that Donne was inclined to satirize. Tyard also uses his many conceits to sing (largely though not wholly), in contrast with Donne, of Platonic love. He translated Leone Ebreo's Platonizing dialogues on Love into French, and dedicated his translation to his mistress; and even followed this with dialogues of his own on the same theme. It is interesting that Donne should have evidently read Ebreo, but used him less whole-heartedly.

The next poet who fully merits extensive comparison with Donne as love-lyrist (indeed, more extensive than is possible in this short discussion) is Ronsard, whose first volume of *Amours* (the *Amours de Cassandre*) appeared in 1552. Ronsard drew far more from Petrarch than Du Bellay had. He also borrowed quite heavily from Bembo, and was influenced by Bembo's gift for development and care for mellifluousness. He probably also knew already the *quattrocentisti*, whom he later warmly regarded. There are certainly plenty of ingenious conceits in this first volume. Compared with Petrarch Ronsard is, here as elsewhere, more frankly and permissively sensual. He was very familiar with the Classical love poets; and far more of a pagan than Petrarch. Again, unlike Petrarch, and (incidentally unlike Donne) he loads his sonnets with mythology. Yet the poems ring true with passion and sensuality; and they are not rent by radically divisive impulses like many of Petrarch's poems. As noted earlier in this Introduction, the *Songs and Sonets* are seldom markedly sensual. Here they differ from Ronsard, as they also do in their deliberate avoidance, in general, of obvious mellifluousness.

It was at this time that Du Bellay performed something of a volte-face. In *L'Olive* Du Bellay had been markedly Bembist and imitative. However, he now brought out a brilliant poem, *A une dame*, later retitled *Contre les Pétrarquistes*, an anti-Platonic poem attacking what Du Bellay now saw as the hollow rhetoric both of Platonizing and of Bembist Petrarchizing. He frankly asserts that what he seeks in love is enjoyment. Ronsard in places implied the same. Bembist Petrarchism had, actually, already been satirized in Italy for some twenty years for its obvious borrowings, and the monotony of its ideas, images, references and language. Niccolò Franco (1515–70) and Pietro Aretino (1492–1556) attacked head on. Francesco Berni (?1497–1535) parodied both Petrarchism and Petrarch, and this became a favourite pastime with cynical wits. Berni also assaulted directly, brushing aside the Petrarchists to allow a true poet to speak – Michelangelo, 'who', writes Berni, 'says things, while you speak words'. Du Bellay was probably aware of these Italian manifestations of anti-Petrarchism. It seems to me more than likely that Donne would have been aware both of the Italian satirists and also of Du Bellay's poem.

Yet Ronsard and other members of the Pléiade continued to Petrarchize. Ronsard's further *Amours* (1555) contains many fresh and delightful poems, very natural and lyrical. Compared with the *Songs and Sonets* these poems, though generally lively, are far more sensuous and even sensual. They are also less complicated than most of Donne's lyrics, both intellectually, and in mood. Ronsard's subsequent continuation (1556) included many songs, some of very great charm. The poems are still unrepentantly voluptuous. There are also signs that Ronsard was becoming more interested in Tebaldeo and Serafino.

Soon after, in Italy, there was a marked reversion to the préciosité of the *quattrocentisti*. Bembist purism began to seem a trifle dull. The new favourites came from Naples: Angelo di Costanzo (1507–?91), Berardino Rota (1508–75), and Luigi Tansillo (1510–68). Costanzo scored the highest immediate success, though all he did really was to revive the conceits of the earlier poets in more tuneful verse. Tansillo was a more gifted poet, with a strong feeling for nature, of which his impressions are sometimes stark, as in his sonnets after a volcanic eruption in the Phlegrean fields. There is also a sonnet in which he startlingly compares himself with a snake dying a painful death, in contrast to himself who is dying deliberately through the delight of love. This is an intensification of the mixture of sweet and painful found often in Petrarch. It also points forward to the masochism sometimes found in Tasso. This kind of Petrarchism is conspicuously absent from the *Songs and Sonets*. Rota sang exclusively of his wife, over a period of more than twenty-five years, and beyond her death. His poems make frequent use of unusual comparisons, such as that the tears on his wife's face are flowers, and her face a garden. Some of the poems are moving, especially those on his dead wife, whom he compares to 'a night-flower touched by the sun'. Such comparisons are, I think, significantly different from those typical of the *Songs and Sonets*. Donne's comparisons even when far-fetched strike one generally as compellingly apt. Such comparisons as these of Rota strike one rather as emotionally touching than as wittily appropriate.

The new fashion passed to France and reached its height with Philippe Desportes (1546–1606). First published in 1573, his poems were a resounding success with the public, and ran through four editions by 1577, and another four by 1583, by which time the collection contained 432 sonnets. Desportes then produced a further collection of 89. His poems continued to appeal and sell right up to his death in 1606. Desportes was an imitator of the Italians, and often a slavish one. Two years before his death an anonymous writer published a book exposing his Italian borrowings. The story has it that when someone showed him the book he laughed the matter off saying: 'Why didn't he consult me? I would have pointed out plenty of others.' Yet he refrained from revealing them. With the help of his Italian sources, Desportes offered his readers a continual firework display of ingenious subtleties and extravagant fantasies. He has, despite his borrowings, something of a wit of his own, and even if he indulges in many periphrases, it is often for the sake of bringing out clearly complex and fantastic conceits. Desportes' poems, though usually displaying a neat turn of wit, nevertheless are bounded within the main lines of Petrarchism: hyperbolical praise of the mistress, complaint at the pains of love and its lack of return, accusations of cruelty against Love and against the mistress, and yet declarations of a certain pleasure in the lover's bitter fate. The poems also deal at every turn in the common currency of Petrarchism: Venus, Love's arrows, the mirror in which the mistress looks at herself, the divine light in her eyes, icy cold, burning heat, storms, floods of tears, worship of the mistress, and her effect on the lover of giving him life and also killing him. Sometimes Desportes adds witty touches which seem original, as when he warns the lady against the danger of looking at herself in the mirror: she may not become a flower like Narcissus, but her Medusa-like glance may turn her into a rock (*Les Amours d'Hippolyte*, poem 18).

Some of Desportes' songs and elegies are masterpieces of their kind. He was, indeed, a poet of considerable talent, and it is not surprising that Ronsard probably underwent his influence in his late *Sonnets pour Hélène* (1578). These were, in any case, strongly affected by the *quattrocentisti*, especially Tebaldeo, whom Desportes so often took as his model. Yet Ronsard does not plagiarize or imitate in a servile fashion, and he even wrote some of his most finely original poems in the fantastic style of those poets. As in his other collections Ronsard makes a fair number of Classical allusions, and the name 'Hélène' naturally prompts many specific conceits. The dominant attitude, however, is the Petrarchan one of the worshipping lover, who often feels frustrated by lack of his beloved's favour, but who also warms at the least sign of regard. Yet in the most famous poem of the series, 'Quand vous serez bien vieille, au soir, à la chandelle', the poet is able to warn his mistress of the coming of old age, to vaunt his prowess as a poet, and to call upon the mistress to pluck the roses of life while she may. He also sometimes shows jealousy of younger lovers (I. xi and xxiv), which is not typical of Petrarch, but slightly reminds one of Donne's poem *The Will*, though Ronsard probably had more reason than Donne to feel in that way. Ronsard also shows a canny wit, and a certain tough resilience not altogether dissimilar to that found in Donne (e.g. in I. xx, xxi, xxii). The *Sonnets pour Hélène* are less physically intimate than Ronsard's earlier love poems; but the longing for physical contact is from time to time powerfully present (e.g. in II. xxix). In the *Songs and Sonets* (as contrasted with Donne's *Elegies*) we find little of this. Extravagant touches are frequent in the *Sonnets pour Hélène*. The poet would like to be Argus to see all the beauties of his mistress, and is ashamed to have only two eyes (I. xvii); and he suggests that talking of love without making love is like seeing the sun without loving its light (I. xviii). This conceit is dexterous. Still more dexterous perhaps is that where Ronsard, at the end of a sonnet, begs his beloved not to take offence if he sometimes touches her hand, but to pardon *herself* for his faults (I. xxxi). This kind of dexterous gallantry is clearly quite alien from the *Songs and Sonets*. Some of Ronsard's extravagances are especially surprising, as when he kisses an orange and lemon which he had from Hélène, and puts them in his breast to make them feel the heat of his love (I. xxxiv). Here, as in many other passages, Ronsard is close to the spirit of the *quattrocentisti*. Yet the detail of the inventions, as here, is often original. Indeed, Ronsard's Petrarchism, in its own way, involves modifications and personal touches as admirable as those of Donne. The content, on the other hand, is quite different from that of Donne's lyrics – a fairly continuous wooing over a period of years, and so, in that respect, much closer to Petrarch; though, in this particular sequence, Ronsard sings the love of an ageing man for a young woman, and so the poems only cover one phase of the span of the *Canzoniere*. As compared with Donne's lyrics, the range of moods in Ronsard is rather narrower. The harsh cynicism of *Love's Alchemy* and the deep confidence of *A Valediction: forbidding mourning* are equally beyond Ronsard's range.

About the same time as Ronsard was writing his final love poems, another less productive but also remarkable French poet, Jean de Sponde (1557–95), was writing love poems which some have considered similar to those of Donne. Sponde's *Amours* do, indeed, contain unusual and subtle images, and their style is firm and dense. There is also a mixture of plain and sophisticated language (and imagery) not dissimilar to that in some of the *Songs and Sonets*. The rhythms are also often those of ordinary speech, and almost wholly anti-oratorical. Moreover, there is even something of the harshness both of language and of movement which we frequently encounter in Donne's love-lyrics. There is also a similar lack of sentimentality, and a certain masculinity in Sponde's poems; and there is nothing of the pastoral in either poet. Yet the moods of Sponde's love-poems are less various than those of Donne, and his guiding star is an irrefragable constancy that Donne only very rarely pretends to. In Donne, moreover, there is most often a sense of a specific dramatic situation, whereas this is rare in Sponde, who also, even seldomer than Ronsard, and certainly than Marot or Donne, gives a sense of close contact with the everyday, workaday world.

A new luminary had begun writing in Italy in the 1560s, Torquato Tasso, who, however, only gained fame with the first performance of the *Aminta* in 1573, which was, moreover, not published until 1581. Tasso had written a considerable array of lyrics in the 1560s, for a Lucrezia Bendidio, and then for a Laura Peperara. He wrote further lyrics for both these good ladies over ten years later. Very imperfect collections of his lyrics came out in the 1580s. Tasso was highly prolific, but also selective, and finally a collection of lyrics sanctioned by him was published in 1591, mainly love poems. This was the only batch of lyrics whose publication he personally approved. Tasso was no literary revolutionary in his lyrics. He followed in the Petrarchan tradition as developed in the sixteenth century, and elaborated within it. He was a very sophisticated poet, and proud of working within the tradition, often using words, phrases, and even whole lines of Petrarch's, and calling attention to his debts in his commentary, according to the most scrupulous practice of imitation. He also elaborated Petrarchan devices, accentuating hyperboles, prolonging metaphors and adorning conceits. He sometimes points out his divergences from some passage or line of Petrarch or one or other of the Petrarchans. Though, indeed, in the Petrarchan tradition, Tasso was no slavish imitator; and he even added further dimensions to love poetry, through absorbing into his poetry many of the ideas of the Italian love treatises. He was also an avid reader of Classical Latin and Greek poets, and of Dante, besides such Petrarchans as Bembo and Giovanni della Casa. The result is a great amalgam of literary influences. Tasso was deliberately eclectic, but generally made something personal out of his picking and choosing. He was especially concerned with the diction of poetry, holding that (except for slight lyric forms like the madrigal) it should be ornate and flowery. This is one point in which his work differs sharply from the *Songs and Sonets*. Tasso is, indeed, in this respect, as Robert Ellrodt has suggested (*Les Poètes Métaphysiques Anglais*, vol. II, p. 215), closer to Spenser than to Donne. He was strongly opposed to the view that the language of poetry should be close to ordinary speech.[1] Furthermore (and here again we have sharp contrast with the *Songs and Sonets*), Tasso characteristically made a strong and successful effort to achieve mellifluousness. It is an interesting fact that, besides writing love poems in his own person,

[1] See e.g. a letter from Tasso to Scipione Gonzaga, 1576, quoted by G. Toffanin, *Il Cinquecento*, Milan, 1935, pp. 603–4.

Tasso wrote a large number for his patrons and friends to present to their ladies. These do not differ greatly in their sensuousness, languorousness, mellifluousness and curiously unpassionate emotionalism from those he wrote on his own behalf. Compared with the *Songs and Sonets* Tasso's love-lyrics are, indeed, for the most part, somewhat lacking in virility, and even show frequent traces of a complacency bordering at times on masochism. Again, their relish of pleasant physical sensations, both in contemplating the beauties of the women, and in experiencing the gentler phenomena of the natural world, marks Tasso's love poems off sharply from the non-indulgence, intellectual keenness, and the frank and specific awareness of harsh physical realities which we find in considerable measure in the love-lyrics of Donne. Furthermore, Tasso is not, characteristically, an argumentative poet. He proceeds by elaborate narration, physical description and emotional exclamation. Like Donne, he is fond of hyperbole, yet the hyperbole is often either directly laudatory of the women's beauty or amatory power, or the expression of conventional Petrarchan complaint at a cruelty which the poet, ultimately, accepts. This is a far cry from most of the *Songs and Sonets*. As to conceits, the two poets share some of the typically Petrarchan ones – the absence of lovers as death, the lady as an angel, or as a sun greater than that in the solar system; but Tasso harps far more on them, and he does not shift as rapidly from conceit to conceit as Donne, or invent such a variety of conceits of his own. His range of reference excludes, for instance, 'low' elements, such as are boldly retained within Donne's literary gamut. Moreover, Tasso's conceits are often elaborated as ends in themselves rather than, as most often in Donne, tools for a highly original and disciplined, frequently self-critical, and sometimes humorous, analysis of a specific love-situation or the poet's reactions to it.

It is virtually certain that Donne knew some of Tasso's work, and it seems clear that he also knew something of the work of Giambattista Guarini (1538–1612). The compass image in *A Valediction: forbidding mourning* is more like that in Guarini's Madrigal 96 than it is to any of the many other uses of the image noted by modern scholars (e.g. by J. Freccero, 'Donne's "Valediction, Forbidding Mourning"', *ELH* 30 (1963), pp. 335–76). Again, in Madrigal 37 the poet's heart is compared to a flitting butterfly that burns its wings in the flame of the mistress's eyes, dies as a butterfly, but rises as a phoenix. It could well be that stanza 3 of *The Canonization* owed something to Guarini's poem. The *Rime* were published in 1598. Guarini's lyrics are courtly and witty. They are slight. There are no lengthy *canzoni* as in Petrarch.

There are over 100 sonnets and 150 madrigals, the longest of which is about 30 lines. The great majority are of less than a dozen lines. Many of the sonnets are praises of the mistress's beauty, complaints at her cruelty, staple Petrarchan material; but some have original turns, e.g. the quite powerful Sonnet 40 in which he compares his growing jealousy to the hydra, and Sonnet 64 against old men who fall in love. The sonnets are, however, miscellaneous. They do not form a sequence. Some are praises of contemporary men, some are political. There is one (84) on the death of Michelangelo, with a conceit on his name in the final line. The madrigals have, on the whole, more character than the sonnets, but they are essentially neat verbal and conceptual pirouetting, very restricted in their reference to life, psychologically rather sentimental, and way behind the *Songs and Sonets* in power and variety of invention. They are pleasant, well-turned little poems, showing a good ear, and a sprightly, somewhat arch, wit. Most of them fall well within the Petrarchan tradition, telling of constant and feverish love for the mistress, her cruelty or coldness, and occasional pity, and the lover's grief at parting as 'death' (85, 88, 89). Yet there are some poems of mutual love, and the 'death' of parting is sometimes seen as that of both lovers. There are also poems in which the lover turns upon the woman and accuses her fiercely of disloyalty (98, 99), and even some in which the lover claims that his love has ceased, though not his desire (101), or even his desire also (106). In one poem he declares that he would rather die in misery than enjoy something not entirely his own (104). In another (107) he expresses entire disillusion with love; but the poem is a slight affair, not comparable in depth, exploration or reference with Donne's *Farewell to Love* or *Love's Alchemy*, nor are there any such poems as Donne's *Love's Growth* with its thoughtful meditation on the nature of love itself. General sensuousness is far more limited in Guarini's work than in Tasso's, but there are strong touches of sensuality, the wish, for instance, to die in the mistress's eyes, and then return alive to her breast (Madr. 11). There are also kisses, possibly mutual (e.g. 71, 72). There is, moreover, a frank awareness that the kiss is a sign of future delight. Such physicalities seldom appear in the *Songs and Sonets*, which are more sharply focused on the nature and status of relationships, and the drift of specific situations, than on their physical frills. Guarini makes elegant miniature use of mythology, e.g. of the contrasting fates of Dedalus and Icarus for his heart flying after his mistress (Madr. 14), or the wish that his mistress should be Cynthia (Diana) in the woods, but Venus in his breast (Madr. 17). In many of the poems there is an epigrammatic final turn of wit, quite charming and simple, generally harmless and pretty. There is none of Donne's irony, sarcasm or cynicism; but also rather little of the mutuality found in some of the finest of Donne's lyrics; and where there is mutuality it is only developed very slightly. We are in a limited, sometimes idyllic world, of little convincing depth. A good many of the poems are variations on general themes, 'a timid lover' (33), 'mortal jealousy' (35), 'cold beauty' (51), 'words and kisses' (77), 'constant love' (84). The general titles rightly suggest a certain impersonality far removed from the personal urgency of many of Donne's lyrics. Some of Guarini's madrigals were set to music by various composers, including Monteverdi. Their comparatively simple and mellifluous character lent them to this. The complex argumentation and personal twists and turns and the 'harshness' of many of the *Songs and Sonets* made those poems generally less fitted for such treatment.

It is high time to turn to English Petrarchism. This could be said to have started with Chaucer, but for the purpose of comparing Donne's love-lyrics with the English Petrarchans it is more sensible to start with Wyatt and Surrey. Dominantly Wyatt is a dissatisfied lover, most often complaining of his treatment by Love or his mistress, though on occasion he exercises firm restraint, as when he determines to regard it as natural for a woman to keep changing her mind ('Divers doth use. . . .'). In some of his poems there are signs that a love has been mutual, but then almost invariably the woman's love has ceased. Compared with Petrarch Wyatt occasionally waxes fierce in his attacks on his mistress. On the whole, moreover, his poems are more exclusively concentrated on his own feelings, and their fate. There is little to correspond to the sensory atmosphere found in much of the *Canzoniere*. There is also extremely little imagery, and in that respect Wyatt differs sharply both from Petrarch and from Donne. There is occasionally argument, though usually there is simply lament; and what argument there is has limited pretensions to ingenuity. There are plenty of the stock Petrarchan properties – tears, sighs, fire, rain, heat, cold, pain and moans; but Petrarch's own storehouse is much richer than Wyatt's. Wyatt does, on the other hand, express his rather limited range of attitudes feelingly and movingly. Yet he was a highly imitative poet, especially in his sonnets, and there are close renderings not only of Petrarch, but also of Serafino and Sannazaro. It would, in any case, be absurd to place his love-lyrics, attractive as some of them are, in the same league as Donne's brilliant creations in the *Songs and Sonets*. They were, however, in any case, pioneering work, as also, in their charming, possibly rather less potently emotional way, were the love-lyrics of Surrey. Both poets were forging language and form. Surrey's love poems are even more unlike Donne's than Wyatt's are. They are somewhat less masculine than Wyatt's, and they are evidently often the result of a dominant occupation with form. On the other hand they reflect many scenes of the English countryside, and some of them have a fresh, open-air character which links them more closely with Petrarch than with either Wyatt or Donne. There are also Virgilian allusions, which one would expect from a translator of the *Aeneid*. The love poems, indeed, sometimes have an oratorical character which renders them less compelling than the more plain-spoken lyrics of Wyatt. They are, however, in any case, generally 'Petrarchan' in their assertion of the pain of love, and they have, indeed, a streak at times of the masochistic element which forms an essential part of Petrarch's own attitudes, and which reappears in some of the later Petrarchans, e.g. in Tasso. Yet in Surrey's lyrics there is seldom a sense of the particularity of a relationship or situation; and that constitutes a sharp contrast with Petrarch, and Wyatt, and Donne; and, one may add, with Sidney.

In Sidney we have at last an English love-lyrist of the first rank. The poems he interspersed in his prose *Arcadia* are mostly little more than experiments, but they include 'My true love hath my heart', and one or two other poems of distinction. Sidney writes in plain language, and already shows an alert wit. It is, however, *Astrophel and Stella* (1591, rev. 1598) that is Sidney's triumph in love poetry. It is the first English sonnet sequence, with the addition of some dozen lyrics in other forms. Like the *Canzoniere* it follows through the whole course of a love relationship. The poems have most often a spontaneity and an alertness that matches Donne. Yet Sidney was also an imitative poet. He drew heavily not only on Petrarch and other Italian poets, but also on the Pléiade, and neo-Latin writers, as well as on Classical Latin and Greek work. In this respect *Astrophel and Stella* must be regarded as less original than the *Songs and Sonets*. Yet the result gives the impression of authenticity. Though Sidney culled ideas, thoughts, conceits and phrases from a whole array of writers, what he writes is alive with a personal voice. Moreover (and this is a point sometimes overlooked) he was not imitating all the time. There are plenty of ideas, thoughts, conceits and phrases in *Astrophel and Stella* for which no source or analogue has yet been discovered. How far is Sidney a 'Petrarchan'? His temperament is, at all events, unlike that of Petrarch – less vulnerable perhaps, partly because not totally committed to his love; certainly less hesitant, and freer both from a sense of sin and from an obsessional fixation on past moments of fatefulness and future possible calamities than Petrarch was. As a poetic lover he is also rather less passive, and in this respect somewhat more like Donne. Furthermore, Sidney is distinctly of this world, less transcendental than Petrarch in his thoughts of his beloved and of love. Their reactions are both individual, but Petrarch's sometimes have, naturally enough, a religious dimension, whereas Sidney's collateral preoccupations are moral and social. Petrarch is sometimes haunted by phobias of illness and death, and fear pervades much of the *Canzoniere*. Sidney shows a strong sense of pain, but little of apprehensive brooding. It may also be fair to say that, though Petrarch is ingenious, and has his fair share of wit, Sidney's turns are often more rapid, and more effervescent, less ruminative, and more playful. Yet basically Sidney's attitude is serious, and though his internal struggles are differently orientated from Petrarch's, being in the end a fight between love and his aspirations for self-realization outside love, there is nevertheless internal conflict at a deep level. No such conflicts appear in the *Songs and Sonets*. There are ambivalencies in places on particular issues, but, in general, there is no conflict between love and other impulses in Donne's love-lyrics. There is, indeed, in *Farewell to Love* and *Love's Alchemy*, the expression of a revulsion from love and, indeed, sexuality, but there is nothing tangible indicated as a substitute or alternative aspiration. As to language, Sidney's is often racier than Petrarch's, and less studiedly elegant; though Sidney's conceits are deftly turned. Sidney is moreover, inventive, but not so inventive as Donne, nor so rich in allusion to the full life of the time. In comparison with Donne, furthermore, the variety of the moods is narrower. This is no doubt partly due to the change in poetic attitudes towards the end of the sixteenth century in England, in favour of a harsher, more cynical stance, both towards the world and towards love, as comes out in the satirists near the turn of the century, including Donne himself.[1] Donne did, however, as we know, eventually transcend this type of attitude, and wrote those magnificent poems of mutual love, which were beyond the scope of Petrarch and of Sidney, because beyond the scope of their experience. In these respects, as in others already mentioned, Sidney was more of a 'Petrarchan' than Donne.

What are we to say of Spenser's love-lyrics? Spenser for a long time

[1] See the excellent extended treatment of this topic in Robert Ellrodt, *Les Poètes Métaphysiques Anglais*, vol. II, chs I–IV.

used Petrarch, and also Du Bellay and Tasso, among other continental poets, for moralizings and reflections on the world and its mutabilities. Spenser was, of course, also under the spell of pastoral poetry, ancient and renaissance. He was, besides, an inveterate allegorist, which the poet of *Astrophel and Stella* was not, any more than his master Petrarch. Spenser's relation to Petrarchism is, indeed, complicated. We are only concerned with the *Amoretti* (1595), but one cannot simply dub those poems 'Petrarchan'. More needs to be said. For Spenser the aim of courtship, both in *The Faerie Queene* and in the *Amoretti*, is sacramental marriage. This is not the aim of Petrarch's courtship. Spenser's courtship in the *Amoretti* lasts for over a year without making much progress, then gains ground and the pair are engaged; but suddenly the poet claims that he has been slandered, and the sequence breaks off after three sonnets lamenting the lovers' separation. We are left in the air. The body of the sequence is, however, in any case, an odd and at times inconsistent mixture of pagan and Christian conceptions of love and its effects. The poet's attitude is, at all events, ambivalent, the lady being sometimes seen as a siren-like threat, and at others as angelically beneficent. This is not wholly unlike Petrarch's ambivalence. Yet, according to one view, Spenser may have bundled together sonnets written at different times, and tried to form them into a unity, but without convincing success. His *main* concern, though, was probably to point towards betrothal and marriage. In this respect he is un-Petrarchan. Yet much of the courtship is conducted with such Petrarchan means as praise of physical and moral beauty, pleas for reciprocated love, and sometimes, though not persistently, in terms of conceits to be found in Petrarch or in his Italian and French followers, including such recent poets as Tasso. Spenser is, however, often a good deal 'higher-minded' than some of the Italian and French Petrarchists, dwelling on the moral virtues of his lady with great insistence. This is somewhat reminiscent of Bembo. Spenser's poetry is often highly derivative, even at times closely imitative. He has, for example, a penchant for comparisons of parts and features of the beloved to jewels and flowers, in the manner of Ronsard, Pontus de Tyard and Desportes, and, indeed, Tasso. There are also plenty of examples of the pastoral strain, though it is generally of a less personal nature, and more of a cult phenomenon, than Petrarch's references to country scenes. Stock images are taken over from Petrarch and Petrarchists. The storm-tossed ship of Petrarch and many of his imitators appears more than once in Spenser's sequence, but not, ultimately, in a spirit of despondency. When the first kiss has taken place (Sonnet 64), the lady commits herself to the keeping of her lover. This is, of course, quite un-Petrarchan, yet (and the distinction is important) not contrary to the doctrines of Neo-Platonism spelt out, both in some of the Italian love treatises, and in Castiglione. Spenser, moreover, in the ensuing sonnets endows the betrothal with a spirit of fully Christian piety. The poet of this sequence was doing something impossible for Petrarch. The outburst in Sonnet 86 against the 'venomous tongue' with its 'forged lies', and the final three sonnets of separation remain a mystery which scholars have not yet convincingly solved. Those three poems do not, however, blur the dominant Spenserian values; and they leave the Spenser of the *Amoretti*, I believe, more 'Petrarchan' than Sidney in respect of religious transcendentalism, and also, perhaps, in the solemnly thoughtful cast of the poems. Spenser, on the other hand, is generally less brilliant than Sidney, and than Petrarch, in his turns of thought and handling of conceits. In their undoubted mellifluousness, on the other hand, his poems are perhaps closer to the master than Sidney's, where so much is staked on the dazzling twists of the sense. In point of diction, Spenser's archaisms are celebrated. He was trying to create an atmosphere of antiquity. This was not an especially Petrarchan procedure; but, in any case, it differentiates Spenser sharply from Sidney, and from Donne. The same is true of his deliberate distortions of natural word-order for the sake either of smoothness or of some form of stately artificiality.

Among the host of other songs and sonnets included in the Elizabethan anthologies or in the collections of poems by single poets there are occasional happy successes, both in sophisticated, courtly style, and in plain language. Yet in quality, apart from Shakespeare, none of the lyric poets other than those already discussed reach Donne's level. The best are probably the sonneteers Samuel Daniel and Michael Drayton, and, in other lyric forms, Ben Jonson, Fulke Greville and Thomas Campion. The sober and finely turned lines of Daniel's sonnets are less similar to Donne's lyrics than the lively, conversational sallies of Drayton; but in neither do we find the fantastically plentiful invention of the *Songs and Sonets*, and the attitudes of both poets, moreover, fall well within the bounds of Petrarchism. Jonson, Greville and Campion all wrote lyrics which generally lent themselves to music. They all had wit, but none used their lyric talents for the argumentative complexities or for the wide range of attitudes which we find in the *Songs and Sonets*. Nor do any of these poets set their lyrics in such definite situations as we generally find in Donne, or weave them round such specific central themes with such subtle variations as we encounter in Donne's lyrics. This kind of feature we do find in George Herbert's religious lyrics, but not in any love-lyrist of the period besides Donne.

The present discussion is not concerned with comparing the structural and textural characteristics of Donne's love-lyrics with those of his immediate predecessors and contemporaries; but such comparisons do yield very interesting results, as can be seen from the work of some recent German critics trained in the school of Professor Wolfgang Clemen.[1] Their detailed analyses establish clearly that Donne took over many of the devices of Elizabethan lyric writers, but generally developed them considerably, often to extremes, and tended towards greater complexity, compression and density, and often towards asymmetricality. Donne is also shown as standing conventional conceits on their heads, and reversing logical figures, with the object of surprising the reader with original effects. The original effects are, however, shown to depend on the existence already in Elizabethan poetry of normal procedures from which the original effects are artistic deviations. It is also indicated in detail how Donne combines textural and structural features which had hitherto existed in other lyric poetry of the Elizabethan period as distinct and even separate.

We have been digressing here somewhat from our main theme, the relation of the *Songs and Sonets* to Petrarchism, and we must return to it. What seems clear is that to the Petrarchizing and pastoralizing sonneteers and song and madrigal writers, what appear to be Donne's earlier lyrics look like a vigorous reaction. Those conventional, courtly poetizings may well have sickened Donne, and this may even account for some of the deliberate coarseness of a number of those lyrics, as well as for some of their harsh realism and freely vented bitterness and fury. In a few cases we actually find Donne affecting to conform to such conventions and then implicitly rejecting them in the same poem. Examples with varying degrees of violence are *The Apparition*, *The Message* and *The Bait*. These strong reactions against a tame and insipid adherence to threadbare conventions may well correspond to a more general shift of taste towards the end of the century, from what would appeal to the Court to what would appeal to the Inns of Court, as several modern critics have suggested. (See, in particular, Ellrodt, op. cit., vol. II, pp. 9–93.)

---

[1] See for instance the works by Werner von Koppenfels and Volker Deubel listed in the bibliography and also Professor Clemen's own *Das Problem des Stilwandels in der englischen Dichtung*, Munich, 1968.

It is probably necessary to say something, albeit brief, about Shakespeare's *Sonnets*, in comparison with Donne's lyrics. If, as seems most likely, Meres's reference in 1598 to Shakespeare's 'sugred Sonnets among his private friends' was to some of the poems we now know as Shakespeare's *Sonnets*, then it is quite possible that Donne may have seen some of them in the late 1590s (one cannot help wondering, conversely, whether Shakespeare may have set eyes on any of Donne's lyrics circulating in manuscript). There are certainly images and allusions in the *Sonnets* which resemble images and allusions in the *Songs and Sonets*, e.g. legal, military, mercantile, alchemical and medical images and allusions, as well as images from food and drink, and from home life. Yet, though the ranges of images and allusion overlap, they are not coincident. There is more imagery in Shakespeare of the countryside and its life, of gardens and trees and flowers, and there is less of a theological character and less from the world of scholarship. But our present question concerns comparison of the *Sonnets* with Donne's lyrics in relation to Petrarchism. Like Michelangelo's, Shakespeare's poems are evidently bisexual. Donne's and Petrarch's, and those of most Petrarchans, are heterosexual. Michelangelo's poems, both to Tommaso Cavalieri and to Vittoria Colonna, are highly sublimated, especially those to Vittoria Colonna. Shakespeare's poems to or about the Friend are also, for the most part, highly sublimated, but those to or about the Dark Woman are strongly sexual, and involve a large measure of hatred. In so far as admiration is a Petrarchan attitude, Shakespeare's poems to or about the Friend are dominantly Petrarchan. Only a few of the *Songs and Sonets* are dominantly Petrarchan in this respect. In Donne's lyrics it is rather love than the beloved that is glorified. Shakespeare's poems to or about the Dark Woman are generally not Petrarchan in this regard. On the other hand, Sonnet 130, which seems to have affinity with Francesco Berni's work, is a parody of conventional Petrarchism, and yet ends with a natural, commonsensical admiration of the woman's beauty, which could justly be termed 'Petrarchan'. In contrast, the fascinatingly sophisticated Sonnet 138, with its wonderfully humorous balance, is totally un-Petrarchan without being hostile to the woman.

In another respect, Shakespeare's *Sonnets* are more Petrarchan than Donne's lyrics, in that the great bulk of them (most of those to or about the Friend) follow out a complex relationship over a period of time. They involve estrangement, jealousy, unfaithfulness on the lover's part, adverse judgements of character as well as admiration, shame at inferiority or insufficiency, all within a total framework of a deep friendship which can equally be called passionate love. This range of attitudes, moreover, is greater than Petrarch's, and involves some which are absent in Donne's lyrics, e.g. estrangement, and shame at inferiority or insufficiency. Mutuality, on the other hand, *is* to be found in some of the *Sonnets*, no less than in Donne's lyrics, yet the social superiority of the Friend adds an element which is absent in Donne's poems as it is in Petrarch's. The glorification of the mutuality of love, which we find in some of Donne's finest lyrics, is almost absent from Shakespeare's *Sonnets*, no less than from Petrarch, though love is glorified in general terms in Shakespeare's Sonnet 116. But Petrarch's and Shakespeare's (and Ronsard's) promises of glory for the beloved from their poetry are not to be found in Donne's lyrics. As for tone, there is a good deal more violence in the *Songs and Sonets* than in either Petrarch's *Canzoniere* or Shakespeare's *Sonnets*. This is not to say that the feelings expressed by Donne are stronger. The strong feelings in Petrarch's and Shakespeare's poems are absorbed within a smoother texture and more regular structure of writing.

There is a group of themes in Petrarch and in the work of many Petrarchans (for instance, Du Bellay, Ronsard and Spenser) which is strongly present in Shakespeare's *Sonnets*, but plays rather little part in Donne's lyrics: the poignant sense of the passing of time, of the havoc wrought by a personified Time, and the apprehension of the threat of death (or Death) to the beloved. In Donne's lyrics the poet seems to live more in the moment. There are occasional apprehensions about the death of the beloved (or of the poet), but it is interesting that in the most powerful poem referring to the beloved's death, the *Nocturnal*, the death has already taken place. As to time, it comes in for little mention, and, on occasion, as in l. 10 of *The Sun Rising*, and, more covertly, in stanza 1 of *The Anniversary*, it is treated with contempt. Parting from the beloved is, however, a theme for sorrow in Petrarch, many Petrarchans, Shakespeare and Donne. Yet, again, Donne differs in laying greater stress on the *moment* of parting, whereas in Petrarch and in Shakespeare the pain of *absence* is more strongly emphasized.

A further distinction between Shakespeare, Petrarch and many Petrarchans, on the one hand, and Donne on the other, is that Donne does not seem to focus much on the physical beauty of the beloved, whereas for Shakespeare and the others it clearly counts for a great deal.

It is, of course, natural enough that within the restrictions of the sonnet form Shakespeare seldom develops a dramatic situation, as Donne does in, for instance, *The Flea* or *The Dream*, or a more or less straightforward narrative such as we find in *Love's Diet*, or a more complicated narrative like that in *The Ecstasy*. Yet narrative is not incompatible with the sonnet form. We find instances, for example, in Spenser's *Amoretti* (e.g. Sonnet 67). The underlying fact, however, is that, roughly speaking, Donne's lyrics correspond to Petrarch's *canzoni* and Shakespeare's sonnets to Petrarch's sonnets.

One final point in this sketchy comparison between the *Songs and Sonets* and Shakespeare's *Sonnets* in relation to Petrarchism: Donne and Petrarch and many of the Petrarchans clearly believe in personal immortality, and show this in their lyrics. There is no indication of such a belief in Shakespeare's *Sonnets*, with the possible exception of Sonnet 146.

With regard to Spain, Donne wrote in 1623 in a letter to the Marquis of Buckingham, then in Spain, that he had more Spanish books in his library, both of poetry and of divinity, than of 'any other nation' (Nonesuch Donne, p. 479). Yet no books of Spanish poetry from his library have so far been found. Out of over seventy of Donne's Spanish books discovered to date, only one is in Spanish, the *Jósefina* of Gerónimo Gracián, found by my old and valued friend José-Antonio Muñoz-Rojas (see his article in the *Revista de Filología Española* 25 (1941), pp. 108–11). The rest are in Latin. It by no means follows, however, that Donne had no books of Spanish poetry, and, still less, that he had not read any. It is quite certain that he had read some literature in Spanish, since the motto in the top right corner of the Marshall portrait of Donne (1591), 'Antes muerto que mudado' ('Sooner dead than changed') is an adaptation, into the masculine gender, of four words in the *Diana* of Jorge de Montemayor (?1520–61).[1] Yet the pastoral tale is in prose, and its pastoral character would have had little appeal for Donne. Donne does, however, also refer in a letter of 1616 to a poem in Montemayor's *Cancionero*, and this, as Robert Ellrodt has rightly said (op. cit., vol. II, p. 226), seems to imply a more extensive and closer acquaintance with Spanish poetry than the mere motto could.

As far as Petrarchism is concerned, two poets writing well before Donne virtually imported it into Spain from Italy, Juan Boscán (c. 1493–1542) and Garcilaso de la Vega (1503–36). Earlier attempts by the Marqués de Santillana (1398–1458) and others had proved abortive. Both Garcilaso and Boscán spent some time in Naples, and cultivated Italian poetic forms, and to some extent, Petrarchan attitudes. Garcilaso, a formidable soldier, accomplished courtier, and highly cultivated

[1] See T. E. Terrill, *MLN* 43 (1928), pp. 318–19.

man, persuaded his friend Boscán to translate Castiglione's *Cortegiano* into Spanish. The lyrics of both poets are mainly songs (*canciones*) and sonnets, as in Petrarch's *Canzoniere*, though Boscán used traditional Spanish forms before coming under Italian influence. Typical of Garcilaso, both in his songs and in his sonnets, are love complaints, in finely elegant and musical lines, at his sufferings and the coldness and cruelty of the mistress who causes them. The language is most often general and abstract, but his tortures and despondency are often described and expressed in strong terms. There is no lack of passion, or of firm linguistic control. Yet the range of feeling expressed is narrow. We have an intense, but a restricted, Petrarchism. The introspection is highly concentrated. There are turns of wit, but they are almost all verbal or purely logical, and there is nothing comparable to the surprising images, or the realistic reference to the life of the everyday world, or the humour, of Donne's lyrics. Nor is there the mutuality found in some of the finest of the *Songs and Sonets*. Boscán, though not so fine a poet as Garcilaso, is perhaps slightly more like Donne, even in the Petrarchan lyrics of Book II of his collected poems, in his spontaneity and colloquial language, and his fondness for paradoxical turns of phrase; and the attitudes expressed are sometimes joyful and hopeful like some of Donne's, in contrast with the pervasive and brooding melancholy of Garcilaso's. Yet it is a very far cry from Boscán's somewhat tedious, conventional Petrarchizings, to Donne's compressed, wittily agile creations. Boscán's lyrics also lack variety of reference, and the range of feelings expressed is narrowly restricted, both in its negative and in its positive phases.

There is, however, a fair measure of invention of ideas and images in Spanish lyric poets writing before Donne. One notable cultivator of the conceit was Fernando de Herrera (?1534–97), but the dominant attitude in his love-lyrics is not only Petrarchan, but even 'Platonic'. There is not much parody of Petrarchism, or, indeed, much humour in the love-lyrics of the Spanish poets of the sixteenth century before Lope de Vega (1562–1635), though the delightfully humorous lyrics of Baltasar de Alcázar (1530–1606) form an exception. There is, on the other hand, subtle argumentation and a taste for paradox in the work of writers who might otherwise have had little attraction for Donne. This is, indeed, the case with Montemayor. Yet nowhere do we find before the last years of the century anything to come within reach of Donne's brilliant harnessing of images from far-flung areas, 'realistic' allusion, and mercurial variety of mood, including modes of humour from the whimsically piquant to the savagely satirical. It is with Lope de Vega, Góngora (1561–1627), and his arch-enemy Quevedo (1580–1645), different as they are from one another as love-lyrists, that we find lyrics sufficiently like those of Donne, both in quality and in kind, to make comparison of much interest.

Even this field of comparison is, however, vast, and I cannot pretend to do more than to scratch the surface, offering my impressions for what they may be worth. It is perhaps better to scratch the surface here than to leave the field untouched. It needs to be cultivated by scholars and critics more deeply versed in both literatures than the present editor. At the outset it is important, I believe, to be clear that in the work of all three Spanish poets many of the poems which could properly be called 'love-lyrics' are in traditional Spanish forms, which are a cross between lyrics and short narrative poems: 'romances' (ballads), 'letras' and 'letrillas'. There are also simple and more elaborate 'canciones'. None of these forms correspond closely enough to those of the *Songs and Sonets* to be fruitfully comparable formally, and their formal character does, to some degree, condition the texture of the writing, the use of images, conceits and allusions, and the thematic nature of the poems. All three poets also wrote many love sonnets, and there are none among Donne's lyrics. Nevertheless, it seems possible to make some meaningful comparisons between the *Songs and Sonets* and the love-lyrics of each of the three poets in relation to the general topic of Petrarchism, especially in point of themes, attitudes and devices.

Let us first consider Lope's love-lyrics in relation to Petrarchism. I shall not attempt to discuss the formal elements of Petrarchism which have been so brilliantly treated in many studies by Dámaso Alonso. Thematically, many of the earlier lyrics of Lope, e.g. both the sonnets in his *Arcadia* (1598) and those published in his *Rimas* of 1602 (200 sonnets, mostly love sonnets), are within the Petrarchan tradition. Some of them are quite close to the work of Petrarch himself (e.g. *Rimas* Sonnet 4); but, as modern research has shown (e.g. the work of J. G. Fucilla in *Estudios sobre el petrarquismo en España*, Madrid, 1960), the main models of the 'third generation' of Spanish Petrarchans, Lope, Góngora and Quevedo, were Tebaldeo, Serafino, Tansillo and Tasso. In his early sonnets Lope is, however, just as in his later work, no slavish imitator. Close comparisons of his poems with what were clearly their models show fascinating modifications.[1] These are most often made in the

---

[1] See, for example, the interesting detailed analyses by Sibylle Scheid in *Petrarkismus in Lope de Vegas Sonetten*, Wiesbaden, 1966.

interests of either a strong turn of wit or an increase in the power of an overall impression, for instance, of the total destruction of a past greatness, or the superiority of renown over survival. Lope typically makes sonnets with strong endings, and in this respect they are like Donne's lyrics. Thematically, on the other hand, they are widely divergent. The two themes just mentioned, for instance – total destruction of a past greatness, and the superiority of renown over survival – are recurrent in Lope's sonnets, but wholly absent from the *Songs and Sonets*. Lope, moreover, makes an extensive use of Classical myth. For example, the fall of Troy, and the catastrophes of Ixion and Phaethon, are used repeatedly by him, and they are used as symbols of amorous disaster. Sometimes this is made explicit (as in Sonnets 29, 52, 123). In other cases the myth is expressed without any explicit reference to the poet's love (Sonnet 35). The objectivity can be regarded, however, as a still more powerful embodiment of the poet's tragic dismay, or of his sense of triumph in having undertaken a bold enterprise, than when the significance is spelt out. Both the typical use of Classical mythology, and the explicit or covert symbolism, are quite untypical of Donne, and so are the tragic sense of catastrophe, and the exhilaration of the feeling that the renown of having undertaken a hazardous love and failed was more than a compensation for the failure. The tragic sense can be regarded as Petrarchan. The sense that renown compensates for failure is not typically so. There is another, very fine, Troy sonnet (172) which comes close to Petrarch in expressing the hope that the poet's amorous sufferings may eventually find relief. A man looks at the field of Troy which is now a meadow. The conflagration and the suffering have vanished, and have been replaced by grass and flowers: so one day the fire of the man's passion may be mitigated and become tolerable. The extended use of a myth for any such purposes is not characteristic of the *Songs and Sonets*, which, when they use myth at all, tend to pause upon it only momentarily, and then to move rapidly to other allusions and images.

The rich sensuousness of many of Lope's lyrics affords another contrast with Donne's. The sensuousness is often pleasurable, but may be dominantly horrific, as in Sonnet 78 of the *Rimas* (*Al Triunfo de Judit*), or a mixture of the agreeable and the painful, as in Sonnet 71 (*De Europa y Júpiter*). Lope has a strong sense of colour and form, and also of movement, as in the depiction of Silvia gathering shells on the shore at Cadiz (*Arcadia*, Sonnet 'Esparcido el cabello por la espalda'). The sensuousness is at least as strong and rich as Petrarch's, and a good deal more so than that in Donne's lyrics. Typical of Lope also, as of Petrarch, are the open-air settings, but in Lope one is aware of an abundance of flowers, trees, fields, birds, animals, fish, as well as of the rivers, the sea, the wind, the sky, the sun, the moon, the stars. These are dwelt on for their own sake, with a *joie de vivre* that is magnetic. There is far less of this in the *Songs and Sonets*, where, indeed, quite a number of the settings are indoor.

Like the *Canzoniere* and the work of most Petrarchans, and unlike the *Songs and Sonets*, Lope's love lyrics often praise the beloved's beauty, and sometimes the 'points' include her voice, and her intelligence, as in Sonnet 127 of the *Rimas*, in praise of Lucinda (Micaela Luján, probably the object of Lope's most passionate love, who bore him several children). Incidentally, it seems clear that Lope's most powerful love lyrics (whether in sonnet form or in traditional Spanish forms) had as their subject one or other of his mistresses (unlike Petrarch), and not either of the women who became his wives (unlike Donne).

As compared with entertainers like Serafino or Desportes, Lope writes with convincing passion. The feelings expressed are as strong as those in Petrarch or in Donne. In range of mood his lyrics stretch beyond the *Canzoniere*, and almost match Donne's, though there is nothing quite to correspond to the mutuality and the glorification of it blazoned in some of Donne's poems. Nor is there the buoyant, un-Petrarchan endorsement of inconstancy found in *The Indifferent*, or the morose refusal of love expressed in *Love's Usury*. Nor are women as a sex scarified in the manner of *Love's Alchemy*. There is, on the other hand, a bitterness in the later *romances* about Filis and in the later sonnets in the *Rimas* (e.g. 190, 191), which is as potent as anything in the *Songs and Sonets*.

As for conceits, Lope considered them to be the highest creation of the Spanish spirit. Like Donne he uses many typically Petrarchan devices (e.g. comparison of the mistress's eyes to the sun, contrast between spring and the lover's sufferings), and he is fond of such things as adunata (*Rimas*, Sonnet 99), hyperboles (such as those piled up about Lucinda in *Rimas*, Sonnet 170), antitheses, puns, paradoxes and asyndeta, as Petrarch was, and also Donne. With regard to 'conceited' metaphors and similes, there are less of these in Lope than in Donne. Lope's 'conceits' are often simply 'fancies', as when he asks the waves of the sea not to cover up Lucinda's footprints in the sand, because he is jealous and wants to read in them (*Rimas*, Sonnet 13), or when he makes the armed Venus boast to Pallas that she will conquer her when in armour still better than she did when naked (*Rimas*, Sonnet 139). When Lope does use similes they seem to come largely from the world of myth (falling from heaven, being a tortured devil), or from a Petrarchan store-house (having fire in one's soul, or being burnt like a butterfly in the rays of the 'sun' mistress); or simply from rustic nature, as when he implores Lucinda to take him in her arms as the ivy tenderly embraces the poplars (*Rimas*, Sonnet 67); or again, from the great world of seas, stars, sun, moon, volcanoes and sandy wastes. Donne uses that world far less for metaphor or simile, though he does occasionally, and he does, of course, refer literally to seas, the sun and the moon among other natural phenomena. Lope, on the other hand, does not draw for his metaphors and similes on the world of commerce, or exploration, or law, or the everyday life of the home, or upon Scholastic philosophy, or subtle theological doctrine. In all this he is more like Petrarch than like Donne.

In what I have said I have been confining attention to Lope's lyrics written by 1602, when the *Rimas* were first published. Those lyrics are considered by high authorities to be his best work of that kind. In general one can say that they fall within the Petrarchan tradition much more than do the *Songs and Sonets*. Lope sometimes tries to define love, and he notably does so in *Rimas*, Sonnet 126, in a series of paradoxes, which are an original development of Petrarchan perplexity, and form a striking contrast to the firm attitudes expressed in Shakespeare's Sonnet 116. There is no attempt in the *Songs and Sonets* to define love, though diverse attitudes to it emerge in various poems. There is, on the other hand, probably more of Italian love philosophy in the *Songs and Sonets* than in Lope's early lyrics. It is only later, e.g. in *La Dorotea* (1632), that we find a neo-Platonic philosophy of love. Lope had by then taken deep draughts of Leone Ebreo. As for parody of Petrarchism, we find it in a pure form in some of Lope's later lyrics. There is, for instance, a sonnet from a comedy of 1625 in which hyperbolical praises of a mistress are couched in terms of vegetables ('Rábano os juzgo, oh Laura, muy lavado'). As we have seen, there is no pure parody of Petrarchism in the *Songs and Sonets*, though there are elements of parody in some of them, e.g. *The Bait*.

Comparison of the *Songs and Sonets* in point of themes and attitudes with the love-lyrics of Góngora may reasonably start by considering the sonnets written by Góngora in 1582–5. These generally have the Petrarchan characteristics of high praise for the woman's beauty, abasement of the lover before her (even more 'Petrarchan' than Petrarch), pastoral setting, powerful sensuousness, and amorous complaint at the beloved's cruelty. Some of them go so far as to idolize the woman. One line, 'Idolo bello a quien humilde adoro' (from Sonnet 217 in the Millé edition of Góngora's *Obras Completas*, Madrid, 1943, hereafter referred to as 'Millé'), was roundly condemned by the Jesuit father Juan de Pineda as disgraceful in the mouth of a priest. (Actually Góngora was not yet a priest when he wrote the poem.) Donne, also not yet a priest, wrote even more boldly in *The Dream*. One of these sonnets by Góngora (Millé 240), incidentally, comes quite close, in another respect, to that poem of Donne. The poet urges himself to banish the vain longings which prevent him from sleeping; arguing that if he yields himself up to real dreaming he will both sleep and see his beloved. Another sonnet (Millé 224) also touches *The Dream* (and, very slightly perhaps, *The Sun Rising*), when it curses the sun for waking the poet just at the moment when he was dreaming that his beloved had ceased being cruel to him. In both cases, however, Góngora's poem stops short of the sexual boldness of Donne. There is, indeed, virtually no close approach to physical contact in any of these sonnets. On the other hand, there is rich descriptive sensuousness, even richer than in any of the Italian sonnets of which some of these are imitations or reminiscences (sonnets by Torquato and Bernardo Tasso, Molza, Sannazaro, Groto, Tansillo, and Petrarch himself). Góngora uses a great range of colour words. He also refers profusely to light, and to sound, usually gentle sound. There is much reference to the song of birds, the glory of flowers, and the greenery of meadows. Gold and silver and precious stones, marble, ivory and ebony enrich the scenes and the comparisons. There is an abundance of sheer love of the beauty of the physical world. This is not matched in the *Songs and Sonets*. Góngora's passion for nature, on the other hand, seems to absorb him to such an extent that the beauty and other characteristics of the beloved appear often to be relegated to the background. There seems, indeed, to be more passion in his famous sonnet to his native Córdoba (Millé 244) than for the women in *most* of these sonnets.

Góngora's sonnets also often contain mythological allusions, and these seem to attract the poet for their own sake rather than for their contribution to the expression of love. Sometimes he seems to take delight in the neat fancy which mythology can afford, as in Millé 216 when he makes the Guadalquivir shed weary tears for the death of two young sisters, and declare that he will follow them to heaven, where they will become Gemini and he Aquarius.

To at least as great an extent as Petrarch, Du Bellay, Ronsard, Spenser and Shakespeare, and much more than Donne in his love-lyrics, Góngora seems deeply concerned with the passing of beauty; and with the corollary, *carpe diem*. I know of no finer descendant of Ausonius' famous epigram on this theme than Góngora's celebrated sonnet 'Mientras por competir con tu cabello' (Millé 228), with the darker tone which Góngora adds in the final line, warning the young woman that both her beauty and herself will be turned into 'earth, humus, dust, shadow, nothing' ('en tierra, en humo, en polvo, en sombra, en nada'). This element of Petrarchism is virtually absent from the *Songs and Sonets*.

On the other hand, the amorous complaints in the sonnets of Góngora, though finely expressed, yet seem to me often to lack real conviction. There are, however, exceptions, for instance Millé 242, where mourning for the rash Phaethon becomes mourning for the poet's hardihood in undertaking the mad enterprise of love (cf. Lope); and Millé 238 (an improvement on Tasso) with its stern warning that Love hides like a poisonous snake behind the roses of the woman's lips. The roses are not roses, but Tantalan apples which fly away from the man they incite, and all that remains of Love is the poison. Other exceptions are Millé 239 and the last sonnet of the series, Millé 247, where Góngora, again imitating Tasso, but improving on him, takes love to be a sea which appears calm, with a gentle breeze blowing, the stars favourable, and all seeming to be set fair, yet the poet has seen the sands whitened with so many unburied bones that he does not venture upon the waters without the protection of Arion with his lyre or skilful Palinurus with his hand on the helm. In all these cases, however, Góngora is working generally within the limits of Petrarchism, and in many instances the ideas of the sonnets are suggested, sometimes very closely, by Italian Petrarchists, though Góngora modifies them with some original touches which seem to show characteristic attitudes, such as a great love of nature and beauty, a fear of the emotional dangers of love, and a horror of death and destruction. The poems do not reveal any great passion (or antipathy) for a particular woman. Nor do they constitute a series in any respect analogous to the *Canzoniere*.

Very few of the 135 sonnets printed in Millé and dated after 1585, when Góngora took deacon's orders, and became Prebendary of Córdoba Cathedral, can be called love sonnets. In Millé 261 (1596), after the vivid description of a cataclysmic storm and overwhelming flood, Góngora assures his reader that when witnessing such phenomena he feared nothing in comparison with his own (presumably amorous) troubles. The description is rather more convincing than the assurance. In Millé 262 (1596) he does reproach a woman for her infidelity to him, comparing himself to a 'volcano of water [tears]' and a 'fountain of flames'. These typical mixed hyperboles are very different from Donne's conceits; but they do seem to express in their curious way a fairly strong resentment at the woman's unfaithfulness. (Góngora had, incidentally, by now been a priest for some years.) Góngora was obviously fascinated by experiments in virtuosity, like Donne. There is a sonnet of 1602 (Millé 268) which compares a woman to Diana hunting in the mountains, and shooting with *one* bow at the wild animals, but with *two bows* (not arrows), her eyes, at the poet's life. The conceit is simply a bold elaboration of a Petrarchan turn, and the theme and attitude entirely Petrarchan. The value of the poem lies largely in its diction, which is handpicked. The theme and attitude are, of course, quite alien to the *Songs and Sonets*. In a charming poem (1603), Millé 274, using Petrarchan and Classical properties, Love is the naked winged Cupid, and the poet is wounded by a snake. Yet Góngora's conception is original. The snake wounded the poet long ago when it was lurking among some violets (i.e. when the woman was a child). Now that the woman is an adult it dwells among lilies (her breasts). She was as powerful, the poet says, when she was the dawn, as she still is as the sun in her full splendour. Her beauty makes the birds sing, but it makes people weep. These conceits are clearly very different from those in the *Songs and Sonets*. They are just as inventive, but they depend upon a fancy which is arbitrary to some degree, and also covert, rather than clear and convincingly just in intellectual terms.

This is probably more than enough to give some idea of the differences in themes, attitudes and devices between Góngora's love sonnets and Donne's love-lyrics. Góngora's sonnets are for the most part typically Petrarchan in themes and attitudes, but he extends them by original touches, and he shows a strong sensuous delight in physical objects. Like Donne he clearly wished to surprise his reader. His conceits are, however, sometimes more arcane, and his hyperboles are frequently mixed. Yet their provenance is almost always from within the Petrarchan tradition. Donne's are drawn from a far wider field.

Though Góngora's sonnets are generally Petrarchan in their themes and attitudes, the poet did not always regard women so favourably. There are satirical and burlesque poems in which women come under fire, and others in which his target is love. Góngora is clearly not a misogynist, and his attacks are on particular types of women: courtesans, adventuresses, loose girls in search of pecuniously advantageous marriages or affairs, bawds, go-betweens, widows who pretend to be chaster than they are, and falsely pious prudes. Góngora also attacks love as a form of slavery, from which deliverance is a great relief. He had tasted Court life both at Madrid and at Valladolid, and his ultimate reaction was highly critical (like Petrarch's of the Papal Court at Avignon), though he himself played the courtier for a fair while. His depreciation of the Court in comparison with simple country life comes out in many poems, though most elaborately and splendidly in the *Soledades* (1613–14), which fall outside the scope of our present comparison. Satires on, or burlesques of, particular women or types of women do not occur in the *Songs and Sonets*. A few poems, e.g. *The Sun Rising* and *The Canonization*, do imply some contempt for the Court and its activities; but there is no contrasting paean of simple, country life. On the other hand, there are attacks on the tyranny of love in a number of Donne's love-lyrics (e.g. *The Will, Love's Exchange, The Broken Heart, Love's Deity, Love's Diet*). Góngora also attacks love because of women's natural weakness, attractiveness, and consequent liability to be unfaithful. Yet one detects a certain tolerance in Góngora towards women as such for these infidelities. Moreover, in contrast, as we shall see, to Quevedo, he never makes the women he attacks ugly or repulsive. In this respect he is more like the Donne of the *Songs and Sonets* (though not of the *Elegies*).

Góngora's most impressive short treatments of love occur, however, in some of the *romances* (ballads). These poems, as already mentioned, are usually partly narrative and partly lyrical. In some of Góngora's a strong sympathy is shown for the claims and aspirations of young lovers inflamed by natural passion. The most outstanding example, perhaps, is the *romance* of *Angelica and Medoro* (1602, Millé 48), based on an episode in Ariosto's *Orlando Furioso* (canto XIX, stanzas 16–37). This wonderfully wrought ballad shows Angelica, the hard-hearted Princess of Cathay, falling in love with the dying young Moor, Medoro, as she tends his wounds. The two are taken by a passing peasant to his hut. Medoro recovers, and the couple then make love among all the delights of an idyllic country setting. The ballad ends with an apostrophe to heaven by the poet, to protect the hut, bower, bed, breezes, fields, springs, meadows, caves, tree-trunks, birds, flowers, ash-trees, poplars, mountains and valleys, which have witnessed the love of the lovers, from the jealous fury of Orlando, who has been fruitlessly chasing Angelica. This powerful impulse to protect genuine young love is typical of Góngora's enthusiasm for authentic, uncorrupt life. Góngora's warm sympathy with the young lovers could, I suppose, be a sublimation of his own conscious or subconscious urges towards a satisfactory sexual relationship rendered virtually impossible by his calling as a priest. Whatever the explanation of the sympathy, however, it is an attractive feature of this ballad, and of a number of Góngora's other ballads, e.g. the touching *romancillo* 'La mas bella niña' (1580, Millé 3), as well as of the great *Fabula de Polifemo y Galatea* and the *Soledades*. In Donne's lyrics, as in Petrarch's, the poet is so absorbed in his own situations that there is no case of the objectification which would be a prerequisite of sympathy with other lovers.

As to anti-Petrarchism, there is at least as much in Góngora's ballads as in the *Songs and Sonets*. Góngora's ballads on Hero and Leander (1589, Millé 27, and 1610, Millé 64) and on Pyramus and Thisbe (1618, Millé 74) are as scathing of type love as any anti-Petrarchan could wish, though it is, interestingly, the men rather than the women who are satirized. In the Letrilla 'Andeme yo caliente' (1581, Millé 96) Góngora even announces that rather than cross the sea at midnight like Leander he would prefer to draw some red and white wine from the gulf of his cellar; and since Love was so cruel as to make Pyramus and Thisbe's bridal bed a sword to join them, he would rather his Thisbe were a pasty and the sword his tooth. It is evident that Góngora shared with Donne a lively humour, and that he could direct it at conventional love patterns just as effectively as Donne. Góngora's humour at times reminds one of Donne's, and both are very different from the mad humour of Quevedo, to whom I must now turn.

From a bio-critical standpoint Quevedo can be sharply differentiated from Lope, Góngora, Donne and Petrarch. As a young man he had a number of affairs with women. Later he had one with a woman who bore him children. He also had a long Petrarchan passion lasting for twenty-two years (1609–31) for a high-born lady who seems to have kept him at arm's length. That passion cannot be described as 'Platonic', either in a strict philosophical, or in a more current, sense. Moreover, during the course of those years he did have other affairs, and not without some measure of satisfaction. At fifty he married another high-born lady, but the marriage collapsed after a few months; and there are apparently no poems referring to that relationship. Quevedo, like Lope, was never a priest, but he was clearly more fervently religious than Góngora who was, and he had a strong sense of sin which tortured him at times excruciatingly. He was also less enthusiastically attached to the beauties of nature than Góngora, and more stridently critical of people in general, and of women in particular. A large proportion of his poetry is satirical, some virulently so, and not unlike Swift in its expression of physical disgust.

Let us now, however, take a brief look at Quevedo's love-lyrics in relation to Petrarchan themes and attitudes, and add, if possible, a side-glance at his poetic devices in comparison with those in the *Songs and Sonets*.

The love-lyrics Quevedo wrote between 1598 and 1609, when he started writing the important series of poems to Lisi, were evidently addressed to a number of different women, and they vary somewhat in tone and considerably in attitude. Some are lachrymose, some, such as the Canción to Aminta (1603), are very sensual, with an abundance of tender kisses and embraces. Others express a charming intimacy, for instance the sonnet to Aminta (VII) who had a carnation in her mouth and bit her lip by mistake. There are plenty of Petrarchan commonplaces: fire-ice effects, phoenixes, hyperbolical praises of the women's beauty; but, like Góngora, Quevedo often adds original touches, as when he says that just as the sun when it sets leaves stars, so Aminta should leave him stars, sparks of her passion, when she goes from him (Sonnet VI). Sometimes Quevedo's attitude is more querulous, but sometimes reconciled to harsh treatment or cold rebuff. In one case we find him reflectively writing in an Idilio of what he had learned by loving Tirsis, stating, somewhat cryptically, that after giving her the palms of victory, he had been able to find in affection for souls the secret passage from one body to another. As time goes on Quevedo seems to make an ever sharper distinction between consciousness of a woman's virtue and physical longing, which he condemns as gross and degenerate (e.g. in Sonnet III to Flora). The development of his attitudes is not, however, linear. In a subsequent sonnet, to Floralba (IV), he tells frankly how he dreamt that he enjoyed her, and he recognizes in the experience a conjunction of heaven and hell. An Idilio to Casilina of 1606 is, contrastingly, Anacreontic, and relishes a sexual mingling of their loves with the 'mortal ambrosia' of wine.

The most important of Quevedo's love-lyrics are the sixty-five sonnets which, with a handful of other poems, form his *Canta Sola a Lisi y la Amorosa Pasión de su Amante* (1609–31). These come closest to being a Petrarchan sonnet-cycle. The series starts with a recognition of the complete enslavement of his will by a frown, a smile, some eyes and some hands. There is soon a great deal of Petrarchan water and fire, which do not destroy each other, so as to allow themselves to destroy him (Sonnet III). There is high praise for Lisi's great beauty, but fear and suffering at her 'cruelty'. In one sonnet (XVI) Quevedo disclaims physical desire, and declares that his love is for eternal hierarchies of virtue, and will not end with his life. The flame of his love, moreover, will not be subject to shadows or eclipses (XVII). He recognizes his sufferings as sent by heaven. Like Petrarch he marks the years they have endured (six by Sonnet XXI, ten by XLIV, twenty-two by LXIV). The poems are sprinkled with wire-drawn conceits, as in XXVI, where Quevedo imagines a hell in which Lisi's victory and amorous spoils will burn, and so, love will give them eternal fire; she will burn in his heart, and he in her eyes. Sometimes, however, the conceits are more interesting, as in XXVIII, where he writes that he knows what it is to love, and that Love knows that he does, but he does not know what love is, and Love ordains that he does not. (The convolutions here remind one of stanza 3 of *Love's Exchange*.) There are also dexterous turns of wit, as where the poet presents Lisi with a dog who saved a lamb from the jaws of a wolf, and begs her not to disdain to take something so deserving just because it is he who sent it. There is, on the other hand, something faintly ridiculous about Quevedo's comparison of himself (in XXXIV) to a jealous bull, though it is, I suppose, possible that the poem may have been intended as a joke. There are some unusual combinations of objects in sonnets in praise of the beloved – burning mines united with a garden, Hyblan sweetness embellishing Parian marble. Such combinations are a far cry from those in the *Songs and Sonets*. They foreshadow surrealism, though not so fully as do Quevedo's satirical and burlesque poems, to which I shall come a little later. In the poems to Lisi the attitudes are generally those of the faithful and complaining Petrarchan lover, which the poet expresses in a variety of images. His love is like the ivy which adorns and destroys (XXXIX); Lisi's eyes do not temper the ice of her disdain as the sun tempers the snow on the mountain peaks (XL). Some of the poems, however, achieve greater intensity. The high points are, I think, Sonnets XLIV and XLV. In XLIV Quevedo states that ten years of his life have been carried away since he first saw the East duplicated in beauty in Lisi's eyes. For ten years the sweet fire has persisted in his veins. For ten years her lights have reigned imperially in his mind:

> Basta ver una vez grande hermosura;
> que, una vez vista, eternamente enciende,
> y en l'alma impresa eternamente dura.

(It is enough to see a great beauty once; once it is seen it fires one for ever, and lasts for ever in the soul which took its stamp.)

In XLV Quevedo imagines his last day closing his eyes. On the other shore his memory will not cease to burn. His flame knows how to swim through the cold water, and although his body will be destroyed, his mindfulness will not. The parts of his body will be ashes, but will have feelings. They will be dust, but dust in love: in one of Quevedo's finest lines:

> polvo serán, mas polvo enamorado.

This bold and passionate thought is probably beyond anything in the *Songs and Sonets*. In those lyrics Donne seldom follows seriously through the idea of his own death, and where he does (as in *The Anniversary* and *The Dissolution*) it is his soul that survives his body and joins the beloved. He does not, like Quevedo, envisage the splendid paradox of love inhering in the relics of physical decay. In some of the sonnets which follow this climax Quevedo still remains the adoring lover, kept at a distance. In one he envies a little girl asleep in Lisi's lap (L). In another (LI), however, he warns other lovers not to follow blindly in his footsteps. Yet his mood again changes (LII), and he calls for torments, since they are required for the glory of the beloved. This degree of abasement, if we are to take it seriously, seems to outdo anything in Petrarch. There is, of course, nothing similar in the *Songs and Sonets*. Quevedo even declares (LVI) that he repudiates with abhorrence that part of his life when he was not suffering the pangs of love for Lisi. His heart is, however, reduced to a realm of fear (LVIII). On the twenty-second anniversary of his love he rejects the idea that it is the god of Love that has held him in thrall. He was held in chains of idolatry by the beauty of Lisi. In the last sonnet of all he laments that remaining alive forestalls him from seeing her. This is the only sonnet *in morte*, and it is something of an anti-climax. Its thinness contrasts unfavourably with Donne's great *Nocturnal*, and even with the ingenuities of *The Dissolution*. Although the love embodied in the poems to Lisi has all the signs of being a great love, one has the impression that perhaps the poet has been exhausted by it. Indeed, the poems to Lisi are not only more obsessional than the *Canzoniere*, they have at times the marks of a passion intense to the point of insanity. Quevedo here does not seem able to see himself critically, as Donne so often does in the *Songs and Sonets*.

Quevedo's few poems to his 'common-law wife' Floris (1621–3) belong almost entirely to the phase of courtship, and follow conventional Petrarchan lines; though there is a typical reference in one of them, a brief ballad 'A la sombra de un risco', to the paradoxical identity of life and death. There is, however, a genial poem (1623) in which Quevedo describes for Floris 'a bull fight with darts, attended by the Prince of Wales, when it rained a great deal'. This is a narrative and not a love-lyric; but its tone is intimate and friendly. It evinces an attitude to a particular woman rather different from those attitudes so far described, and also from the attitudes of Quevedo's satirical and burlesque poems, which call for at least brief comment.

Satirical and burlesque attitudes actually predominate in Quevedo's poetry, and his best work is in these modes. There are, moreover, many poems in which the objects of the satire or burlesque are women: women posing as pure, but worthy of citizenship of Sodom; women corruptible by money, as he takes most women to be; women who cuckold their husbands, as he takes most women to do (the difference between women and hens being that hens lay eggs while women lay horns: Letrilla VI, 1604); women who thirst for gold and take it at all times (Letrilla XV); women who are bawds or thieves; women whose beauty, if they ever had any, has fallen into a decay which Quevedo contrives to make grotesque. Quevedo, indeed, succeeds in making all these kinds of women, and a number of other kinds too, into grotesque objects. His uses of imagery and wordplay to produce these grotesque effects are often brilliantly ingenious. Within the scope of the grotesque the effects vary from the dominantly disgusting to the dominantly comic.[1] Quevedo distorts the human body by fierce caricature. He describes women in coarse terms usually applied, for instance, to cows or sows. He jumbles parts of women's bodies, and their functions, and he dissects their bodies and reconstructs them, so as to demean them. Women are feared and hated by him as leading to sin, and putting men in peril of damnation; and he takes a grim or ferociously comic revenge upon them. He also writes many palinodes towards the end of his life.

In comparison with Donne's love-lyrics Quevedo's are typically either ultra-Petrarchan or ultra-satirical or burlesque. He is a poet of extremes. Donne's blend of controlled irony or humour with predominantly positive or negative feelings is quite different, as is, for instance, also his restrained realism about the endurance of love. As for mutual love, Quevedo only very occasionally expresses it, or writes in a

---

[1] For excellent detailed analyses of many instances see J. Iffland, *Quevedo and the Grotesque*, London, 1978.

vein which presupposes it. A number of the finest *Songs and Sonets* therefore fall outside his scope. They are also, we need to remember, un-Petrarchan. Quevedo's scurrilous satires on women and burlesque poems about them must, of course, be reckoned as 'anti-Petrarchan'. They are often immensely powerful, and they spring in part from his naturally malicious and aggressive temperament, and in part from his fanatically religious outlook. What aggressiveness we find in the *Songs and Sonets* (and we do find it) is, even in *The Apparition*, less intense; for Quevedo's aggressiveness has often the intensity of madness, or at least of a genius closely allied to it. These negative poems of Quevedo's come sometimes close to nihilism, at least in relation to earthly life. To borrow D. H. Lawrence's phrase, they 'do dirt on life'. Yet they do it with superb force and subtlety. The strange conceits which contribute so much to Quevedo's characteristic effects are very different from Donne's. The associative power of both poets is great and fantastic. Yet the justice of the often far-fetched conceits is generally clear in Donne without the need to solve puzzles in order to admit it, whereas in Quevedo unexpected and even arcane ambiguities and associations play their part. Puns weave between images, and images between puns, in complex chain-reactions.

One final word: Quevedo's negative reactions to life are sharply opposed to the almost pagan love of life and nature so typical of Góngora. Góngora in this respect is closer to Petrarch. As for the *Songs and Sonets*, they are, in any case, far from nihilism, but their positive reactions to life are concentrated on specific personal relationships, and their negative reactions are generally limited in scope. Though the view of women in *Love's Alchemy* perhaps points in the direction of Quevedo, it is a mere velleity.

Notes on the text and canon

THE TEXTUAL SITUATION AND ITS PROBLEMS

The vast majority of Donne's poetry was not printed in his lifetime. The first collected edition came out in 1633,[1] two years after Donne's death. A very few of the *Songs and Sonets* had already been printed with

---

[1] I shall refer to the 1633 edition as *1633*, and in the same way to the other early editions.

musical settings in collections of songs,[1] but almost all Donne's love-lyrics only reached the public in print in 1633, and two did not appear until the second collected edition of Donne's poems was published in 1635.[2] As often at the time, however, many of these lyrics had circulated in manuscript. Donne had, from early days, a considerable number of friends of both sexes, and may naturally be supposed to have given copies to them, or even dictated poems to them (or to amanuenses for them) from time to time. Since these lyrics were, for the most part, very striking and much admired, what more natural than that copies should be made of copies, further copies taken from these, sometimes to many removes, and that they should be collected by admirers, and collections lent and copied? We may also reasonably conjecture, I believe, that friends would sometimes rely on memory, and faultily record or transmit the text; and also that the poet himself may well have communicated different texts at different times, whether through deliberate revision, or simply spontaneously. It would seem that at least soon after the turn of the century, manuscript collections of Donne's poems may have begun to be made. This process continued until *1633* was published, and even after. Moreover, copies were taken of whole collections. The publisher of *1633* seems to have used at least two manuscript collections, and another was extensively used for *1635* – often with unfortunate effects, but not always.

The text of *1633* is good, and Grierson rightly made it the basis of the text of his great edition of Donne's poems (1912). As he saw, however, *1633*'s text is by no means perfect, and needs emending from manuscripts. Controversial is how much, and on what principles; and, of course, what readings should be adopted in specific cases. I shall presently offer a short survey of the most important manuscript material available.

In point of canon, *1633*, though it presents problems in other classes of poem, for instance the *Elegies*, presents none in the *Songs and Sonets*. It contains 52 out of the 54 printed in this edition, and none which is not generally accepted as authentic. *1635* added the other two poems, *A Lecture upon the Shadow* and *Farewell to Love*. The *Lecture* is found in many manuscripts; *Farewell to Love* in extremely few: yet there is no need to doubt its authenticity. Its omission from the two main manuscript collections used for *1633* may well have occurred because Donne thought the poem too strong meat for publication, or for wide circulation.

---

[1] See Appendix XII, pp. 341–3.
[2] *A Lecture upon the Shadow* and *Farewell to Love*.

THE MANUSCRIPTS

Only one autograph manuscript of any of Donne's poems is known to exist, and it is not of one of the *Songs and Sonets*.[1] With this one exception the extant manuscripts are all copies of other manuscript material, or possibly, in some cases, the result of dictation. They comprise (1) lone copies of a single poem or of a few poems, sometimes in excruciatingly corrupt texts, (2) copies of poems by Donne scattered here and there within miscellanies containing poems by other poets, (3) collections of Donne's poems in miscellanies, (4) collections purporting to be wholly of Donne's poems (though sometimes containing a few inauthentic poems), (5) collections of single classes of Donne's poems (e.g. the *Satires*). Although, occasionally, interesting readings are found in (1) and (2), it is clear that little authority can be accorded them unless they are supported by readings in (3), (4) or (5). Now, in the case of the *Songs and Sonets* there is no extant manuscript of type (5). In attempting to establish an authoritative text, therefore, we can substantially confine our attention to manuscripts of types (3) and (4).

Grierson, in his elaborate textual introduction, classified manuscript collections of Donne's poems into three groups, according to their textual similarities:

Group I contained three manuscripts, closely related: *D* (Dowden MS); *H49* (British Library, Harleian MS 4955); *Lec* (Leconfield MS).[2] Grierson noticed that these manuscripts clearly derived from a common source. They contained roughly the same poems, and there were striking similarities of order. Furthermore, their texts, with some divergencies, especially in *Lec*, were virtually identical.

Since 1912, the date of Grierson's edition, two other manuscripts belonging to this group have come to light: *C57* (Cambridge University Library, Add. MS 5778); *SP* (St Paul's Cathedral Library MS). *C57*

---

[1] It is the original verse-letter 'To the Lady Carey, and Mrs Essex Riche, from Amyens' (in *Gr*, I, p. 221). The manuscript was discovered in April 1970 by Mr P. J. Croft of Sotheby's among the family papers of the Duke of Manchester. It was auctioned at Sotheby's in June 1970 for £23,000, but its first buyer was refused an export licence. It was then acquired by the Bodleian Library, where it now is. (See for further details of the manuscript A. J. Smith in *TLS*, 7 January 1972.)

[2] For further details of manuscripts mentioned in my account see the list of sigla on pp. ix–x. Many of the manuscripts in the Leconfield collection belonged at one time to Henry, 9th Earl of Northumberland (1564–1632), the friend of Donne who communicated the news of Donne's marriage to his father-in-law (see *Gr* II, p. lxxxiv).

is very closely related to *Lec*, and *SP* to *D*. I am not, however, convinced that *SP* is actually a copy of *D*.

The Group I manuscripts are entirely canonical, but contain no poem datable after 1614. As to the dates of the manuscripts themselves, all that is yet clear is that *H49* must have been written late in 1629, or soon after. My impression from examining these manuscripts is that the most careful and reliable text is that of *D*. Even *D*, however, is by no means free from inaccuracy; and, in any case, we cannot properly expect any marked correlation between excellence of text and nearness in date to the writing of the exclusive common ancestor of the Group. Professor Gardner, in her edition of the *Divine Poems*, establishes a stemma showing the descent of Group I manuscripts from an exclusive common ancestor *X*:

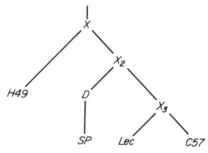

It is important to realize that this stemma leaves open the possibility that the line of descent between *X* and *H49*, between *X₂* and *D*, and between *X₃* and *Lec*, and *X₃* and *C57* involves an intervening manuscript or manuscripts. Moreover, *X₂* could well be a more reliable transcript, whether immediate or mediate, of *X*, than *H49*. It would therefore be a mistake, for example, to assume that *H49* is nearer to the root of the Group I tradition than *D*.

Of the 54 *Songs and Sonets* printed in this edition *D*, *SP* and *H49* contain 45, and *Lec* and *C57* 44.[1]

Professor Gardner (*ESS*, pp. lxv–lxvi) has established the important fact that the collection of Donne's poems (almost all lyrics) in another manuscript, *H40* (British Library, Harleian MS 4064), is closely related to the corresponding poems in Group I manuscripts. *H40* contains 34 lyrics. All are in Group I manuscripts, and there is considerable textual agreement. Only 11 have titles, but those agree with Group I; and Group I only entitles 3 of the remaining 23 shared with *H40*. *H40* is a

---

[1] *Lec* and *C57* omit *The Prohibition*.

manuscript containing a fair number of poems by other writers of the time. The Donne lyrics occur mainly in batches, but sometimes singly. Their text is very good. It is free from typical Group I errors; and so cannot descend from X. Yet it has enough distinctive mistakes to imply that it is not an ancestor of X. Professor Gardner holds that $H40^1$ and X descend from a common ancestor β_2. This seems quite possible; but I do not believe that it must necessarily be so. It is possibly worth adding that, as Grierson pointed out, Harleian 4064 contains an unusually large number of poems addressed by various poets to the Countess of Bedford, and seems to have other conections with her family.

Grierson's Group II contained four manuscripts, also closely related to one another: *A18* (British Library, Add. MS 18647); *N* (Norton MS); *TCC* (Trinity College, Cambridge, MS); *TCD* (Trinity College, Dublin, MS). No fresh manuscript definitely belonging to this group has come to light since 1912. On the other hand, one manuscript already known to Grierson, British Library, Lansdowne MS 740 (*L74*), is closely related to the group, as are three manuscripts which have more recently been discovered, the Dolau Cothi MS (*DC*), and the Dalhousie MSS I and II in the Scottish Record Office.[2] I shall say more of *L74* and *DC* presently.

As Grierson indicated, *A18* seems to be a copy of *TCC*; and *N* a copy of *TCD*. *TCD* contains a larger collection of Donne's poems than *TCC*. Grierson also pointed out that *TCC* and *TCD* seemed to be in the same hand; but he rightly observed that neither manuscript is a copy of the other, even in the case of poems common to both. My own scrutiny of the lyrics contained in both manuscripts has convinced me that the copyist, when he wrote *TCD*, was, sometimes at least, copying a different manuscript from that from which he took *TCC*.

It looks as if *TCC* was earlier than *TCD*; but both must have been written after the death of the Marquis of Hamilton in March 1625, since they both contain the 'Hymn' that Donne wrote in his memory. They also contain some of the other poems that Donne wrote after ordination, together with the early prose *Paradoxes and Problems*, none of which material occurs in Group I manuscripts.

---

[1] It should be noted that Professor Gardner reserves the siglum *H40* for the Donne collection of 44 poems (including the 34 lyrics), and uses the siglum *H40** for the miscellany in Harleian 4064 that it shares with Bodleian MS Rawlinson Poetical 31 (*RP31*).

[2] I have collated *L74* and *DC*. The Dalhousie MSS came to my notice too late for collation. They are reported by Dr Peter Beal (in T. Hofmann and J. Horden (eds), *Index of English Literary Manuscripts*, London, 1980, Donne section), as Δ 11 and 12, and are evidently related to *L74*. I am grateful to Dr Beal for the sight of some specimen pages.

Of the lyrics *TCC* contains only one poem not by Donne, and *TCD* is only a little less accurate in canon. The text of the lyrics is very similar in the two manuscripts, but *TCD*'s is somewhat better, and, in particular, more carefully punctuated. *TCC* contains 51 of the poems printed here; *TCD* only 49, two having apparently been torn out.

The Group II texts of many of the poems differ in some details from the Group I texts; and for a few poems (e.g. *The Flea, A Lecture upon the Shadow, The Good-morrow* and *The Relic*) the two groups offer different versions. Sometimes Group I's seems superior (e.g. for *A Lecture upon the Shadow* and *The Good-morrow*); sometimes Group II's (e.g. for *The Flea*); sometimes Group I's seems better for some lines and Group II's for others (e.g. *The Relic*).

Grierson noticed that *L74* was textually connected in the *Satires* with Group II manuscripts. *L74* is a composite manuscript containing an interesting collection of Donne's poems (mainly early ones) together with a few by contemporary poets. Professor Gardner has closely analysed *L74* and its relations with Group II, and has pointed out that the poems by Donne in the relevant part of *L74* are almost identical with the opening poems of *TCD*. She has indicated that the immediately following poems in Group II are 27 of the 31 poems of Donne which appear further on in *L74*. Furthermore, she has observed that textually *L74* agrees very closely with Group II, while avoiding distinctive Group II errors. *L74* contains 25 of the lyrics printed in this edition. Twenty-four of these occur also in the Group II manuscripts. *L74*'s text is definitely good. It might be important to know to whom this collection belonged. In any case, however, it is clear from Grierson's Introduction and from Professor Milgate's work on the text of the *Satires* that the heavily revised text of the *Satires* in *L74*, Group II and certain other manuscripts was probably already in existence by 1610.

The Dolau Cothi manuscript (in the National Library of Wales) has come to the notice of scholars fairly recently.[1] Except for the *Satires* it contains almost all Donne's poems, and only one poem of doubtful authenticity. It omits only two of the *Songs and Sonets* printed here. Professor Gardner has indicated some important connections with Group II

---

[1] This manuscript was deposited in the Library in 1927 by Herbert Johnes Lloyd, of Dolau Cothi, Camarthenshire. My late cousin Kenneth Redpath, of Newport, Pembrokeshire, pointed out to me that the Johnes family seem to have had a long run at Dolau Cothi, at least from the seventeenth century; and he suggested that, since the Cothi is a tributary of the Towry, and communications would tend to be down the river valleys, there might well be some links between the Johneses and the Donnes, who came from Kidwelly, near the mouth of the Towry.

(*ESS*, p. lxx): that *DC* contains the same verse-letters as *TCD* and *N*; that it contains poems elsewhere only found in Group II, *Lut* and *O'F* (two very late manuscripts in Group III, to be discussed in due course); that in it the *Songs and Sonets* have, with two exceptions, the Group II titles; and that it groups six of the poems under a heading 'Songs which were made to certaine Aires which were made before', which also appears in Group II as a heading to a group of three of the same poems. My own examination of *DC* reveals that in the *Songs and Sonets* the manuscript often reads throughout a poem with *H40* and all Group I against *L74* and Group II; sometimes throughout a poem with *L74* and Group II against *H40* and some or all of Group I; occasionally at certain points in a poem with *H40* and some or all of Group I and at others with *L74* and Group II; very seldom with manuscripts outside both groups against Groups I and II; in one or two instances with *1633* against all other extant manuscripts. There are, however, a few more complicated cases in particular poems. *DC*'s text is often good, and punctuation seems, in general, unusually careful. On the other hand, in places, e.g. in *A Nocturnal*, which does not appear in any other extant manuscript except Group II, *Lut* and *O'F*, *DC*'s text is plainly corrupt at a number of points. It is hard to tell whether the copyist of *DC* had before him one manuscript to copy, or several texts from which he could often make a choice of readings. If it was one manuscript, it was certainly very unlike any other that is yet known. It seems more probable that the copyist had more than one manuscript to work from.

It is now time to pass to Grierson's Group III. This contained nine manuscripts: *A25* (British Library, Add. MS 25707); *B* (Bridgewater MS); *Cy* (Carnaby MS); *JC* (John Cave MS); *O'F* (O'Flaherty MS); *P* (Phillipps MS); *S* (Stephens MS); *S96* (British Library, Stowe MS 961); *W* (Westmoreland MS).

Grierson noticed that *B* resembled *P*, *S96*, *S* and *O'F* rather than Group I or Group II; and that *Cy* and *P* read together in a number of cases. He recognized, however, that his Group III manuscripts could not be traced in their entirety to a single head, though he rightly maintained that in some classes of poems, such as the *Elegies* and the *Holy Sonnets*, they tended to follow a common tradition which might or might not be that of one or other of the first two groups. He did not comment specifically on the case of the *Songs and Sonets*. Summarizing his findings, he held that only Groups I and II and *W* had the appearance of being derived from some authoritative source, that is, from manuscripts in the possession of Donne's own circle. The rest seemed to him to be work of amateurs to whom Donne was not known, or who belonged to a generation that knew Donne as a divine, but only vaguely as a wit (*Gr*, II, p. cxii). As far as the *Songs and Sonets* are concerned Grierson was too sweeping here, since at least two of the other manuscripts known to him, *H40* and *L74*, seem to possess authority comparable to that of Groups I and II. As for *W*, it contains only one of the *Songs and Sonets* (*A Jet Ring Sent*), and therefore only comes minutely into our picture. Moreover, though there is considerable corruption in some of the manuscripts (especially in *S* and *B*, but also in *JC* and *P*, and even in *Cy*) all of them deserve some consideration, since in certain poems they may preserve early readings differing from those in Groups I and II, and from those in *H40* and *L74*. Most of these manuscripts may derive ultimately from copies of poems or small groups of poems given by Donne from time to time to friends (possibly in somewhat differing texts), the copies then being copied, further copies being taken, and so on, until one copy and another found their way into collections. In the case of the *Songs and Sonets* the generally most authoritative among these manuscripts of Grierson's Group III are undoubtedly *S96* (which may have been written in the mid-1620s), and *O'F*, a very full and well-arranged, but far from canonical collection, which was completed on 12 October 1632 (i.e. over a year and a half after Donne's death), and clearly intended for imminent publication. The publisher of *1633*, who forestalled this, evidently used other manuscripts, though his collection was not so full as that in *O'F*. On the other hand, Grierson noticed that *O'F* was pretty certainly used by the publisher of *1635*, who seemed to have taken a number of fresh poems from it, some spurious, some doubtfully authentic, and also to have altered the text in many places to its readings. More recently Professor Gardner and Professor Milgate have demonstrated in detail that in the poems edited by them virtually all the textual innovations in *1635*, in poems common to it and *1633*, are to be found in *O'F*; so that for these poems *1635* has virtually no textual authority independent of the authority of *1633* and *O'F*.

Grierson also mentioned two duplicates of manuscripts in his Group III: one of *JC*, namely *D17* (Dyce MS), and one of parts of *A25*, namely *C29* (Cambridge University Library, Add. MS 29D). These add nothing textually, but are perhaps worth mentioning again here because of their accessibility to scholars in Great Britain.

Grierson knew of another manuscript which concerns us, *HK* (The Haslewood-Kingsborough MS),[1] which he might well have placed in

---

[1] For fuller descriptions of this manuscript see Gardner (*ESS*, pp. lxxvi–lxxx) and C. M. Armitage, 'Donne's poems in Huntington MS 198', *SP* 63 (1966), pp. 697–707.

his Group III had he obtained access to it and collated it. Both parts of this manuscript are miscellanies, and both contain sizeable collections of Donne's poems. It would appear that the first part (*HK1*, not collated for this edition) was probably copied in the late 1630s. The text of the 24 *Songs and Sonets* it contains is described by Professor Gardner as 'respectable' (*ESS*, p. lxxx), and as reading on the whole with *H40* and Group I, but showing occasional connections with *JC* and *S*. The second part (*HK2*) seems to have been written much earlier. Though all but a few of the *Songs and Sonets* it contains are also in *H40*, it reads usually with *L74* and Group II against *H40* and Group I, occasionally with *L74* against both groups, and sometimes with one or more other manuscripts. Professor Gardner (*ESS*, p. lxxvi) considers that in the 23 lyrics *HK2* shares with *L74* its text is an inferior version of *L74*'s, and this has disinclined her from taking seriously its readings in the other lyrics it contains. Her disinclination may be slightly hazardous; though some of *HK2*'s readings are, indeed, inferior, and others plainly corrupt.

. Since Grierson's edition there have come to light several other manuscripts which he would undoubtedly have classified in Group III: *Dob* (Dobell MS); *K* (King MS); *Lut* (Luttrell MS); and *O* (Osborn MS). Of these the most important are *Dob* and *Lut*. *K* is reported to contain 26 of the *Songs and Sonets* in what Professor Gardner describes as the worst text she has seen. *O*, which contains 43 of the *Songs and Sonets* here printed, is apparently very similar in text to *P*, which I have collated, and which, though it sometimes has interesting readings, is often corrupt. *Dob* contains a large collection of Donne's poetry, but also the *Paradoxes and Problems* and some of the *Sermons*. The poems include 48 of the *Songs and Sonets* printed here. Its text is very like that of *S96*, which includes only poems. I have little doubt that these two manuscripts are closely related. The hand is similar, and the same ornament appears at the end of individual poems. *S96* contains only 43 of the *Songs and Sonets* here printed. I should not be surprised if it represents an earlier stage of the collection found in *Dob*. Since *S96* may well have been written about 1625, *Dob* was probably written late in the 1620s. *Lut*, on the other hand, was written between Donne's death and 12 October 1632, the date of *O'F*, which was probably largely copied from it. *Lut* has all but one of the *Songs and Sonets*, and *O'F* has them all. Their text is like that of *S96* and *Dob*, but sometimes diverges. All four manuscripts contain a number of inauthentic poems. Professor Gardner has restricted the term 'Group III' to these four manuscripts, and classified the rest of the manuscripts in Grierson's Group III, together with

HK2, *O*, *D17* and *K*, into two new categories, IV (containing only *W*), and V, which she subdivides into four subgroups. Since, however, Professor Milgate, for the poems he has edited, has reclassified Professor Gardner's category V manuscripts as Group III, the situation has become somewhat confusing. I propose to accept Professor Gardner's classification of *W* as forming a category (IV) on its own; but, since it contains only one of the most trivial of the *Songs and Sonets*, I shall not be concerned with it here. For the others I do not propose to revert to Grierson's terminology ('Group III') for the considerable array of manuscripts which Professor Gardner heads 'V'; but to adopt her terminology for this edition. ('V' would also cover *C29*, the duplicate of part of *A25*.) On the other hand, I do not find Professor Gardner's subgroups rigid enough for me to adopt them. I am therefore regarding the ten manuscripts in her category V (*A25*, *JC*, *D17*, *Cy*, *O*, *P*, *HK2*, *B*, *S*, *K*) as a miscellaneous set of manuscripts with complex relations between some of them, and simple relations between others. *JC* certainly goes with its copy *D17*; but they often diverge from the better text in *A25*, which Professor Gardner subgroups with them. Again, *Cy*, *O* and *P* often read together, but *Cy* too often deviates from *O* and *P* for a subgrouping of the three to be wholly advisable. *P* (and presumably *O*) are, in any case, far poorer texts than *Cy*. Moreover, as to the relation of these three manuscripts, it seems to me hard to accept Professor Gardner's stemma making *HK2* their exclusive common ancestor in the same way as *X* and *Y* would be the common ancestors of Groups I and II respectively. It is, indeed, possible that the collections of *Songs and Sonets* in *Cy*, *O* and *P* largely derive from the same collection represented by *HK2*, but that is another matter. Furthermore, *HK2* would appear to have close links both with *L74*, on the one hand, and fairly close links with *A25* and *JC*, on the other. *B*'s text of the *Songs and Sonets* is evidently related to *L74*, Group II, and *HK2*, but also to *Cy*, *O* and *P*. *S*, whose text is very corrupt, has various affiliations in various poems. *K* is evidently negligible. Some of these manuscripts in category V can be dated, at least roughly: *JC* must have been written between 3 June 1620 and 1625, the date of its copy *D17*. *P* belonged to Henry Champernowne in 1623. *S* is dated 19 July 1620.

I am glad to be able to report some further manuscript material not, as far as I know, used in any previous edition of Donne. This is a sizeable collection of Donne's poems contained in a commonplace book known to have belonged at one time to Sir John Wedderburn (1599–1679), who, after holding the Chair of Philosophy at St Andrews University, followed a medical career, and served both Charles I and Charles II as a royal physician. This manuscript is in The National Library of Scotland at Edinburgh.[1] The book contains a variety of material, including other poetry of the early and late seventeenth century, and political and medical writings; but, at one end (ff. 3a–49b) there is to be found this Donne collection transcribed in a neat Secretary hand. The Donne collection contains 29 of the *Songs and Sonets*. These are all expressly attributed to 'J.D.'. The text is generally excellent. There are occasional lapses, but very few. The readings mostly agree with those of some or all of the manuscripts of Group I, or with some or all of the manuscripts of Group II; very seldom with Group III against either. Sometimes the manuscript comes closest to *H40*. Sometimes it reads, interestingly enough, with *H40* and *L74* against Group I; and sometimes with *L74* and Group I against Group II. Its textual position is, in fact, very complicated; but its affiliations are clearly with Groups I and II rather than with Group III or category V. My impression is that it is a manuscript with a status not dissimilar to that of *H40* or *L74*, probably representing a collection of Donne's poems made in 1610 or soon after. Only twelve of the lyrics have titles of any kind. None of the poems in the manuscript can be dated with certainty after 1609. Moreover, the text of the two *Satires* it includes (II and IV) is most similar to that in *W*, which, in Professor Milgate's view, represents the ?1598 version, in contrast to that of 1593–8 on the one hand, and that of ?1607, on the other. In point of fact, *Wed* (to give the manuscript its siglum) is probably higher in the line of descent than *W*, since it includes l. 46 of *Satire II*, which *W* omits. *W*, a manuscript of very high authority, was almost certainly written about 1620. I should not be surprised if *Wed* was written substantially earlier.

I propose to classify the manuscript collections as indicated in the list of sigla on pp. ix–x.

Before going on to discuss the early editions I now want to consider briefly the topic of textual transmission in the manuscripts, and, in particular, the possible origins of Groups I and II (on which Professor Gardner has advanced an interesting theory); and the possible relations

[1] I discovered the manuscript there in September 1967, and was kindly supplied with a photocopy of the collection. A year or so ago I found a short description of the manuscript by Mr Alan MacColl in a note in *RES* n.s. 19 (1968), pp. 293–5, which I had missed. In a footnote he says that Sir William Arbuckle had reported this manuscript to Professor Gardner, who passed the information to him. Mr MacColl hazards as a pleasant speculation (which had also occurred to me) the thought that the manuscript might at one time have belonged to Charles I, who much admired Donne's verse.

between the manuscripts of those two groups and some of the other collections. These are difficult matters, and, in our present state of knowledge, one needs to be tentative at a number of points.

The possible origins of the Group I and Group II manuscripts
We know that in the winter of 1614–15, that is, shortly before he was ordained (23 January 1615), Donne, with some reluctance, was preparing to print a collection of his poems. In a letter dated 20 December 1614 to his old friend Sir Henry Goodyer he told him in a hushed whisper ('so softly that I am loath to hear myself') that he was 'brought to a necessity of printing' his poems, and addressing them to the Lord Chamberlain. It was a matter of printing a few copies at his own expense. Now, Donne seems not to have kept copies of a number of his poems, and was clearly finding it hard to obtain manuscript copies (or, possibly, *reliable* manuscript copies) from other people. This should not cause us surprise, since several of his poems had been written between fifteen and twenty-five years earlier, and the early copies may have been taken soon after the poems were written, while more recent copies may frequently have been very corrupt. Yet although, as already mentioned, quite a few manuscript collections were made between 1620 and the publication of the first printed edition in 1633, Donne's letter to Goodyer suggests that, at least as far as Donne himself knew, there were hardly any collections available for him to draw on in 1614. He did, however, know that Goodyer himself had such a collection in an 'old book', and he urgently asked to 'borrow' it. The inner story of Donne's project to publish remains obscure. In any case, it came to nothing, though why it did so is equally uncertain.

Professor Gardner stated in her edition of *The Divine Poems* that she believed that X, the ancestor of the Group I manuscripts, was 'a copy of Donne's own collection', which he 'speaks of' in that letter to Goodyer. This description suffers from a certain ambiguity; but it is clear from a later passage that Professor Gardner meant that on her theory the text of X was substantially 'the text of the "edition" of 1614', and that the Group I manuscripts substantially represent that text (pp. lxiv, lxvi). Thirteen years later Professor Gardner expresses herself more tentatively (*ESS*, p. lxv): 'I have suggested it might be a copy of the collection that Donne himself was putting together in 1614 when he was considering publishing his poems'. This is quite unambiguous, and its tentativeness is, I believe, wise; for it is hard to see how one could hold this view with any confidence, while believing, as Professor Gardner does, (1) that it is extremely unlikely that Donne revised any of these poems after ordination, and (2) that the Group II manuscripts descend from a collection made by someone who had access to Donne's papers after 1625. There are certainly considerable differences between Group I and Group II readings in a number of poems, and if the differences are due to revision (whether of a deliberate or of a less intent variety), and if that revision did not take place after ordination, then the latest version in existence at the time of ordination could have been that of Group II, not that of Group I. Indeed, this alternative possibility seems at least to deserve serious attention, and I offer it tentatively (simply as an alternative) for the consideration of scholars and general readers alike. As already mentioned, Professor Milgate's work on the text of the *Satires* has brought out clearly that the heavily revised text of the *Satires* in *L74*, Group II, and certain other manuscripts, was already in existence by 1610. Why should not the *L74* text of the love-lyrics it contains also in many instances embody revisions by Donne of earlier texts of the poems? And what is there to exclude the further possibility that in the 24 lyrics which Group II share with *L74* certain further revisions by Donne are preserved in the Group II texts? There are not many variations in those poems between *L74* and Group II, and the comparatively few revisions, including the addition of titles,[1] could have been made quite rapidly.

On this alternative theory, however, what would the Group I tradition represent? One possibility, I think, would be that it could represent substantially the collection of Donne's poems up to 1614 in the 'old book' which he asked Goodyer for, in the form in which they were *before* Donne started to prepare an edition for the press. An alternative possibility is that it could represent a stage reached at some point in 1614/15 before Donne made the final revisions which are embodied in the Group II tradition. In any case, the collection behind Group I was very incomplete. Its text, moreover, differed considerably, in many poems, from that represented in the Group II manuscripts, which, if they derive ultimately from Donne's papers after 1625, as Professor Gardner has suggested, would presumably spring from the collection which he regarded as containing the final versions of his poems.

Now, if the Group I manuscripts do, in fact, derive from a collection of Donne's poems up to 1614 *before* he started to prepare his projected

[1] Nearly all the lyrics have titles in Group II. Only four have titles in *L74*.

edition, or before the stage of final revision, then some of those revisions might, I suppose, have been suggested by the arrival, from friends, of texts embodying revisions which he had already made some years before, including some of those contained in *L74*. Furthermore, it does not seem unreasonable to suppose that he may have kept both the revised and the unrevised collections, and that copies may have been made from both at some time or times from 1614 until 1633. On the other hand, he may well have given the 'old book' back to Goodyer, and copies from that text and from his own may have been made during that period. Yet a further possibility is, I imagine, that because the project of publishing in 1614 came to nothing, what revisions there were remained incomplete in one or both of the manuscripts represented by the Group I and Group II manuscripts forming the basis of *1633*. The whole matter would appear to be shrouded in uncertainty.

Groups I and II in relation to some other manuscript collections
It is clear that all the manuscript collections in Group III (*S96*, *Dob*, *Lut*, *O'F*) preserve mainly a tradition independent of Groups I and II, though *Lut* and *O'F* sometimes read with Group II, when it varies from Group I. *S96* and *Dob* are very close to each other, and *Lut* and *O'F* do mainly derive from a similar text. If Group I descends from a manuscript in Donne's possession in 1614, and Group II from a manuscript belonging to him in 1625, then it would seem likely that all other extant manuscript collections, with the exception of *DC*, which is clearly close to Group II, and also to Group I, derive from manuscript material outside the tradition of both Groups, and *in circulation before 1614*. Professor Milgate's analysis of the manuscripts of the *Satires* suggests that the Group III manuscripts, and the following manuscripts of Professor Gardner's category V – *A25*, *JC*, *D17*, *Cy*, *O*, *P*, *S* and *K* – in general represent the earliest version of the *Satires* (1593–8), whereas Groups I and II represent later versions. It seems quite possible that this is true also of the Group III and the category V versions of the *Songs and Sonets*, though, as I have already said, there is certainly much corruption in some of those category V manuscripts.

The relations between *H40* and Group I, and between *L74* and Group II, have already been briefly discussed; likewise those of *Wed* to the groups and to category V; so have the relations of *DC* to the other manuscripts. The origin of *DC* is, however, a problem of some interest. A possible theory might be that it was a copy taken from Donne's papers at some time towards the end of Donne's life, and that the copyist used ancestors of the Group I and Group II manuscripts, making a choice of versions and of particular readings. Professor Gardner interestingly notes that where there was a choice between a Group I and a Group II version of a poem, *DC* makes the same choice as *1633*. On the other hand, *DC* very frequently reads differently in specific details from *1633*. It was certainly not the manuscript which *1633* followed.

THE EARLY EDITIONS

As already indicated, the first printed edition of Donne's poems came out in 1633, two years after the poet's death. Grierson demonstrated the superiority of this edition to that of any extant manuscript or single group of manuscripts.[1] Its text of the *Songs and Sonets* was mainly printed from a Group I manuscript closely resembling *C57*; but partly from a Group II manuscript; and partly from some other source or sources. The editor may possibly have been the printer, Miles Fletcher, who was evidently a man of technical skill. Whoever the editor was, he certainly appears on occasion to have used some critical judgement in deciding between readings. The printer gave careful attention to punctuation; but there is no good reason to suppose that the result coincided with the punctuation of the manuscripts from which the text was printed, and still less justification for assuming that the punctuation of the edition is identical with Donne's own punctuation of any of the poems. On the contrary, there is good ground for supposing that Donne's own punctuation may well have been very different. As Professor A. J. Smith pointed out in 1972 in his article[2] on the only known autograph manuscript so far discovered of any Donne poem,[3] there are over forty differences of punctuation, in that poem of sixty-three lines, between Donne's autograph and the 1633 edition. This is not surprising. Printing houses had their own house styles, and a dead man could not lift a finger to infringe them.

The second edition appeared in 1635. Prefixed to the title page in a number of copies is the so-called 'Marshall portrait' of Donne. This is an engraving by William Marshall, apparently from a medallion, which may have been a miniature painting by Nicholas Hilliard. The portrait is in an oval frame, outside which, in the top left-hand corner, is engraved

ANNO DNI.1591.
AETATIS SVÆ · 18 ·

[1] *Gr*, II, pp. cxiv–cxxi.
[2] 'A John Donne poem in holograph', *TLS*, 7 January 1972, p. 19.
[3] *A letter to the Lady Carey and Mrs Essex Riche. From Amyens.*

and in the top right-hand corner a band bearing the motto ANTES MUERTO QUE MUDADO ('sooner dead than changed') and a coat of arms. The motto was taken, presumably by Donne, from the *Diana* of Jorge de Montemayor, where, however, it appears in the feminine ('. . . muerta. . . . mudada'). Underneath the portrait is a poem by Izaak Walton. In this edition the *Songs and Sonets* are grouped together for the first time. Two not included in *1633* are added (*A Lecture upon the Shadow* and *Farewell to Love*), but two poems almost certainly not by Donne are included. The text of the *Songs and Sonets* is, on the whole, inferior to that of *1633*, though not always. The edition was clearly influenced by the Group III manuscript *O'F*, badly in point of the canon of Donne's poems, and often for the worse, though not always, in point of text.

Other editions were issued in 1639, 1650, 1654 and 1669.[1] Textually, only *1669* shows any distinct independence of the earlier editions, as far as the *Songs and Sonets* are concerned. In general, however, its text is definitely inferior to that of *1633*, to whose readings it does, nevertheless, often revert.

Finally, Jacob Tonson published an edition in 1719. It was printed from *1669* and, like Grierson, I have found no definite evidence of recourse by its editor to any manuscripts, or to *1633* or *1635*.

---

[1] An edition was prepared in 1649, and a few copies were printed; but it was not published. According to Grierson the text of the poems is identical with *1650* and *1654* (Gr, II, pp. lxx).

NOTE ON THE USE OF THE SLUR

In the early editions and in the manuscripts an apostrophe is often inserted between two words, where there is no question of its standing for a missing letter. In many cases this device is clearly intended to indicate that the two words should be pronounced with scarcely any interval between them. It seems possible that this was Donne's own intention. There is no modern typographical equivalent for the device; and the elision of a letter together with the use of an apostrophe would not generally meet the case. Therefore, in those instances where a modern reader might well fail to obey what may have been Donne's wishes, I have inserted a slur (instead of the old apostrophe), to indicate that there should be virtual continuity in pronunciation.

SONGS AND SONETS

The Apparition

When by thy scorn, O murd'ress, I am dead,
    And that thou thinkst thee free
From all solicitation from me,
Then shall my ghost come to thy bed,
And thee, feign'd vestal, in worse arms shall see;   5
Then thy sick taper will begin to wink,
And he, whose thou art then, being tir'd before,
Will, if thou stir, or pinch to wake him, think
    Thou call'st for more,
And in a false sleep will from thee shrink;   10
And then, poor aspen wretch, neglected thou
Bath'd in a cold quicksílver sweat wilt lie,
    A verier ghost than I:
What I will say, I will not tell thee now,
Lest that preserve thee; and since my love is spent,   15
I had rather thou shouldst painfully repent,
Than by my threat'nings rest still innocent.

In 1633–1719. L74; Wed; HK2 omit.

Text: Title The Apparition *1633–1719; I; DC; Cy.* An Apparition *H40; II; III; S.* Apparition *A25, P.* Another Sonnett *B.* An: ~~inspiration~~ Aparitione [sic] *S962.*

5 fain'd vestal] fond virgin *S96, Lut, O'F* (faynd vestall *in margin); P.* fond vestal *S962.*

10 in a false . . . *II; Lut, O'F (both omit* will*); A25, P (both omitting* will*); 1669–1719 (reading* even *for* will*).* in a fain'd . . . *D17, B (*fayned*).* in false

sleep will *1633–54; (1635–54 omit* will*); I; H40; DC; S96, Dob; Cy, S; S962.*

11 And then poore . . . thou *1633–1719; Lut, O'F; A25, B.* And there poore . . . thou *S96, Dob; D17.* Then poore . . . thou *S.* Thou poore . . . then *I; H40; II; Cy; S962.* And thou poore . . . then *DC.* And there poore . . . then *P.*

17 rest still] keepe thee *Lut, O'F; A25, Cy, P, D17.*

General note. As Professor Donald Guss says (*John Donne, Petrarchist*, Detroit, 1966, p. 54), three conceits place the poem within the Petrarchan tradition: 'death through unrequited love; supernatural punishment of obdurate ladies; and the rejected lover's desire for vengeance'. See also Guss's analysis of Donne's special achievement here (op. cit., pp. 53–60). Guss quotes passages from Serafino Ciminelli dall'Aquila very close to some of Donne's poem. It is important, however, to note that at the end of the poem Donne is very much alive, yet at least affects not to feel, and most probably does not feel, any further love, but only the desire that the woman should undergo the tortures of repentance. Petrarch (*Canz.* 126) had imagined that there would come a time when Laura would turn eager and joyful eyes towards where she caught sight of him originally, but would then see him already as dust beneath the stones, and would sigh and weep for pity of him. The idea of the dead lover was taken up by many Petrarchans, some of whom, e.g. Serafino, described the actual death or the funereal aftermath (see Guss, op. cit., pp. 54, 198). They often attributed the death to the beloved's failure (or even cruel refusal) to return the love, and sometimes called on higher powers to punish the lady, and sometimes imagined themselves exacting a satisfying revenge. Petrarch himself, in an unusually fierce sonnet (*Canz.* 256), had expressed a strong desire for vengeance against Laura for little by little consuming and sapping his afflicted and weary spirits, and at night roaring over his heart like a cruel lion when he ought to be at rest. He there goes on to say that his soul, which death thrusts out of its dwelling-place, yet goes off after her, and speaks to her and weeps and then embraces her, and he wonders if perhaps on some such occasion her sleep may be broken, and she may listen to him. Petrarch's resentment is clear enough, but his final reaction is typically mild and loving. Not so, of course, Donne's in this poem. There was, however, plenty of precedent for sharper reactions than Petrarch's, particularly among Petrarchists but also in Classical poetry. It has been rightly pointed out, for instance, that the tone and theme of *The Apparition* are close to Propertius's *Elegy* IV.7 (W. von Koppenfels, *Das Petrarkistische Element in der Dichtung von John Donne*, Munich, 1967, p. 105, n. 18). Sometimes a Petrarchan will threaten some form of earthly punishment, for the crime of murder or theft, possibly administered by the law, possibly by the poet himself or his ghost. Often, however, the threat of punishment yields to an expression of love not weakened even by death, though on occasion the vengeful impulse remains inexorable (as in Serafino's *strambotti* 103 and 194 quoted by Guss, op. cit., p. 57). Donne's poem does, however, seem to me more 'realistic' than Serafino's.

A further point of interest is raised by Professor H. M. Richmond (*The School of Love*, Princeton, 1964, p. 87), who maintains that the poet's declaration in l. 15 that his love 'is spent' contradicts the implication at the start of the poem that the woman's scorn could and would kill him. I wonder, however, whether beneath the controlled fury of the poem, with its apparently radical hatred and contempt, there does not lurk a forlorn hope that the poem itself may 'convert' the woman to a more favourable attitude. Why should the poet wish that she would 'painfully repent'? Not, one may fairly safely imagine, for the sake of any other lover; and if for the sake of the poet, then the ending of the poem may, after all, perhaps, subtly cohere with its beginning.

3 *solicitation*] '-ation' trisyllabic.
6 *wink*] grow dim or flicker before going out.
10 *in a false*] This reading of *II* seems slightly superior to *1633*'s 'in false'; partly for the suggestively jerky rhythm, and partly because it more vividly

suggests specifically deliberate action by the tired new lover. The article has considerable MS support.

12   *quicksílver*] so accented even as late as Johnson's time (see his *Dictionary*). The accentuation has not been unheard in the present century – e.g. in the music-hall song:

> I've often said to myself, I've said:
> 'Cheer up, Quicksilver, you'll soon be dead;
> It's a short life and a gay one!'

cold quicksílver sweat] *OED* wrongly quotes this as 'cold quicksilver bath', chilling enough, though within the context of the poem a ludicrous exaggeration. The metallic allusion in the true text is potent enough, especially as there may be a strong hint of poison here, since mercury vapour was even then known to be highly poisonous (see E. Grimston's *D'Acosta's History of the Indies*, 1604, IV. x. 235).

The Message

Send home my long-stray'd eyes to me,
Which, oh, too long have dwelt on thee;
Yet since there they have learn'd such ill,
    Such forc'd fashions,
    And false passions,   5
      That they be
      Made by thee
Fit for no good sight, keep them still.

Send home my harmless heart again,
Which no unworthy thought could stain;   10
But if it be taught by thine
    To make jestings
    Of protestings,
      And cross both
      Word and oath,   15
Keep it, for then 'tis none of mine.

Yet send me back my heart and eyes,
That I may know, and see, thy lies,
And may laugh and joy, when thou
    Art in anguish   20
    And dost languish
      For some one
      That will none,
Or prove as false as thou art now.

General note. This lively poem is an admirable example of Donne's use of ternary form. In point of structure it also affords a striking instance of Donne's exploitation of what is known in rhetorical and poetic theory as the convention of 'revocatio', the renunciation by the orator or poet of an attitude adopted earlier in the same speech or poem. See the excellent treatment of Donne's use of the convention in comparison with that by other Elizabethan poets in Dr Volker Deubel's *Tradierte Bauformen u. lyrische Struktur*, Stuttgart, 1971, pp. 139–49, which also discusses many other aspects of the structure of Donne's lyrics as compared with the lyrics of his Elizabethan predecessors. As Volker Deubel points out (p. 145), we have in *The Message* cases of *revocatio* within the first two stanzas, and then, in the final stanza, a *revocatio* of these *revocationes*.

The Message is one of six poems grouped in *DC*, and of three grouped in *II* as 'Songs which were made to certaine Aires that were made before'. A setting by Giovanni Coperario appears in Tenbury Wells MS 1019, f 1ᵛ. The text there involves a few variants from that here printed. For musical settings of *Songs and Sonets* see Appendix XII, pp. 341–3.

3   *learn'd*] taken on, acquired.
3–4 *such ill, / Such forc'd fashions*] such affected habits. (As Mr W. G. Ingram has suggested to me, the association of fantastically stuffed garments, belying the form beneath, is probably present in the phrase.)
8   *Fit for no good sight*] possibly 'No longer able to tell [or 'appreciate'] genuineness if they saw it'.
     still] for ever.
11] *But*] The reading of *1633* and the vast majority of MSS was rejected by Grierson in favour of 'But', and he defended his decision in a note:

> It seems incredible that Donne should have written 'Which if it' etc. immediately after the 'Which' of the preceding line. I had thought that the *1633* printer had accidentally repeated from the line above, but the evidence of the MSS points to the mistake (if it is a mistake) being older than that. 'Which' was in the MS used by the printer. If 'But' is not Donne's own reading or emendation it ought to be, and I am loath to injure a charming poem by pedantic adherence to authority in so small a point. *De minimis non curat lex*; but art cares very much indeed. *JC* and *P* read 'Yet since it hath learn'd by thine'. (*Gr* II, p. 37)

Professor Gardner, however, retains the *1633* reading 'Which'. She justifies her decision by the weight of manuscript authority:

> It is impossible, having regard to the agreement of *I*, *II*, *Dob*, *S96*, to regard 'But' as anything but an emendation in *Lut* to avoid the repetition that Grierson disliked. The remaining manuscripts rewrite the line to make it conform to l. 3, *HK2* and *A25* showing a first stage in a process completed in *P*, *B*, *JC*. (*ESS*, p. 154)

The last sentence of Professor Gardner's note refers to the reading of *HK2* and *A25*:

> Yet since there 'tis taught by thine

and the reading of *P*, *B*, and *JC*:

> Yet since it hath learn'd by thine

Now, is it really impossible to regard 'But' as anything but an emendation in *Lut* to avoid the repetition that Grierson disliked? Such an assertion is surely too confident? Admittedly, *I*, *II*, *Dob* and *S96* amount to eleven reputable MSS, and one may add *DC* for good measure; but errors are often enough perpetuated in manuscript traditions, especially by faithful copyists; and 'Which' could easily have been caught from the previous line by some copyist early in the tradition. (Can we even totally rule out the possibility that it was a mistake by Donne himself in a careless moment?) Surely the question is not to be settled simply by counting pieces of paper, however respectable their authority may be? On semantic and aesthetic criteria, and possibly even on the ground of syntax, 'But' is here far superior to 'Which'. Grierson was entirely right; and I am glad to see that Professor A. J. Smith in his Penguin edition of Donne's poems has also adopted the reading 'But'.

14 *cross*] literally 'cancel' (Grierson), or possibly 'contravene'. Both senses were current in Donne's day (see *OED*). There is not much to choose between them in the present context, and 'break' would probably be the best modern equivalent.

23 *That will none*] The sense is probably: 'That will have no truck with you'.

A Jet Ring Sent

Thou art not so black as my heart,
  Nor half so brittle as her heart, thou art;
What wouldst thou say? Shall both our properties by thee be spoke,
  Nothing more endless, nothing sooner broke?

Marriage rings are not of this stuff;   5
  Oh, why should aught less precious or less tough
Figure our loves? except in thy name thou have bid it say:
  'I'm cheap, and naught but fashion, fling me away.'

Yet stay with me since thou art come,
  Circle this finger's top, which didst her thumb.   10
Be justly proud, and gladly safe, that thou dost dwell with me,
  She that, oh, broke her faith, would soon break thee.

In 1633–1719. Among MSS collated for this edition only II; DC; W; Lut, O'F; S962 include.

Text: Title A Je(a)t(e) Ring sent *1633–1719; II; Lut, O'F; S962.* To a Jeat ring sent to me *W.* A Jeat Ringe *DC.*

6 Oh, *1633–69; DC (no comma); W; Gr; Gar.* Oh! *1719.* Or *II; Lut, O'F (b.c.); S962.*

7 loves *1633–1719; II; DC; W; S962; Gr; Gar.* love *Lut, O'F.*

A Jet Ring Sent

General note. The only one of the *Songs and Sonets* occurring in *W*, the MS copy of Donne's poems belonging to his friend Rowland Woodward. As Professor Gardner indicates, this makes it safe to regard the poem as an early one, written before 1598.

Jet rings were common, and often lined with silver engraved with inscriptions ('posies', cf. *Hamlet*, III. ii. 155).

1 *black*] probably (cf. l. 4) 'constant', because true black has no shades; this would be a bold stroke of wit, in view of the usually sinister figurative implications of 'black'. Cf., however, a close precedent in one of the black ring sonnets of Serafino:

> Chiara è la fé se ben mio nome è nera
> Benché tal nome assai forte me avante,
> Ch'ogni nero color dice constante,
> E questa afferma assai mi fé sincera.
>
> (Sonnet 49, ll. 1–4)

2 *brittle*] i.e. liable to break faith.
3 *spoke*] i.e. symbolized.
4 *endless*] eternally faithful.
6 *less precious or less tough*] i.e. than gold.
7 *Figure*] Represent.
8 *naught but fashion*] 'mere pretence', 'mere show' (cf. *OED*, sb. 7 *obs.*).
fling me away] a pun on 'jet' and French 'jette' ('throw away'), as F. L. Lucas suggested to John Hayward (see Nonesuch Donne, p. 766), or English to 'jet'. *OED* gives (vb 2, II. 3) an English verb 'jet' = 'to throw, cast, toss' (*obs. exc. dialect*), though the first instance it quotes is dated 1659.
10 *her thumb*] Chambers points out that thumb-rings were commonly worn by prosperous citizens, and quotes *1 Henry IV*, II. iv. 335; and this passage suggests that women also wore them.

The Legacy

When I died last (and, dear, I die
  As often as from thee I go),
  Though it be an hour ago,
And lovers' hours be full eternity,
I can remember yet, that I   5
  Something did say, and something did bestow;
Though I be dead, which sent me, I should be
Mine own executor and legacy.

I heard me say: 'Tell her anon,
  That my self' (that is you, not I)   10
  'Did kill me'; and when I felt me die,
I bid me send my heart, when I was gone;
But I alas could there find none,
  When I had ripp'd me, and search'd where hearts should lie;
It kill'd me again, that I who still was true   15
In life, in my last will should cozen you.

Yet I found something like a heart,
  But colours it, and corners had;
  It was not good, it was not bad,
It was entire to none, and few had part.   20
As good as could be made by art
  It seem'd; and therefore, for our losses sad,
I meant to send that heart instead of mine:
But oh, no man could hold it; for 'twas thine.

In 1633–1719. D17 omits.
Text: Title The Legacy *1633–1719; DC.*
Legacy *L74.* Elegy II. Song *or no title other*
MSS.
  1–2 *So parenthesized in several MSS, e.g.*
  L74; Wed; HK2, Cy.
  3 be *H49, D, SP; H40; II; L74; Wed;*
  DC; S96, Lut, O'F; HK2, A25, Cy, P,
  B, S; S962; Gar. be but *1633–1719;*
  Lec, C57; Dob; Gr; Ed (1956).
  4 And] For *D, SP, Lec, C57; S96.*
  10 (that is you, not I) *Lut; Gr; Hayward*

(both printing a comma after I*); Ed (1956).*
(that is, you not I) *O'F.* that is you,
not I *1635 – 1719.* (that's you, not I)
(some MSS without apostrophe, some
without comma) II; L74; Wed; DC; Dob;
HK2, Cy, P. that's you, not I *1633;*
Gar. thats you, not, I *A25.* that you,
not I *H49 (no comma), D, Lec, C57;*
H40; B; S962. that thou, not I *SP.* not
you not I *S96 (with* that *in margin as*
alternative or correction to first not*); S.*
  12 bid] bad *Dob; S962.*

14 rip(p)'d me *1633; I; H40; A25, B* (ript), *S; S962.* rip(p)'d *II; L74; DC; Wed; III; HK2; Cy, P; 1635–1719.* h(e)arts should *II; L74; Wed; Lut, O'F; HK2, Cy, P; 1635–1719; Gar.* h(e)arts did *1633; DC (s possibly added later); Gr; Ed (1956).* hart did *I; H40; S96, Dob; B, S; S962.* harts doe *A25.*

16] In life, should in my death thus cozen you *A25.*

22 our losses sad *1633–54; TC, N; L74; Wed; DC; III; HK2; A25, P; Gr; Ed* *(1956); Gar.* our loss(e) be(e) ye(e) sad *H49, Lec, C57; H40; Cy (yo^w), B (yo^u), S; S962.* our losse, bee yee had *D.* yor loss, be ye sad *SP.* yor losses sad *A18.* our loss be sad *1669–1719.*

23 me(a)nt *1633–1719; I; H40; DC; S96; A25, Cy, B, S; S962; Gr; Ed (1956).* thought *II; L74; Wed; Dob, Lut, O'F; HK2, P; Gar.* that *II; L74; Wed; Lut, O'F; HK2, A25, Cy, P; 1635–1719; Gar.* this *1633; I; H40; DC; S96, Dob; B, S; S962; Gr; Ed (1956).*

General note. A most ingenious and amusing exploitation of Petrarchan conventions (parting of lovers as death; an hour's absence as eternity; the lover's last will; exchange of hearts). The fantastic transition, through patent impossibilities, from the hyperbolically laudatory beginning, through the mock-search, to the depreciatory 'something like a heart', and finally the exposure of the slipperiness of the woman, is conducted in masterly fashion. It is also worth noting in the imagery the combination of law and surgery, unusual in lyric poetry, but characteristic of Donne's bold, masculine strength.

1–2] The parentheses appear in several MSS, e.g. *L74; Wed; HK2, Cy.*

1–5] A difficult passage, variously punctuated in modern editions. The sense is: 'When I died last (and, dear, I die every time I leave you), even though it was an hour ago, and lovers' hours are each a whole eternity, I can still remember that . . .'.

3] The MS evidence for omitting 'but' is so strong that *1633* should, I think, be emended, as Professor Gardner has done. Yet she seems to me to go too far when she writes (*ESS*, p. 172) that *1633*'s reading 'gives eight syllables at the cost of sense'. If 'but' were taken to mean 'only', that would be true; but if we took it to mean 'actually', 'neither more nor less than', 'just' (*OED* B.adv. 6b), a use then current, the line would make perfectly reasonable sense. It would also yield an octosyllabic line parallelling ll. 11 and 19.

6 *bestow*] give away (*OED* 6).

7–8] 'Though I, who sent myself, am dead, I was to be my own executor and my own legacy.'

9–16] A stanza which has caused great difficulty. My own reading agrees partly with Chambers and partly with Grierson. I entirely concur with Grierson against Norton and Chambers that the stop at the end of l. 14 should be heavier than that at the end of l. 13, and that ll. 15 and 16 are a comment on the whole incident. On the other hand, I believe Chambers was right against Grierson in ending the inverted commas after 'me' in l. 11. The sense seems to me to be: 'I heard myself say: "Tell her presently

that it was my self'' (my self being you not me) "that killed me"; and then
when I felt myself dying I told myself to send you my heart when I was
dead; but when I ripped my body open, and looked in the place where
hearts ought to be located, I failed to find one there; and the thought that
I, who was always true to you during life, should cheat you in my will,
killed me all over again.'

10 *(that is you, not I)*] The contraction 'that's' printed in *1633*, and adopted by
Professor Gardner, is well supported in MSS, and gives a lively line, with
stresses where required. Yet the uncontracted form 'that is' is also well
supported, and gives the right stresses too, besides matching metrically the
corresponding lines in stanzas 1 and 3. In any case, moreover, it is worth
adding the parentheses, which are also well supported by MSS.

14 *hearts should*] seems the best reading, at least for a modern edition. 'hearts
did' has only *1633* as definite support, with the doubtful backing of *DC*.
'hart did' seems quaint, though just possibly it could have been a light-
hearted use. Alternatively it could be a corruption of 'harts did', in which
case *1633* would have much more support. Neither reading is wholly satisfactory, nor is 'harts doe', which, though sensible enough, reads lamely.

18 *colours*] probably meaning that it was a painted heart, i.e. a hypocritical
one, not a 'true plain' one. This heart was, of course, that of his mistress
(cf. l. 24).

corners] The circle and sphere were considered the most perfect forms.
Donne writes in a sermon: 'And of all formes, a Circle is the perfectest'
(*Sermons*, IV. 51). 'Corners' are often mentioned by Donne in association
with untoward secrecy, suspiciousness, and lack of straightforwardness,
e.g. 'God is a circle himselfe, and he will make thee one; Goe not thou
about to square eyther circle, to bring that which is equall in it selfe, to
Angles, and Corners, into dark and sad suspicions of God, or of thy selfe
. . .' (*Sermons*, VI. 175); and, praising James I, Donne writes: 'He is too
Great, and too *Good* a *King* to seeke corners, or disguises, for his actions'
(*Sermons*, IV. 201).

20 *It was entire to none*] It was not given wholly to anyone.
and few had part] and few had a share in its affections.

22 *for our losses sad*] The sense is: 'being sad for our losses'; probably, that is,
for his loss of his heart and her loss of him and his heart. Though the poem
may imply that his mistress has his heart, it does not say so; and, in any
case, the poet did not think so, but was desolated by the idea that *he* had
cheated *her* (ll. 15–16).

our losses sad] This reading seems to make the best sense, though *H49*'s is
lively, and could be appropriate to the impending announcement to the
mistress of the loss of her own heart. Yet I wonder whether it might not
be a corruption of 'our losse beynge sad', or even of 'your losse beynge
sad'.

23 *meant*] The sense is: 'intended'. 'meant' seems slightly better than

'thought', which suggests a passing idea, whereas 'meant' more appropriately implies an intention, which was only frustrated by the slipperiness of the heart. MS support for 'meant' is considerable, and there seems no need to emend *1633*.

that] Group II has some more support here, and 'that' seems slightly preferable to 'this', as suggesting greater critical detachment on the part of the poet, and avoiding the least suggestion that the heart might be his own.

24] 'I could not send it, for no one could hold such a fickle heart as yours.'

Song

Go and catch a falling star,
    Get with child a mandrake root,
Tell me where all past years are,
    Or who cleft the Devil's foot,
Teach me to hear mermaids singing,   5
Or to keep off envy's stinging,
        And find
        What wind
Serves to advance an honest mind.

If thou be'st borne to strange sights,   10
    Things invisible go see,
Ride ten thousand days and nights,
    Till age snow white hairs on thee,
Thou, when thou return'st, wilt tell me
All strange wonders that befell thee,   15
        And swear
        Nowhere
Lives a woman true, and fair.

If thou findst one, let me know,
    Such a pilgrimage were sweet;—   20
Yet do not, I would not go,
    Though at next door we might meet;
Though she were true, when you met her,
And last, till you write your letter,
        Yet she   25
        Will be
False, ere I come, to two, or three.

In 1633–1719 and all 25 MSS collated for this edition.

Text: Title Song *1633–1719 and some MSS. No title other MSS.*

3 past years] past hours *S96; S; S962.* past times *P.* times past *1669–1719.*

11 go(e) see *S96, Dob; S; S962; 1669–1719.* to see *1633–54; N; DC; Wed; Lut, O'F; HK2, A25, Cy, P, B; D17, Gr; Ed (1956); Gar.* see I; *H40; TCC, A18, TCD (to deleted); L74.*

14 when thou return'st] at thy return *III; S.*

15 wonders that] things that e're *Lut, O'F.*

21 not, I] not, for I *III; S; S962.*

24 last] *om. TCC, A18.* last so *S96, Lut, O'F; A25, D17; S962.* lasts so *Dob; S.*

25 Yet] Greate *A25.*

26–7 Will . . . come] Would . . . came *D17.*

Song

General note. The device of the 'impossibility' (*adunaton*) was used both in Classical and in medieval poetry (see E. R. Curtius, *Europäische Literatur und Lateinisches Mittelalter*, 3rd edn, Berne/Munich, 1961, pp. 104–8), and Petrarch employed it both when expressing recognition of the impossibility of ever being loved by Laura (e.g. *Canz.* 239, 10 ff.) and when affirming his own irrefragable constancy (e.g. *Canz.* 195, 5 ff.). These uses were continued by Petrarchists. As Werner von Koppenfels points out, however, anti-courtly exploitation of the same device is found in poetry of the late Middle Ages, e.g. poem 125 (fifteenth century) in R. T. Davies (ed.), *Medieval English Lyrics*, London, 1963, 'Whan nettiles in winter bere roses rede', where each stanza lists *adunata*, with the refrain 'Than put in a woman your trust and confidence' (Koppenfels, op. cit., p. 52).

Donne's poem is one of six grouped in *DC* as 'Songs which were made to certaine Aires that were made before'. It is not among three so grouped in *II*. There is a musical setting in BL Egerton MS 2013, f58^v. Only one stanza of text is given. It reads 'tymes' for 'yeares' in l. 3. See Appendix XII, pp. 341–3.

2 *Get with child a mandrake root*] The meaning is: 'Beget a child on a fork-rooted plant'. The forked root of *atropa mandragora* resembles the human form: sometimes the female form, sometimes the male, according to whether the roots are twofold or threefold. It is not the case that they all resemble the male form, and so I do not think there is the additional idea here of the impossibility of a male begetting a child on a male. See D. C. Allen, 'Donne on the mandrake', *MLN* 74 (1959) for further information.

10] The sense is: 'If you *do* feel carried away by an urge to see strange sights.' As Mr W. G. Ingram has pointed out to me, the emphasis is on 'be'st'.

11] Though Professor Gardner retains the reading of *1633*, she had felt some misgiving about doing so, and conjectured that the true reading has possibly been preserved by *S96* and *Dob*. I think this is very probable. Though 'to see' would not result in nonsense, it would attribute to the addressee of the poem the knowledge of what 'strange sights' he wanted to see, instead of making this part of the advice being tendered by the poet. That would take away part of the point of the stanza. With the reading 'go see' the sense will be: 'If you do feel carried away by an urge to see strange sights, go and have a look for some invisible things . . .'. Though I agree with Professor Gardner about the attractiveness of the reading 'go see', however, I do not feel altogether happy about her explanation of the origin of *1633*'s reading 'to see'. She suggests that *1633* 'made an obvious correction of the defective line in Groups I and II'. Now that 'to see' has the additional support of *DC* and *Wed*, it seems less likely that this is the explanation; but even on earlier evidence the situation would seem to have been more complicated. We do not know what Group II manuscript the editor of *1633* had at his disposal. It is noteworthy that *N* reads 'to see', and that *TCD* did so before correction. 'To' could, in any case, have been caught from l. 10 at some stage in transmission.

12–13] Professor Gardner refers us to Miss K. M. Lea's interesting suggestion in an article entitled 'Harington's *Folly*' (in H. Davis and H. Gardner (eds), *Elizabethan and Jacobean Studies presented to F. P. Wilson*, Oxford, 1959, pp. 51–2) that this may echo Ariosto's *Orlando Furioso*, XXVII. 123–4, where Rodomonte's railings at women's inconstancy are interrupted by the poet saying he is sure good women can be found, though none have yet come his way. He will not give up, and before more white hairs come he will go on looking in the hope of saying one day that one woman has kept her word.

23] The sense requires trochaic feet throughout.

24] *1633*'s reading is best, allowing a stress on 'And'.

The Will

Before I sigh my last gasp, let me breathe,
Great Love, some legacies: Here I bequeath
Mine eyes to Argus, if mine eyes can see,
If they be blind, then, Love, I give them thee;
My tongue to Fame; to ambassadors mine ears;   5
    To women or the sea, my tears:
Thou, Love, hast taught me heretofore
By making me serve her who had twenty more,
That I should give to none but such as had too much before.

My constancy I to the planets give;   10
My truth to them who at the Court do live;
Mine ingenuity and openness,
To Jesuits; to buffoons my pensiveness;
My silence to any who abroad hath been;
    My money to a Capuchin: 15
Thou, Love, taught'st me, by appointing me
To love there, where no love receiv'd can be,
Only to give to such as have an incapacity.

[My faith I give to Roman Catholics;
All my good works unto the Schismatics   20
Of Amsterdam; my best civility
And courtship, to an University;
My modesty I give to soldiers bare;
    My patience let gamesters share:
Thou, Love, taught'st me, by making me   25
Love her that holds my love disparity,
Only to give to those that count my gifts indignity.]

In 1633–1719 and all MSS here collated except TCD, from which a leaf almost certainly containing the poem has been torn out.

Text: Title The Will *1633–1719; I; H40; Wed; DC; Lut, O'F; HK2, Cy, P.* A Will *A25.* Loues Will *L74 (in another hand?).* Loues Legacies *TCC, A18, N.* Testamentum *S96, Dob.* Testamentum / Or Loves Legacy *S962.* Loves Legacie *S. No title D17.*

9 That ... as] Only to give to those that *Dob; S; S962.* Only to give ...

which *Lut, O'F.* Only to give ... who *S96.*

16 by appointing] by making *III; S; S962.*

17 can *1633–1719 and some MSS, e.g. I.* co(u)ld *some MSS, e.g. L74; Dob; S; S962.*

18 such as] those which *Dob, Lut, O'F; S962.* those who *S96.* those yt(= 'that') *S.*

19–27 *Whole stanza om. in I; H40; II; L74 (here added on verso in another hand);*

121

The Will

I give my reputation to those
Which were my friends; mine industry to foes;
To Schoolmen I bequeath my doubtfulness;   30
My sickness to physicians, or excess;
To Nature, all that I in rhyme have writ;
    And to my company my wit:
Thou, Love, by making me adore
Her, who begot this love in me before,   35
Taught'st me to make as though I gave, when I do but restore.

To him for whom the passing bell next tolls,
I give my physic books; my written rolls
Of moral counsels, I to Bedlam give;
My brazen medals, unto them which live   40
In want of bread; to them which pass among
    All foreigners, mine English tongue:
Thou, Love, by making me love one
Who thinks her friendship a fit portion
For younger lovers, dost my gifts thus disproportion.   45

Therefore I'll give no more; but I'll undo
The world by dying; because love dies too.
Then all your beauties will be no more worth
Than gold in mines, where none doth draw it forth;
And all your graces no more use shall have   50
    Than a sun-dial in a grave:
Thou, Love, taught'st me, by making me
Love her, who doth neglect both me and thee,
To invent, and practise, this one way to annihilate all three.

Wed; DC; HK2, A25, Cy, P, D17 (indicates lacuna), B. Stanza included in III; S; S962.

28 I . . . reputation] My reputation I give III; S; S962.

32 r(h)yme *variously spelt;* verse (rime *in margin as alternative or correction*) B.

35 who] that III; S.
this love in me] in me this love HK2.

36 as though I gave] as I did give D17.
do but restore III; S; 1635–1719. did but restore 1633; I; H40; TCC, A18,

N; L74; Wed; DC; A25, Cy, P, D17, B; Gr; Gar. but restore HK2. restore S962.

49 doth] do(e) TCC, A18, N; L74; Dob; Cy, S. dare D17.
where . . . forth] when no man drewes it forth S96; A25. when none do draw it forth S962.

52–3 making mee / Love her, who doth neglect] appointing mee / To loue her who neglects S96, Dob; S962. appointing . . . who doth neglect S.

General note. The poem is in the tradition of *Le Lais* (Legacy) or *Petit Testament* of Villon. There are many such poems by Continental and English poets of the sixteenth century. Probably no poem in Donne's collection is so closely packed with references to contemporary life. Yet this poem also embodies traditional Petrarchan attitudes towards the recalcitrant woman, which Donne expresses with delightful ingenuity. At the end, however, it is his own death that is to destroy the world. (Contrast *A Fever*, ll. 7–8, which follows the Petrarchan tradition.)

The omission of stanza 3 from the great majority of MSS presents a problem. Grierson thought that probably in James I's reign its references to religion were thought too outspoken and flippant; but Professor Gardner (*ESS*, p. 175) argues that such a consideration would be relevant to publication rather than to circulation in MS among friends. Yet it is surely possible that the exclusion by Donne was made either with a view to publication, or when circulating his poem to friends who might be offended? I believe stanza 3 would have been likely to give offence to more people than stanza 2. On the other hand, I find attractive Professor Gardner's idea that stanzas 2 and 3 were not both intended to stand in the poem. As she points out, in the MSS that preserve stanza 3 (*III*, *S*, *S962* and *L74* – added on the verso – among those I have collated), stanza 1, like the next two, ends with the formula 'Only to give to . . .', whereas in the other MSS and in *1633* it ends as here printed. The result, as she says, is that in *III*, etc., we have a poem in six stanzas, of which the first three end with variations on the same pattern, and the last three abandon the pattern. This is certainly untypical of Donne's work. For that reason, though she prints all six stanzas, she does not adopt the reading of *III*, etc. in l. 9, and she believes it possible that stanzas 2 and 3 are alternatives. I would go further, and conjecture that this is even probable. There is a certain overlap between the material and also between the general drift of the two stanzas, which lends colour to this.

3 *Argus*] The Greek mythological character who was appointed by Hera to guard Io after her metamorphosis into a heifer. Argus had a hundred eyes, and was therefore surnamed 'Panoptes' (the all-seeing).

5 *Fame*] Rumour.
  ambassadors] possibly a hit at the spying activities of some contemporary ambassador or ambassadors in London.

10 *planets*] which are, as the name signifies, essentially wandering.

12 *ingenuity*] ingenuousness, freedom from dissimulation.

15 *Capuchin*] A Franciscan friar of the new rule inaugurated in 1528. Like all Franciscans he would have taken the vow of poverty. Capuchins derived their name from the pointed *capuche*, the hood of their cloaks. This line may be a quip at the abuse of begging by the Friars. It seems similar in form to La Fontaine's stroke (at the end of the fable *Le Rat qui s'est retiré du Monde*):

¯ Un moine? Non, mais un dervis:
Je suppose qu'un moine est toujours charitable.

Donne, I suggest, is ironically affecting to believe in the sincerity of the Friars' vows, just as La Fontaine is pretending to believe in the charity of monks.

18 *have an incapacity*] i.e. are unable to make use of the gifts.

19] If this is, as seems possible, an attack on the Jesuit doctrine that faith alone is insufficient for salvation without co-operant good works, then it is a very poor one, since the Jesuits did not deny the efficacy of faith, and even maintained, like all orthodox Catholics, its necessity for salvation.
Catholics] It is essential to pronounce the word as a trisyllable here.

20] This shot at the extreme Puritan Schismatics of Amsterdam, who believed in justification by faith alone, is more effective, since they considered good works entirely inefficacious for salvation.

21–2 *my best civility . . . University*] seemingly an attack on the boorishness of some of the contemporary dons.

22 *courtship*] courtly manners.

23 *bare*] scarcely covered in rags.

24 *patience*] trisyllabic.

26 *disparity*] i.e. beneath her.

28 *reputation*] '-ation' trisyllabic.

29 *mine industry to foes*] probably because hard work is often the result of attacks or unscrupulous rivalry by enemies.

30 *Schoolmen*] Scholastic philosophers who raised puzzling questions.
doubtfulness] perplexity.

36 *do*] Grierson and Professor Gardner follow *1633*'s 'did', and that reading is, indeed, supported by the great majority of MSS, but 'do' (*III*; *S*, followed by *1635–1719*) seems to cohere better with the present tenses strewn throughout the first five stanzas of the poem. The poet is *now* restoring his reputation, industry, and so on, to their rightful owners, by his will.

38 *physic*] medical.

40 *brazen medals*] old bronze coins, not current cash.

41–2] An allusion to continental ignorance of the English language.

42 *mine English tongue*] not well known abroad at that time.

43–5, 52–3] These lines present something of a puzzle. They could imply that the woman does not return Donne's love because he is too old (Professor A. J. Smith's view); or they could imply that she is chaste, and incapable of offering anything but friendship, suitable as a portion for older men, but not for 'younger lovers' (Professor Gardner's view). Lines 43–5 seem to favour Professor Smith's view, since 'youn*ger*' would naturally imply 'younger than the writer of the will'. In that case 'friendship' would, of course, need to be construed in a broad rather than a 'Platonic' sense. On the other hand, l. 53 might seem to support Professor Gardner's view. Yet I do not think that it need, since 'Love' here could be taken as meant in a serious, high sense, which the lady would be falling short of by preferring the more sensual attractions of younger lovers. I therefore incline to Professor Smith's view.

44 *portion*] trisyllabic.

45 *disproportion*] make inappropriate ('-portion' trisyllabic).

46–7] A stroke of pyrotechnical *panache*, not, I think, to be taken too seriously, but to be seen as leading up to the *aesthetic* climax of the final fourteener, in which Donne brings off a *coup* somewhat similar to that in *The Flea*, ll. 16–18.

49 *none*] no one, nobody.

Love's Diet

To what a cumbersome unwieldiness
And burdenous corpulence my love had grown,
    But that I did, to make it less,
    And keep it in proportion,
Give it a diet, made it feed upon   5
That which love worst endures, *discretion*.

Above one sigh a day I allow'd him not,
Of which my fortune, and my faults, had part;
    And if sometimes by stealth he got
    A she-sigh from my mistress' heart,   10
And thought to feast on that, I let him see
'Twas neither very sound, nor meant to me:

If he wrung from me a tear, I brin'd it so
With scorn or shame, that him it nourish'd not;
    If he suck'd hers, I let him know   15
    'Twas not a tear which he had got,
His drink was counterfeit, as was his meat;
For eyes which roll towards all, weep not, but sweat.

Whatever he would dictate, I writ that,
But burnt my letters; when she writ to me,   20
    And that that favour made him fat,
    I said: 'If any title be
Convey'd by this, ah! what doth it avail
To be the fortieth name in an entail?'

Thus I reclaim'd my buzzard love, to fly   25
At what, and when, and how, and where I choose;
    Now negligent of sport I lie,
    And now, as other falconers use,
I spring a mistress, swear, write, sigh and weep:
And the game kill'd, or lost, go talk, and sleep.   30

In 1633–1719. Wed; D17 omit. Leaf almost
certainly containing poem torn out from TCD.
Text: Title Love's Diet (variously spelt)
1633–1719; I; H40; TCC, A18, N; L74
(added later); Lut, O'F; HK2, Cy, P, S.
Amoris Dieta S96, Dob; S962. The Diet
DC; A25.

8 fortune] fortunes III; A25, P; S962.
faults] fates DC.

11 feast] feede III; S962.

12 me(a)nt to me(e)] ment to bee Lut.
meᵃnt for me [sic] S962. meat to me
Sparrow conj.
mee: 1635–1669. mee; 1633. mee.
1719; Gr; Gar.

13 wrung(e) (or wroung) 1633; most
MSS. wrought HK2, Cy, P, S.
so 1633–1719; L74 (corrected from too
to soe in ?later hand); DC (soe); S96, Dob
(both soe), Lut, O'F (both so); HK2 (soe),
A25 (so), Cy (soe), P, S (soe); S962
(soe). too I; H40 (to); TCC, A18, N;
L74 (before correction); B.

18 which 1633–1719; I; H40; N; L74;
DC; A25, B. that TCC, A18; III;
HK2, Cy, P, S; S962.

19 What ever he would] Whatsoever he
would TCC, A18, N; L74; DC. What
he would ever S962.
dictate] distast(e) TCC, A18, N; L74
(corrected to dictate); O'F (in margin as
alternative or correction), P.
writ(t)] wrot(t)e L74; III; Cy, S; S962.
write Lec, C57; A25.

20 But] And L74.
when] If or if or yf Dob, Lut, O'F;
S962.
writ(t)] wrot(t)(e) III; S; S962.

21 that that] if that O'F (in margin as alternative or correction); Cy, P. yet that
S962.

24 name] man Lec, C57; S962; 1669–
1719.

25 reclaim'd] redeem'd 1633; Lec, C57.

27 sport(e)] sports 1633.

29 swear, write, sigh] sigh, swear, write.
III; S962.

30 go talk] goe, talke, TCC, A18 (no
comma after talke), N; L74.
and sleep] or sleepe III; Cy, P, S; S962;
1635–1719.

General note. One special originality of this poem is its detached treatment of the
poet's love, as if it were an object quite independent of the poet – some kind of
animal or bird (by l. 25 it has become a 'buzzard', but it is not clear whether it
has been that all along, what with its dictating letters and receiving them!).
Donne, in one way, remains within the Petrarchan conventions by dealing in
sighs (stanza 2), tears (stanza 3), and letters (stanza 4) (cf. Lovers' Infiniteness,
l. 17); but he invents superbly within this framework, with a range of
references from unsound food to the law of real property. The coarseness of the
physical terms, combined with the sophisticated, abstract language, and the
nonchalance of the ending, help to make the poem a masterpiece of lively
humour.

W. von Koppenfels (op. cit., p. 125) draws attention to some striking
similarities of ideas and language between this poem and two poems by George
Turberville, 'To a fickle and inconstant Dame' and 'To a friend that refused
him without cause' (in Chalmers' English Poets, London, 1810, vol. II,
pp. 636–7). Turberville even calls his unsatisfactory lady a 'buzzard'.

4 proportion] pronounced as four syllables.
6 discretion] pronounced as four syllables.

8] in which allowance, sighs for my ill-fortune and for my own faults had their share.

12 *sound*] sincere.

to] for.

12] John Hayward (Nonesuch Donne, p. 765) pointed out two difficulties: (1) that if the sigh was not meant for Donne, it would not seem to matter whether it was 'sound' or not; (2) that 'meant to me' in the sense of 'meant for me' is not quoted in *OED*. This made Hayward incline to adopt Sir John Sparrow's suggested emendation 'nor meat to me'. He did not, however, do so. Point (1) does not actually seem all that strong. It seems quite sensible to say: 'The sigh was not very sound, and, in any case, it was not meant for me.' Point (2) seems stronger, and Hayward supported it by saying that even if *OED* had overlooked the use, it seems odd that Donne should have preferred it to the more common 'meant for'. In point of fact, *OED* does quote two passages (1d) which would support 'meant to me': '1580 Sidney *Ps.* 27: 5. When greate griefes to me be ment, In tabernacle his, he will hide me.' and '1634 Milton *Comus* 765. She [sc. Nature] good cateress Means her provision onely to the good that live according to her sober laws.' In itself, Sparrow's suggested emendation still has considerable attractions in the context of the poem. Stanza 2 clearly deals with the 'meat' which the poet's love would like to feast on, while stanza 3 deals with the drink (l. 17 clearly refers back to the sighs of stanza 2). On the other hand, this is not conclusive in favour of the emendation, since stanza 2 would still be referring to the meat for Donne's love, even if it did not mention the meat by name. Moreover, Hayward's second objection to 'meant to me' now seems to me to fail. For this reason, and in view of the lack of textual support from the MSS and old editions, I would not feel justified in adopting Sparrow's attractive suggestion. It is perhaps worth, finally, drawing attention to the readings of *Lut* and of *S962*, though neither can be accepted.

13 *brin'd*] salted.

17 *meat*] i.e. the sighs referred to in the preceding stanza.

21] We should, in modern English, of course, simply say: 'And that favour made him fat'.

24] The fortieth person named as a remainderman in an entail would have a very slender chance of coming into possession.

25 *buzzard*] a rapacious but sluggish species of hawk. Here the word has possibly also the secondary sense of 'blockhead' or 'dunce'. (Dr Johnson quotes a passage from Ascham in which it is used in that sense.)

27 *sport*] both hawking and also, of course, sexual play (as in *Love's Usury*, l. 13).

27–8 *Now . . . now*] sometimes . . . sometimes. . . .

29 *spring*] The sense is: 'start' or 'rouse' (the correct hawking term); but, as Werner von Koppenfels suggests (op. cit., p. 126), it may well have a

further sexual sense of 'to cover'. *OED* quotes a passage of 1585: '[They] sought the fairest stoned horses to spring their mares.'

swear. . . . weep] the love-falconer's methods of killing his game.

30   *go talk, and sleep*] This reading (*1633, I*, and a few other MSS) is probably not worth disturbing. The reading of *TCC, N* and *L74* is, however, attractive, if we construe 'go' as = 'walk'. Either reading, moreover, seems slightly superior to 'go talk, or sleep', as suggesting a definite routine.

The Triple Fool

I am two fools, I know,
For loving, and for saying so
   In whining poetry;
But where's that wiseman, that would not be I,
   If she would not deny?   5
Then, as the earth's inward, narrow, crooked lanes
Do purge sea-water's fretful salt away,
   I thought, if I could draw my pains
Through rhyme's vexation, I should them allay:
Grief brought to numbers cannot be so fierce;   10
For he tames it, that fetters it in verse.

But when I have done so,
Some man, his art and voice to show,
   Doth set and sing my pain,
And, by delighting many, frees again   15
   Grief, which verse did restrain.
To love and grief tribute of verse belongs,
But not of such as pleases when 'tis read;
   Both are increasèd by such songs:
For both their triumphs so are publishèd,   20
And I, which was two fools, do so grow three;
Who are a little wise, the best fools be.

In 1633–1719. A25 omits.

Text: Title The Triple Fool *1633–1719; II; DC.* Song *or no title other MSS.* The Triple Fool *added in L74; Dob, in later hand.* Triple Fool *added in S962.*

6 inward, narrow, crooked *1633–1719 (without commas) (variously punctuated in MSS).* narrow, inward, crooked *Lec.* inward crooked narrow *III; S962.* inward crooked *P.* inward narrow *B.*

13 art(e) and voice *1633–54; I; H40; N (seems corrected from* act*); Wed; DC; Cy,* P, D17, B, S. act and voice *TC, A18, N (b.c. seemingly); L74 (possibly corrected from* arte *to* act *but leaving in terminal* e*).* voice and art *III; S962.* art or voice *1669–1719.* art and his voyce *HK2.*

14 set(t) *1633–1719; I; H40; Wed; DC; D17.* sit(t) *II; L74; III (O'F b.c.); HK2, Cy, P, B, S; S962.*

20 triumphs] trialls *S96, Lut, O'F; HK2, P, Dob (reads* triumphs *but has* trialls *written above as alternative or correction).* tortures *Cy.*

General note. The poet is trebly a fool because (1) he loves, (2) he expresses his love in verse, (3) he thereby enables someone to set the verse to music and by singing it to reawaken the suffering in the poet which poetical composition had brought within bounds. The humour of the start and of the end and the self-critical (?affected) sarcasm about 'poetry', with its undoubtedly satirical shot at *flabby* Petrarchism, are combined here with a seemingly genuine recognition of the painfulness of unsatisfied love, and the poet's shame at having his unrequited love known to others (cf. *Love's Exchange*, ll. 19–20).

4   *wiseman*] meaning both (1) something similar to the modern American 'wise guy', or to the still current English word 'wiseacre' (cf. Mr Worldly Wiseman in *The Pilgrim's Progress*), and (2) wise man. Donne uses the single word in sense (2) elsewhere, e.g. in a passage in one of the Sermons (VI. 99).

6   *Then*] 'thus', 'so'; alternatively 'then (when I berhymed my lady)'.

6–7] This curious, false explanation of the freshness of fresh water in inland rivers was offered in a number of Renaissance compendia, particularly those undistinguished by up-to-date scientific information. Professor Don Cameron Allen (*MLN* 65 (1950), 102) refers us for a gloss to a passage from Caxton's translation of the *Image du Monde*:

> Alle watres come of the see; as wel the swete as the salt, what somever they be, alle come out of the see, and theder agayn alle retorne. Wherupon somme may demande: 'Syth the see is salt, how is it that somme water is fresshe and swete?' Herto answerth one of the auctours and sayth that the water that hath his cours by the swete erthe is fresshe and swete, and becometh swete by the swetnes of therthe whiche taketh a way from it his saltnes and his bytternes by her nature; ffor the water whiche is salt and bytter, whan it renneth thurgh the swete erthe, the swetnes of therthe reteyneth his bytternes and saltnes.
>
> (Op. cit., ed. O. H. Prior, *EETS* (e.s. CX (1913), 109–10)

The 'auctour' is Honorius Augustodunensis, whose *Imago Mundi* is, according to Professor Allen, followed here.

Professor Gardner tells us that such an explanation had been rejected by Aristotle (*Metaphysica*, 354b and 355b), but adopted by Seneca (*Quæstiones Naturales*, III. v), and that Jerome's gloss on Ecclesiastes 1:7 agrees with it. She notes that the popular encyclopaedias adopting it stressed the 'endless winding channels' (Seneca) and 'hidden veins' (Jerome) through which the waters passed. In view of this it is perhaps worth drawing attention to the reading 'veins' in l. 6 in some MSS.

14   *set*] The sense is: 'set to music'. 'set' is better than 'sit'. It pairs with 'art' as 'sing' does with 'voice'. It might be argued that the singer was often a different person from the composer; but at that time he was also frequently one and the same.

Woman's Constancy

Now thou hast lov'd me one whole day,
Tomorrow when thou leav'st, what wilt thou say?
Wilt thou then antedate some new-made vow?
     Or say that now
We are not just those persons which we were?   5
Or, that oaths made in reverential fear
Of Love, and his wrath, any may forswear?
Or, as true deaths true marriages untie,
So lovers' contracts, images of those,
Bind but till sleep, death's image, them unloose?   10
     Or, your own end to justify,
For having purpos'd change, and falsehood, you
Can have no way but falsehood to be true?
Vain lunatic, against those 'scapes I could
     Dispute, and conquer, if I would;   15
     Which I abstain to do,
For by tomorrow, I may think so too.

In 1633–1719. S96; A25, Cy, D17 omit.
Text: Title Womans Constancy 1633–
1719; II; DC; Lut, O'F; S962. No title rest.
in L74; Dob Woman's Constancy added
later.
10 Bind] altered in C57 to Last.
13 Can have no] altered in C57 to Have

now no.
14 Vain] altered in C57 to Fond.
those H40; II; L74; DC; Dob, Lut;
HK2, P (but possibly reads these), B, S;
S962. these 1633–1719; I; Wed; O'F;
Gr; Ed (1956); Gar.

2 *when thou leav'st*] when you stop loving me.
4–5] Donne here imagines a preposterously sophistical argument based on the philosophical view that flux excludes personal identity. The doctrine of total flux goes back, of course, to Heraclitus, and probably beyond.
8 *true*] real.
14 *Vain*] Futile.
    lunatic] (1) 'madwoman'; but probably also (2) 'fickle creature' (because influenced by the moon).
    those] the balance of MS authority favours 'those', which is also perhaps preferable intrinsically as referring to the morrow.
    'scapes] subterfuges.
17 *I may think so too*] I may want to end our relationship too.

Confined Love

Some man unworthy to be possessor
Of old or new love, himself being false or weak,
   Thought his pain and shame would be lesser,
If on womankind he might his anger wreak;
     And thence a law did grow,   5
     One should but one man know;
     But are other creatures so?

Are sun, moon, or stars by law forbidden
To smile where they list, or lend away their light?
   Are birds divorc'd, or are they chidden   10
If they leave their mate, or lie abroad a-night?
     Beasts do no jointures lose
     Though they new lovers choose,
     But we are made worse than those.

Who e'er rigg'd fair ship to lie in harbours,   15
And not to seek new lands, or not to deal withal?
   Or built fair houses, set trees, and arbors,
Only to lock up, or else to let them fall?
     Good is not good, unless
     A thousand it possess,   20
     But doth waste with greediness.

In 1633–1719. H40; Wed; S96; A25 omit.
Text: *Title* Confined Love *1635–1719.* To
the worthiest of all my Lovers *Cy.* To the
wor: of al my Lou my virtuous Mrs. *P.* A
Songe *Dob (with* Confined Love *added by
later hand).*
  3 lesser] the lesser *Dob; HK2, Cy, P,
    D17.*
  6 should *MSS; Gar.* might *1633–1719;
    Gr; Ed (1956).*
11 a-night *Ed.* anight *L74.* a night *most
    MSS (probably meaning* a-night) *(SP
    nearly joins the two words); 1633–54.* all
    night *Cy; 1669–1719.*
12 do(e) no(e) *1633–1719; L74; Lut, O'F;*

S962; Gr; Gar. doe not *D17, B; Ed
(1956).* did no(e) *I; II; DC; Dob; HK2,
S.* did *Cy.* did not *P.*
13 choose *1633–1719; H49, SP, Lec, C57
    (has one* o *possibly added); L74; TCC,
    A18, N; Lut, O'F (has one* o *possibly
    added); Cy, D17; Gr; Ed (1956); Gar.*
    chuse *HK2, S.* chose *D; TCD; DC;
    Dob; P, B; S962.*
15 ship(p)] shipps *B; S962.*
17 built *1633–5; L74; Dob, Lut, O'F;
    HK2, Cy, P, D17, B, S; S962; Gr; Ed
    (1956); Gar.* build *I; II; DC;
    1639–1719.*

Confined Love

General note. This poem, put into the mouth of a woman, argues with remarkable freedom for female promiscuity. The idea that sexual liberty is natural, and that an upstart law has restrained it, occurs also in *The Relic*, l. 30, and in *The Progress of the Soul*, ll. 191–203, in respect of incest. The idea probably came to Donne from Ovid (see my note on *The Relic*, ll. 29–30). In Ovid, *Metamorphoses* x. 329 ff. the sexual freedom of animals is favourably contrasted with the fetters imposed on humanity by spiteful laws. In *Confined Love* Donne enlarges the field of comparison, brilliantly taking in sun, moon and stars, with their 'smiles', and in stanza 3 ships, houses and gardens.

The title 'A Songe' in *Dob* suggests that the poem was probably intended to be set to music or to fit an already existing air. No setting has, however, yet to come to light.

11 *a-night*] Though *1633–54* and most MSS read 'a night', I believe Grierson and Hayward were right to take the meaning to be 'at night' rather than 'for a night, from time to time'. It certainly fits better with l. 20, and, indeed, with the vigorous sweep of the whole poem.
12 *jointures*] A jointure was originally a joint estate limited to husband and wife, or in tail, as a provision for the wife in her widowhood; later, an estate settled on the wife alone, for the same purpose. Coke on Littleton (1628) describes it as 'a competent livelihood of freehold for the wife of lands and tenements, to take effect upon the death of the husband for the life of the wife at least' (36b).
14 *we*] we women (cf. l. 6).
16 *deal withal*] trade with it.
20 *it possess*] possess it.
21] But is wasted if someone keeps it greedily to himself.

The Indifferent

I can love both fair and brown,
Her whom abundance melts, and her whom want betrays,
Her who loves loneness best, and her who masks and plays,
Her whom the country form'd, and whom the town,
Her who believes, and her who tries,   5
Her who still weeps with spongy eyes,
And her who is dry cork, and never cries;
I can love her, and her, and you, and you,
I can love any, so she be not true.

Will no other choice content you?   10
Will it not serve your turn to do as did your mothers?
Have you old vices spent, and now would find out others?
Or doth a fear, that men are true, torment you?
Oh we are not, be not you so.
Let me, and do you, twenty know.   15
Rob me, but bind me not, and let me go.
Must I, who came to travel thorough you,
Grow your fix'd subject, because you are true?

Venus heard me sigh this song,
And by love's sweetest part, variety, she swore   20
She heard not this till now; and it should be so no more.
She went, examin'd, and return'd ere long,
And said: 'Alas, some two or three
Poor heretics in love there be,
Which think to establish dangerous constancy.   25
But I have told them: "Since you will be true,
You shall be true to those, who are false to you!" ' '

In 1633–1719. L74; A25, Cy omit.
Text: Title The Indifferent *1633–1719; II;*
DC. Song *I; S96, Dob (has* The Indifferent
added probably later). A Song *H40; B.*
Sonnet *P. P reverses stanzas 2 and 3.*
 3 masks] sports *Wed; HK2, S; 1669–*
1719.
10 choice *H40 (choyse); Dob (with* vice *in*
 margin as alternative or correction); B
 (choyce). vice *(with* choyce *written*

above as alternative or correction) S962.
vice *or* vyce *1633–1719; I; II; Wed;*
S96, Lut, O'F; HK2, P, D17, S; Gr; Ed
(1956); Gar.
12 Have you old *H49, D, Lec, C57 (olld);*
H40 (ould); III; D17, B (ould); Gar.
Have you all *SP.* Or have you all old
1633–1719; II; Wed; DC; HK2, P, S;
S962; Gr; Ed (1956).(Gar quotes a read-
ing from Cy, but that MS omits the poem).

spent] worn(e) *Wed; S96; HK2, S; Dob (with* worne *in margin as alternative or correction).*

13 a fear] fear *H40; B.* a shame *Wed; S96; HK2, S.* shame *Dob (with* fear *in margin as alternative or correction). Line omitted P.*

16 Rob(b) *1633–1719; II; DC; III; HK2, P, S; S962; Gr; Ed (1956); Gar. Line omitted Wed.* Reach *H40.* Racke *H49, D, SP* (Rack), *Lec* (Rack), *C57* (Rack); *D17, B* (Wracke *corrected from* Back).

17 who came *1633–1719; Lec, C57; Wed.* which came *H49, D, SP; H40; II; DC; Dob, Lut, O'F; D17, B; S962.* which come *S96.* that came *HK2, S.*

20 part] sweet *Wed; Dob (has* part *in margin as alternative or correction); HK2, P, S; 1669–1719.* part, Sweet *S96.*

21 and it should be so *TCD, N; DC; S96 (spells it as* t'[= 't]), *Dob; S962; Gar (spells it as* 't, *i.e. substantially as S96).* and that should be so *H49; D17* (y'[= 'that']). and that it should be so *1633; D, SP (both* y'[= 'that']), *Lec, C57* (y'[= 'that']); *H40; B, S; Gr; Ed*

(1956). and it should be *TCC, A18; Lut, O'F.* it should be so *Wed; HK2, P; 1635–1719.*

23 some *1633–1719; Wed; III; HK2, P.* but *I; H40; II; DC; D17, B, S; S962.*

24 there] they *H40; Wed; S.*

25 to establish *Ed.* to'establish *TCD, N.* to stablish *1633–1719; Lec, C57; Gr; Ed (1956); Gar.* to establish *H49, D, SP; H40; TCC, A18; DC; S96; HK2, P, B, S; S962.* t'establish *Wed; Dob, Lut, O'F; D17.*

26 you] they *Lec, C57; P, S.*

27 You shall . . . those, who are *Wed.* You shall . . . them, who'are *1633–54; (*who're *1669–1719); II (but only TCD has an apostrophe); DC (no apostrophe); S96 (no apostrophe); Dob* (wh'are), *Lut, O'F (both without apostrophe); HK2* (which are); *P* (who're); *S962 (no apostrophe); Gr; Ed (1956) (no apostrophe); Gar.* You shall . . . them, who we(a)re *I; B (no comma), S.* You should . . . them, who weare *H40.* You shall . . . them that will be *D17.*

Note on the printing of the poem. The layout here printed is that of *1633–1719* and most MSS. A few MSS have various different layouts, involving some indentation; but they do not seem to improve on that of the early editions, which matches the speed of the poem.

1 *brown*] i.e. not merely the conventional Elizabethan beauty, who was fair.

1] Professor Gardner rightly refers to Ovid, *Amores*, II. iv, where the poet tells how he can be captivated by women of very various and even contradictory kinds. The sting at the end of stanza 1 of Donne's poem is, however, entirely his own.

2] The woman who is made amorous by living in luxury, and the woman who gives herself because she needs money.

3 *loves*] also governing 'masks and plays'.
   masks] either (1) Court masques (the dramatic performances) or (2) masked balls.

5] The woman who trusts her lover, and the woman who tests him.

10 *choice*] the subtler reading, leaving the quip at fidelity as a 'vice' until l. 12, instead of making it twice.

11 *to do as did your mothers*] i.e. to be promiscuous (the word 'do' may even have a strong sexual sense).

136

12 *Have you old*] The Group II reading adopted by *1633* would give an extra foot. As Professor Gardner suggests, it looks as if 'Or' had been caught from the next line, and the unmetrical result patched up by inserting 'all'.

16 *Rob*] A textual crux. See Appendix I, pp. 304–5.

17 *travel*] The *1633* spelling 'travaile' suggests more strongly a possible *double entendre*.

   thorough] through.

21 *and it should be so no more*] I have hesitated between this MS reading and that of *H49*, which is lively, and which contains the word 'that', for which there is much MS authority. *1633*'s 'and that it' gives a weaker line with an extra foot.

22 *examin'd*] i.e. like an inquisitor.

23 *some*] Professor Gardner reads 'some' with a certain reluctance, since MS authority favours 'but'. Yet semantically 'some' seems justifiable. Venus is not lamenting that there are only two or three 'heretics', she is, if anything, deploring the fact that there are any at all. *H40*'s reading 'but . . . they' would be better than 'but . . . there', since Venus would be saying '*it is* only two or three heretics', not '*there are* only . . .'.

25] The sense is probably: 'Who are planning [or 'Who fancy they may manage'] to establish the dangerous doctrine of constancy'.

26 *will be*] insist on being.

27] There is extensive support for the substantive reading of *1633*, and its elision mark represents a reasonable compromise between 'who are' and 'who're'. The Group I reading is, however, of some interest, and its past tense 'were' is supported by *H40*, as well as by *B* and *S*. If we were to take it as more than a corruption, the sense would have to be understood as being that the heretics were to be deceived even before they started to be faithful. This bold meaning would be possible in Donne; but 'are' makes the ending quite strong enough, and the more difficult sense which 'were' would offer might puzzle a reader unnecessarily, and distract him from clarity of response. Moreover, 'were' could well be a corruption, and it could especially easily have arisen if dictation had occurred at some point in the transmission to *H40* and Group I. *H40*'s own reading offers perhaps a more attractive alternative, Venus shrewdly twitting the heretics with the mock obligation which implies that their fidelity is only designed to ensure the reciprocal fidelity of their lovers. I do not, however, feel that the reading is so attractive as to warrant adopting it against the strong textual support for *1633*. *Wed*'s reading is an interesting variation of *1633*'s, and offers what is a more usual construction nowadays. Though there is no support for it in other MSS, and the sequence 'them, who' was common enough at the time (and is not incorrect even now) yet 'them' could easily have been caught from l. 26, and 'those' offers both a pleasing variety, and a somewhat stronger line.

Community

Good we must love, and must hate ill,
For ill is ill, and good good, still,
   But there are things indifferent,
Which we may neither hate, nor love,
But one, and then another prove,   5
   As we shall find our fancy bent.

If then at first wise Nature had
Made women either good or bad,
   Then some we might hate, and some choose:
But since she did them so create,   10
That we may neither love, nor hate,
   Only this rests: All, all may use.

If they were good it would be seen,
Good is as visible as green,
   And to all eyes itself betrays: 15
If they were bad, they could not last,
Bad doth itself, and others, waste;
   So, they deserve nor blame, nor praise.

But they are ours as fruits are ours,
He that but tastes, he that devours,   20
   And he which leaves all, doth as well:
Chang'd loves are but chang'd sorts of meat;
And when he hath the kernel eat,
   Who doth not fling away the shell?

In 1633–1719. A25, D17 omit.
Text: Title Community *1635–1719.*
  3 there] these *(variously spelt) I; Cy*
  (corrected in a modern hand to there).

21 he which *almost all MSS; Gar.* he that
  1633–1719; HK2, B; Gr; Ed (1956).
  that *TCC, A18.* which *Cy.*

General note. Possibly the most cynical of the *Songs and Sonets*, if we are to take it, as I think we should, straightforwardly, and not, as has recently been suggested, as an argument, deliberately full of fallacies, and intended to condemn male promiscuity. Actually, in any case, the poem is not full of fallacies. The concatenation of the argument is tight enough. What makes the whole argumentative edifice unsound is the inclusion of more than doubtful premises, e.g. that 'good is as visible as green' and that 'bad doth itself and others waste'.

A passage closely related to this poem occurs in one of Donne's *Paradoxes* (IV):

> And of *Indifferent* things many things are become perfectly good by being *Common*, as *Customs* by use are made binding *Lawes*. But I remember nothing that is therefore *ill*, because it is *Common*, but *Women, of whom also: they that are most Common, are the best of that Occupation they profess.* (Nonesuch Donne, p. 340)

1 *ill*] evil.
2 *still*] always.
5 *prove*] try.
12] this is the only possibility left, that all men may use all women.
13–15] In *Paradox IV* Donne writes of Good as more plenteous and more common than Evil. Likewise, green is the most common colour in the natural world.
17 *waste*] in the old spelling 'wast', the rhyme being perfect.
21 *which*] a common alternative for 'who' at the time.
    doth as well] do equally well.
22 *meat*] food (*OED* 1, now archaic or dialectal).

Love's Usury

For every hour that thou wilt spare me now,
        I will allow,
Usurious God of Love, twenty to thee,
When with my brown, my gray hairs equal be;
Till then, Love, let my body reign, and let   5
Me travel, sojourn, snatch, plot, have, forget,
Resume my last year's relict: think that yet
        We had never met.

Let me think any rival's letter mine,
        And at next nine   10
Keep midnight's promise; mistake by the way
The maid, and tell the lady of that delay;
Only let me love none, no, not the sport;
From country grass, to comfitures of Court,
Or city's quelque-choses, let report   15
        My mind transport.

This bargain's good; if, when I am old, I be
        Inflam'd by thee,
If thine own honour, or my shame, or pain
Thou covet, most at that age thou shalt gain.   20
Do thy will then, then, subject and degree
And fruits of love, Love, I submit to thee;
Spare me till then, I'll bear it, though she be
        One that loves me.

In 1633–1719. II; A25, D17 omit.
Text: Title Love's Usury *1633–1719; DC.*
Added later in L74; Dob. Elegy *S96.*

  5 reign (raigne *or* raygne *in all MSS I*
    have seen)] range *III; 1635–1719.*
  6 snatch, plot] plot snatch *S.* match,
    plot *Lut, O'F; 1635–54.*
 15 let report] let not report *III; 1635–54.*
 19 or pain] and pain *Lut, O'F.*
 20 covet, most *Sparrow conj., Hayward; I;*
    H40; L74; Wed; DC; Lut, O'F; B;
    S962; Ed (1956); Gar. covet most,

    1633, 1669–1719; Gr. covet most *S96;*
    Dob; HK2, Cy, P, S; 1635–54.
    age] age; *S96.* age, *DC; Dob; S.*
 21 then, then, subject *H40; B; S962.*
    then, then subject *1633–1719; most*
    MSS; Gr; Ed (1956); Gar. then, the
    subject *III (O'F b.c.).* then, thou sub-
    ject *S.*
 22 fruit(e)s *I; III; B; S962.* fru(i)t(e)
    1633–1719; H40; L74; Wed; DC
    (fruict) *HK2, Cy, P, S; Gr; Ed (1956);*
    Gar.

5 *let my body reign*] 'let physical passion rule me'.
6 *snatch*] seize opportunities of physical gratification.
7–8] 'Take up again the woman I cast off last year, and imagine we had never
met before.'
9–12] I believe that Professor Gardner is right in interpreting 'at next nine' to
mean the nine o'clock after Donne gets hold of the letter. It is possibly
worth trying, however, to get a clearer picture of the situation Donne is
describing, of how the intrigue he is imagining would work. The language
is pretty sketchy, but Donne's mind usually has precise ideas. Let us
suppose, first, that the letter is *from* the rival *to* the lady appointing or
agreeing to the midnight assignation, and that the poet intercepts it and
simply pockets it. In that case the lady would not expect the assignation to
be kept. So that could not be the situation. If the letter were *from* the rival,
then for the lady to expect the rival, the letter would have to be sent on to
the lady after interception. If, however, it were sent on unchanged, the
lady would then expect the rival at midnight; and if the poet turned up
before midnight there would be no 'delay' (l. 12) for him to explain. If,
then, the letter were *from* the rival, it would also be necessary for the poet
either to alter the letter or to substitute one of his own, in either case fixing
the time for the tryst at nine instead of midnight. In either case, however,
it would be straining language to say that there would be a 'promise'
(either by the rival or by the poet) to meet the lady at midnight. The
possibility, therefore, that the imagined letter would be *from* the rival *to*
the lady does not seem to fit the case very well.

Now let us consider the possibility that the letter would be *from* the lady
to the rival. If Donne simply pocketed it, and then appeared three hours
early, what advantage would he obtain? The lady would not be expecting
anyone till midnight, so he might well not have any opportunity of
enjoying her company before then. The rival would not have received the
letter, and so would know nothing of the assignation, so Donne could do
just as well for himself (probably, indeed, better) if he turned up at midnight. If, on the other hand, Donne, after intercepting the letter, sent it on
to the rival unaltered, he would fare no better. If he appeared at nine he
might not see the lady at all, and the rival would come on the scene at midnight, and might cause a tiresomely unpleasant scene. If the letter were
from the lady *to* the rival Donne would need to keep it, but send an answer
to the lady either purporting to come from the rival, or else, impudently,
from himself, appointing nine as the hour of meeting. He could then turn
up somewhat late, after seducing the maid, and brazenly explain to the
lady the reason for the delay.

11–12 *mistake by the way the maid*] meaning (1) take the maid to be the lady, and
(2) seduce the maid.
13 *no, not the sport*] The sense is: 'let me not even fall in love with the physical
play itself'. This may be taken either generally, or, as is the view of Mr

Edward Gillott with whom I have discussed this passage, as referring to
the pleasure of sexuality with any *particular* woman. The latter interpretation seems to me the better.

14 *comfitures*] literally 'sweetmeats'.

14–16] Donne is here using 'grass', 'comfitures', and 'quelque-choses' figur-
atively, for the various types of women on his large playground.

15 *quelque-choses*] (*choses* disyllabic) literally 'dainties', 'fancy dishes', also,
more generally 'insubstantial trifles' – another spelling of 'kickshaws'.
This use by Donne to characterize dressed-up dolls (married or otherwise)
of the city families was possibly a characteristically bold touch. He uses the
term again, as a specifically culinary metaphor, in a letter to Sir Henry
Goodyer (1609?), with reference to some aphoristic observations in the
letter: 'These, Sir, are the salads and onions of *Mitcham*, sent to you with as
wholesome affection as your other friends send Melons and Quelque-
choses from Court and London' (Nonesuch Donne, p. 460).

15–16] *let . . . transport*] 'let information as to the women to be found in these
localities switch my attention from one to another'.

17 *This bargain's good*] i.e. from the point of view of Love the usurer.

19 *If*] Whether.

20] The MS support for Sir John Sparrow's conjectural emendation (adopted
by John Hayward) turns out to be extremely strong. The meaning of
ll. 19–20 on that reading is, of course: 'If what you want is to increase
your own honour, or my shame or pain, you will gain most by making me
fall in love when I am past middle age'. This makes better sense than either
1633's reading, or that of *S96*, *Dob*, etc., though neither of those actually
yields nonsense.

21 *then, then, subject*] The punctuation adopted emphasizes that 'then' is
temporal, and keeps the focus on that future time.

21–2] 'When that time comes, do just what you like with me: I will abide then
by what you lay down as to whom I shall love, how much I shall love, and
what the results [e.g. children] of my love shall be.'

22 *fruits*] I slightly prefer the plural as suggesting a brood of children; and it is
well supported.

23–4 *though she be . . . me*] Cynical indeed: when that time arrives (but not
now), Donne will even stand loving someone who is in love with him.

Mummy

OR

Love's Alchemy

Some that have deeper digg'd love's mine than I,
Say, where his centric happiness doth lie:
    I have lov'd, and got, and told,
But should I love, get, tell, till I were old,
I should not find that hidden mystery;   5
      Oh, 'tis imposture all:
And as no chymic yet the Elixir got
      But glorifies his pregnant pot,
      If by the way to him befall
Some odoriferous thing, or med'cinal,   10
   So, lovers dream a rich and long delight,
   But get a winter-seeming summer's night.

Our ease, our thrift, our honour, and our day,
Shall we for this vain bubble's shadow pay?
     Ends love in this, that any man   15
Can be as happy as I can, if he can
Endure the short scorn of a bridegroom's play?
     That loving wretch that swears
'Tis not the body's marrow, but the mind's,
      Which he in her angelic finds,   20
      Would swear as justly, that he hears,
In that day's rude hoarse minstrelsy, the spheres.
     Hope not for mind in women; at their best
     Sweetness, and wit, they are but Mummy, possess'd.

In 1633–1719 and all MSS collated for this edition.

Text: Title Mummy *or* Love's Alchemy *Ed (1956);* Loves Alchymie *DC; 1633–1719.* Mummy *(in original hand, with* or Alchymy *added in another hand) L74.* Mummy *(*Loves Alchymy *added in another hand) Dob.* Mummy *all other MSS collated except Wed; A25, P, which have no title.*

15 any *Sir Charles Tennyson conj; S96,* Dob; S962. my *1633–1719; rest of MSS; Gr; Ed (1956); Gar.*

19 marrow *S96; HK2* (marrowe); mar/ry–/rowe [*sic*] *Dob.* marry *rest of MSS; Gr; Ed (1956); Gar.*

23 women] woman *H49, D, SP; TC, N; L74; Wed; Lut, O'F; ?S.* woeman *A18.* no man *HK2.*

24 *variously punctuated in the early editions and MSS (see note).*

143

Mummy or Love's Alchemy

Note on the title. Mummy is the title given in most MSS; *Love's Alchemy* in *DC*, and *1633–1719*.

General note. A scarifyingly anti-Platonic and anti-Petrarchist poem, expressing contempt both for love and for women. It is, however, also a strong expression of disillusion with sexuality itself. The poem is a fine flower of that *fin de siècle* nausea well described by Professor Robert Ellrodt in *L'Inspiration Personnelle et l'Esprit du Temps chez les Poètes Métaphysiques Anglais*, Paris, 1960, part II, ch. II.

1–2] The direct reference of these lines is to the ethereal claims of high-minded lovers. Donne's scepticism as to the validity of such claims may, however, be latent here in the coarse secondary implications of some of the language. 'Centric', for instance, is used in *Elegy XVIII* with an obviously sexual sense:

> Although we see Celestial bodies move
> Above the earth, the earth we Till and Love:
> So we her ayres contemplate words and heart,
> And virtues; but we love the Centrique part.
>
> (ll. 33–6)

'Digg'd' in l. 1 of the present poem is also clearly paralleled by 'Till' in the above passage.

2 *his centric happiness*] the core of love's happiness.

3 *told*] The sense is probably: 'counted' (the successful love affairs) or, possibly, 'calculated' (the essence of love) like an alchemist.

6] i.e. love has no 'centric happiness' such as the 'deeper' lovers had boasted it had.

7 *chymic*] alchemist.
the Elixir] the *Elixir Vitae*, which was supposed by believers in it to be a substance capable of curing all diseases and indefinitely prolonging life.

7–10] Grierson quotes from a letter to Goodyer: 'I am now, like an alchemist, delighted with discoveries by the way, though I attain not mine end' (*Letters to Severall Persons of Honour*, 1651, p. 172).

9] If during his quest he happens to hit on . . .

12] i.e. a short and cold time of it.

13 *day*] life (*OED* 14).

15 *any*] In a letter to me dated 30 April 1960 Sir Charles Tennyson wrote: 'The text here seems queer – so very clumsy. . . . Could "my man" be a mistake for "any man"?' This conjecture receives interesting support from *S96* and *Dob*, and the miscellany *S962*. I have never been quite happy with 'my man' (= 'my servant'). It coarsely manifests a *social* snobbery quite diverse from Donne's often expressed belief in the special superiority of true lovers to *everyone else*.

17] Endure the short humiliation of a wedding ceremony.

144

18–20] With the text here offered, a paraphrase might run: 'That loving fool who swears that it is not the innermost substance of the woman's body, but the central core of her mind, that he finds angelic in her . . .'.

19 *marrow*] *1633* prints 'marry', and most MSS read the same. 'Marry' was, however, a possible spelling for 'marrow' at the time; so that MS support for 'marry' is not conclusive evidence that a verb was intended. The spelling 'marrowe' in three MSS, on the other hand, offers some evidence that the word was meant as a noun. Moreover, as Professor Gardner says, 'marrow' gives easier sense, since it provides a proper antecedent for 'which'. On balance she nevertheless prefers to take 'marry' as a verb, because of the references in ll. 17 and 22 to a wedding ceremony. I am more impressed by the awkwardness of the absence of a proper antecedent to 'which', if 'marry' be taken as a verb. Donne might, I suppose, have intended a play on both senses.

22 *In that day's rude hoarse minstrelsy*] In the crude and raucous scrapings and blowings at the wedding day celebrations.

the spheres] i.e. the music of the spheres.

24 *wit*] quick and lively fancy.

Mummy] 'body without mind'; but, more than that, 'mere lumps of dead flesh'. The belief that Egyptian mummies had been prepared with bitumen or asphalt had led medieval physicians in the East to prescribe first the scrapings off mummies, and then the mummified flesh itself, both for external and internal use. The term 'mummy' in time came to be applied to this dead flesh. A considerable trade in such 'mummy' was carried on between the Near East and Western Europe throughout the Middle Ages, and indeed, despite denunciation by eminent physicians like Paré, until the eighteenth, and in parts of Europe, the nineteenth century. Often enough the 'mummy' came to be a spurious manufacture from dead bodies of recent date, especially those of felons and suicides, doctored with bitumen and aloes, and baked until the embalming matter penetrated.

punctuation] *1633* punctuates:

Sweetnesse, and wit they'are, but, *Mummy*, possest.

This gives a slow, carefully calculated line, which also makes sense. There is, however, no MS support for a comma after 'are' nor after 'but' or 'Mummy'. There is, on the other hand, plenty of support for commas after 'Sweetness' and 'wit'; and a comma after 'Mummy', though unsupported by MS evidence, helps to achieve maximum impact for the ending.

possess'd] I doubt whether this has multiple meanings here. I believe the only sense to be 'sexually enjoyed'.

Negative Love

OR

The Nothing

I never stoop'd so low, as they
Which on an eye, cheek, lip, can prey;
   Seldom to them, which soar no higher
   Than virtue or the mind to admire:
For sense, and understanding, may   5
   Know what gives fuel to their fire.
My love, though silly, is more brave,
For may I miss, whene'er I crave,
If I know yet, what I would have.

If that be simply perfectest   10
Which can by no way be express'd
   But *negatives*, my love is so.
   To All, which all love, I say no.
If any who deciphers best
   What we know not, our selves, can know,   15
Let him teach me that nothing; this
As yet my ease and comfort is:
Though I speed not, I cannot miss.

In 1633–1719. Among MSS collated for this edition only II; DC; Lut, O'F; A25 include. Text: Title Negative Love, or The Nothing Lut, O'F; Ed (1956). Negative Love 1633–1719; II; Gr; Gar. The Nothing A25. Negative Loves DC.

5 For] Both A25.
6 their 1633–1719; II; DC; Lut, O'F. the A25.
8 may I 1633–1719; DC; A25. I may II; Lut, O'F (b.c.).
11 way] means Lut, O'F.
14 who deciphers best TCC, A18, N omit. Added in TCD by apparently same hand.
16 teach me that nothing; this 1633 (This); II; DC. tell me what nothing 'tis Lut, O'F (b.c.). tell that nothing; this A25. tell me that nothing. This 1635–1719.

Note on the title. I have preserved both titles, as each seems to make a distinct contribution to understanding the poem.

General note. The poet declares that he has never descended to mere lust of the flesh, and seldom to 'Platonic' admiration. His love does not know what it wants, and so, in a sense, it wants nothing. He refuses to identify his love with that of the general run of lovers. He justifies its superiority by a characteristically bold comparison of it with God; and, asking sceptically to be told the solution of the mystery of the 'nothing' he wants, wittily concludes with the thought that at least his love cannot fail to be satisfied.

1–2 *they . . . prey*] completely physical lovers (cf. the 'dull súblunary lovers' of
   A Valediction: forbidding mourning, l. 13).
3 *Seldom*] contrasting with the 'never' of ll. 1–2.
   to them] as far as those.
3–4 *them . . . admire*] 'Platonic' lovers.
5–6] Implying that neither lust nor 'Platonic' admiration is true love, since
   both lack its mystery.
7 *silly*] probably 'ignorant' (*OED* adj. 3 *obs.* or *arch.*).
   more brave] probably 'finer' (see *OED* adj. 3 *arch.*), because of the point
   made in ll. 10–12.
8 *miss*] fail to obtain what I want.
   whene'er I crave] whenever I want a woman.
8–9] Difficult lines. The sense may be that he hopes he will be disappointed if
   his love is ever of the kind that knows what it wants. Any 'love' of that
   kind would fall short of the 'mystery' which is the hallmark of the superior
   love which he values (cf. *A Valediction: forbidding mourning*, ll. 17–18).
10–12] Like God, according to Thomist philosophy. There are plenty of passages in early Christian and in Scholastic writings which suggest that the
   nature of God can only be expressed by *negatives*, or, at least, can be best expressed that way. The Pseudo-Dionysius Areopagita (*De Mystica Theologia*,
   c. 2) prefers expressing the attributes of God by *negatives*, e.g. that He has no
   imperfection. Cf. also Augustine, *Tractatus in Johannis Evangelium* 3 (see
   Oeuvres de S. Augustin, Paris, 1969, vol. 71), and *De Trinitate* 5, c. 1 in
   Migne, *Patrologia Latina*, Paris, 1845, vol. 42, pp. 819–1098, and many
   other passages. Aquinas writes even more strongly, in *Summa Theologica*, Ia
   pass., q.iii, to the effect that we cannot know what God is, but only what
   He is not. Yet there are passages to the contrary, even in Aquinas himself, as
   when he writes of God as simple, or as the first being (*Summa Theologica*, I,
   3, 7). There is, however, enough in the theologians to enable Donne to
   borrow quite scrupulously for his witty conceit.
13] A not altogether easy line. It probably means: 'I decline all the positive per-
   fections of women, which are what everybody loves'.
14–16] 'If any subtle psychologist, able to read our enigmatic hearts for us, can
   find out the answer, let him tell me what that nothing is which I want.'
15 *What we know not, our selves*] Grierson (II, p. 50) quotes pertinently from
   Donne's *Sermons* a passage where Donne suggests that the reason why
   Adam did not name himself when he named creatures, was that he knew
   himself least. (*Sermons*, IX. 256).
17 *As yet*] In the meanwhile.
18] A paraphrase might run: 'Though I make no progress, I cannot fail to
   obtain what I want' (because he wants nothing definite – cf. note on
   ll. 8–9, above).

Farewell to Love

Whilst yet to prove,
I thought there was some deity in love,
So did I reverence, and gave
Worship; as atheists at their dying hour
Call (what they cannot name) an unknown power,   5
As ignorantly did I crave:
Thus when
Things not yet known are coveted by men,
Our desires give them fashion, and so
As they wax lesser, fall, as they size, grow.   10

But, from late fair
His Highness, sitting in a golden chair,
Is not less cared for after three days
By children, than the thing which lovers so
Blindly admire, and with such worship woo;   15
Being had, enjoying it decays:
And thence,
What before pleas'd them all, takes but one sense,
And that so lamely, as it leaves behind
A kind of sorrowing dullness to the mind.   20

Ah, cannot we,
As well as cocks and lions, jocund be
After such pleasures? Unless wise
Nature decreed (since each such act, they say,
Diminisheth the length of life a day)   25
This, as she would man should despise
The sport,
Because that other curse, of being short
And only for a minute made to be
Eager, desires to raise posterity?   30

1633 omits. 1635–1719 include. All MSS collated omit except S96, O'F; S962.
Text: Title Farewell to Love *1635–1719; S96, O'F; S962.*
  5 (what . . . name) *Ed (1956).* ,what . . . name, *1635–1719.*

10 size *1635–1719* (sise); *O'F* (size). rise *S96.* seize *S962.*
11 late *1635–1719; O'F.* last *S96; S962.*
21 Ah] Oh *S96.*
27 sport, *1635–1719; Ed (1956); Gar.* sport; *Gr.* sport *S96* (Sport); *S962.*

> Since so, my mind
> Shall not desire what no man else can find;
> I'll no more dote and run
> To pursue things which, had, endamage me.
> And when I come where moving beauties be,   35
> As men do when the summer's sun
> Grows great,
> Though I admire their greatness, shun their heat;
> Each place can afford shadows. If all fail,
> 'Tis but applying wormseed to the tail.   40

28 that] the *S962.*
 curse, *S96.* curse *1635–1719; Gr; Ed (1956); Gar.*
 short *S96, O'F (x in the margin might even be a deleted comma).* short, *S962; 1635–1719; Gr; Ed (1956); Gar.*
29 minute *1635–1719; S96, O'F; Gr; Ed (1956).* minute, *S962; Gar.*
29–30 be / Eager, desires *1635–1719; S96, O'F; S962; Gar.* be, / Eagers desire / *Gr.* be / Eager desires, *Hayward.* be, / Eagers desire *Ed (1956), tentatively*

accepting Gr.
31 so, *1635–1719; O'F (maybe full stop).* so: *S96.* so! *S962.*
34 things which, had, endamage me. *Ed.* things, which had, indamage me *S96.* things which had, indammage me *Gar.* things which had indammag'd me *1635–1719 (1719:* endamag'd); *O'F (*endammag'd); *Gr; Ed (1956) (*endamag'd). things which had endaⁿger me *S962 (though possibly no* r, *and that what is meant is* endamage).

General note. In one miscellany (Harvard College Library, MS. Eng. 966/17) 'Mr. An: Saintleg'' is written beside the title. Yet, though the poem does not occur in *1633,* and only occurs in *S96, O'F* and *S962* among MSS collated for this edition, it accords entirely with Donne's style, and also with his spirit in one of his many moods.

This poem is, indeed, a renunciation of love, and it is also a renunciation of sex. The first stanza prepares the reduction of love to sexuality. The second effects that reduction, and goes on to characterize the disillusioned aftermath of the act of love. Stanza 3 then tries to account for this, and stanza 4 expresses the poet's resolve not to want that impossibility, love, nor to chase after sexual play, but to steer clear of attractive women. If these measures fail, that will only be natural. They will have been as futile as using wormseed as an antaphrodisiac by applying it to the penis (see note on ll. 39–40).

For an interesting full-length discussion of the poem see A. J. Smith, 'The dismissal of love' in *John Donne: Essays in Celebration,* London, 1972.

1 *Whilst yet to prove*] While I still had no experience of love.
2–4 *I ... Worship*] I thought that there was something divine in love, and therefore I reverenced and worshipped it.
5 *Call*] Call upon.

6] So ignorant were my longings.

9 *fashion*] form, shape. (Here trisyllabic.)

9–10 *and . . . grow*] Somewhat obscure. Grammatically 'they', in each case, should refer to 'things not yet known'; but the resulting sense is not entirely satisfactory, since there is clearly no method of gauging the size of the 'things' other than by the size of the 'desires'. On the other hand, to take 'they' to refer to 'desires' makes the passage not merely tortuous, which would be typical enough of Donne, but also untidy, and untidiness is highly uncharacteristic of him. I think, therefore, that of these two the former interpretation is preferable. Yet neither is satisfactory, and it has therefore occurred to me that the sense is possibly more complex, namely (starting at l. 7): 'Thus when we wish for things as yet unknown to us, our desires give them a form, and then in turn dwindle or increase as that form grows less or bulks larger'. There may well be a ribald suggestion in l. 10, as Professor Smith maintains (op. cit., p. 116).

10 *wax lesser*] grow less.

fall] abate.

size] get larger, swell.

11–15] The sense is probably: 'But lovers, after a short while, no more bother about the act of love which they wonder at so blindly, and court with such worship, than children do about some prince sitting on a gilt throne, bought for them at a recent fair'. If the prince was made of gilt gingerbread, the children might well even have eaten him.

16] Once the experience has taken place, the enjoyment of it peters out.

18 *them all*] all the senses.

takes but one sense] 'appeals only to one of the senses', probably the sense of touch.

19 *lamely*] feebly.

as] that.

21–3] The idea that only the lion and the cock remain brisk after the act of love is at least as old as Galen. Dr T. R. Henn provided me a modern reference to Galen's pronouncement, in a poem entitled 'After Galen' by Oliver St John Gogarty:

> Only the Lion and the Cock,
> As Galen says, withstand Love's shock.
> So, Dearest, do not think me rude
> If I yield now to lassitude,
> But sympathize with me. I know
> You would not have me roar, or crow.

24–5] Aristotle held that sexual acts shorten life; but he did not quantify this. The quantifying was probably a popular superstition.

23–30] A hard passage, not made easier by the fact that the poem is not in

1633, and is only in a few MSS. John Hayward has called the lines 'the most unintelligible in the whole canon of Donne's poetry' (Nonesuch Donne, ad loc.). The difficulty lies in ll. 28–30, which have been variously interpreted (see Appendix II, pp. 306–11).

In ll. 29–30 the reading of *1635–1719* and the MSS:

> And only for a minute made to be
> Eager, desires to raise posterity.

was cleverly emended by Grierson to:

> And only for a minute made to be,
> Eagers desire to raise posterity.

but his explanation of his emended text does not seem satisfactory (see Appendix II, pp. 306–7). In my 1956 edition I adopted Grierson's emendation, and an attractive explanation of that text suggested to me by F. L. Lucas; but I am now convinced, as I then hoped to be, that good sense can be made of the old reading. Taking (as Grierson did) 'that other curse' to refer to humanity's living only for a short while, and construing 'And only . . . eager' to mean 'for a minimal period at a high pitch of life', the sense could be: 'since humanity's other curse, of living only for a brief period, and only for a mere minute at a high pitch of life (including sexuality), demands the procreation of children'. I had thought that this type of explanation involves too vigorous construction of 'desires', but if we take 'desires' in *OED* sense 3, '*trans*. Of things: To require, need, demand', this objection is, I believe, overcome. Professor A. J. Smith seemingly adopted this sense in his article 'The dismissal of love' (in *John Donne: Essays in Celebration*), though in his Penguin edition (1971) he glossed as 'prompts the urge', which appears open to the objection I have indicated.

31 *Since so*] Since this is the situation.

34 *which, had, endamage*] The reading of *S96*, adopted by Professor Gardner, seems preferable to the other variants; but the sense perhaps comes out more clearly if we add a comma after 'which'.

35 *moving beauties*] devastatingly attractive women.

39–40 *If all fail. . . . tail*] John Hayward noted on l. 40: 'This line is obscure unless we remember that wormseed . . . is a powerful anaphrodisiac, and that the Latin word for tail is *penis*. "Tail" in this sense is common in Elizabethan literature'. There is no doubt that in the Renaissance some people regarded 'wormseed', which was primarily a remedy against intestinal worms, as also an anaphrodisiac ('antaphrodisiac' might have been a more accurate term for what they meant). It is not clear, however, whether they believed that to act as an antaphrodisiac wormseed should be taken orally or spread on the penis. Donne himself could easily have learned from his medical stepfather what exactly the belief was; and he could also have known which method could conceivably have been efficacious. I have consulted my friend Dr Gordon Simpson, and he tells me that, in any case, spreading the preparation on the penis would have been useless, and might even have acted as a stimulant. It seems somewhat more probable, therefore, though by no means certain, that the belief was that it would act as an antaphrodisiac if taken orally. Furthermore, it would seem that Donne, with his chance of being especially well informed, may well have had good reason to believe that 'applying wormseed to the tail' would be quite futile.

All this appears to support Professor Katherine Emerson's interesting suggestion (*MLN* 72 (1957), p. 95) that the meaning of this passage is not that if all else fails one can always resort to antaphrodisiacs, but that if 'all' the expedients mentioned in ll. 31–9 fail, the reason why is that they are as futile against natural instincts as spreading wormseed on the penis would be as an antaphrodisiac.

The Damp

When I am dead, and doctors know not why,
    And my friends' curiosity
Will have me cut up to survey each part,
When they shall find your picture in my heart,
      You think a sudden damp of love   5
      Will through all their senses move,
And work on them as me, and so prefer
Your murder, to the name of massacre.

Poor victories; but if you dare be brave,
      And pleasure in your conquest have,   10
First kill the enormous giant, your *Disdain*,
And let the enchantress *Honour* next be slain,
      And like a Goth and Vandal rise,
      Deface recórds, and histories
Of your own arts and triumphs over men,   15
And without such advantage kill me then.

For I could muster up as well as you
      My giants, and my witches too,
Which are vast *Constancy*, and *Secretness*,
But these I neither look for, nor profess;   20
      Kill me as woman, let me die
      As a mere man; do you but try
Your passive valour, and you shall find then,
Naked you've odds enough of any man.

In 1633–1719. H40; L74; Wed; HK2, A25, Cy omit.
Text: Title The Damp *1633–1719; MSS except P, D17.*

6 through *1633–1719; I; TCC, A18; DC; S96, Lut, O'F; P, B, S; S962; Gr.* thorough *TCD, N; Dob; D17; Gar.*

9 Poor victories; *1633–39; I; TC, A18; DC; B; Ed (1956).* Poor Victory; *P.* Poor victories: *S96, Dob.* Poor victories, *Lut, O'F; S962.* Poor victories *N; S.* Poor victories! *D17; 1650–1719; Gr; Gar.*

15 arts *1633–54; I; II (TCD has* c *written above* r, *but* r *not deleted; N reads* arts*); III; S.* acts *P, D17, B.* parts *(or, possibly,* arts*) S962; 1669–1719* (parts).

24 Naked *1635–1719; I; III; P, D17, B, S; S962; Hayward; Ed (1956); Gar.* In that *1633; II; DC; Gr.*

The Damp

Title and 5 *Damp*] 'chill depression'; a metaphor taken from cold foggy night air, and ultimately from noxious vapour.

General note. In a number of the other lyrics Donne projects beyond his death, either in the whole of the poem (*The Legacy, The Apparition, The Funeral, The Relic, The Computation, The Paradox*), or in part of it (*The Canonization, The Anniversary, A Valediction: of my name in the window, Love's Exchange, The Prohibition, The Expiration*). In *The Damp* Donne projects wholly beyond his death; and the poem starts with his friends' demand for an inquest, and the strong image of an autopsy. Donne then attributes to the woman, in a hyperbolical fiction, the thought that when the dissection reveals her picture in his heart, a chill of love will infect the doctors and the curious friends, so that they too will all die for love of her. Donne is within the Petrarchan tradition here. Professor Guss (op. cit., p. 76) refers us to two *strambotti* by Serafino (89 and 126) which foreshadow Donne's conceits of the inquest and autopsy, with the discovery of the woman's picture in the dead lover's heart. Serafino even suggests that her picture may harm whoever sees it. Donne continues within the Petrarchan tradition in stanza 2 and the first four lines of stanza 3, though the world is also peopled with medieval personifications; but in the last four lines of the poem he is writing in an erotic vein deriving ultimately from the *Greek Anthology*. W. von Koppenfels (op. cit., p. 84) cites the epigram on the Armed Aphrodite attributed to Leonidas of Alexandria (*GA*, XVI. 171), which asks Aphrodite why she is bearing the arms of Ares, when she had when naked disarmed Ares himself. This conceit was used by sixteenth-century poets, Continental and English. Donne, indeed, in this poem, takes elements from hyperbolic quattrocentism, from medieval romance, from historiography, as well as from erotic literature and Elizabethan slang; and the compound is entirely his own, a sparkling display of wit, ending (in the better text) as strongly as it began. It is essentially a poem of seduction which works by accumulation of subtle detail to achieve its aim by cajoling the woman avid of conquest into deciding on the *kind* of conquest most welcome to her lover.

1–8] Professor Donald Guss (op. cit., p. 76) convincingly indicates anticipations in Serafino of the conceits in stanza 1. Serafino's Strambotto 89 'Quando sero portato in sepoltura' describes the funeral procession which will follow his body when he has died for love, while he says in Strambotto 126, 'Felice specchio hor che madonna godi', that if his breast were cut open everyone would recognize the image of his lady on his heart. He even suggests that the sight of this image may do harm to people; and the same dangerous character of the lady's picture appears in Serafino's Sonnet 35 'Ciascun vuol pur saper che cosa è quella' (Serafino, *Opere*, Venice, 1502; I have used the 1530 edn in which the sonnet is no. 105).

6 *through*] This reading is far more strongly supported by the MSS and early editions than the form 'thorough', which Professor Gardner adopts for the

sake of the metre. I doubt, moreover, whether the metre does require the extra syllable. There is certainly no need (and it may even be better not) to emphasize the word 'through'. A slight stress may well rather fall on 'Will'; though the main stresses fall later in the line.

7 *prefer*] promote.

8 *massacre*] W. von Koppenfels (op. cit., p. 105) notes Spenser's reference in *Amoretti* 10.6 to 'huge massacres' which the eyes of the lady make.

9 *victories;*] There is no need to alter *1633*'s semicolon, which is supported by some MSS. Grierson's and Professor Gardner's 'victories!', the reading of *1650–1719*, has only the support of *D17* among MSS here collated. The exclamation mark may make the line too strident. Possibly the right tone is reflective.

brave] possibly playing on the senses (1) 'courageous' and (2) 'splendid', both senses subtly preparing the subsequent evolution of the poem, as does 'pleasure' in l. 10.

9–20] Professor Guss (op cit., pp. 77–8) indicates that the martial conceits somewhat resemble those in some poems of Tasso. W. von Koppenfels (op. cit., p. 104) notes some precedents in Elizabethan sonneteers for Donne's battles of personified abstractions. The allegorical figures seem to come from medieval romance, on which, of course, both Tasso and Spenser drew considerably.

10 *pleasure*] probably hinting covertly at the sexual pleasure which the woman will finally obtain if she follows the instruction given in ll. 22–3.

11–12, 19–20] Donne presses into poetic service the giants and enchantresses of medieval and Renaissance allegory. Cf. *The Dream*, stanza 3.

13–14] cf. *A Valediction: of the book*, ll. 23–7.

16 *kill*] to the initiated the word might well already involve a sexual sense.

20 *neither look for, nor profess*] i.e. neither look for in you nor profess in myself.

21–4] an ingenious transition to a clear invitation to sexuality.

23 *passive valour*] strength as a woman, taken as the passive sex. Professor Gardner compares *Love's Deity*, l. 12.

then] One of the awkward cases in modernization of the spelling. The reading of the old editions and MSS is 'than' (meaning 'then'). I have, however, felt bound to print 'then' since 'than' in this sense is not a modern word: but I have felt equally bound to point out that the faulty rhyme which results is not Donne's.

24 *Naked*] This bold reading has even stronger support in the MSS than I thought when I adopted it in 1956. The tamer 'In that' *may* have been a correction by Donne. It is hard to say.

Witchcraft by a Picture

I fix mine eye on thine, and there
  Pity my picture burning in thine eye;
My picture drown'd in a transparent tear
    When I look lower I espy;
      Hadst thou the wicked skill   5
By pictures made and marr'd, to kill,
How many ways mightst thou perform thy will!

But now I have drunk thy sweet salt tears;
  And though thou therefore pour more I'll depart:
My picture vanish'd, vanish fears   10
    That I can be endamag'd by that art;
      Though thou retain of me
One picture more, yet that will be,
Being in thine own heart, from all malice free.

In 1633–1719. I; L74; A25, S omit.
Text: Title Witchcraft by a Picture *1633–1719; II; DC.* Song *H40; Wed.* A Songe *B.* The Picture *Cy, P.* Picture *III; HK2.*
7 will! *Ed (1956).* will? *1633–1719; Gr; Gar.*
8 sweet(e) salt *1633–1719; H40; II; DC; B; S962.* swete-salt *Wed.* sweetest *III; HK2, Cy, P, D17.*
9 thou therefore . . . I'll depart *Ed.* thou therfore pouer more, will departe *H40 (no comma after more); Wed.* thou therfore powre, more, Will depart *B.* thou poure (*or* powre) more I'll (*or* Ile) depart *1633–1719; II; DC; III; HK2, Cy, P, D17; S962.*

10 picture] pictures *H40.* picture's *Wed.* vanish'd, vanish feares *1633;* most MSS. vanished, vanish all feares *Lut; O'F; 1635–54, 1719.* vanish, vanish fears *1669.*
11 that art(e) *1633–1719; H40; II; Wed; DC; HK2, Cy, P, B; S962.* thy art(e) *III (Dob has* that *written above as alternative or correction).* thine arte *D17.*
14 thine (*or* thyne) owne *1633–1719; H40; Wed; DC; III; HK2, Cy, P, D17, B.* mine (*or* myne) owne *II; S962.* from all *1633–1719; II; DC; HK2, Cy, P, D17; S962 (with* thy *written above).* from thy *H40; B.* from *Wed; III.*

Textual note. Unlike Professor Gardner (*ESS*, pp. 160 and lxv–lxvi) I am counting this poem as part of the Donne collection in *H40*, because of its position in the MS. (Curiously enough, she quotes a reading from *H40* for l. 14.)

General note. Burning, drowning and freezing (the last not mentioned here) as fates of the lover were commonplaces of Petrarchism.

3–4] cf. *A Valediction: of weeping.* Professor Guss (op. cit., p. 69) cites a fairly closely related image from Serafino, Sonnet 36 ('Mentre che amore in me non abitava'), where Serafino says that his lady, who used to enjoy seeing her picture in his eyes, has ceased to look kindly on him, because he is weeping, and this distorts her picture.

6] The sense is: 'To kill people by making pictures of them, and then destroying the pictures'. This was one reputed method of witchcraft. For another reference by Donne to the device see *Sermons*, I. 160. In *Heroides*, VI. 91 ff. Ovid tells of Medea making a wax image of someone she wants to kill, and driving a slender needle into its heart; and, adds Ovid, doing other deeds better for him not to know about. W. von Koppenfels (op. cit., p. 90) quotes Daniel's Sonnet 10 in the *Sonnets after Astrophel*, where a 'sly enchanter' pricks a magic wax image to upset the person he wants to kill; and refers to a passage rather more similar to Donne's poem in Sonnet 2 of Decade II of Constable's *Diana*. Donne's treatment is, however, as usual, more compact than the sonneteers', and he fits the conceit better into a specific situation, and exploits it more wittily.

7 !] In the seventeenth-century editions this appears as a question mark, a common typographical equivalent at the time for a mark of exclamation.

9–11] There is an interesting metrical feature here. The three lines, as printed in *1633*, not only do not correspond to ll. 2–4, but lack one foot overall. I am inclined to believe the reading 'therefore' (*H40*, *Wed*, *B*) genuine, and more likely to have been dropped by other MSS than inserted by these. *H40*'s 'pictures' (which possibly receives some support from *Wed*, and might seem also more consonant with stanza 1 and with l. 9) is not really, in my view, more consonant with these parts of the poem, and certainly does not fit so well as 'picture' with the well-attested title. *Lut* and *O'F*'s addition of a foot in l. 10 are, I suspect, a clumsy attempt at revision.

14 *from all malice free*] This may simply be a tender joke on Donne's part. The sense seems on the surface to be that her heart is so free from malice that nothing lodged there could come to harm. Yet Donne may also intend the sense that his lady will not attack that picture, simply because to do so would be to attack her own heart.

The Paradox

No lover saith: 'I love', nor any other
    Can judge a perfect lover;
He thinks that else none can, nor will agree
    That any loves but he:
I cannot say I lov'd, for who can say   5
    He was kill'd yesterday?
Love with excess of heat, more young than old
    Death kills with too much cold;
We die but once, and who lov'd last did die,
    He that saith twice, doth lie: 10
For though he seem to move, and stir a while,
    It doth the sense beguile.
Such life is like the light which bideth yet
    When the light's life is set,
Or like the heat, which fire in solid matter   15
    Leaves behind, two hours after.
Once I lov'd and died; and am now become
    Mine epitaph and tomb.
Here dead men speak their last, and so do I:
    Love-slain, lo! here I lie.   20

In 1633–1719. Among MSS collated for this edition only II; L74; S96, Lut, O'F; S; S962 include.

Text: Title The Paradox *1635–1719. No title 1633; MSS.*

3 can, nor will agree *H40*; II; L74; S; S962; Gr; Ed (1956).* can or will agree, *1633–1719.* can nor will agree *S96, Lut, O'F.* can nor will agree, *Gar.*

7 heat, more young than old *L74; S96; H40*; Ed.* heat, more young than old, *1633–54; Lut, O'F; Gr; Gar.* heat, (more young than old) *TCC, A18* (reads) heates), *TCD, N (no comma after* heat*); S962.* heat more young than old *S.* heat, more young, than old, *Ed (1956).* heat more young than old; *1719.*

14 light's life *L74; (given in margin as ? alternative) Lut; S; H40*; Gr.* life's light *1633–1719; II; S96, Lut (but with* light's life *as ? alternative), O'F; S962.*

17 lov'd *MSS; Gr.* love *1633–1719.*

20 lie *S96, Lut, O'F; H40*; Gr.* die *1633–1719; II; L74; S; S962.*

General note. The paradox seems to be that no lover while alive can say that he loves or that he has loved. The only solution of the paradox is by means of an epitaph. That solution, however, implies another paradox, viz. that dead men speak their last in their epitaphs.

The style of the poem is that of an epigram, in the manner of Martial. Donne, here as ever, is no waster of words; but the compression in this poem results in obscurity in places, e.g. in ll. 7–8.

1 *No lover saith: 'I love'*] possibly because as soon as he loves he is at once struck dead (see below), or possibly because no true lover will reveal his love to others (the idea might be a relic of the code of courtly love).
any other] anyone but the lover himself.

3 *can, nor will agree,* punctuation] The occurrence of punctuation marks in MSS is more significant than their absence. The comma after 'can' in seven of the collated MSS is therefore significant.

3–4] The probable meaning is: 'The man who is completely in love thinks that no one else can judge his love'. This is no mere repetition of 'nor . . . lover'. That was an objective statement; this is the lover's view on the point.

5–6] Nor can I say that I did love (using the past tense), for a man who was killed yesterday does not live to tell the tale.

1–6] The paradoxical situation therefore is that it is impossible for love to be attributed to anyone either (1) by himself (a) in the present tense, or (b) in the past tense; or (2) by anyone else. The 'solution' of the paradox, which is itself another paradox, comes in ll. 17–20.

7 *Love with . . . heat*] Love kills by excess of heat.

7–8] F. L. Lucas suggested to me as the most likely interpretation: 'Love kills more of the young with too much heat than Death kills of the old with too much cold'. In my 1956 edition I therefore retained *1633*'s comma after 'old', but inserted a comma after 'young' to bring out that sense. I now believe this is best done by simply removing *1633*'s comma after 'old'.

9 *who lov'd last did die*] slightly obscure; it probably means: 'even the very last person who has been in love, has already died.'

10] Whoever says that he died twice, first through love, and then through death, is simply lying.

12] It is merely an illusion that he is still alive.

13–14] The sense is: 'This sort of life is like the light that lingers on after sunset' ('the light's life', being, as Grierson says, the sun).

17–20] The sense is: 'The only thing that I can say [as an attempted solution of the paradox] is that I loved at one time [probably playing on this meaning and the meaning 'once only'] and died, and have now become my own epitaph and tomb'. Line 17 actually seems to contradict l. 5.

19 *Here*] i.e. in the epitaphs on their tombs.

20] This is, of course, the epitaph. Whether there is a pun on 'lie' is a question. For there being a pun it may be said that anyone who says that he loved cannot be telling the truth (cf. l. 5), and as it was the speaker himself that has said that, he must know that what he is now saying is untrue, and so must be lying. Against there being a pun it could be argued that the ending has quite enough point without a pun, and that this would even distract from the neatness of the 'solution'. Moreover, 'here I lie' would, if there were a pun, be modifying 'Love-slain, lo!', which would be very clumsy; besides which 'love-slain, lo!' by itself has scarcely any claim to be called an assertion at all, and, if it is not one, then it cannot be a lie.

The Bait

Come live with me, and be my love,
And we will some new pleasures prove
Of golden sands, and crystal brooks:
With silken lines, and silver hooks.

Then will the river whispering run   5
Warm'd by thine eyes, more than the Sun;
And there the enamour'd fish will stay,
Begging themselves they may betray.

When thou wilt swim in that live bath,
Each fish, which every channel hath,   10
Will amorously to thee swim,
Gladder to catch thee, than thou him.

If thou to be so seen be'st loath
By Sun, or Moon, thou dark'nest both,
And if my heart have leave to see,   15
I need not their light, having thee.

Let others freeze with angling reeds,
And cut their legs with shells and weeds,
Or treacherously poor fish beset,
With strangling snare, or windowy net: 20

Let coarse bold hands, from slimy nest
The bedded fish in banks out-wrest;
Or curious traitors, sleave-silk flies,
Bewitch poor fishes' wand'ring eyes.

For thee, thou need'st no such deceit,   25
For thou thyself art thine own bait;
That fish, that is not catch'd thereby,
Alas, is wiser far than I.

In 1633–1719. L74; Wed; Dob; A25, B, S omit.
Text: Title The Bait *1635–1719.*
5 Then *II; DC.* There *1633–1719; I;*

H40; S96, Lut, O'F; HK2, Cy, P, D17;
S962.
6 thine *or* thyne *TCD, N; Lut, O'F;*
HK2, Cy; *1669–1719; Gar.* thy

160

1633–54; I (excl. H49); H40 (thie); TCC, A18; DC; S96; P, D17; S962; Gr; Ed (1956). the H49.

7 there 1633–1719; I; H40; II; DC; S96; P, D17; S962. then Lut, O'F; HK2, Cy (with there written above).

11 to 1633–1719; I; H40; II; DC; S96; S962. unto Lut, O'F; HK2, Cy, P, D17.

15 my hart or heart II; DC. my self(e) 1633–1719; I; H40; S96, Lut, O'F; HK2, Cy, P, D17; S962.

20 windowy] winding D17.

23 sleave-silk almost all MSS. sleave-sicke 1633. sleavesilke 1635. sleave silke 1639–1719. with silke Cy, P.

25 thee, thou needst 1633–1719; II; DC; Lut, O'F; HK2, Cy, P. thee, there needs (some without comma) I (excl. H49); H40; S96; D17. though there needs S962. those there needs H49.

27 catch'd or catcht 1633–1719; I; H40; Lut, O'F; D17. caught II; DC; S96; HK2, Cy, P; S962.

General note. A sequel to Marlowe's 'Come live with me, and be my love'. Marlowe's poem had been partly printed in *The Passionate Pilgrim*, 1599, and fully in *England's Helicon*, 1600, where it is followed by 'The Nymph's Reply', ascribed to 'Ignoto', and generally believed to be by Raleigh. Professor Gardner plausibly suggests that Donne's poem may have been inspired by an anonymous parody which comes next in the 1600 anthology, and is also ascribed to 'Ignoto'. Walton, in *The Compleat Angler*, 1633, quotes Donne's poem (somewhat inaccurately), and makes one of the characters say that Donne wrote it to show the world that he could write softly and smoothly when he thought it fit and worth the trouble. There is, however, a good deal more to the poem than that. It is a masterpiece of complex invention and wit, weaving in and out of the Petrarchan and Pastoral traditions.

Professor Guss (op. cit., pp. 82–4) points out close similarities in a sonnet by Tasso (no. 84), but rightly indicates the absence in Tasso's poem of the unpleasant naturalistic details in Donne's poem. He also contrasts the wholly laudatory character of Tasso's sonnet with the self-critical stance adopted by Donne. I would wish to add a further point: the contrast between Donne's humour and Tasso's dazzled fulsomeness. W. von Koppenfels (op. cit., pp. 54–8) draws attention to many touches in Greek poetry, Petrarch and Petrarchans, including English sonneteers, which Donne could well have absorbed into his highly original poem. It is especially interesting to compare Spenser's curiously masochistic sonnet (*Amoretti* 57).

The poem is one of six grouped in *DC*, and three grouped in *II*, as 'Songs which were made to certaine Aires that were made before'. A tune is included in William Corkine's *Second Book of Ayres*, 1612, with words starting 'Come live with me, and be my love'. Marlowe's poem and its various parodic successors, including Donne's, may well have been sung to it. (See Appendix XII, pp. 341–3.)

3–4] Possibly a parody on Petrarchan decoration.

punctuation] I have strengthened the comma at the end of l. 3 in the early editions to a colon, because I think it probable that Donne intended l. 4 as a sharp recoil from the trend of Marlowe's poem. It would be especially so to any reader who remembered Nashe's words (see next note).

4] cf. Nashe, *Terrors of the Night*, 1594, where the devil fishes 'with silken nets and silver hooks'.

5 *Then*] This reading of *II*; *DC* seems to indicate more cogently than the *1633* reading the effect mentioned in l. 6 of the woman coming to live with the poet; and I adopt it despite the greater MS support for 'There'. It could well be a deliberate revision by Donne.

7 *stay*] probably = 'stop'.

8 *Begging*] Begging that.

11–12] A strangely amusing conceit, an extreme and, almost certainly, intentionally preposterous hyperbolical reversal.

13–14] A typically original touch, outdoing the normal Petrarchan references to the superiority of the woman to sun or moon.

15 *my heart*] This bold reading of *II*; *DC* bears the stamp of a revision by Donne. It is also *difficilior lectio*, and so, *potior*.

17 *reeds*] rods.

17–25] A typical Petrarchan contrast between lovers and laymen; but drawn with Donne's vigorous realism.

23 *curious*] strangely and ingeniously made.
   sleave-silk] This means: 'made from sleave-silk', which is defined by *OED* as 'silk thread capable of being separated into smaller filaments for use in embroidery, etc.'

25 *For thee*] As for thee.

27 *catch'd*] I retain *1633*'s form here, as verbally more interesting, and better suggesting the suddenness of the catch.

27–8] A comic ending, in a similar spirit to the start and ending of *The Triple Fool*.

The Prohibition

Take heed of loving me;
At least remember, I forbad it thee:
Not that I shall repair my unthrifty waste
Of breath and blood, upon thy sighs and tears,
By being to thee then what to me thou wast;   5
But so great joy our life at once outwears:
Then, lest thy love, by my death, frustrate be,
If thou love me, take heed of loving me.

Take heed of hating me,
Or too much triumph in the victory: 10
Not that I shall be mine own officer,
And hate with hate again retaliate;
But thou wilt lose the style of conqueror,
If I, thy conquest, perish by thy hate:
Then, lest my being nothing lessen thee,   15
If thou hate me, take heed of hating me.

Yet, love and hate me too;
So, these extremes shall neither's office do:
Love me, that I may die the gentler way;
Hate me, because thy love's too great for me;   20
Or let these two, themselves, not me, decay;
So shall I live thy stay, and triumph be:
Then, lest thy love, hate, and me thou undo,
Oh, let me live; yet love, and hate me too.

*In 1633–1719. Lec, C57; L74; Wed; A25,
S omit. II; DC; Dob, S96 omit stanza 3. In B
stanzas 1 and 2 headed J.D. and stanza 3
headed T.R.*
Text: Title The Prohibition *1633–1719;
II; DC; Dob; S962.*
  2 forbad(d) *H49, D, SP; H40; II; DC;
    D17; S962.* forbade *1633; Gr; Gar.*
    forbid(d) *III; HK2, Cy, B, P.*
  5 By . . . wast *1635–1719; S96, Lut,
    O'F; Cy, D17; Gr.* By being to me
    then what to me thou wast *Dob, O'F
    (b.c.); HK2, P, B.* By being to me then

that which thou wast *1633. om. H49,
D, SP; H40; II; DC; S962.*
  6 our life at once] at once our life *Dob;
    Cy, D17.*
  7 be] thee *HK2, Cy (corrected from* be),
    D17, B.* ~~th~~ be [*sic*] *SP.* be/thee *Dob.*
 18 neither's] neythers *H49, D; H40; D17;
    Gar.* neithers *SP; Gr.* neyther *O'F.*
    neither *Lut.* neither their *Cy.* ne'r their
    1633–1719; B. ne're their(e) *HK2 (no
    apostrophe), P, B; S962.*
 20 thy] my *Lut, O'F; 1633 (some copies).*
 22 I live thy stay, and triumph be *Ed.* I

live thy stage, and triumph be *H40*. I live thy staye, not triumph be *H49, D; Lut (but possibly* stage). I live thy stay, not triumph be *1633; SP; O'F (b.c.) (though possibly* stage); *D17 (omits comma).* I live thy stage, not triumph be *1635–1719; Lut (but possibly* staye), *O'F (though possibly only after correction from* stay); *Cy (omits* I live), *HK2, P (both omit comma); S962.* I, live, thy stage, not triumph be *Gr.* I live, thy stage, not triumph be *B; Gar.*

23 Then, lest thy love, hate, and me thou undo *Lut (comma after* me), *O'F; Cy (but omits comma after* Then), *D17 (omits commas after* Then *and* hate); *Ed (1956); Gar (omits comma after* hate). Then lest thy love hate, and me thou undo *H49, D, SP; H40.* Then lest thou thy love hate, and me thou undo *1635–54.* Then lest thy Love thou hate, and me undo *1719.* Lest thou thy love, and

hate; and me undo *HK2, P (no stops), B (comma after* hate); *S962; 1633 (no stops); Gr (no stops).* Lest thou thy love, and hate, and me thou undo *1669.*

24 Oh, let me live; yet love, and hate me too *Ed.* Oh, let me live, yet love and hate me too *Ed (1956).* O let me live, yet love and hate me too *1635–1719; Cy; Gar* (Oh *not* O). Oh let me live; yet love and hate me too *Lut, O'F (reads* O *not* Oh). O let me live, yet love, and hate me too *H40.* Oh let me live, O love, and hate me too *H49.* O let me live, O love, and hate me too *D.* O let me live, oh love, and hate me too *SP.* Oh let me live, oh love and hate me too *D17.* To let me live, Oh love and hate me too *1633* (Oh *corrected from* Of); *HK2* (o *for* Oh), *P (no stops), B (semicolon after* live); *S962* (O *not* Oh).

General note. The fact that *B* (the Bridgewater MS) heads the first two stanzas *J.D.* and the third *T.R.* suggests that the third was either written or mooted by one of Donne's friends, possibly Sir Thomas Roe. Yet however large a part the friend may have played in creating the excellent third stanza, it is certainly of a piece with Donne's own work.

1 *Take heed of*] Beware of.

3 *repair*] replenish.

4 *upon*] 'from', i.e. by drawing upon.

5 *what to me thou wast*] viz. cold.

6 *joy*] i.e. the joy of mutual love.

10 *victory*] i.e. the victory of having captured him without having lost her own heart.

11 *mine own officer*] The sense is not very clear. Possibly the meaning is that he will not, like an officer of the law, simply mete out justice, i.e. repay hatred with hatred; or possibly the phrase means simply 'not that I shall take my own part', as a representative (officer) takes the part of the person or power he represents.

13 *style*] title, appellation (*OED* 18b); with, no doubt, the concomitant glory.

15 *lessen thee*] diminish your glory.

18] The sense is: 'In that way, these extremes of love and hate will not perform their respective functions' (*not* 'each other's functions').

19 *the gentler way*] The sense is probably: 'through excess of joy in your love'. There may, however, be a play on 'die' as 'have a sexual orgasm'.

19–20] In any case, he is asking her to love him so that he shall not die in the way described in stanza 2: and to hate him so that he shall not die in the way described in stanza 1.

21 *decay*] here used transitively.

22 *live*] remain alive.

22] For my full reasons for proposing this new reading for the line see Appendix III, p. 312. Here suffice it to say that MS support for 'stay(e)' is at least as strong as that for 'stage'. Moreover, 'stay' (i.e. a support) makes much better sense in the total context of the poem. Stanza 1 warns the beloved not to love her lover, because the excess of joy which that would give him might kill him, and so frustrate her love for him. Stanza 2 warns her not to hate him, for that would kill him too, and so she would lose the glory of her triumph. The challenge therefore is that she must neither love nor hate him, since both will kill him. This challenge stanza 3 attempts to meet. 'Stage', however, would be irrelevant to stanza 1, which involves nothing about the mistress wishing for 'victories' over her love, or 'displaying her power' over him. She is imagined as *loving* him, and this love would be frustrated by his death. Contrariwise, if he were to remain alive, he would be a 'stay' for her. Similarly, in stanza 2, what she would lose by his death (which would be the result of triumphing *too much* in her victory) would be the 'style of conqueror', including, no doubt, the glory of the lover's being led alive in the triumphal procession. Stanza 3 would meet the challenge either in the way described in ll. 19–20, or in that indicated in l. 21, the result, in either case, being that she will have him *both* as her 'stay' (as stanza 1 supposes she would wish) *and* as her 'triumph' (as stanza 2 supposes her wish would be).

23–4] As will be seen from the apparatus there is strong MS support for 'Then' as the first word of l. 23 (paralleling ll. 7 and 15). There is also sufficient support for 'yet' in the middle of l. 24. 'Yet' also avoids the rather monotonous repetition of 'Oh' or 'O' in that line. The force of 'yet' seems to be as follows: If the mistress is to preserve all three things (1) her love, (2) her hate, (3) Donne, she must preserve *him* ('Oh, let me live' thus corresponds to, and ties up, stanzas 1 and 2); but those stanzas suggest that she cannot do this if she loves or hates him. Stanza 3, however, shows how she can preserve him, and *yet* love and hate him too.

23] F. L. Lucas suggested to me that it is perhaps worth pointing out that if my proposed text of ll. 23–4 be adopted, both metre and logic demand that the word 'and' before 'me' be stressed in reading. This would presumably apply to Professor Gardner's text also, in which she has since adopted substantially the same reading.

The Broken Heart

He is stark mad, who ever says
   That he hath been in love an hour;
Yet not that love so soon decays,
   But that it can ten in less space devour:
Who will believe me, if I swear   5
That I have had the plague a year?
   Who would not laugh at me, if I should say
   I saw a flask of powder burn a day?

Ah, what a trifle is a heart,
   If once into love's hands it come!   10
All other griefs allow a part
   To other griefs, and ask themselves but some;
They come to us, but us Love draws,
He swallows us, and never chaws:
   By him, as by chain'd shot, whole ranks do die;   15
   He is the tyrant pike, our hearts the fry.

If 'twere not so, what did become
   Of my heart, when I first saw thee?
I brought a heart into the room,
   But from the room I carried none with me: 20
If it had gone to thee, I know
Mine would have taught thy heart to show
   More pity unto me: but Love, alas,
   At one fierce blow did shiver it as glass.

Yet nothing can to nothing fall,   25
   Nor any place be empty quite,
Therefore I think my breast hath all
   Those pieces still, though they be not unite;
And now, as broken glasses show
A hundred lesser faces, so   30
   My rags of heart can like, wish, and adore,
   But after one such love, can love no more.

In 1633–1719 and all MSS here collated.

Text: Title The Broken Heart *1633–1719;*
DC. Elegie *(corrected later to* Broken Heart*)*
L74; Elegie *S96, P.* Song *I; H40; Dob; Cy;*
S962. No titles other MSS. The Broken
Heart *inserted in Dob by later hand.*

8 flask(e) *1633; D, SP, Lec; H40; Wed;*
O'F (after correction); A25, D17, B, S;
S962; Gr; Ed (1956); Gar. flash *H49,*
C57; II; L74; DC; S96, Dob (with flask
in margin as alternative), Lut, O'F (cor-
rected to flask*); HK2, Cy (*flashe*), P;*
1635–1719.

15 chain'd shot *(variously spelt) 1633–*
1719; I; L74; Wed; S96; D17, B; Gr.
chain shot *(variously spelt, sometimes*
hyphenated) H40; TCC, A18; DC; Dob,
Lut, O'F; HK2, A25, Cy, P; S962; Gar.
a chain shot *(variously spelt) TCD*
(hyphenated), N; S.

17 did *1633–1719; I; H40; DC; D17;*
S962; Gr; Ed (1956); Gar. could *II;*
L74; Wed; III; HK2, A25, B. would
Cy, P, S.

20 But *1633–1719; I; H40; III; S; S962;*
Gr; Ed (1956); Gar. And *II; L74; Wed;*
DC; HK2, A25, Cy, P, D17, B.

21 thee *1633–1719; I; H40; S96, Dob;*
D17; S962; Gr; Ed (1956); Gar. thine
II; L74; Wed; DC; Lut, O'F; HK2,
A25, Cy, P, B, S.

22 thy *almost all MSS; Gar.* thine
1633–1719; HK2, B; Gr; Ed (1956).

24 one fierce *II (*feirce *A18, N);* B *(in*
margin); Ed (1956). one first *1633–*
1719; almost all MSS (incl. B in text); Gr;
Gar. first *S96.* the first *Dob; S962.* one
flint *HK2.*

30 hundred *1633–1719; I; H40 (An*
hundred*); DC; III; D17; S962; Gr; Ed*
(1956); Gar. thousand *II; L74; Wed;*
HK2, A25, Cy, P, B, S.

General note. The only poem in the collection expressing a *coup de foudre*.
Petrarch's own love for Laura started in that way, and Petrarchans generally
wrote of their love as in that respect like their master's. Sidney, in Sonnet 2 of
Astrophel and Stella, is a notable exception. In Donne's poem the violent images
– plague, battle, the predatory pike, and the shivering of glass by an aggressive
blow – represent a harsher process than the imagery of Petrarch or any of the
Petrarchans.

8 *flask*] Although 'flash' is also well supported by MSS, and was, indeed,
adopted by all the early editions subsequent to *1633*, I have no doubt that
'flask' is the better reading. If a 'flash' could mean a quantity of powder,
then 'flash' might have the advantage over 'flask' of referring directly to
powder, and so making the supposition of seeing the burning last a day
even more incredible. 'Flash' does not seem, however, to have borne any
such meaning. A 'flask' was a powder-horn. Grierson aptly quotes from
Romeo and Juliet, III. iii. 130:

> Thy wit, that ornament to shape and love,
> Mis-shapen in the conduct of them both:
> Like powder in a skilless soldier's flaske,
> Is set a fire by thine own ignorance,
> And thou dismembred with thine owne defence.

14 *chaws*] chews.

15 *chain'd shot*] cannon balls or half-balls chained together, which normally

separated in flight to chain length, and could cut down whole ranks of men.

16 *fry*] swarm of small fish, forming the pike's prey.

17–24] It is a turn of great wit that Donne diverges from the typically Petrarchan idea that the vanished heart had gone to the woman, and insists that it had simply been smashed to pieces by Love. Donne is, however, even also able to use the Petrarchan idea indirectly for the appeal implied in ll. 21–3.

24 *fierce*] This reading is recorded by Grierson as that of *II* and of *B*. Actually *B*'s text reads 'first', but 'feirce' [*sic*] is given in the margin as an alternative or correction. Professor Gardner does not mention the reading 'fierce' in her apparatus, but does so in her commentary, where she rejects it on the ground that *L74* agrees with 'all the other MSS in reading "first"'. I question the validity of the ground (see *ESS*, pp. lxviii–lxx, for the argument); and I would also urge that semantically 'one fierce' has the advantage over 'one first' of avoiding needless and awkward redundancy. Other MSS avoid the redundancy in different ways. *S96* reads 'At first' (giving a poor line), while *Dob* and the miscellany *S962* have 'At the first', which would be a quite acceptable reading. 'Fierce' (spelt 'feirce' in *A18* and *N*), however, is, in any case, a good strong word, according well with the violence of the explosion in stanza 1, and of the battlefield and the predatory pike in stanza 2.

24] with the result that his heart never reached his lady.

25] alluding to the belief that matter is indestructible.

25–30] Superbly original again in using the images from physics, and that from the homely idea of a shattered mirror, to arrive at the distinction between the impossibility of ever *loving* again, and the possibility of more limited attitudes.

26] alluding to the belief that an absolute vacuum is impossible.

29 *glasses*] mirrors.

30 *hundred*] As Professor Gardner says, the hyperbolic 'thousand' is in Donne's manner. She retains 'hundred', however, and so do I, though not because a copyist would be more likely to enlarge than diminish, but because I believe Donne could well have written 'thousand' and later corrected it to 'hundred', since it might have seemed absurd to imagine anyone seeing as many as a thousand faces in the pieces of a shattered mirror. Even a 'hundred' might strain credulity; though perhaps not so severely. In a not wholly parallel, yet relevant, image in a sermon, Donne contents himself with a 'hundred':

> As in a mirror, in a looking glasse, that is compassed and set about with a hundred lesser glasses, a man shall see his deformities in a hundred places at once, so hee that hath sinned thus shall feele his torments in him selfe, and in all those, whom the not covering of his sins hath occasioned to commit the same sins.   (*Sermons*, IX. 270)

If Donne originally wrote the more hyperbolical 'thousand', it may possibly have derived from some strikingly similar lines in a *strambotto* by Serafino:

> Meravigliome assai specchio, c'ha intorno
>   Madonna ognihor quando in belta piu vale,
> Che non ti frangi al suo bel viso adorno
>   Essendo un vetro pur caduco e frale,
> Che quando la vidi io quel primo giorno
>   Subito mi senti nel petto un strale
> Non so sel colpo lo facesse Amore,
>   Che mi fe drento in mille parte il core.

(Serafino, the fourth Specchio (Mirror) strambotto (1530 edn, f 129^v).)

31–2] The sense comes out most clearly if the words 'like', 'wish', 'adore', and the two words 'love' in the last line, are emphasized.

Love's Exchange

Love, any devil else but you
Would for a given soul give something too.
At Court your fellows every day
Give the art of rhyming, huntsmanship, or play,
For them who were their own before;   5
Only I have nothing which gave more,
But am, alas, by being lowly, lower.

I ask not dispensation now
To falsify a tear, or sigh, or vow,
I do not sue from thee to draw   10
A *non obstante* on nature's law;
These are prerogatives, they inhere
In thee and thine; none should forswear
Except that he Love's minion were.

Give me thy weakness, make me blind,   15
Both ways, as thou and thine, in eyes and mind;
Love, let me never know that this
Is love, or, that love childish is;
Let me not know that others know
That she knows my pain, lest that so   20
A tender shame make me mine own new woe.

If thou give nothing, yet thou art just,
Because I would not thy first motions trust;
Small towns, which stand stiff, till great shot
Enforce them, by war's law condition not.   25
Such in love's warfare is my case;
I may not article for grace,
Having put Love at last to show this face:

This face, by which he could command
And change the idolatry of any land;   30
This face, which, whereso'er it comes,
Can call vow'd men from cloisters, dead from tombs,
And melt both poles at once, and store
Deserts with cities, and make more
Mines in the earth, than quarries were before.   35

170

For this, Love is enrag'd with me,
Yet kills not. If I must example be
To future rebels; if the unborn
Must learn, by my being cut up, and torn:
Kill, and dissect me, Love; for this   40
Torture against thine own end is,—
Rack'd carcasses make ill anatomies.

In 1633–1719. L74; *Wed; S96; A25, Cy,
S; S962 omit.*
Text: Title Love's Exchange *1633–1719;
II; DC. Inserted in Dob later.*
4 or *1633–1719; Gr; Ed (1956).* and
MSS; *Gar.*
5 who *MSS; Gar.* which *1633–1719; Gr;
Ed (1956).*
8 not *H49, D, SP; H40; TCD, N; DC;
Dob, Lut, O'F; HK2, P, B; Gar.* no(e)
*1633–1719; Lec, C57; D17; Gr; Ed
(1956).* but *TCC, A18.*

9 a tear, or sigh, or vow] a tear or vow *I;
H40; II; DC; Lut, O'F (b.c.); D17.* a
tear, a sigh, a vow *HK2; 1669–1719.* a
sigh, a tear, a vow *Dob; P (no commas),
B.*
10 from] for *N; Dob, Lut, O'F (b.c.); D17.*
(*TCD has* from *written in by the same
hand in the space evidently left for it*).
20 paine *or* payne *MSS; Gar.* paines
1633–1719; Gr; Ed (1956).
38 future rebels] fortune's rebels *Lut,
O'F.*

General note. Complaints against Love were frequent in Petrarch, and in the poems of many and various Petrarchans. Donne lodges such complaints in some of the other lyrics, e.g. *Love's Deity, The Will, Twickenham Garden,* in varying tones. In *Love's Exchange* the tone is especially sharp. Shame at being in love without it being returned is found in Petrarch, but Donne's turns in stanza 3 are original and typically vigorous. The combination in stanza 4 of military imagery with knowledge of the law of war is also original. The last two stanzas take up some ideas found in Petrarch and some Petrarchans, but richly extend them. Remarkable too is the recognition, beautifully timed just half-way through the poem, of the 'justice' of Love in giving nothing to the lover who would not trust the first stirrings of Love now evidently recognized as a god rather than a devil.

3–5] 'At Court your colleagues [i.e. the devils who preside over rhyming, hunting, and gambling] bestow every day the art of rhyming, huntsman-ship, or gambling, on those who are already their devotees'.
4 *or*] Despite the MS support for 'and', 'or' seems the better reading, fitting the singular 'art'.
6] 'I alone have received nothing, although I gave more of myself than did those devotees of the devils of rhyming, hunting, and gambling.'
8 *dispensation*] i.e. suspension of the law of nature in his particular case.
8–14] A stanza of some difficulty. Possibly the meaning is: 'I am not asking now for any dispensation to counterfeit a tear, sigh, or vow; I am not

asking you for an exemption from the law of nature. Such counterfeiting and unnatural actions are exclusive privileges belonging by nature to you and your favourites; nobody should perjure himself unless he is one of Love's darlings' (which the poet himself is not).

11 *non obstante*] The first two words of a clause (*non obstante aliquo statuto in contrarium*) used at the time in statutes and letters patent to give a licence from the sovereign to do something notwithstanding any statute to the contrary. The Bill of Rights, when passed into law in 1689, abolished all such licences. The form was more loosely used to connote exemption from laws in a wider sense.

15 *thy weakness*] Cupid being blind.

23 *motions*] probably a play on two of the senses in use at that time: (1) 'proposals', (2) 'impulses communicated'.

24–5] 'It is one of the laws of war that small towns which hold out against a siege until reduced by heavy artillery, may not attach conditions to their surrender.'

27–8] 'I cannot stipulate for mercy, when I have caused Love in the end to adopt this atttude towards me' (with a play on 'show this woman's face to me', the sense which is taken up fully in the next stanza).

29–35] W. von Koppenfels may well be right in seeing here a measure of parody of Petrarchan hyperbole.

28] As F. L. Lucas suggested to me, the continuation of the sense in the next stanza seems to require a lighter stop than the full stop printed by the early editions and all modern editors. I have therefore ventured to print a colon, which has the added advantage of emphasizing the anaphora.

29 *This face*] i.e. his mistress's face.

30] 'And make any country adopt a new and true worship' [i.e. of this woman, or of Love]. There may possibly be a jibe here (and in l. 32) against Roman Catholicism.

31–5] The vitalizing force of the woman is what is here particularized in the sequence of references: to renunciation of celibacy, reanimation of dead bodies, thawing of the frozen poles into fertility, filling of deserts with the teeming life of cities, and increase of the earth's rich active mineral deposits. It is not inconceivable that Donne may have intended to contrast the animating and constructive power of this 'face' with the destructiveness of the 'face' of Marlowe's Helen. I owe this last suggestion to Mr W. G. Ingram.

34–5] There may be a reference here to beliefs then current that the heat of the sun's rays could purify minerals, and even transmute baser into more precious minerals (cf. *Sermons*, I. 163–4; III. 372–3). Donne puts the belief into the mouth of Allophanes in the *Ecclogue. 1613 December 26*, ll. 61–4 (*Gr*, I, p. 133):

The earth doth in her inward bowels hold
   Stuffe well dispos'd, and which would faine be gold,
But never shall, except it chance to lye,
   So upward, that heaven gilds it with his eye.

36 *For this*] i.e. for holding out against him for so long.

36–9] Punishment of the recalcitrant lover by Love as an example for others appears in Petrarch, *Canz.* 23, 5 ff., as W. von Koppenfels points out (p. 96). The gruesome references also have some precedent in Drayton, Sonnet 50.

40] W. von Koppenfels (loc. cit.) also cites Petrarch, *Canz.* 207, 79 ff., where the poet asks Love for a quick death. On the other hand, the sardonic reference to Love's self-interest (cf. *Love's Usury*) and the snap of the harsh phraseology are Donne's own creations.

41 *against thine own end is*] militates against your own purpose.

42] 'Bodies which have been tortured on the rack do not make good subjects for dissection.'

The Flea

Mark but this flea, and mark in this
How little that which thou deny'st me is;
Me it suck'd first, and now sucks thee,
And in this flea our two bloods mingled be;
Confess it, this cannot be said   5
A sin, or shame, or loss of maidenhead,
    Yet this enjoys before it woo,
    And pamper'd swells with one blood made of two,
    And this, alas, is more than we would do.

Oh stay, three lives in one flea spare,   10
Where we almost, nay more than married are:
This flea is you and I, and this
Our marriage bed, and marriage temple is;
Though parents grudge, and you, we're met
And cloister'd in these living walls of jet.   15
    Though use make thee apt to kill me,
    Let not to this, self-murder added be,
    And sacrilege; three sins in killing three.

Cruel and sudden, hast thou since
Purpled thy nail in blood of innocence?   20
In what could this flea guilty be,
Except in that drop which it suck'd from thee?
Yet thou triumph'st, and say'st that thou
Find'st not thyself, nor me, the weaker now:
    'Tis true; then learn how false, fears be;   25
    Just so much honour, when thou yield'st to me,
    Will waste, as this flea's death took life from thee.

In 1633–1719. D17 omits.
Text: Title The Flea 1633–1719; I; DC;
III; Cy, P, S; S962. Flea Wed; No title other
MSS. Wed omits stanza 3.
3 Mee it suck'd H40; II; L74; Wed;
    HK2, Cy, P, A25, B, S; S962; 1669–
    1719; Ed (1956); Gar. It suck'd me
    1633–54; I; DC; III; Gr.
5 Confesse it, H40; II; L74; Wed; III;

HK2, P, B, S; S962; Gar. Confess it.
1669–1719. Confess it: Ed (1956).
Thou know'st that 1633–54; I; DC;
Gr. Confesse that A25. Confesse it:
thou know'st that Cy.
6 A sinne, or shame, or losse (some
    without commas) H40; TC, A18; L74;
    Wed; S96, Dob, O'F; HK2, A25, B;
    S962; Ed (1956); Gar; 1669–1719. A

sinne, nor shame, nor losse *1633–54 (1633* shame); *H49, D, C57; DC; Gr.* A sinne or shame, nor losse *SP, Lec.* No sinne or shame, or losse *N.* Or sinne, or shame, or losse *Lut; Cy, P.* A synne, a shame, a losse *S.*

11 nay *H40; II; L74; Wed; III; HK2, A25, Cy, P, B, S; S962; 1669–1719; Ed (1956); Gar.* yea *1633–54; I; DC; Gr.*

14 we're *Ed.* w'are *1633–1719; H49, D, SP; Gr; Gar.* were *DC.* we(e) are *Lec, C57; H40; TCC, A18; L74; Wed; A25, S.* ~~yet~~ wee are [*sic*] *TCD.* yet we(e) are *N; III; HK2, Cy, B; S962.*

grudge . . . met] grudge yet we are met *P.*

16 thee *H40; II; L74; Wed; III; HK2, A25, Cy, B, S; S962; Gar.* you *or* yee *1633–1719; I; DC; P; Gr; Ed (1956).*

17 to this *Lut, O'F; HK2, A25, Cy, P, B, S; Gar.* this *H40; Dob; S962.* to that *1633–1719; I; DC; Gr; Ed (1956).* to thy *II.* to thie *L74.* (sweet) this *S96. Wed reads* to thyselfe murther.

20 innocence] Innocents *B.*

21 In what *H40; II; L74; III; HK2, A25, Cy, P, B, S; S962; Ed (1956); Gar.* Wherein *1633–1719; I; DC; Gr.*

Textual note. It seems likely that this poem underwent revision. At all events the Group I and *DC* text, adopted by *1633*, differs from that of *H40*, Group II, and most other MSS, at a number of points. The Group II version gives a more finished and vital poem, and I have therefore followed it in both my editions.

General note. Marcel Françon, in his informative article 'Un motif de la poésie amoureuse au XVIe siècle', *PMLA* 56 (1941), 307–36, makes clear that the flea had already been used widely in Europe in the sixteenth century in erotic, facetious and satiric poetry. A notable model was apparently the *Carmen de Pulice*, long attributed to Ovid, but most probably written by a late-medieval poet, Ofilius Sergianus. There the poet, envying the flea's exploits on his mistress's body, longs to be changed into one. Fleas also joined the band of creatures, from elephants to ants, which were subjects of mock *encomia*. A certain Coelius Calcagninus wrote an *Encomium Pulicis* in 1519, and this evidently sparked off a number of similar pieces. In 1553 Ronsard wrote a sonnet ('Ha, seigneur dieu, que de graces écloses') in which he expressed the wish to be transformed into a flea and bite his mistress's teats during the day, and to be changed back into a man at night. (Later, however, in 1578, Ronsard altered the lines concerned, replacing them by a comparison between women's breasts and the rondure of the sky.) In 1579 the scholar, historian, and lawyer Étienne Pasquier, visiting the Dames des Roches at Poitiers, noticed, while chatting with Catherine des Roches, that a flea had installed itself right in the middle of her bosom. To commemorate the occasion there was eventually published in 1582 *La Puce de Madame des Roches*, a collection of poems on fleas in French, Spanish, Italian, Latin and Greek. Poems on fleas were common in neo-Latin, and instances can be found in the collection of burlesque pieces *Amphitheatrum Sapientiae Socraticae Joco-Seriae* by Caspar Dornavius (Hanover, 1619), which includes poems on fleas by J. J. Scaliger and Rapin. Donne's ingenious and bold turns, and the lively tones of the words addressed to the woman, afford a typical instance of his original exploitation of a basic traditional theme.

5 *said*] called.

9 *alas*] because she will not yield to him.

10–15] Preposterous boldness reaches its climax in these lines, and incredible originality in the close-packed l. 15.

11 *more than married*] possibly because their bloods are mingled in the flea; possibly because the flea is also their marriage-bed and marriage-temple; possibly for both reasons.

16] The sense is probably: 'Though you are used to killing me with your coldness, and so are well fitted to kill me again now'.

18 *sacrilege*] because she will be attacking a temple (cf. l. 13).

three sins in killing three] murder in killing him, suicide in killing herself, and sacrilege in killing the flea.

The Dream

Dear love, for nothing less than thee
Would I have broke this happy dream;
    It was a theme
For reason, much too strong for phantasy,
Therefore thou wak'dst me wisely; yet   5
My dream thou brok'st not, but continuedst it,
Thou art so true, that thoughts of thee suffice
To make dreams truths, and fables histories;
Enter these arms, for since thou thought'st it best
Not to dream all my dream, let's do the rest.   10

As lightning, or a taper's light,
Thine eyes, and not thy noise, wak'd me;
    Yet I thought thee
(Thou lov'st truth) but an Angel, at first sight,
But when I saw thou sawest my heart,   15
And knew'st my thoughts, beyond an Angel's art,
When thou knew'st what I dreamt, when thou knew'st when
Excess of joy would wake me, and cam'st then,
I do confess, I could not choose but be
Profane, to think thee anything but thee.   20

Coming and staying show'd thee, thee,
But rising makes me doubt, that now
    Thou art not thou.
That love is weak, where fear's as strong as he;
'Tis not all spirit, pure, and brave,   25
If mixture it of *fear*, *shame*, *honour*, have.
Perchance, as torches which must ready be
Men light and put out, so thou deal'st with me,
Thou cam'st to kindle, goest to come; thus I
Will dream that hope again, but else would die.   30

In 1633–1719. H40; Wed; D17 omit. A25
omits stanza 3.
Text: Title The Dream *1633–1719; I; II;*
DC; Lut, O'F. Dream *L74 (? in another*
hand); S96, Dob; HK2, B, S; S962. A
Dream *Cy, P. No title A25.*

7 true *III; HK2, A25, Cy, P, B, S; S962;*
1635–1719; Gar. Truth *H49, D, Lec,*
C57; TCD, N. truth *1633; SP; TCC,*
A18; L74; Gr; Ed (1956). (DC reads
Thou art soe truth, *and* fables
Histories, *omitting latter part of line 7*

and first part of line 8. It is impossible to say whether truth belongs to line 7 or to line 8).

8 truth(e)s *1633–1719; TCC, A18; L74; A25, Cy, P; Gr; Ed (1956)*. Truths *O'F (but possibly corrected from* Truth*)*. Truth *H49, D, C57; TCD, N; Lut.* truth *SP, Lec; S96; HK2; Gar.* true *Dob; B, S; S962. (For DC see apparatus to line 7).*

9 for] and *Lut, O'F.*

10 my] the *HK2.*
   let's] Ile *B.*
   do(e) *I; L74; III; HK2, A25, B, S; S962; Gar.* act(e) *1633–1719; II; DC; Ed (1956); Gr.* to *Cy, P.*

11 light(e)ning(e) *1633–1719; II; L74; DC; III; A25, Cy, B, S; S962.* lightnings *I; HK2, P.*

14 (Thou lov'st truth) but an *I; II; L74* (louest . . .); *DC; Ed (1956).* (For thou lov'st truth) an *1633–1719; III; HK2, Cy, P, B, S; S962; Gr; Gar.* (For thou louest truthes) An *A25.*

19 do(e) *MSS; Gar.* must *1633–1719; Gr; Ed (1956).*
   I *HK2, A25, Cy, P, B, S; S962.* it *1633–1719, and rest of MSS.*

20 Profane *or* Prophane *1633–1719; Lut;*

HK2, A25, Cy, P, B, S; S962. Profanenes *or* Prophannes *or* Prophanenes(s)(e) *or* Profaness *I; II; L74; DC; S96, Dob; Ed (1956). (O'F possibly corrected twice, from* Profane *to* Profanesse *and back again.)*
   to] and *S.*

24 That *I; II; DC; L74; S96; HK2.* For *Cy, P, B, S; Dob (with* that *in margin as alternative or correction); S962.* Yet *Lut, O'F.*
   fear(e)'s as strong *1633–54; 1719; H49, D, SP, Lec, C57 (after correction); TCC, A18; L74; DC; Cy (no apostrophe).* fear(e)s are strong *III; HK2, P, B, S; S962; 1669.* feare is strong *C57 (b.c. to* feare's *as strong); TCD, N.*

28 thou deal'st] thou do(e)st *III; B.* dost thou *S.*

29 Thus *I; II; L74; DC; Ed (1956).* Then *1633–1719; III; HK2, Cy, P, B, S; S962 (Some MSS with lower case t); Gr; Gar.*

30 hope] love *(corrected from* hope*) B.*
   but] or *Dob; HK2, Cy, P, S; S962.* would *1633–1719; H49; II; L74; DC; III; HK2, Cy, P, B, S.* will *D, SP, Lec, C57; S962.*

General note. Sexual dreams are found in the *Anacreontea*, the *Greek Anthology* and medieval Latin poetry, as well as in the Petrarchan tradition. Donne's originality in this poem lies in several features: (1) making the girl appear in reality just when his sexual excitement had reached a high pitch in his dream; (2) the philosophical fascination of the relations between the dream world and the real world; (3) the bold exaltation (in stanza 2) of the girl above the angels; (4) the narrative vividness as the situation and Donne's reactions to it develop through the poem; (5) the timing of the various phases in relation to the formal structure, in which this poem must surely stand high among the *Songs and Sonets*.

It is interesting to compare the final resolution of this poem, in its proposed return to the dream world, with the resolution of [*Picture and Dream*] which renounces the self-indulgence of fantasy for the more dangerous encounter with reality.

3–4] 'It was a suitable subject for a fully wakened consciousness and much too convincing to form part of a mere dream.'

7 *Thou art so true*] 'You are so much of a reality.' 'True' here can scarcely mean 'faithful'. That would be irrelevant to the immediate context and, indeed, to the whole poem.

true] Grierson argued for *1633*'s reading, 'truth', quoting from Aquinas a passage in which it is asserted of God that truth is not merely *in* Him, but He is himself the highest and first Truth. Grierson maintained that Donne was here giving the lady the divine attribute of identity between being and essence. I have, however, searched in vain for a parallel use of 'so' to qualify a noun. I think it probable, as Professor Gardner suggests, that 'truth' may have been caught from the line below. This could have happened whether in that line the reading was 'truth' or 'truths'.

8 *truths*] The balance of MS readings favours 'truth', but 's' is so often dropped in transmission that the absence of 's' in MSS cannot be regarded as definitive; and I see no strong reason to emend *1633* here. In any case, the singular 'truth' does not fit the line so well.

10 *Not to dream all my dream*] 'For me not to dream all my dream.'

do] This strong reading is well attested. It seems not impossible that Donne toned it down.

11–12] Grierson quotes from two sermons: 'A sodain *light* brought into a room doth awaken some men; but yet a *noise* does it better' (*Sermons*, IV. 211); and 'A Candle wakes some men, as well as a noyse' (*Sermons*, IX. 366).

14 *(Thou lov'st truth) but*] Professor Gardner argues against this reading that 'but' here and 'But' at the start of l. 15 would be awkward; and also that the reading makes the point of the divine attribute of the mistress too early, spoiling 'the fine hyperbole of the close'. Yet the presence of 'but' in the highly authoritative MSS in which it appears needs explaining. Professor Gardner's suggestion that it may have been inserted to fill out the line after a loss of the initial 'For', through the opening in some MS being carelessly made, and seeming to cancel the word, though it is ingenious and possible, does not seem very convincing. Another possibility is that Donne revised the reading one way or the other. The question would then arise: which was the revision? Professor Gardner herself suggests that Group III MSS are further from Donne's papers than the MSS of Groups I and II. On the other hand, *1633* reads 'For thou lovest truth'. The problem is a hard one. The editor of *1633* may have been baffled (or embarrassed) by the reading in his Group I and Group II MSS, and have had recourse to a Group III or some other MS. On textual grounds the claims of Groups I and II are probably somewhat superior here, though perhaps not much. Aesthetic factors may be decisive. Professor Gardner's point about the 'buts' does not seem to me a strong one (cf. *A Lecture upon the Shadow*, ll. 23–4; and *The Anniversary*, l. 17). As to her view that the reading of *I* and *II* would reveal the secret too early, I suggest that the reading here adopted not only makes a wittier line (as she admits) but an intriguing one, which, as the

poem unrolls, leads up to the climax without immediately suggesting its full character.

but an angel] merely an angel.

16] Grierson's note has thrown much light on this line. As he points out, the sense is not that she could read his thoughts better than an angel, but that she could read his thoughts whereas an angel could not: the reading of thoughts being beyond the power of angels, according to the view of Aquinas, which Donne preferred to the opposite view of the Scotists (see *Sermons*, IV. 315 and X. 82–3).

19 *do*] The reading of the early editions, 'must', might seem preferable, despite its lack of MS support, since 'do' could appear to break the sequence of tenses, whereas 'must' could possibly = 'had to'. Yet 'do' need not really conform to the past tenses of ll. 11–18. It is probably to be taken as an interjection outside the sequence. Moreover, as to 'must', *OED* records no instance of 'must' in the past indicative between 1471 (Caxton) (*OED* I. 2a) and 1691 (Shadwell) (*OED* II. 1d). Furthermore, the past tense here would be less vivid than the present. 'Must' could, of course, be present, but then it would have no advantage over 'do', which is far better supported.

could not choose but be] could only be.

19–20 *I . . . Profane . . . thee*] The MS readings suggest that two versions were current before the publication of *1633*:

> I doe confesse, I could not chuse but bee
> Prophane, to thinke thee any thing but thee.

and

> I doe confesse, it could not chuse but bee
> Prophanesse, to think thee any thing but thee.

The *1633* version seems an eclectic one; though *Lut* actually has the same reading. As things stand, however, I believe we should choose between the two versions quoted above; and the version here adopted seems to me the stronger. It is, moreover, possible that 'Prophanesse' (or one of the other spellings of that word) was caught from 'confesse' in l. 19 at some stage in transmission. (For fuller treatment of this crux see Appendix IV, pp. 315–17.)

21 *show'd thee, thee*] showed you to be yourself.

22 *doubt*] suspect.

25 *pure*] unadulterated.

brave] splendid.

27–9] A paraphrase might run: 'Perhaps, in the same way as when torches have to be dry enough to light at once when required, people light them beforehand, and then put them out, so you came to set me alight, and are now only going away for a short while before you return to light me again.' Donne uses the simile more than once in the *Sermons*, e.g. 'As a *Torch* that hath been lighted, and used *before*, is easier lighted than a *new torch*, so are the branches, and parts of this Text, the easier reduced to your memory, by having heard former distributions thereof' (II. 131).

29 *thus*] This well-supported reading seems to have somewhat more finality than *1633*'s 'then'.

[Picture and Dream]

Image of her whom I love, more than she
    Whose fair impression in my faithful heart
Makes me her medal, and makes her love me
    As kings do coins, to which their stamps impart
The value, Go, and take my heart from hence,   5
    Which now is grown too great and good for me:
Honours oppress weak spirits, and our sense
    Strong objects dull; the more, the less we see.

When you are gone, and Reason gone with you,
    Then Fantasy is Queen, and Soul, and All: 10
She can present joys meaner than you do,
    Convenient, and more proportional.
So, if I dream I have you, I have you,
    For all our joys are but fantastical:
And so I scape the pain, for pain is true;   15
    And sleep, which locks up sense, doth lock out all.

After a such fruition I shall wake,
    And, but the waking, nothing shall repent;
And shall to love more thankful sonnets make
    Than if more honour, tears, and pains were spent.   20
But dearest Heart, and dearer Image, stay!
    Alas, true joys at best are dream enough:
Though you stay here, you pass too fast away;
    For, even at first, life's taper is a snuff.

Fill'd with her love, may I be rather grown   25
Mad with much heart, than idiot with none.

In 1633–1719 among the Elegies. HK2, Cy, A25; S962 omit.

Text: Title [Picture and Dream] *Ed.* [Image and Dream] *Gar.* Elegie *1633.* Eleg. X. The Dreame. *1635–54; Gr.* Elegie X. *1669–1719.* Elegie *or no title MSS excl. S96.* Picture *S96. Not divided into stanzas in MSS or early editions. First printed in stanzas by Professor R. E. Bennett (1942).*

1 whom] w^{ch} *P.*
she] thee *P.*

16 up] out *Lec.* our *D17.*
out] up *P, B, S; S962.*

17 a such] such a *Lec, C57; H40; B, S; S962; 1669–1719.*

20 honour, tears, and pains] hono^r; paines; teares *P.* honour, teares, or pains *D17.*

21 dearer Image] dearest Image *A18; P.*   heart] love *P.*
22 dream] dreamt *S96.*   than idiot with none] rather than fool
26 much] such *D17.*   with none *P.*

Note on the title. I tentatively propose the title *Picture and Dream* for the reasons given below.

General note. The meaning of this poem seems to me by no means wholly clear. The only titles in the old editions and MSS other than 'Elegie' are 'The Dream' (*1635–54*) and 'Picture' (*S96*). A basic question is the meaning of the word 'Image' (ll. 1 and 21). The main possibilities are (1) 'picture', (2) 'mental representation'. Professor Gardner adopts (2), and interprets the poem in terms of the love philosophy of Leone Ebreo. I feel more inclined, like Grierson, to (1), which has some backing in *S96*'s title; and seems to cohere better with stanza 2, which describes the situation which would result if both the 'image' and Donne's 'heart' were to be sent away. Dr Paul Hammond has suggested to me the attractive possibility that the 'image' was a miniature painting of the beloved.

1] Syntactically puzzling at first; but I believe 'she' is accusative = 'her' (cf. *OED* 4a). At this stage of the poem the poet loves the picture more than the woman because it offers a less overwhelming and less painful experience (cf. l. 20 and ll. 25–6) (see also note on ll. 3–5).

3–5] The suggestion is possibly that at this stage the beloved only loves him because she has impressed him and made him love her.

4–5] cf. *A Valediction: of weeping*, ll. 3–6.

5–8] The poet seems to be sending away the picture, and with it his heart, which is overwhelmed by the beauty of the beloved and the honour of the possession of her impression in his heart (cf., possibly, with regard to her beauty, *Air and Angels*, l. 22).

7–8] cf. ll. 5–8 of a strambotto by Serafino, 'Quanto una lingua piu brama laudarte':

> Non scerno ingegno human minima parte
> De la beltà, che in tal sol si raduna,
> Perche guardando il Sol nostri occhi offende,
> Et tanto il vedi men quanto piu splende.
>
> (1544 edn, p. 114)

9 *you*] the picture. (The mistress seems only to be referred to in the third person in this poem.)
   Reason] the heart, according to the Aristotelian theory, being the seat of Reason.

10 *Fantasy*] the faculty presiding over the world of dreams.

11 *meaner*] more moderate.

12 *Convenient*] possibly (1) 'comfortable' (*OED* 6) because less exposed to

pain; or possibly, simply (2) 'suitable to the circumstances' (*OED* 4b).
more proportional] more appropriate in quantity (? to the poet's capacity)
(*OED* 2).

13] It is hard to be sure how strong a sexual sense the line has; if, indeed, any.

14 *fantastical*] i.e. figments of the imagination.

15–16] In contrast the poet takes pain to be a reality; from which, however, sleep, which occludes sensation of the external world, delivers one.

17 *a such fruition*] such an enjoyment of possession.

21 *dearest*] 'most dear' (not the dearest thing of all, because the picture is itself dearer).
dearest Heart] i.e. his own heart, which is most dear to him because it contains the beloved's impression.
dearer Image] Why is the picture still dearer? Possibly because it was a gift from the beloved.

21–3] The poet tells the heart and picture to stay after all, since even joys in waking life are really little better than dreams; and both 'heart' and 'picture' (presumably in so far as it has meaning for him) are all too transient.

24 *at first*] when life starts.
taper] candle.
snuff] mere candle-end.

25–6] i.e. he would rather go mad with love for her through his capacity for joy and pain, than become mentally deficient through lack of sensibility.

A Valediction: of my name, in the window

I

My name engrav'd herein
Doth cóntribute my firmness to this glass,
  Which, ever since that charm, hath been
  As hard as that which grav'd it was;
Thine eye will give it price enough to mock   5
  The diamonds of either rock.

II

'Tis much that glass should be
As all-confessing, and through-shine as I;
  'Tis more, that it shows thee to me,
  And clear reflects thee to thine eye.   10
But all such rules love's magic can undo,
  Here you see me, and I am you.

III

As no one point, nor dash,
(Which are but áccessary to this name),
  The showers and tempests can outwash,   15
  So shall all times find me the same;
You this entireness better may fulfil,
  Who have the pattern with you still.

In 1633–1719. L74; A25 omit.
Text: Title A Valediction of my name, in
the window 1633–1719; variously punctuated I; H40; Cy (Glass Window). Valediction . . . window II; DC. A valediction to
. . . window B. A Valediction of his
Name in a Window Wed. Valediction 4:
of a Glass. Upon the engraving of his
name with a Diamond in his Mistress
window when he was to Travel Lut, O'F
(which reads Of Glass). Upon the engraving
of his name . . . travel S96. Valediction
on glass P. The Diamond and Glass S. A
Valediction of his name in the window
Dob; S962. No title HK2, D17.

5 eye 1633–1719; I; Gr. eyes rest of MSS;
  Gar.
6 diamonds] diamond H40; S96, Lut,
  O'F; D17, S; S962.
9 thee to me S96, Lut, O'F (b.c.). it to me
  S. thee to thee 1633–1719; I; H40; II;
  Wed; DC; Dob; HK2, Cy, P, D17, B;
  S962; Gr; Ed (1956); Gar.
10 thee to thine 1633–1719; I; H40; II;
  Wed; DC; Dob; Cy, P, D17, B; S962;
  Gr; Ed (1956); Gar. me to thine S96;
  HK2, S; Lut (has in margin or/thee to
  mine). thee to mine O'F (b.c.) (mee . . .
  thine written above, mee then deleted).

185

IV

Or, if too hard and deep
This learning be, for a scratch'd name to teach,　　　　20
 It as a given death's head keep,
 Lovers' mortality to preach,
Or think this ragged bony name to be
 My ruinous anatomy.

V

Then, as all my souls be　　　　25
Emparadis'd in you (in whom alone
 I understand, and grow, and see),
 The rafters of my body, bone,
Being still with you, the muscle, sinew, and vein,
 Which tile this house, will come again.　　　　30

VI

Till my return, repair
And recompact my scattered body so,
 As all the virtuous powers which are
 Fix'd in the stars, are said to flow
Into such characters as gravèd be　　　　35
 When those stars have supremacy:

13 nor] or *TCD, N; III; HK2, Cy, P, D17, B, S; S962*.

14 *Parentheses in S96, Lut, O'F.*
accessary *(or* -ie) *or* accessory *almost all MSS; Gar.* accessaries *or* accessories *1633–1719; Dob, Lut, O'F; S; Gr; Ed (1956)*.

31 return, *1633–1719; Wed; DC; Dob; Gr; Ed (1956).* return *1633 (in uncorrected state); almost all MSS; Gar.*

32 so, *1633 (in uncorrected state); 1639–1719; some MSS incl. C57; H40; N (seemingly); Wed; S96, Dob; Gar.* so. *1633–5; Gr; Ed (1956).* ,so *Lut, O'F; S.* so *HK2, D17, B; S962.*

36 those *almost all MSS; 1635–1719; Gar.* these *1633; Lec, C57; S; Gr; Ed (1956).* supremacy: *1633–39; S96, Lut, O'F; Gr; Ed (1956).* supremacy. *almost all MSS; 1633 (uncorrected); 1650–1719.* supremacy, *Gar.* supremacy *a few MSS generally careless of punctuation, e.g. A18; S962.*

39–end.] om. *Cy.*

44 out *I; H40, II; Wed; DC; Dob; HK2, P, D17, B, S; S962; Ed (1956); Gar.* ope *1633–1719; S96, Lut, O'F; Gr.*
this] the *III (O'F possibly b.c.); P, B; S962.*

45 on] at *S96, Lut, O'F.*

VII

So, since this name was cut
When love and grief their exaltation had,
  No door 'gainst this name's influence shut;
  As much more loving, as more sad,   40
'Twill make thee; and thou shouldst, till I return,
    Since I die daily, daily mourn.

VIII

When thy inconsiderate hand
Flings out this casement, with my trembling name,
  To look on one, whose wit or land   45
  New battery to thy heart may frame,
Then think this name alive, and that thou thus
    In it offend'st my Genius.

IX

And when thy melted maid,
Corrupted by thy lover's gold, and page,   50
  His letter at thy pillow hath laid,
  Disputed it, and tam'd thy rage,
And thou begin'st to thaw towards him, for this,
    May my name step in, and hide his.

X

And if this treason grow   55
To an overt act, and that thou write again,
  In superscribing, this name flow
  Into thy fancy, from the pane.
So, in forgetting, thou rememb'rest right,
    And, unawares, to me shalt write.   60

---

50 and] or *S96, Lut, O'F; D17.*

53 towards] to *S96, Lut, O'F.*

55 grow(e) *Lec, C57; S96, Lut, O'F; D17, S.* go(e) *all other MSS here collated; Gr; Ed (1956); Gar.*

58 pane] pen *Lut, O'F; S.*

60 unawares *SP; II; Wed; DC; III; HK2, P, D17, B, S; S962; (punctuation from III).* unaware *1633–1719; H49, D, Lec, C57; H40; Gr; Ed (1956); Gar.*

XI

But glass and lines must be
No means our firm substantial love to keep;
   Near death inflicts this lethargy,
   And this I murmur in my sleep;
Impute this idle talk to that I go,   65
   For dying men talk often so.

64 this] thus *III; HK2, P, S.*

Note on the title. of] on.

General note. Unlike *A Valediction: forbidding mourning* and the *Song* 'Sweetest love', this poem does not spring from a settled reciprocal love. It is a courting poem by a lover not confident that the woman's love for him will last. It seems to mark a more apprehensive moment in a love relationship than *A Valediction: of the book*, despite the last stanza of that poem. It is part of the poet's apprehensiveness that he wishes the woman to be sad every day he is away, and also that he should imagine a more favourably placed rival, a corruptible maid arguing on that rival's behalf, and finally the horror of his beloved actually writing that rival a love letter.

3 *charm*] 'spell' (laid upon the glass by engraving his name in it).
4 *that which grav'd it*] i.e. a diamond.
5 *eye*] 'attentive look' (*OED* 6). If we take 'eye' in this sense there is no need to emend *1633* (which is supported by Group I) to the vaguer reading of the other MSS. The singular is also more elegant; and cf. l. 10.
    price] value.
    mock] 'set at naught', rather than 'simulate', which would be less typical of Donne's forthright style.
6 *diamonds*] trisyllabic.
    of either rock] Professor G. Blakemore Evans, in an excellent note (*MLR* 57 (1962), pp. 60–2), has thrown much light on this passage. He points out that John van Linschotten's account of his travels in the East and West Indies (1596), translated into English in 1598, when discussing places where oriental diamonds were to be found, refers to a place in the Deccan called 'the old Rocke', from which the best diamonds came, and another place in Malacca, similarly called, where many excellent small diamonds were to be found. Linschotten does not mention any contrasting 'new rock', but Anselmus Boetius de Boodt does so, in his standard mineralogical work, *Gemmarum et Lapidum Historia*, Hanover, 1609, which owes much to Linschotten. Boetius de Boodt divides oriental diamonds into those of the old rock, and those of the new rock, according to their provenance, but does not suggest any contrast in quality, though he does

make such a distinction concerning turquoises. John Fryer, however, in *A New Account of East India and Persia*, 1698, writes: 'Of Diamond Mines there are two sorts, the Old and New Rock, the latter the Larger, the other the Best; the first in *Deccan*, the other in *Golconda*' (ed. W. Crooke, Hakluyt Society, ser. II, vol. XX (1912), p. 97). Professor Evans's conclusion is that Donne may have meant to refer either (1) to the best oriental diamonds (i.e. those of 'either' of the two rocks known as 'old rocks'); or (2) to the diamonds of both the 'old' and the 'new' rocks. Professor Evans prefers (1), but concedes that it is quite possible that Donne, while referring to 'old' and 'new' rocks, understood no special value distinction in the two terms, thinking simply of the best oriental diamonds as being of two kinds.

8 *through-shine*] transparent.

9–10] The reading 'thee to me' (*S96*, *Lut*, *O'F* (*b.c.*)) in l. 9, not noted by Grierson or Professor Gardner, seems to make excellent sense, suggesting, as it does, the situation of the lover looking, possibly from outside the house, and seeing his mistress through the window-pane. *1633*'s 'thee to thee' makes l. 10 tamely repetitive of l. 9. In l. 10, on the other hand, *1633*'s reading 'thee to thine' fits in well. 'Me to thine' (*S96*; *HK2*; *S*; *Lut* (*b.c.*)) could conceivably refer to the reflected glint of the scratched name. Yet the more usual optical phenomenon suggested by 'thee to thine' (the reflection of the mistress's image in the pane) seems to make clearer sense.

11–12] The working of 'love's magic' here may not be altogether clear in concrete terms, but I believe Professor D. L. Peterson is probably right in taking the point to be that if the lady looks concentratedly at the name, she will see simultaneously 'Donne' and her own image (*The English Lyric from Wyatt to Donne*, Princeton, 1967, p. 322).

13 *point*] dot or stop.

14 *áccessary*] the only accentuation in Donne's time.

17–18] 'You may complement this utter devotion better by having the pattern [of the durable letters of the name in the window] always with you.'

21 *as a given death's head*] like a present of a *memento mori* in a ring, as Chambers pointed out.

22] primarily (1) 'as a declaration that the absence of lovers is death'; but possibly also (2) 'as a declaration that death must close even the lives of lovers'.

23 *ragged bony name*] Dr Henn suggested to me that the name 'John Donne' would have presented a particularly ragged appearance.

24 *ruinous*] dilapidated, through having lost the flesh, muscle, sinews and veins.
   anatomy] skeleton.

25 *all my souls*] i.e. the vegetative, sensitive and intellectual souls of Scholastic philosophy.

25–30] These are difficult lines. I think perhaps the sense is that, since all his souls are in her paradise, the scratched name, which she is to think of as his skeleton, will regain from her the 'muscle, sinew, and vein', which it has lost; and become eventually again a complete body.

29 *sinew*] could mean at that time 'nerve' or 'sinew' (see *OED* 1 and 2).

31 *return,*] I follow Grierson against Professor Gardner here, in retaining the corrected *1633* reading, followed in all the early editions, and supported by a few MSS, including the generally well punctuated *Dob*. The absence of stops in MSS is less significant than their presence.

31–6] On the punctuation here adopted 'repair' and 'recompact' are imperatives, and the reconstitution of the body is thought of as proceeding supernaturally during the poet's absence, not simply occurring upon his return. There is a parallel imperative in stanza VII 'shut' in l. 39. A rough paraphrase of stanza VI could be: 'Till my return, repair and fit my body together again, just as, according to astrologers, the forces inhering in particular stars are said to flow into letters engraved when these stars are in the ascendant.' This is wholly in the spirit of occult philosophy, as exemplified in, for example, the work of Cornelius Agrippa.

32 *recompact*] fit together again.

   so,] There is no support, from MSS here collated, for a full stop after 'so'. Moreover, among early editions only *1635* follows *1633* in printing one. I follow Professor Gardner here in adopting the punctuation of *1633* before correction.

36 *supremacy:*] I follow Grierson in adopting *1633*'s colon. This stop suggests a parallelism between stanzas VI and VII. Professor Gardner's comma has no support in the MSS or early editions, which mainly have a full stop. Her reason for printing a comma – that it is hard to see how, during the lover's absence, his lady could 'repair' and 'recompact' his body merely by cherishing his soul and keeping his skeleton with her – may, I hope, be met by the explanation that this would be supernatural.

37 *So,*] Likewise.

37–42] Stanza VI has asked the mistress to 'repair and recompact' the lover's 'scattered body', just as astral forces are supposed to communicate themselves to letters engraved when the stars concerned are in the ascendant. Stanza VII, I believe, considers the reverse effect – that of the scratched name on the feelings of the lady. Since it was cut when 'love and grief' were in the ascendant, the poet asks her to expose herself to its influence, so that the sadness it causes her will make her love him all the more; which, he adds, will be appropriate, since (in true Petrarchan tradition) he dies every day he is absent from her, and she should therefore mourn him every day.

44 *out*] Stronger than 'ope', and better supported by the MSS. It also describes the action unambiguously, which 'ope' does not.

46] may lay fresh siege to your heart.

48 *Genius*] protecting spirit.

49 *melted*] 'softened', i.e. into supporting the new lover's cause.

52 *Disputed it*] argued in favour of it.

53 *for*] because of.

55–6] An allusion to the legal distinction between treasonable intent and treason manifested in an overt act. 'Grow' brings out better than 'go' the greater gravity of the overt act. It also gives an eye-rhyme.

57 *In superscribing*] When writing his name and/or address.
this name flow] i.e. 'may this name flow'.

60 *unawares*] rather better supported by MSS than *1633*'s 'unaware'.

61–4] 'But this is all absurd. We mustn't rely on glass and lines to preserve our firm, substantial love; it is the fact that I am nearly dead that has made me fall into this coma, and I'm murmuring all this in my sleep.' Cf. in a letter from Donne to Sir Henry Goodyer (*Letters*, 1651 edn, p. 57): '. . . and I may die yet, if talking idly be an ill sign'. As Professor R. Ellrodt (op. cit., vol. II, p. 235) has pointed out, it is just possible that Donne may have taken the general idea from some lines of Lope de Vega (*Poesias Liricas*, Madrid, 1941, 2 vols, vol. I, p. 63). If so, as Ellrodt says, Donne's poem would have been written in 1598 or later. I would add, however, that if Lope's lines sparked off Donne's, Donne has, typically, transformed what Lope wrote, which speaks only of love for his absent mistress making him talk deliriously.

62 *our firm substantial love*] a rather surprising phrase after all the persuasion, exhortation and apprehension. It could itself be a persuasive suggestion; or it could be a genuine dismissal of the poet's phantoms of uncertainty.

65–6] A scintillating flash of wit – to excuse himself for all he has said in the poem by making it all out to be a *consequence* of the sole reason for his saying it (the parting)!

66 *dying*] He is 'dying' because he is a departing lover. I do not believe for one moment that there is a sexual pun on the word here. It would hopelessly blur the sharp and clear ending of the poem.

A Lecture upon the Shadow

Stand still, and I will read to thee
A lecture, love, in love's philosophy.
    Those three hours which we have spent
    In walking here, two shadows went
Along with us, which we ourselves produc'd;   5
But, now the Sun is just above our head,
      We do those shadows tread;
        And to brave clearness all things are reduc'd.
    So, whilst our infant love did grow,
    Disguises did, and shadows, flow   10
From us, and our care; but now 'tis not so.

That love hath not attain'd the high'st degree,
Which is still diligent lest others see.

Except our love at this noon stay,
We shall new shadows make the other way.   15
    As the first were made to blind
    Others, these which come behind
Will work upon ourselves, and blind our eyes.
If once love faint, and westwardly decline,
      To me thou, falsely, thine,   20
        And I to thee mine actions shall disguise.
    The morning shadows wear away,
    But these grow longer all the day,—
But oh, love's day is short, if love decay.

Love is a growing, or full constant light;   25
And his first minute, after noon, is night.

1633 omits. In 1635–1719. Cy omits.
Text: Title A Lecture upon the Shadow
1650–1719. Song *1635.* Lecture upon the
Shadow *II.* Lecture upon Shadow *DC.*
Love's Lecture upon the shadow *L74
(added in later hand).* Shadow *S96, Dob;
HK2; S962.* The Shadow *Lut, O'F; P.*
Love's Lecture *S. No title I; H40; Wed;
A25, D17.*
  3 Those *I; H40; Wed; DC; S96; D17, B;*

S962. These *1635–1719; II; L74; Dob,
Lut, O'F; HK2, A25, P, S; Gr; Ed
(1956); Gar.*
which *I; H40; Wed; DC; III; A25,
D17, B, S; S962.* that *1635–1719; II;
L74; HK2, P; Gr; Ed (1956); Gar.*
  4 In walking *I; H40; Wed; DC; S96,
Dob; D17, B, S; S962; Ed (1956).*
Walking *1635–1719; II; L74; Lut,
O'F; HK2, A25, P; Gr; Gar.*

9 love *1669–1719; I; H40; Wed; DC; III; D17, B, S; S962; Ed (1956)*. loves *1635–54; II; L74; HK2, A25, P; Gr; Gar*.

11 care *I; H40; Wed; DC; S96, Dob; A25, D17, B; S962 (reads and from our care); Gar*. cares *1635–1719; II; L74; P; Gr; Ed (1956)*. eares *Lut, O'F; HK2. S reads and from our fears*.
but now 'tis not so] now it is not so *Lut, O'F; B, P*. but now it is not so *S; S962*. but now not so *A25*.

12 the high'st *1635–1719; II; L74; DC* (highest); *HK2* (Highest), *A25; Gr; Ed (1956); Gar*. the least *H49, D, Lec;*

H40; Wed; III; D17, B, S; S962. the last *SP, C57*. his highest *P*.

13 diligent] vigilant *Lut, O'F*.

14 love *(most with capital L) I;. H40; Wed; DC; III; A25, P, D17, B, S; S962; Ed (1956)*. loves *1635–1719; II; L74; HK2; Gr; Gar*.

19 If once love *(some with capital L) I; H40; Wed; D17, B; S962; Ed (1956)*. If love once *S*. If our love *(with once as alternative or correction) Dob*. If our love *S96 (? capital L), Lut, O'F (both capital L)*. If one love *DC*. If our loves *1635–1719; II; L74; HK2, A25, P; Gr; Gar*.

26 first *MSS; Gr*. short *1635–1719*.

Textual note. This poem was first printed in *1635*. The MSS diverge interestingly, Group I and *H40* differing at several points from Group II and *L74*, which *1635* closely follows, save in l. 26. Grierson follows *1635*, except in l. 26; and so does Professor Gardner, except in l. 11, where she rightly adopts the Group I and *H40* reading 'care', in preference to 'cares'. The Group I and *H40* readings, except possibly in l. 12, seem to me to make a more coherent poem, and I should not be surprised if they represent revisions by Donne. The crucial differences are in ll. 9, 14 and 19, on which I comment below.

General note. The whole poem is what it says it is (l. 2), a 'lecture . . . in love's philosophy', and this is perfectly embodied in the imagery of sun and shadows and the walking and standing figures. At the same time it is evident that the poet is deeply concerned that the love between him and his beloved shall last. The concern is similar to that expressed in the final lines of *The Good-morrow* and *The Anniversary*. It would be a mistake, I believe, to take the strong final couplet as expressing a pessimistic outlook. It simply issues a warning that any 'slackening' in love means the end of it. Nothing in the poem denies the possibility that love, unlike the sun, could remain indefinitely at the noon which it has reached. Its day will, indeed, be short, if it decays; but the poem nowhere suggests that it need decay. In fact, the rhetoric of the poem can be seen as an attempt by the poet to bring home to the beloved the precious but vulnerable character of their love, and so to make its decay less probable.

2 *love*] his lady, not the god of love, and therefore, in a modern version, better spelt with a small 'l'. Since writing this note I have seen that Sir Desmond MacCarthy suggested to John Hayward that the line should read: 'A Lecture, love, in Loves philosophy'. I am slightly disinclined to give a capital to 'love's', because the word then suggests the god of love: though I would admit that that reading may be correct. Hayward says that the MSS and editions do not support that reading, though he is inclined to

think it correct. It is true that the seventeenth-century editions give the reading no support. The 1719 edition, however, does give it partial support by printing: 'A Lecture, Love, in Love's Philosophie'.

3 *Those*] slightly superior to 'These', because the hours are now past.
which] I adopt the Group I reading here for uniformity.

4 *In walking*] This reading seems to fit better walking to a particular place, whereas 'Walking' would fit better walking to and fro. Professor Gardner believes that the lovers must be thought of as simply strolling to and fro, with their shadows sometimes behind them, sometimes in front (*ESS*, p. 208). She calls it 'absurd' to suppose that the lovers had spent three hours walking steadily in one direction. Surely this is questionable? When I was young I often walked for hours in one direction with a girl friend, and I see no reason to believe that this was impossible for a pair of lovers in the time of Donne. It seems to me that to think of the lovers as strolling to and fro, with their shadows sometimes behind them, and sometimes in front, is to miss a great mathematical beauty in the poem. As I see it, stanza 1 describes the walk of the lovers for three hours from 9 a.m. till noon, from West to East. Their shadows would fall behind them, and the strange shapes would act as disguises from other people. The lecture is then delivered at noon, when the lovers are thought of as not casting any shadows. The poet says that if their love declines from its zenith, then their shadows will fall in front of them – i.e. come from behind, or come after noon, according to whether we take 'behind' in l. 17 as an adverb of place (= 'from behind') or of time (= 'later') – and would distract *them*, and upset their relationship. Professor Gardner considers that 'behind' cannot be an adverb of place implying that the shadows of stanza 1 which were 'before' them will now be 'behind', and gives as her reason the 'absurdity' of walking for three hours in one direction, which I have already questioned. Even, however, if 'behind' be taken as temporal, Professor Gardner would need to explain 'the other way' in l. 15. Surely that must refer to place? After the noon of their love, if it started to decline, the shadows would fall 'the other way', i.e. in front of them, and would baffle the lovers themselves just as the shadows before noon had baffled others. This would happen whether they were (either actually or fictively) to continue walking from West to East, or simply stood still (either actually or fictively) facing East.
here] probably = 'to here'.

8 *brave*] splendid.

9 *love*] The singular is superior to 'loves' here and also in ll. 14 and 19. Donne is clearly comparing the love between himself and his lady with the sun, not with the shadows, as ll. 9 and 25 show. Furthermore, no provision is made in the poem for one of the two 'loves' declining and not the other, so that the plural would not only risk confusion, but also be irrelevant; and I see no compensating advantages.

11 *care*] meaning, as Professor Gardner suggests, their care to hide their love from others; and so, better than 'cares', which would suggest troubles or anxieties.

12] The fact that *SP* and *C57* both read 'the last' makes me wonder whether further back in the tradition the converse mistake of writing 'the least' for 'the last' may have occurred: 'the last' seems to make far better sense than 'the least', and just as good sense as 'the high'st', to which it is phonally superior. Perhaps, however, as the extant MSS stand, one must stick to 'the high'st'.

14 *love*] see note on l. 9 above.

15 *the other way*] see note on l. 5 above.

19 *If once love faint*] see note on l. 9 above.

  faint] grows less powerful.

24] The drift seems to be: 'But, alas, there wouldn't even be the chance of the shadows growing longer and longer in *love's* afternoon; for it is too short!'

26] The violent image of darkness immediately after high noon occurs several times in the *Sermons*, e.g. at III. 362: 'Their light [that of worldly men] shall set at noone . . .'.

Air and Angels

Twice or thrice had I loved thee,
Before I knew thy face or name;
So in a voice, so in a shapeless flame
Angels affect us oft, and worshipp'd be;
    Still when, to where thou wert, I came,   5
Some lovely glorious nothing I did see:
    But since my soul, whose child love is,
Takes limbs of flesh, and else could nothing do,
    More subtle than the parent is
Love must not be, but take a body too;   10
    And therefore what thou wert, and who,
        I bid Love ask, and now
That it assume thy body, I allow,
And fix itself in thy lip, eye, and brow.

Whilst thus to ballast love I thought,   15
And so more steadily to have gone,
With wares which would sink admiration
I saw I had love's pinnace overfraught;
    Every thy hair for love to work upon
Is much too much, some fitter must be sought;   20
    For, nor in nothing, nor in things
Extreme, and scattering bright, can love inhere:
    Then, as an Angel, face, and wings
Of air, not pure as it, yet pure, doth wear,
    So thy love may be my love's sphere;   25
        Just such disparity
As is 'twixt Air and Angels' purity,
'Twixt women's love, and men's, will ever be.

In 1633–1719. L74; Cy, A25 omit.
Text: Title Air and Angels *1633–1719 and*
almost all MSS. ffire an angells [*sic*] *P. No*
title H40; Wed; B; S962.
  5 Still] Till *Lec, C57; Wed.*
13 assume] assumes *I; Wed; HK2, P, D17.*
   assures *S.*

14 lip(p)e] lip(p)s *III;* B (lyppes); *S962;*
   1669–1719; Chambers.
   eye] eyes *1669–1719; Chambers.*
24 it(t)] yet(t) *Lec, C57; B; S962.* yt
   [probably = that] *H49, D.*
28 love] loves *Wed; III; HK2; P, D17, S;*
   S962 (but has s struck through).

General note. As this poem is notoriously difficult, it is perhaps best to start by offering a possible paraphrase, and then to try to justify controversial points in notes on specific lines. The sense seems to me to be as follows:

'I had loved the idea of you (as manifested incompletely in other women) several times before I actually met you. (Angels often affect us like that. They appear in a voice or a formless flame, and we worship them in that guise.) Whenever I came to the place where you were, what I saw was some beautiful and splendid, but quite indeterminate thing. But [I thought that] since my soul has taken on a body, and would be incapable of action without it, my love, which is my soul's child, ought not to be more rarefied than its parent, but should also assume a body: and so I told my love to enquire what sort of a person and who you were, and then I permitted it to take on your body, and stay permanently in your face.

'I intended by this means to keep my skimming craft of love steady, by ballasting her, but to my dismay I saw that I had not merely ballasted the little boat, but overloaded her with wares which would sink even wonderment; [then the metaphor suddenly changes] even a single hair of yours presents too great a task for love to work upon it. I must look for some more suitable body for my love than your physical body. For love cannot inhere either in nothing or in things which are too concentrated and destructively brilliant. So the solution must be that just as an angel (to appear to human beings) takes on a face and wings of air (not as pure as the angel itself, of course, but pure all the same), so my love must take your love as its sphere, just as an angel moves in and exerts control over a sphere. In point of fact, indeed, the perennial difference between male and female love is that women's love, though pure like air, is not quite so pure as men's love, which is of angelic purity!'

The angel, which was the woman at the start of the poem, has thus at the end become the poet's love for the woman, which will depend upon its being returned.

If this interpretation is on the right lines, then the typically Petrarchan worship of the beloved as angelic is somewhat impudently (but I do not feel insultingly) qualified, if not precisely overturned, by the reversal in ll. 23–5 of taking the poet's love as like an angel, and by the final declaration that women's love is less pure than men's. The final lines are possibly something of a piece of banter. I do not believe that the joke (if joke it be) is to be read as an insult, or that it would have been taken as such by an intelligent woman. The image (23–5) is delightfully subtle and intricate; and the tone is one of humorous teasing. Moreover, as Professor A. J. Smith has pointed out ('New bearings in Donne: "Air and Angels"', *English* 13 (1960), reprinted in H. Gardner (ed.), *Twentieth-Century Views: John Donne*, Englewood Cliffs, 1962), about fifty years earlier Sperone Speroni had held men's love to be superior to women's, and Professor Gardner quotes a passage to the same effect from Leone Ebreo. There was nothing outrageously new in Donne's concluding assertion.

1–2] cf. *The Good-morrow* (ll. 6–7): '. . . a dream of thee'; cf. also Hardy's *The Well-Beloved*, as Grierson suggested to me.

3] i.e. manifested very incompletely and temporarily.

3–4] It appears from the interesting researches of Miss Mary Paton Ramsay (*Les Doctrines Médiévales chez Donne*, Oxford, 1917, 2nd edn 1924), that Donne fairly certainly accepted the view that angels are immaterial. This view had to face the problem how such immaterial beings could communicate with men. To solve it certain Christian philosophers, including Dionysius the Areopagite and, later, St Thomas Aquinas, had adapted a neo-Platonic doctrine found in Plotinus. That doctrine concerned the human soul, and it was that the human soul, when it descends into the world, first joins itself to an ethereal body, viz. 'spirit' ($\pi\nu\epsilon\hat{\upsilon}\mu\alpha$), which acts as its vehicle. Plotinus did not clarify this view: but his disciples Porphyry and Jamblichus did. The notion descended to the seventeenth-century philosopher, Cudworth. Dionysius and St Thomas did not hold this view about the human soul; but they did hold a somewhat analogous view about angels, namely, that they might take more or less rarefied bodies, in order to communicate with and influence men. Miss Ramsay herself thinks that this is the view that Donne is putting forward in these lines. I am not convinced that this is so. I certainly think Donne is probably alluding to this Thomist doctrine in the latter part of stanza 2; but in ll. 3–4, it seems to me, he might at least equally well be alluding to the view held by Moses Maimonides, whose work he also knew, that angels only *appear* to have bodies, e.g. flames or human bodies (see *Guide des Egarés*, I. ch. xlix). St Thomas Aquinas, in the passage from the *Summa Theologica* (I. li. 2) quoted by Grierson (II, p. 21), writes that angels cannot assume bodies of fire, for if they did they would burn everything they touched. In that case it would not seem that it could consistently be Thomist doctrine that an angel should really appear in a flame.

5 *Still when*] Whenever.

9 *subtle*] rarefied.

15–16] I think these lines mean that Donne thought by this means to keep his love steady instead of flighty.

15–18] I believe that the subtlety of these lines is not generally appreciated. Donne had, I think, a sharp distinction in his mind between what we should call 'capsizing', and 'sinking without capsizing'. He puts the distinction in his own terminology in a letter to his friend Sir Henry Goodyer (possibly dated 1608). (This letter is reprinted in the Nonesuch Donne, p. 450.) The relevant passage is as follows:

> The pleasantnesse of the season displeases me. Every thing refreshes, and I wither, and I grow older and not better, my strength diminishes, and my load growes, and being to passe more and more stormes, I finde that I have not only cast out all my ballast which nature and time gives,

Reason and discretion, and so am as empty and light as Vanity can make me; but I have over fraught myself with Vice, and so am riddingly subject to two contrary wrackes, Sinking and Oversetting, . . .

'Sinking', then, i.e. sinking through too great a cargo, is distinguished from 'Oversetting', i.e. capsizing through lack of ballast. Donne wanted to keep his little ship of love steady, to prevent it from *capsizing*: but he found he had gone to the opposite extreme, overloaded it, and so exposed it to the 'contrary wracke', *sinking*. He had thought he was simply ballasting the pinnace; he had loaded it with more than a full cargo. There is another parallel passage in *The Second Anniversarie*, where Donne writes about Elizabeth Drury (ll. 316–17):

> (For so much knowledge, as would over-fraight
> Another, did but ballast her).

17 *admiration*] pronounced as five syllables.

18 *pinnace*] a small light craft, sometimes used for reconnaissance, and I think that is relevant here. Donne himself uses the word 'pinnace' with that force in a letter to Mrs Herbert (11 June 1607) in which he calls the letter itself 'a Pinnace to discover'.

22 *Extreme*] Probably 'exceedingly intense' (*OED*, adj. 1b); but it could be simply the obsolete adverb = 'extremely' (*OED* B), as Professor Gardner suggests.

24 *it*] The vexed point here is whether 'it' refers back to 'Angel' (l. 23) or to 'air' (l. 24). There are arguments in favour of each interpretation. (See Appendix V, p. 318). My own view is that it most probably refers back to 'Angel'. If, however, it be taken to refer to 'air', then the reference is, in my view, merely parenthetical, and does not affect the point of the last three lines of the poem, namely, that women's love, though pure as air, is not quite as pure as men's love, which is as pure as an angel. It is possible, however, in any case, that the right reading is 'yt' (*H49, D*), which probably equals 'that'. If so, it would refer back quite naturally to 'Angel', and the problem of the sex of angels, discussed in Appendix V, would not arise. With regard to the MS reading 'yet(t)', it is perhaps worth mentioning that 'yat' was a common spelling of 'that' in the fifteenth to seventeenth centuries. The reading may therefore give some support to 'that'. The reading 'yet(t)', though possible, is, I believe, unattractive for the reasons given in Appendix V, p. 318.

25 *sphere*] probably 'Ptolemaic sphere'; but it could alternatively mean 'element'.

26–8] The controversy about these lines is as to whether they imply that women's love is purer than men's, or that men's love is purer than women's. My own view is that the implication is almost certainly that men's love is purer than women's. (For my arguments in favour of this view, see Appendix V, p. 320.) It seems that this was the prevailing view among sixteenth-century love theorists, such as Leone Ebreo and Sperone Speroni. (See A. J. Smith, 'New bearings in Donne: "Air and Angels"', *English* 13 (1960), reprinted in Helen Gardner (ed.), *Twentieth Century Views: John Donne*, Englewood Cliffs, 1962, and Helen Gardner, *ESS*, pp. 205–6.) Professor Gardner makes the attractive suggestion that Donne may here be aiming to attenuate the prevailing distinction rather than simply to endorse it.

The Expiration

(A VALEDICTION)

So, so, break off this last lamenting kiss,
    Which sucks two souls, and vapours both away;
Turn thou, ghost, that way, and let me turn this,
    And let ourselves benight our happiest day:
We ask'd none leave to love; nor will we owe   5
Any so cheap a death, as saying: 'Go':

Go; and if that word have not quite kill'd thee,
    Ease me with death, by bidding me go too:
Oh, if it have, may my word work on me,
    And a just office on a murderer do.   10
Except it be too late to kill me so,
Being double dead, going, and bidding go.

In 1633–1719. I; H40; L74; Wed; Cy omit.
Text: Title The Expiration *1633–1719; II;*
DC. Valedictio *S96, Dob, O'F.* Valediction
Lut; B. Valedice *HK2.* Valedico *P.*
Valedictio Amoris *S; S962. No title A25,*
D17.
1 break *1633–1719; II; DC; D17.* leave
III; HK2, A25, P, B, S; S962.
4 our selves *1633–1719; II; DC; HK2,*
A25. our soules (*or* sowles) *III; P, D17,*
B, S; S962.
    happiest *1633–1719; II; DC.* happy *III;*

HK2, A25, P, D17, B, S; S962 (spells
happie).
5 ask'd *II; DC; III; A25, D17; S962.* ask't
B. aske *1633–1719; HK2, P, S.*
9 Oh *1633; II (no comma in TCC); DC (no*
comma); A25, D17 (reads Oh!*); Gr; Gar.*
Or *III; HK2, P, B, S; S962; 1635–1719;*
Ed (1956).
    may *II; DC.* let *1633–1719; III; HK2,*
A25, P, D17, B, S; S962; Gr; Ed (1956);
Gar.
    word] words *TCD, N; D17.*

Note on the title. The title in the early editions and in *II; DC* does not by itself make clear the character of the poem. I have therefore introduced as a subtitle the idea given by the nine other MSS here cited.

General note. This superb lyric, highly charged with feeling, and closely packed with thought, starts with the conceit of the kiss of parting killing both the lovers (see note on l. 12, below). It then takes the conceit literally, and develops it, imagining the two lovers as spirits, with the poet's ghost urging the woman's to turn away, and let his turn away, and so transform their happiest day to black night. They refuse, he suggests, to be parted by anyone else. The splendid anadiplosis of the imagined command of some third party: 'Go', followed by the lover's command 'Go' is one of the poem's striking features.

The Expiration

(In this connection it is worth bearing in mind John Wesley's remark that the second word of an anadiplosis is spoken louder than the first. That should certainly be done in reading this poem aloud.)

After the second 'Go' we find, curiously, that the lovers seem not to be departed spirits, but to be still alive. Still more curiously, however, this inconsistency does not seem to matter. We are sufficiently stirred by the powerful emotions of the lover to engage with the present painful situation and forget the earlier conceit. We are also delighted by the ingenuity of the new conceit (ll. 9–10) of the word 'Go' being hypothetically used by the woman to punish the lover for 'murdering' her. The acme of wit is, however, reserved for the final couplet with its suggestion by the lover that he may well be already dead twice over, through leaving the beloved, and through telling her to leave him. The final 'go' could even be another 'Go', a further command.

The poem was set to music for voice and lute by Alphonso Ferrabosco, and first printed in his *First Book of Ayres* (1609), making it the first of Donne's poems to appear in print, though, as with the other musical settings in the book, the poet's name is not given. Ferrabosco's text follows the readings of Group III and of the looser class denominated *V* by Professor Gardner. The setting is finely expressive. There is also an anonymous MS setting in the Bodleian (MS. Mus. Sch. f. 575, *f*. 8ᵛ). See Appendix XII, pp. 341–3.

1 *break*] As Professor Gardner says, 'break' is the more powerful word, while 'leave' is the more musical, giving perhaps excessive alliteration to the line. I find the explosive 'break' more consonant with the high tension of the poem. Since *L74* omits the poem, 'break' may well be a revision by Donne.

2 *sucks two souls*] There is an implied play on 'soul' = *anima* = 'breath'. Cf. the well-known passage about Helen's kiss in Marlowe's *Dr Faustus*. The pun already exists in the title of the poem. Stephen Gaselee ('The soul in the kiss', *Criterion* 2 (1924), pp. 349–59) cited many instances from Classical poetry of the conceit that the soul is in the kiss, starting with an epigram in the *Greek Anthology* attributed to Plato (*GA*, V. 78) which could be translated as follows: 'When I was kissing Agathon, my soul was on my lips. The poor thing came as if it were meaning to pass over to him'. Professor Gardner (*ESS*, p. 159) cites a passage from one of Donne's sermons where he refers to Plato's epigram (*Sermons*, III. 320). It seems clear that from Ancient and Late Latin poetry the kiss theme passed into the Petrarchan cycles in the fifteenth century (see H. Pyritz, *Paul Flemings Liebeslyrik – Zur Geschichte des Petrarkismus*, 2nd edn, Göttingen, 1963, pp. 194 ff.). Some of the English sonneteers use the kiss theme. W. von Koppenfels (op. cit., pp. 109–10) cites Watson, *Hekatompathia* 20, and Sidney, *Astrophel and Stella* 79, 81. They also broaden it into a love-death conceit, e.g. Sidney 79, 11. As W. von Koppenfels points out, this had already been done by Ronsard in a number of poems, e.g. *Amours de*

Cassandre, 79, 213; *Amours de Marie*, Chanson 'Harsoir, Marie' and Chanson 'Douce Maistresse' (*Oeuvres complètes*, ed. G. Cohen, Paris, 1950, vol. I., pp. 162, 173).

vapours] evaporates.

3 *ghost*] because, having parted from her lover, she will Petrarchanly have died.

4 *benight*] (1) shroud in darkness, and (2) cloud over with sadness.

happiest] 'happy day' is something of a jingle, and I should not be surprised if Donne had revised it. 'Happiest' also gives greater moment to the occasion.

5–6] 'We didn't ask anyone for permission to love each other when our love began; and we will not give anyone the easy task of killing us by telling us to part.'

9 *Oh*] 'Oh' is more emotional, 'Or' more logical. I now think that, as Professor Gardner says, 'Oh' is better, because more in keeping with the emotional tone of the poem.

may] The reading of *II*; *DC*, like other readings of these MSS in the poem, seems superior to that of *1633* and the other MSS, 'let'; and may well be the result of revision by Donne. Semantically it has the advantage of clearly connoting an ardent wish, without the intrusion of implicit reference to a third party who would do the 'letting'. In phonal terms it coheres well with 'my', 'me' and 'murderer'.

me] the word bears the stress here.

11 *Except*] Unless.

11–12] 'Unless it is too late to kill me in this way, since I am already doubly dead, through leaving you and through telling you to leave me.'

The Computation

For the first twenty years, since yesterday,
    I scarce believ'd thou couldst be gone away;
For forty more, I fed on favours past,
    And forty on hopes, that thou wouldst they might last;
Tears drown'd one hundred, and sighs blew out two;   5
    A thousand, I did neither think, nor do,
    Or not divide, all being one thought of you;
    Or, in a thousand more, forgot that too.
Yet call not this long life; but think that I
Am, by being dead, immortal; can ghosts die?   10

In 1633–1719. I; H40; L74; Wed; S96; A25, Cy, D17 *omit.*

Text: Title The Computation 1633–1719; II; DC; Dob; S962. *No title* Lut, O'F; HK2, P, B, S.

1 the 1633; II; DC; S962. my Dob, Lut, O'F; HK2, P, B, S; 1635–1719.

2 thou could'st 1633–1719; TCD, N; DC; S962. thou would'st TCC, A18. you could Dob, Lut, O'F; HK2, B. you would P, S.

3 For 1633–1719; II; DC; S962. And Dob, Lut, O'F; HK2, P, B, S.

4 thou would'st they might 1633 *(comma after* would'st*)*; 1635–1719; II *(no comma)*; DC *(no comma)*; S962 *(no comma)*. you wish they may Dob; B. you wish they might Lut, O'F; P. *(possibly)* your wish may ever S. you with they

might HK2.

5 Tears drown'd one hundred, and sighs blew out two 1633–1719; II; DC *(comma after* blew*)*; S962. Tears have one hundred drown'd, sighs blown out two Dob, Lut, O'F; HK2, P *(omits* sighs . . . two*)*, B, S.

6 A 1633–1719; II; DC; S962. One Dob, Lut, O'F; HK2, P, B, S. neither think, nor 1633–1719; TCC, A18 *(both omit comma)*, TCD, N *(omits comma)*; DC; S962. nothing think nor Dob; HK2, P, B. nothing think or Lut, O'F. think nothing nor S.

8 a 1633–1719; II; DC; B; S962. one Dob, Lut, O'F; HK2, P, S.

9 call 1633–1719; II; DC; S962. think Dob, Lut, O'F *(b.c.)*; HK2, P, B, S.

General note. The drift of the poem is roughly: 'Each hour since I left you has seemed like a hundred years'. A strong feeling is being expressed, for which Donne, like many of us, brings into play large numbers. Here there is, however, also wit, and it lies in the precise calculation which fits a full twenty-four-hour day. The playful spirit of the wit, and the paradoxical shifts of the final lines are not far removed from the work of the fifteenth-century Italian Petrarchans; but the mathematical slant is typical of Donne.

1] Another allusion to the length of 'lovers' hours' in absence (cf. *The Legacy*, ll. 3–4).

4] *that . . . last*] 'that you might be willing for the favours to continue'.

6–7] 'For a thousand years I neither thought of anything nor did anything, or else it was that I didn't distinguish one thought or act from another, because all my activity consisted in thinking a single thought, the thought of you.'

8] A difficult line. Possibly it takes up the two previous lines, and continues: 'Or perhaps what happened was that in another thousand years I even forgot about that thought of you.' Alternatively it may mean: 'Or perhaps in the next thousand years I forgot what happened in the previous thousand years [being so concentrated on thinking about you].'

9–10] The sense is: 'Don't call this long life, though; think of me rather as having died [through being absent from you], and therefore become immortal. It was only by being incapable of dying again, because I was already a departed spirit, that I was able to subsist for that length of time.'

Lovers' Infiniteness

If yet I have not all thy love,
Dear, I shall never have it all;
I cannot breathe one other sigh, to move,
Nor can intreat one other tear to fall;
All my treasure, which should purchase thee—   5
Sighs, tears, and oaths, and letters—I have spent:
Yet no more can be due to me,
Than at the bargain made was meant;
If then thy gift of love were partial,
That some to me, some should to others fall,   10
    Dear, I shall never have thee all.

Or if then thou gav'st me all,
All was but all which thou hadst then;
But if in thy heart, since, there be or shall
New love created be, by other men,   15
Which have their stocks entire, and can in tears,
In sighs, in oaths, and letters, outbid me,
This new love may beget new fears,
For this love was not vowed by thee:
And yet it was, thy gift being general;   20
The ground, thy heart, is mine; whatever shall
    Grow there, dear, I should have it all.

Yet I would not have all yet,
He that hath all can have no more,
And since my love doth every day admit   25
New growth, thou shouldst have new rewards in store;
Thou canst not every day give me thy heart,
If thou canst give it, then thou never gav'st it:
Love's riddles are, that though thy heart depart,
It stays at home, and thou with losing sav'st it: 30
But we will have a way more liberal
Than changing hearts; to join them: so we shall
    Be one, and one another's All.

In 1633–1719. *II; L74; Cy omit.*

Text: Title Lovers Infiniteness *1633–69.*
Lover's Infiniteness *1719.* A Lovers
Infiniteness *DC.* Mon Tout *A25.* Elegy
S96. No title other MSS. Love's Infiniteness
Gr conj.; Gar. Lours Infineniteness *[sic]*
added in Dob in later hand.

1 thy *1633–1719; DC; S96, Lut, O'F;*
HK2, A25, P, D17. your *I; H40; Wed;*
Dob; B, S. thy *(with* your *written above*
as alternative or correction) S962.

5 All *MSS; Gar.* And all *1633–1719; Gr;*
Ed (1956).

6 Sighs, tears, and oaths] Sighs, tears,
oaths *Lec, C57.* Tears, sighs, and oaths
HK2, A25, P.

12 then thou] thou then *H40.* thou *A25,*
D17, S; S962.

14 heart] bre(a)st *HK2, A25, P.*

16 Which] Who *III; HK2, A25, P.*

17 in oaths, and *1633; I; H40; Wed; DC;*
S96, Lut, O'F; Gr; Gar. in oaths, in
1635–1719; Dob; HK2, P, D17, B, S;
S962; Ed (1956). and oaths, and *A25.*

21 is] was *S96, Lut, O'F; HK2, A25, P.*
Dob reads is *but has* was *in margin as an*
alternative or correction.

25–6 love . . . admit . . . growth] heart
. . . beget . . . love *HK2, A25, P.*

28 it, then] it then, *some MSS incl. H49,*
D, C57; H40. it now, *HK2 (no comma),*
A25, P.

29–30 Love's . . . it] Except mine
come when thine doth depte
[? = depart] / And in such giving it,
thou savest it *HK2 (no comma), A25.*
Except mine come when thine doth
part / And so in giving it thou savest
it *P.* Perchance mine comes when
thine doth part, / And by such losing
it thou savest it *D17.*

31 we] I *B; S962.*
have] find *HK2, A25, P.*

32 joyne them *1633–54; DC; Lut, O'F;*
HK2, D17, B, S; S962. joyne thee *I;*
H40; Wed; S96. winne them *A25, P.*
ioyne *Dob.* joyn us *1669–1719.*

Note on the title. Grierson considered *Lovers Infiniteness* a strange title (Gr, II, p. 17). It was not found in any of the MSS he had collated, and he thought it possibly ought to be *Loves Infiniteness*, though he pointed out that 'Lovers' suits the closing thought in ll. 32–3. Professor Gardner writes that *Mon Tout* is the only title found in manuscript; and adds that, though 'the title supplied by the editor of *1633* was a good one', she has accepted Grierson's suggestion *Loves Infiniteness.*

Actually, the title *A Lovers Infiniteness* appears in *DC.* Moreover, *A25*'s title *Mon Tout* also rightly suggests that it is the capacity for love, rather than simply love, that forms the real subject matter of the poem. Furthermore, since both lovers are concerned, *1633*'s title (which may, of course, have come from some lost or undiscovered MS) is an improvement on those in *DC* and *A25.* Each lover's capacity to love is represented as inexhaustible, and the final joining of their hearts as the source of infinite satisfaction to both of them.

General note. An attempt to solve the teasing paradox of both wanting all the woman's love, and yet wanting a continual increase – the amorous equivalent of the mathematical paradox of the wholeness of infinity. Donne's argument is ingenious, but possibly slightly flawed (see my detailed commentary on pp. 41–3, above).

5 *All*] Quite apart from the MS support for 'All' against *1633*'s 'And all', 'All' is more logical. The 'treasure' which the poet has 'spent' consists in great measure (as l. 6 shows) of the 'sighs' he has breathed and the 'tears' that have fallen. The adoption of 'All' involves changing Grierson's comma after 'fall' in the previous line to a heavier stop; but *1633*'s full stop does seem too heavy.

8 *bargain*] This commercial word, like 'stocks' (l. 16) and 'outbid' (l. 17), is typical of Donne's frequent infusion of hard-headed 'realism' into his love lyrics. It is particularly striking in this fundamentally tender poem.

9 *partial*] trisyllabic.

17 *in oaths, and*] There is not a great deal to choose between the three variants on aesthetic grounds. I still think there may be a slight superiority in the insistence of the threefold 'in' of the *1635* reading; but the MS evidence for *1633* is greater than I had realized in 1956. It may be worth adding that this case is one of the exceptions noted by Professor Gardner to her generalization that changes from *1633* in *1635* (other than obvious misprints) are to be found in O'F.

18] 'This new love may cause me fresh anxiety.'

29–30] Mr Leo Salingar has drawn my attention to the difficulty of seeing just how these two lines fit into the argument of the stanza. I believe they may refer to exchange of hearts between the lovers (cf. Sidney's 'My true love hath my heart and I have his'). This is supported by ll. 31–2, which contrasts the 'more liberal' course of joining the hearts, with the procedure of exchange, as if that had just been referred to. On this assumption ll. 29–30 would grow out of the preceding argument as showing how love evades the logical inference (l. 28) that if the mistress could give the lover her heart then she had never given it to him already. 'Love's riddles are . . .' could then be paraphrased: 'The paradoxical facts about love, however, are that . . .'. *1633* has the two colons at the ends of ll. 28 and 30. These could well indicate two definite shifts of thought. The two 'riddles' could be (1) that even if the mistress gives away her heart it 'stays at home', because it is instantaneously replaced by the lover's heart; and (2) that she saves it by losing it, because it goes to him, where it is not lost but safe. This *could* be the meaning, and the lines would then provide two paradoxes, the second gaining force from the unmistakable allusion to the New Testament (Matthew 10:39; 16:25; Mark 8:35; Luke 9:24). Yet if these are the two 'riddles', the expression of them is not very satisfactory; and the two lines can only be made to follow coherently from what precedes by understanding some such connective as 'however', 'yet' or 'but'. I suspect that the *1633* lines may have been a revision by Donne which gained some local success at the expense of satisfactory sequence. Incidentally, the *1633* lines are both a foot longer than the corresponding lines in stanzas 1 and 2.

Let us therefore consider the MS evidence. *H40*, *I*, *DC* and *III* all support *1633* here. On the other hand, in all these MSS, except *DC*, *Lut* and *O'F*, the text of the last part of this stanza is far from reliable, since they read 'thee', 'Thee' or 'y^e' for 'them' in l. 32 (some even having a comma before 'Thee'). Group II versions omit the poem. However, there was clearly another MS tradition, possibly, as Grierson thought, representing an earlier version or versions of the poem. This is found in *HK2*, *A25*:

> Except mine come when thine doth part,
> And in such giving it thou savest it.

and in *D17*, which reads:

> Perchance mine comes when thine doth part,
> And by such losing it thou savest it.

and also in *P*, which reads like *A25*, but with 'And so in giving'.

These versions all refer to a process of exchange, and fit more clearly into the argument than the more dazzling version of *1633*. The *HK2*, *A25*, *P* readings are the best, since 'Except' (= 'Unless') is the kind of connective required to point the sequence of sense. I have been sorely tempted to adopt that reading; but the authority for the more brilliant but less coherent version is perhaps too strong. In any case, however, the *HK2*, *A25*, *P* version is not wholly satisfactory either, since the beloved would not actually be saving *her* heart, and certainly not *by* receiving his instead, which that version of the lines seems most naturally to imply.

31 *more liberal*] The sense is: 'more generous'. Each lover will transcend the quasi-commercial ethos of exchange in contributing to the mystical union.

The Anniversary

All Kings, and all their favourites,
    All glory of honours, beauties, wits,
The Sun itself, which makes times, as they pass,
Is elder by a year, now, than it was
When thou and I first one another saw: 5
All other things to their destruction draw,
    Only our love hath no decay;
This, no tomorrow hath, nor yesterday;
Running it never runs from us away,
But truly keeps his first, last, everlasting day.   10

    Two graves must hide thine and my corse;
    If one might, death were no divorce:
Alas, as well as other Princes, we
(Who Prince enough in one another be)
Must leave at last in death, these eyes, and ears,   15
Oft fed with true oaths, and with sweet salt tears;
    But souls where nothing dwells but love
(All other thoughts being inmates) then shall prove
This, or a love increasèd there above,
When bodies to their graves, souls from their graves remove.   20

    And then we shall be throughly blest,
    But we no more than all the rest;
Here upon earth, we are Kings, and none but we
Can be such Kings, nor of such subjects be:
Who is so safe as we, where none can do   25
Treason to us, except one of us two?
    True and false fears let us refrain,
Let us love nobly, and live, and add again
Years and years unto years, till we attain
To write threescore; this is the second of our reign.   30

In 1633–1719. L74; Wed; A25 omit.
Text: *Title* The Anniversary *1633–1719;*
II; DC. Ad Liviam *S96.* The Anniversary
added in later hand Dob. No title other MSS.
  3 they] these [or those] *Lut;* these *(with*
  they *in margin in another hand as alter-*
  native or possibly correction) O'F. these
  1635–54. these *(? corrected to* they*)*
  S962.

10 his *1635–1719; II; DC.* the *rest of*
  MSS.
22 we *MSS; Gr.* now *1633–1719.*
23–4 and none but we / Can be *1633–54,*
  1719; II; DC. and but we / None are
  rest of MSS; 1669.
24 nor *1633–1719; II; DC; III; P, B;*
  S962. and *I; H40; HK2, Cy, D17, S.*

General note. There are instances in Petrarch where the poet looks back on the day when he first saw Laura. Yet none of them express any sense of stable mutuality in love between them on earth, either past, present or future. Any hope Petrarch feels able to cherish with a substantial chance of its fulfilment is for some possible return of love in the next world. Here on earth the years pass – seven, ten, eleven, fourteen, fifteen, sixteen, seventeen, and so on, and his longings remain unsatisfied; and then after twenty-one years Laura dies. In contrast, Donne in this poem tells of the steady fixity of a mutual love which has lasted a year, but is thought of as untouched by time. Only death can end it (and, fancifully, could they be buried together, even death could not separate them: ll. 11–12). Death will, however, destroy their bodies. Yet their souls, permanently filled with their love, will, in heaven, continue to love with the same or even greater intensity than now. That will mean true blessedness for them. Yet, since their love is a very special relationship, it seems to the poet to deserve more than the blessedness which (he takes it) will be accorded to every-one else who goes to heaven. (These lines, 21–2, are sometimes misunder-stood, as if Donne were claiming for their two souls something *more* than would be allowed to *all other souls.* He is only, in fact, implying that he would not wish their two souls to have no better fate than *any other souls,* or than *the general run* of souls – quite a different point.) Since he does not relish being lost in the general *mêlée,* he turns back to their time on earth, and what it has to offer; and he affirms the value of their lives and of their earthly love, which depends only on their faithfulness to each other. Here he does seem to exalt their specific personal relationship. Yet, in doing so, he surely recognizes their situation as that of all true lovers, who alone can let each other down, but, as long as they are true, remain invulnerable. The last four lines then express an exhortation to live out their lives, fearless both of phantoms and of harsh realities, and nobly faithful, until they have *loved* for sixty years (not attained the *age* of sixty, as is sometimes thought). This seems to me the expression of a measured but humanly exhilarating hope for a love lasting through life such as that vowed to in the Anglican marriage service (and in the Catholic also) then and now. The final clause is a triumphant announcement of the start of the second year of their love, which, for the poet, stretches before them for years and years and years, *provided that* they are true (cf. *The Good-morrow,* ll. 20–2).

The mutuality is, moreover, explicitly reaffirmed in the last two words of the poem.

2 *honours*] people of rank.
3 *which makes times*] which makes the hours, days, years, and so on.
 they] probably 'times', rather than the people in ll. 1–2.
3–5] i.e. the sun, the time-maker itself, which paradoxically makes times in the very moment of their passing, is now older by a year, a measure of the time sequence it had itself created. Donne uses a similar stroke of wit in *The Second Anniversary*, l. 24:

> Before the sun, the which fram'd days, was fram'd.
> (Gr, I, 252)

4 *Is*] This applies grammatically only to the sun, but Donne is clearly making a similar assertion about everything mentioned in ll. 1 and 2.
10 *his*] 'its', as normally in the written English of the time. (The first instance of the possessive 'its' in *OED* is dated 1598.)
11–12] Professor Gardner says that this implies that their love is clandestine, because they may not, as married lovers may, expect to be 'married in the dust'. On this assumption, however, I cannot see why she holds (*ESS*, pp. xxviii–xxix) that the poem could not have been written to Ann More. Why could it not have been written just a year after Donne had met her? Their love had then not yet been consecrated by the marriage ceremony.
16 *sweet salt tears*] an interesting effect. Possibly 'sweet' because (1) part of life, which is here valued above death ('Alas' in l. 13), and (2) part of the happy element in love; and 'salt', because love had its bitter moments, either intrinsically or through circumstance. The oxymoron is subtly compact (cf. also *Witchcraft by a Picture*, l. 8). W. von Koppenfels draws our attention to a number of 'bitter-sweet' touches in Petrarch, e.g. *Canz.* 118, 5; 175, 4; 229, 14; 270, 22 ff.
18 *inmates*] merely short-term lodgers. Cf. 'In-mate, a short Sojourner' (*Sermons*, VIII. 64); and a letter from Donne to Sir Henry Goodyer (*c*. 1608): 'They [his vices] Inne not, but dwell in me' (Nonesuch Donne, p. 451).
 prove] experience.
19 *there above*] in heaven.
20] i.e. when death comes. Donne seems to be implying here the view he expresses in *Pseudo-Martyr*, 1610, p. 111, and in a number of passages in the *Sermons*, that the souls of the righteous go straight to heaven at death. This was contrary to the opinion of the majority of the early Fathers, but closer to the doctrine later adopted by the Roman Church and declared by Benedict XII in 1336, that the souls of the righteous would not have to wait till the Judgement Day, but would be admitted to heaven either at death or after purification in purgatory. This was amplified and clarified by the

Council of Florence in 1439, which declared that baptized souls which had not sinned, or whose sin had been purged on earth or in purgatory, would be immediately received into heaven, and see God. The question was not an article of faith for Protestants, and Jeremy Taylor, for instance, held the opposite view to Donne, who did not, however, believe in purgatory. On the whole matter see Helen Gardner (ed.), *The Divine Poems*, Oxford, 1952, Appendix A, 'Donne's views on the state of the soul after death', pp. 114–17.

21 *throughly*] thoroughly.

22] 'But in *heaven* we shall be no more blessèd then anyone else.' Grierson, quoting a passage from the *Sentences* of Peter Lombard (IV. Dist. xlix. 4), and referring us to Aquinas, *Summa Theologica*, Supp. Q. XCIII, points out that the Scholastics held that although all are equally content in heaven, not all are equally blest. In the bull *Laetantur coeli*, moreover, issued by the Council of Florence in 1439, it was expressly stated that the vision of God, accorded to those who were sinless or who had purged their sin, would be more or less perfect according to the merits of the souls concerned. Donne may therefore be inadvertently misinterpreting the Catholic view, or he may be wresting it for the sake of the poem.

24 *nor of such subjects be*] 'nor can be Kings of such subjects'.

30 *threescore*] i.e. our diamond jubilee, as this is our anniversary.

Love's Growth

OR

Spring

I scarce believe my love to be so pure
    As I had thought it was,
    Because it doth endure
Vicissitude, and season, as the grass;
Methinks I lied all winter, when I swore   5
My love was infinite, if spring make it more.
But if this medicine, love, which cures all sorrow
With more, not only be no quíntessence,
But mix'd of all stuffs paining soul, or sense,
And of the Sun his working vigour borrow,   10
Love's not so pure, and abstract, as they use
To say, which have no mistress but their muse,
But as all else, being elemented too,
Love sometimes would contémplate, sometimes do.

And yet not greater, but more eminent,   15
    Love by the spring is grown;
    As, in the firmament,
Stars by the Sun are not enlarg'd, but shown.
Gentle love deeds, as blossoms on a bough,
From love's awakened root do bud out now.   20
If, as in waters stirr'd more circles be
Produc'd by one, love such additions take,
Those, like to many spheres, but one heaven make,
For they are all concentric unto thee:
And though each spring do add to love new heat,   25
As princes do in times of action get
New taxes, and remit them not in peace,
No winter shall abate the spring's increase.

In 1633–1719. H40; L74; HK2, A25 omit.
Text: Title Love's Growth *1633–1719; II;*
DC; S962. Spring *I; Wed; S96, Dob.* The
Spring *Lut, O'F; Cy, P, B, S. No title D17.*
  9 paining] vexing *III; Cy, P, S;*
  1635–1719.

  10 working] active *Lut, O'F; Cy, P, S;*
  1635–1719. line om. II; DC; S962.
  11 pure, and] pure an *III; Cy, P, D17, B,*
  S; 1669–1719.
  12 which] who *Lut, O'F; Cy, P, D17.*
  that S96. they *S.*

14 sometimes would] would sometimes *Wed; O'F; Cy.*

15 not *I; II; Wed; III; Cy, P, D17, B; S962; Gar.* no(e) *1633–1719; DC; S; Gr; Ed (1956).*

19 Gentle] Greater *P.*

21 waters *C57; TCC; A18; Wed; III; P, D17, S.* water *1633–1719; H49, D, SP, Lec; TCD, N; DC; Cy, B; S962; Gr; Ed (1956); Gar.*

23 to many *I; II; Wed; DC; III; Cy, D17,*

B; S962; Gar. so(e) many *1633–1719; S; Gr; Ed (1956).* the *P.*

25 though each . . . do(e)] though each . . . doth *Dob.* if each . . . doe *Cy, P.* though new . . . do *D17.* if each . . . doth *S.*

new heat] such state *P.*

26 times of action] time of actions *I.* time of action *Wed; III; Cy, S; S962.* times of actions *P.*

28 the] this *Lut, O'F; Cy, P, S.*

Note on the title. I have printed both titles, because each has considerable authority.

Note on the printing of the poem. 1633 and some MSS break the poem after l. 6. Other MSS do not; and as the asymmetricality is untypical of Donne, I have closed up stanza I. Grierson in his large edition followed *1633*, but in his plain text (Oxford, 1929) he removed the asymmetricality by adopting the break after l. 6 and introducing a corresponding break after l. 20. This alternative has been supported by Sir John Sparrow in a letter to the *TLS*, 21 December 1956. He rightly urges that only one other of the *Songs and Sonets* has stanzas as long as fourteen lines. I have, however, decided to retain the layout I adopted in my first edition. My reasons are: (1) that there is no other lyric in the collection with stanzas of different lengths; (2) that none of the MSS or old editions give a break after l. 20, whereas in some MSS the layout is that here printed; (3) that such a break would not correspond to a break in sense.

General note. This admirable poem may yet, in its complexity, involve some contradiction. The first stanza would appear as firmly anti-Platonic as any utterance in the collection. The poet clearly recognizes his love as dependent upon the natural processes of seasonal change, and as a mixture of spiritual and sexual elements ('do' in l. 14 is probably strongly sexual). Yet even in the first stanza there is a shift from the categorical statement of ll. 1–4 to the hypo-thetical clauses of l. 6 and l. 7, the latter of which governs the rest of stanza 1. These hypotheticals prepare the way for the reversal at the start of stanza 2, where the poet declares that spring did not make his love greater, after all, but only more conspicuous. It now becomes a matter of love's 'root' being 'awaken'd', and showing itself in tender sexuality (ll. 19–20). The simile of ll. 21–4 again mutes the idea of fundamental change, and when we reach the last lines we see that the poet's object is to make it clear that, though each spring *adds* (as if external and not fundamental) 'new heat' to his love, that love will not be subject to domination by winter. The whole process, by sophistical argument, and wonderfully inventive and persuasive imagery (including the political image of ll. 26–7), has been 'shown' to be asymmetrical – growth immune from any reversal. The conclusion then tends towards the Platonic, a recognition that the fundamental love is always there, and independent of the physical 'vicissitude' to which the start of the poem had declared it to be subject.

1 *pure*] not composed of more than one element, and therefore not susceptible of change.

4 *grass*] Professor D. L. Peterson (op. cit., p. 304) is, I feel sure, right in seeing here a reference to the biblical 'All flesh is grass' (Isaiah 40:6; 1 Peter 1:24).

7–8] Paracelsian medicine used chemical remedies which were often as violent in their effects as the maladies they were employed to cure. *OED* quotes from Thomas Burton's *Diary*, 1659: 'It is a paracelsian remedy, that may kill as well as cure'.

8 *quíntessence*] Grierson quotes a key passage from Paracelsus (*The Fourth Book of the Archidoxies. Concerning the Quintessence*) which refers to the quintessence as being a certain matter which could be extracted from all natural bodies, and which was absolutely pure and separate from the four elements. It had the capacity to cure all diseases, and did not do this by means of temperature, but by its own purity. It was not to be extracted 'by the mixture or addition of incongruous matters'. Elsewhere Paracelsus says that it is not a fifth element.

6–14] The sense, then, seems to be: 'But if this medicine, love, which cures all sorrow with more sorrow, is not only not a quintessence, but is not even pure – being a mixture of everything painful to mind or body, and owing its strength to the sun, so that it is stronger in the spring than it was in the winter – then the love is not so pure and abstract as poets are in the habit of saying, who have no mistress except their muse; but being, like everything else, composed of diverse elements, it would sometimes want to contemplate its mistress, and sometimes to make love to her.'

14 *do*] cf. *The Dream*, l. 10.

15 *eminent*] conspicuous.

15–18] Probably alluding to the popular belief that the stars (like the moon) received their light when the sun shone on them, or when they partook of its light. Nancy P. Brown, in 'A note on the imagery of Donne's "Love's Growth"', *MLR* 48 (1953), pp. 324–7, maintains that the suggestion that the light of the planets is reflected from the sun was made by Plato in the *Timaeus* (39 B and C), and affirmed by Proclus' commentary. She tells us that the theory grew in popularity in the sixteenth century, and she quotes a passage (which I had encountered independently) from Thomas Kyd's *Tasso's Householders Philosophie* (tr. 1588) in which a servant is said to be a reasonable creature by participation 'euen as the Moone and the Starres receiue light by participation with the sunne'. Yet as late as the beginning of the seventeenth century Kepler held both stars and planets to be self-luminous (*De stella nova*, 1606, c. XVIII). The theory of the reflected light of the planets was only proved by Galileo's experiments with his telescope in 1609–10, the results of which were published in *Siderius Nuncius*, 1610. In a letter to Kepler dated 26 March 1611, published by Kepler the same year, Galileo writes that his proof depended chiefly on the fact that he had distinctly observed that the planets received greater brightness, and reflected it more intensely, in proportion as they were nearer to us and to the sun.

Donne makes specific reference to the work of Kepler and Galileo in *Ignatius His Conclave* published in 1611. In this poem Donne's point seems to be that the sun does not make the stars larger, but simply makes them visible. Cf. a passage in a sermon:

> The Sunne does not enlighten the Starres of the Firmament, meerly for an Ornament to the Firmament, (though even the glory, which God receives from that Ornament, be one reason thereof) but that by the reflection of those Starres his beams might be cast into some places, to which, by a direct Emanation from himselfe, those beauties would not have come.
>
> (*Sermons*, VIII. 243)

21 *waters*] The plural is more suggestive of an expanse of water, and the reading is well supported.

21–4] 'If love acquires additions of that sort [i.e. 'gentle love deeds'], then, as when water is stirred additional circles are produced by the original one, these new additions will only constitute one heaven, just as the spheres in the Ptolemaic astronomy only form one heaven; and that is because all these additions will be centred on you, just as in that system the spheres are all centred on the earth.'

26–7 *in times of action get / New taxes*] levy new taxes in times of emergency.

The Ecstasy

Where, like a pillow on a bed,
    A pregnant bank swell'd up, to rest
The violet's reclining head,
    Sat we two, one another's best.

Our hands were firmly cémented   5
    With a fast balm, which thence did spring;
Our eye-beams twisted, and did thread
    Our eyes upon one double string:

So to intergraft our hands, as yet
    Was all our means to make us one,   10
And pictures on our eyes to get
    Was all our propagation.

As, 'twixt two equal armies, Fate
    Suspends uncertain victory,
Our souls (which to advance their state   15
    Were gone out) hung 'twixt her, and me.

And whilst our souls negotiate there,
    We like sepulchral statues lay;
All day, the same our postures were,
    And we said nothing, all the day.   20

If any, so by love refin'd
    That he souls' language understood,
And by good love were grown all mind,
    Within convenient distance stood,

In 1633–1719. L74; Wed; Cy; S962 omit.
Text: Title The Extasie *(variously spelt)*
1633–1719; I; DC; III; HK2, A25, P, B.
Extasie *H40; II; D17.* An Extacie *S.*
  9 intergraft *(or entergraft) 1633–1719; I;*
    H40; II; DC; P (entergraffe), *S.* ingraft
    (or engraft) III; HK2, A25, D17, B
    (ingraff).

10 our *H40; II; DC; III; HK2, A25, P,*
    D17, B, S; Gar. the *1633–1719; I; Gr;*
    Ed (1956).
11 on *almost all MSS; Ed (1956); Gar.* in
    1633–1719; P; Gr.
25 knew *almost all MSS; 1635–1719.*
    knowes *1633; D, SP, Lec, C57.*
42 Interinanimates *H49; H40; II; DC; III;*

He (though he knew not which soul spake,   25
   Because both meant, both spake the same)
Might thence a new concoction take,
   And part far purer than he came.

'This Ecstasy doth unperplex,'
   We said, 'and tell us what we love;   30
We see by this it was not sex;
   We see we saw not what did move:

'But as all several souls contain
   Mixture of things, they know not what,
Love these mix'd souls doth mix again,   35
   And makes both one, each this and that.

'A single violet transplant,—
   The strength, the colour, and the size,
All which before was poor, and scant,
   Redoubles still, and multiplies.   40

'When love, with one another so
   Interinanimates two souls,
That abler soul, which thence doth flow,
   Defects of loneliness controls.

'We then, who are this new soul, know   45
   Of what we are compos'd, and made,
For the atomies of which we grow,
   Are souls, whom no change can invade.

'But oh alas, so long, so far
   Our bodies why do we forbear?   50
They are ours, though they are not we, we are
   The intelligences, they the sphere.

A25, P, D17, B. Interanimates *1633–*
1719; D, SP, Lec, C57; HK2, S.
51 They are ours, though they are not
wee, wee are *MSS* They are ours,
though not wee, Wee are *1633–1719.*

52 spheare (*or* Spheare) *H49, D, SP, C57;*
H40; II; DC; S96, Lut, O'F; HK2,
A25, P, D17, B, S. spheares *1633–*
1719; Dob. sphears *Lec.*

'We owe them thanks, because they thus
    Did us, to us, at first convey,
Yielded their forces, sense, to us,   55
    Nor are dross to us, but allay.

'On man heaven's influence works not so,
    But that it first imprints the air;
So soul into the soul may flow,
    Though it to body first repair.   60

'As our blood labours to beget
    Spirits, as like souls as it can,
Because such fingers need, to knit
    That subtle knot, which makes us man:

'So must pure lovers' souls descend   65
    To affections, and to faculties,
Which sense may reach and apprehend,
    Else a great Prince in prison lies.

'To our bodies turn we then, that so
    Weak men on love reveal'd may look;   70
Love's mysteries in souls do grow,
    But yet the body is his book:

'And if some lover, such as we,
    Have heard this Dialogue of One,
Let him still mark us, he shall see   75
    Small change, when we are to bodies gone.'

55 theyre (*or* their) forces, Sense, *D* (Us), *SP.* their forces, Sence, *TCD;* their forces (;Sence;) *N.* theyre (*or* their) forces, sense *H49; H40* (sence); *DC* (sence); *Dob* (sence); *D17* (Sense). theire forces, sences *Lec.* theyre forces, sences, *C57.* their forces sence, *TCC* (Sence), *A18.* theire forces sence *HK2, A25.* theire forces, since, *S96.* these forces, since, *Lut* (i *not dotted*). these forces, Sense, *O'F.* these forces first *P.* their forces since *S.* their senses force *1633–1669 (and 1719, reading* sense's); *B* (sences).

59 So (e)] For *1633–1719; I; O'F (a.c.).*
67 Which *1633–1719; all MSS; Gr.* That *Gar.*
74 Dialogue of One *many MSS.* dialogue of one *1633–1719; other MSS.*
76 to bodies gone] to bodies grown(e) *S96, Dob (with* gone *as alternative or correction), O'F (after correction); 1635– 1719.* two bodies growne *Lut, O'F (before correction); P.*

Note on the title. The predominant meaning of the title is pretty certainly the mystical state in which a soul, liberated from the body, contemplates divine truths. The souls of the lovers, which, during the poem, coalesce through love (ll. 41–8), communicate their thoughts in this state to the understanding listener.

Note on the printing of the poem. Many of the MSS divide the poem into quatrains. The *1633* editor, who was perhaps the printer, did not preserve this division, but printed the poem in one continuous block. This began a long and bad tradition, which may even have contributed to the difficulty of understanding the poem, quite apart from making it needlessly and inelegantly ponderous in appearance. Among modern editors Chambers first broke away, and printed the poem in quatrains.

General note. The poem has been greatly admired, both by critics and by creative writers, including Coleridge and Ezra Pound. It has also received widely divergent interpretations, ranging from the view of the late Professor Pierre Legouis that it is a poem of seduction, through that of Grierson that it is a justification of that natural love which rests on the interdependence of soul and body, to Ezra Pound's downright assertion that the poem expresses 'Platonism believed'. Discussion has been so extensive and crucial that I have reserved my attempt to consider the controversy, as a general problem, for an Appendix. (See Appendix VI, pp. 323–7.)

3 *The violet's*] Professor A. J. Smith aptly quotes a passage from H. Golding-ham's *The Garden Plot*, 1578, bearing out that the violet was emblematic of faithfulness and lack of hypocrisy. Possibly consistent with this (though not necessarily so) is a reference in Mario Equicola's *Libro di Natura d'Amore*, Venice, 1526, f. 164^r, to the violet as 'a pleasing flower dedicated to Venus'.

5 *cémented*] so accented in Donne's time. Probably simply 'united as with cement' (*OED* v. 1) rather than the alchemical sense 'made to penetrate and combine at a high temperature' (see *OED* sb. 2). Like the eyes in ll. 7–8, the hands of the lovers seem to remain distinct.

6 *fast*] i.e. set fast. There is, however, probably also the sense that their steadfastness has contributed to the firmness of the 'balm', and has in turn been contributed to by it.
balm] here simply meaning an aromatic resinous exudation. There is probably also, however, a sense that the balm is soothing and curative for both lovers.

7–8] Professor Gardner refers to a passage from Leone Ebreo's *Dialoghi d'Amore*, translated as *The Philosophy of Love*, by F. Friedeberg-Seeley and J. H. Barnes, London, 1937, p. 215, which reconciles two theories of sight current at the time, 'extramission' (beams projected from the eye on to the object), and 'intramission' (beams received on the eye from the object).

Leone Ebreo holds both necessary, but adds the further requirement that the eye must direct its beam a second time to make the form on the pupil tally with the object. Professor Gardner plausibly suggests that this passage may have stimulated Donne to create his two conceits 'of the twisting of the beams and the reflection of each in the other's pupils'. On the other hand, Professor Mario Praz quotes a passage from Bruno's *Candelaio* (I. x) in which the eye-beams of the two gazing lovers are actually said to meet, and light to join up with light (*John Donne*, Turin, 1958, p. 227). In neither case, however, do we actually *have* Donne's ingenious conceits of the *twisting* of the eye-beams, and the *threading* of the eyes upon one double string. This may be yet another instance of his originality. If the image be fully apprehended the result is *Grand-guignol*. So to take it would, I believe, disturb the tenor of the poem. It seems therefore preferable to take it simply as a diagrammatic optical conceit.

9 *So*] either (1) In that way, or (2) Therefore.

   intergraft] It is doubtful whether Donne meant 'intergraft' to be taken in a strictly horticultural way. In any case, no such two-way flow of sap as he would need for a perfect horticultural image would result from any known process of grafting. Probably therefore, 'intergraft' should be taken in a general figurative sense: 'fix in each other so as to produce a vital union'.

11 *on*] This vivid reading is clearly superior to that of the early editions.

   get] The sense is: 'beget'. Professor Gardner rightly reminds us that these pictures were called 'babies' from the pun on *pupilla*.

12 *propagation*] to be pronounced as five syllables.

13–17] The situation described is somewhat obscure. F. L. Lucas suggested to me that there may be some reminiscence of Homer's Zeus holding the scales of Hector and Achilles (*Iliad*, XXII. 209 ff.). Donne would certainly be familiar with this situation through the passage in *Aeneid*, XII. 725–7, where Virgil imitates the Homeric lines. Lines 13–17 of Donne's poem, however, taken together, seem to give a more active role to the two souls than that of mere destinies which are to be weighed. They seem at least to be parleying from their scale-pans. Indeed, their parleying appears to be neither more nor less than the unanimous 'Dialogue of One', which lasts from l. 29 to the end of the poem.

18] The lovers, who were sitting in l. 4, are now lying. What their precise 'postures' now are is left vague.

21–8] Donne here supposes a neo-Platonic lover who has grasped the essential fact that human love is a union of souls, but has still something to learn about love, which the souls of the two lovers can teach him if he pays good heed to what they say.

27 *concoction*] a purification or sublimation by heat, e.g. of metals in a furnace. According to a common belief at that time, the heat from the sun 'concocted' gold below the earth's surface (cf. *Sermons*, I. 163, 272).

29–36] The ecstasy enables the souls to have a true insight into the nature and cause of their love. It did not spring from physical passion, but from the need for each soul to complement its deficiencies.

32] The sense is: 'We can see that we did not see before what the cause of our love was' (cf. the similar, though not identical, points made in *A Valediction: forbidding mourning*, ll. 17–18, and *The Relic*, ll. 23–4).

33   *several*] separate.

36   *each this and that*] A somewhat obscure phrase, possibly meaning that there is no distinction of 'this' and 'that' between the two souls once love has united them, so that each can equally well be called 'this' or 'that'; alternatively, the meaning may be that by the working of love the two souls become qualitatively indistinguishable, both now consisting of precisely the same mixture of elements. The second interpretation seems to me the more probable.

37   –] I have supplied the dash to make clear that ll. 38–40 are to be taken together, and that 'violet' is not the subject of l. 40.

37–40] This seems a point additional to what has gone before. It foreshadows the point of ll. 41–4, viz. that by 'interinanimation' the two souls grow, as well as being mixed. The working of the image is not, however, wholly clear. Nothing corresponds to the other soul in the case of the violet. Professor Gardner suggests that Donne is referring to the doubling of single flowers by transplantation, a phenomenon referred to by Bacon and other contemporaries of Donne. I am somewhat doubtful whether anything so specific is being referred to here as the main point, since 'strength, colour, and size' are all in question; but it may be part of what Donne had in mind.

39] I have removed the parentheses from round this line for the same reasons as mentioned in note 37 ('All which' = 'All of which').

41–2] ? paralleling 'intergraft' (l. 9).

41–4] The process described in these lines is not clear. There seem at least two possible interpretations: (1) that the two souls are united to form one soul; (2) that the two souls are not actually united, but an oversoul comes into being as a result of their 'interinanimation'. Some support is lent to (2) by the plural 'intelligences' in l. 52; (1) seems in closer accord with ll. 33–48.

42] uses two souls to give a quickening of life to each other.

44] restrains the defects which the two separate souls had before union.

45–8] The argument seems desperately sophistical. The two souls already seem to have undergone change, so what good grounds could there be for believing that they will now be forever immune from it? Donne may have tried to play a trick by suddenly eliciting from an unwary reader the stock response that a soul must be exempt from mutability. On the other hand, it is possible that Donne is here expressing an insight (which we have, of course, to take on trust) that the two souls which are the 'atomies' are, in point of fact, immutable.

47   *atomies*] atoms.

50 *forbear*] do without, dispense with (*OED* 4).

51–2 *we are . . . sphere*] The sense is: 'we are related to our bodies as angels are related to the sphere they control'. In the Christianized Ptolemaic astronomy, various orders of angels each ruled one of the spheres from the moon's (first sphere) to the crystalline (ninth).

53–6] The lovers therefore owe their bodies gratitude, because the bodies yielded their forces, their powers of movement and perception, to the two lovers so that they could come to know each other. I do not believe that the meaning is that the bodies gave these powers up to the souls when these met in ecstasy. Surely such powers would be of little use to them in that state?

55] I feel sure that Grierson was right to prefer the reading of most MSS, 'forces, sense' to 'senses force', the reading of the early editions. After the privilege of discussion with him, moreover, I was quite convinced by his explanation of 'forces, sense' to mean 'their forces, namely sense', in distinction from the mental forces of the *soul*.

56 *dross*] the scum of molten metals, which is a waste product.
   allay] 'The metal of a baser kind mixed in coins to harden them, that they may wear less' (Dr Johnson's *Dictionary*). The modern form is, of course, 'alloy'.

57–8] The sense is: 'The planets and stars can only exert their influences on man by first affecting the air.' Grierson quotes a passage from Du Bartas dated 1581, which refers to Pliny's *Natural History*, Plutarch, Plato and Aristotle, for opinions on the point.

59–60] In Scholastic cosmology the planets and stars were considered to be guided by intelligences which were superior to human souls. In a sense, therefore, 'heaven's influence' on man was the influence of one spiritual substance on another. This fact reveals the parallel with the interaction of human souls through the medium of body.

   Grierson points out that Aquinas himself did not accept the view that intelligences act on man mediately and controllingly. He considered that they illuminated the human intellect without influencing the will (*Gr*, II, p. 44; cf. Aquinas, *Summa Theologica*, I. cxv. 4). It seems to me, then, more natural to suppose that Donne was not referring here to Aquinas's distinction, which would blur his point.

60 *repair*] goes to, resorts to.

61–4] 'Spirits' were thought of as a thin vapour or rarefied liquid, very active in character, either extracted from the blood or a thin part of it, which acted on the soul to produce sensations, and was used by the soul to perform bodily actions. There were various kinds of 'spirits', according to the part of the body in which they had their origin. A clear account of 'spirits' appears in Descartes in the *Principia* and in the *Traité des Passions*. Grierson quotes a passage from Burton's *Anatomy of Melancholy*, 1638, in which it is stated that 'spirits' were currently held either to form a *medium* between soul and body, or, as by Paracelsus, to constitute a fourth soul. There are, however, some passages from a much earlier work, Timothy Bright's *Treatise of Melancholy*, 1586, which are in places strikingly close to this quatrain. Bright writes that God made man's body a 'tabernacle', which contained by his blessing 'a spirituall thing of greater excellencie, then the redde earth, which offered it self to the eye only', and he continues:

> This is that which Philosophers call the spirit: which spirit, so prepareth that worke to the receavinge of the soule, that with more agrement, the soule, and body, have growne into acquaintance: and is ordained of God, as it were a true love knot, to couple heaven and earth together . . .
>
> (p. 34)

and somewhat later:

> . . . without this spirite, no creature could give us sustentation. For it is a knot, to joyne both our soules and bodies together: so nothing of other nature can have corporall conjunction with us, except their spirites with ours first growe into acquaintance. . . .
>
> (pp. 35–6)

and again:

> . . . the soul inspired from God . . . not fettered with the bodie . . . but handfasted therwith, by that golden claspe of the spirite: . . .
>
> (p. 36)

63 *need*] meaning 'are needful' (*OED* I. 3), as the punctuation here adopted from some MSS (e.g. *D*, *SP*) clearly brings out.

63–4] The sense is: 'Because such almost immaterial fingers are needed to tie that extremely complex and elusive knot, holding body and soul together, which makes us into human beings with all our human functions.' (Descartes thought the knot was tied in the pineal gland.) For a passage in the Sermons parallelling the quatrain, cf: 'In our naturall persons, the body and soul do not make a perfect man, except they be united, except our spirits (which are the active part of the blood) do fit this body and soule for one another's working' (*Sermons*, VI. 128).

64] The term *'nodo'* ('knot') for the link between soul and body is used by F. Cattani in one of the sixteenth-century Italian love-treatises, *I Tre Libri d'Amore*, Vinegia, 1561, p. 111, quoted by A. J. Smith, 'The metaphysic of love', *RES* n.s. 9 (1958), p. 366.

66 *affections*] emotions, feelings.
   faculties] powers of action.

67] i.e. within the reach of the senses.

68 *a great Prince*] possibly, as critics and scholars generally hold, the soul; but possibly Love, which can only be set free in the human sphere through the

medium of bodies; and can only be revealed to others (ll. 69–72) in bodily action.

69 *turn*] return (*OED* 21 obs.).

70 *Weak men*] i.e. people who are unable to sustain their faith in love without some outward manifestation of its mysteries.

73–6] i.e. a true lover, having heard the 'dialogue', will observe that the quality of their love once the souls have returned to their bodies will remain the same as they have claimed it to be.

74 *Dialogue of One*] a paradoxical phrase referring to the fact that the two souls were speaking as one.

The Good-morrow

I wonder, by my troth, what thou and I
Did, till we lov'd; were we not wean'd till then?
But suck'd on country pleasures, childishly?
Or snorted we in the Seven Sleepers' den?
'Twas so; but this, all pleasures fancies be: 5
If ever any beauty I did see,
Which I desir'd, and got, 'twas but a dream of thee.

And now good-morrow to our waking souls,
Which watch not one another out of fear;
For love, all love of other sights controls,   10
And makes one little room, an everywhere.
Let sea-discoverers to new worlds have gone,
Let maps to others, worlds on worlds have shown,
Let us possess our world; each hath one, and is one.

My face in thine eye, thine in mine appears,   15
And true plain hearts do in the faces rest;
Where can we find two better hemispheres,
Without sharp North, without declining West?
Whatever dies, was not mix'd equally;
If our two loves be one, or, thou and I   20
Love so alike, that none do slacken, none can die.

In 1633–1719. Cy omits.

Text: Title The good-morrow *1633–
1669.* The Good-morrow *1719. The good
morrow variously capitalized II; DC, S962.
Titles added in later hands: The Good Morrow L74. The Godd Morrow Dob. Elegy
S96. No title other MSS collated.*

2 lov'd; *some MSS incl. TCC, A18, N;
L74; Wed; Dob; HK2, B, S.* lov'd,
*1633–35; other MSS incl. H49, C57;
H40; TCD; S96, O'F; A25, D17;
S962.* lov'd? *1639–1719; Gr; Ed
(1956); Gar.*

3 But suck'd on country pleasures,
childishly *1633–54; MSS, sometimes
without comma: I (C57* country . . .
childishly *altered to* childish . . . sillily);
H40; Wed; DC. But suck'd on childish
pleasures, sillily *(variously punctuated) II;
Dob; P, D17, B, S; S962; 1669–1719.*
But suck'd one childish pleasures sillily
L74; HK2 *(but those MSS often spell* on
as one)*. But suck'd one childish
pleasure sillily S96. But suck'd on
childish pleasure sillily Lut, O'F. Or
suck'd we childish pleasures sillily
A25.*

4 snorted *1633–54; I (C57 altered to*
slumbred); *H40; Wed; DC; III; HK2,
S.* slumb(e)r(e)d *II; L74; A25, P, D17;
S962; 1669–1719. line om. B.*

10 For *1633–1719; I; H40; Wed; DC; III;
D17.* But *II; L74; HK2, A25, P, B, S;
S962.*

227

11 one *1633–1719; I; H40; Wed; DC; III; S.* a *II; L74; HK2, A25, P, B; S962.* no *D17.*

13 to others, worlds on worlds *(some MSS without comma) I; H40; II (excl. A18); Wed; DC; III (Lut possibly* on world.*); HK2, B; Ed (1956); Gar.* to other, worlds on worlds *1633–54; Gr.* to other worlds our world *1669–1719.* to other worlds one world *P, D17, S (but reads* mapp*).* in studies, worlds on worlds *A25.* to other worlds, on worlds *A18.* to others worlds, on worlds *S962.* to others worlds, one worlds *L74 (which often reads* one *meaning* on*).*

14 our *all MSS excl. I; D17; Gar.* one *1633–1719; I; D17; Gr; Ed (1956).*

16 true plain] plain true *II; L74; HK2, A25, P, B; S962.*

17 better *1633; I; H40; Wed; DC; D17; Gr.* fitter *II; L74; III; HK2, A25, P, B, S; S962; 1635–1719.*

19 was *1633–54, 1719; I; H40; Wed; DC; III; D17, S.* is *II; L74; HK2, A25, P, B; S962; 1669.*

20 If our two *1633–1719; I; H40; Wed; DC; III; D17, S.* If both our *II; L74; HK2, A25, B; S962.* If our both *P.* or, *1633; MSS, some without comma: I; II; L74; Wed; DC; S96, Dob; A25, B; S962; Gr.* as *H40.* both *Lut, O'F; HK2, P, D17; 1635–1719.* and *S.*

21 Love so alike, that none do slacken, none can die *1633; I; H40; Wed; DC; Gr; Gar.* Love just alike in all, none of these loves can die *II (; after all); L74 (;); III; HK2, A25 (;), P (no stop), D17, B (:), S (.); S962 (;); 1635–1719; Ed (1956).*

Textual note. Grierson suggested (II, p. 10) that the MSS point to 'two distinct recensions of this poem', and Professor Gardner (*ESS*, p. 197) rightly draws attention to the fact that there are 'clearly two traditions in manuscript, *H40* and Group I reading against *L74*, Group II, *HK2, P, A25* in ll. 3, 4, 10, 11, 16, 17, 19, 20 and 21'. She adds that 'in ll. 3, 17 and 21 *H40* and Group I stand alone (except for the support of *JC* in l. 17)', but that 'otherwise they have the support of Group III'. These observations on the MS readings substantially stand, but need some modification. Professor Gardner might have pointed out that *DC* supports the Group I readings in ll. 3, 4, 10, 11, 16, 17, 19, 20 and 21. I am, moreover, now able to add that *Wed* also supports these Group I readings. Grierson's suggestion that there were two distinct 'recensions' of the poem is very reasonable; and so is the further possibility, mentioned by Professor Gardner as an alternative, that there were three stages, the first being represented by the ancestor of *L74*, Group II and the other manuscripts supporting them, the second being represented by the ancestor of Group III, and the third being represented by the ancestor of Group I and *H40*. There is, however, the additional possibility that the Group I version was toned down in certain places at some stage, to avoid indecency or coarseness. This hypothesis may receive some support from a fact which Professor Gardner does not mention, namely, that in *C57* ll. 3 and 4 are altered to the Group II version. This omission in Professor Gardner's edition was pointed out in Professor Mark Roberts's able review article 'If it were Donne when 'tis done . . .', *EC* 16 (1966), where he argues for the view that the Group I version was the earlier, and was later altered to that of Group II.

In the text printed here I follow the *1633*, Group I readings in ll. 3, 4, 10,

11, 16, 17, 19 and 20. Those readings seem to me far stronger in ll. 3 and 4 than those of Group II, and somewhat stronger or more appropriate in lines 11, 17, 19 and 20; and possibly also, though more doubtfully, in l. 10. In l. 16 there does not seem much to choose. For l. 21, the *1633* Group I version now seems to me possibly superior, for the reasons given in my note below, and I have therefore printed it.

Whether the Group I or the Group II readings were the earlier is controversial. On the assumption that the revisions were Donne's own, it would seem more likely that Group II represents the earlier version. If only ll. 3 and 4 were in question, however, the view that the earlier recension of the poem was that found in Group I would have considerable attraction; but in view of the superiority of Group I in ll. 11, 17 and 19, where no such moral considerations are involved, that hypothesis seems less plausible. Yet it is still necessary to take account of Professor Roberts's point that in *C57* ll. 3 and 4 are altered to the Group II version. One possible explanation might be that the scribe of *C57*, either at the time he was first copying or subsequently, referred to a MS containing the Group II version and copied it in as an alteration, in the belief that it represented a change authorized or made by Donne himself. If so, his belief might have been right or might have been wrong; we cannot say which, in our present state of knowledge. In any case, however, it would seem more likely that the recension of the poem found in Group II is the earlier, even if its version of ll. 3 and 4 were subsequently restored by Donne for moral reasons.

2   *lov'd;*] The lack of MS support for the question mark suggests that the right reading is a stop reflecting a meditative tone. The semicolon seems most appropriate, especially for a modern edition.

3   *country*] primarily 'rustic', and, therefore, unrefined as compared with the pleasures of the Court or City. There would, however, probably be an inevitable sexual overtone (cf. 'country matters' in *Hamlet*, III. ii. 117).

3]   The *1633*, Group I version seems far superior to that of Groups II, III and V, which may well have been the original version, strengthened later. Yet one cannot rule out the possibility that Donne or someone else may still later have found the sexual suggestion inadmissible, and have reverted to the weaker line to preserve decency.

4   *snorted*] i.e. snored. Clearly the stronger reading, which, since *S* has it, must have existed before 19 July 1620, the date at the end of that MS. But since *L74* agrees with Group II, and *A25*, *P* and *D17* also read 'slumbered', that was probably the earlier version, though again one cannot exclude the possibility that 'snorted' was later altered back to 'slumbered' by Donne or some other reviser, to avoid coarseness. The fact that Group III read 'snorted' could, as Professor Gardner says, be explained in two ways, either (1) the ancestor of Group III was a copy of the corrected version incorporating most but not all the corrections already made to the original version of the poem; or (2) the ancestor of Group III

incorporated all the corrections made up till that time, but further corrections were made later, and included in the ancestor of *H40* and Group I.

Seven Sleepers' den] The Seven Sleepers were the heroes of a celebrated legend translated from the Syriac by Gregory of Tours, and included in his *De Gloria Martyrum*. The story tells that in A D 250 or 251 during the persecution of the Christians by the Emperor Decius, seven Christian youths from Ephesus took refuge in a cave in a nearby mountain. Their pursuers walled up the entrance of the cave, with the intention of starving them to death; but the young men fell into a miraculous sleep, from which they did not wake until some time during the reign of Theodosius II (possibly A D 439 or 446). When they woke they thought they had only been asleep for a single night, and one of them, who went to the city for food, was amazed to find on the churches and other buildings, the cross which, when he had fallen asleep, had been an object of execration.

5 *but*] except.

10 *For*] better than 'But', which might suggest a contrast with l. 9 which would work against the true sense.

10] 'For love inhibits all desire to see other people or things.'

11 *one*] makes for a more meaningful and fuller-sounding line than 'a'.

13 *others*] The MS authority for 'others' is decisive; but the *1633–54* reading 'other' adopted by Grierson was a current form of the plural in Donne's time.

    worlds] Either 'continents', or 'worlds' in a sense which would include celestial bodies.

13] 'Allow maps to have revealed worlds on worlds to other people.'

14 *our*] clearly the right reading. I drew attention to it in 1956, but did not then realize how overwhelmingly the MSS supported it. *DC* and *Wed* can now be added to the support cited by Professor Gardner.

    each hath one, and is one] 'each has the world of the other, and is also the other's world'.

17 *better*] Grierson held this reading more appropriate than 'fitter', which would suggest the correspondence of the hemispheres (a matter already covered in stanza 2), whereas what is now in point is that these hemispheres are not liable to coldness or to decline.

18] 'Without the North, with its bitter cold, and without the West, where the sun goes down', i.e. our love is subject neither to coldness nor to decline.

19 *was*] somewhat the better reading, since the mixing took place before the hypothetical death, and 'is' inevitably tends to be taken as a present tense.

19] Grierson aptly quotes from Aquinas (*Summa Theologica*, I, Qu. lxxv. Art. 6) a passage stating that corruption only occurs where there is contrariety.

20 *If our two*] better than 'If both our', since there is some awkwardness in supposing 'both' to be 'one'.

21] Neither of the two variants seems to me wholly satisfactory. If, as I am now inclined to believe, the reading of Group II, *L74*, and the other MSS agreeing with them, is earlier than that of Group I, *H40*, and the MSS agreeing with them, then whoever revised the line must have had some improvement in mind. It seems possible that loving 'just alike in all' may have seemed too vague – not to have focused attention sharply enough on the matter of the intensity of the lovers' love; but there may have been some other reason for the revision. On the other hand, the Group I version is open to the objection that, on the one hand, there seems nothing to prevent two precisely similar loves both slackening to a precisely similar degree; while, on the other hand, if 'loving so alike' necessarily excluded that case, by precluding the possibility of slackening at all, then the mention of slackening would be redundant to the point of absurdity. Donne demands this close kind of reading, and his work usually repays it handsomely. In the present case, however, I cannot help feeling that something may have gone wrong, and prevented this otherwise magnificent poem from achieving a truly satisfying ending. In any case, however, it seems reasonable to ask what 'none' (l. 21) means on the Group I reading. This is a question that may well not occur on a loose reading of the line. Yet looked at closely 'none do slacken' seems most naturally to mean 'neither of us slackens (in our love)'. I believe, however, that 'none do slacken' is most often taken to mean 'neither of *our* loves slackens'. This seems to me to make the construction very awkward. Yet if 'none' in 'none do slacken' refers to the lovers, then 'none' in 'none can die' must surely most probably also refer to the lovers? Now, in that case, what the final lines of the poem will be saying is that if the lovers' love be actually a complete unity, *or* they love so similarly that neither of them slackens off in relation to the other's love, then the *lovers* can never die, i.e. they will achieve immortality. That would certainly give a strong meaning to the final lines, and could well afford a good reason for revising the *L74*, Group II reading in l. 21. It might be contended that l. 19 would more naturally refer to a mixture of loves rather than of lovers; but such a point is far from certain. In *The Ecstasy* there is talk of the mixture and even re-mixture of 'souls' (l. 35), so why should l. 19 of this poem not refer to the 'mixing' (i.e. intermingling) of the lovers? Yet even if 'none' be taken to refer to the 'love(s)' rather than the lovers, though the construction becomes awkward, and there remains some logical difficulty, I prefer now to adopt the Group I reading, since I believe it may represent a revision by Donne, even though not a wholly satisfactory one.

19–21] On the bolder hypothesis the lines as here printed could mean roughly: 'Everything that dies contains some element of contrariety. If our two loves are either numerically one, or if we each love so similarly that neither slackens in love relative to the other, then neither of us can come to an end [i.e. we shall achieve immortality].'

The Sun Rising

Busy old fool, unruly Sun,
      Why dost thou thus,
Through windows, and through curtains, call on us?
Must to thy motions lovers' seasons run?
          Saucy pedantic wretch, go chide   5
          Late schoolboys, and sour prentices,
   Go tell court-huntsmen that the King will ride,
   Call country ants to harvest offices;
Love, all alike, no season knows, nor clime,
Nor hours, days, months, which are the rags of time.   10

Thy beams, so reverend and strong
      Why shouldst thou think?
I could eclipse and cloud them with a wink,
But that I would not lose her sight so long:
          If her eyes have not blinded thine,   15
          Look, and tomorrow late, tell me
   Whether both Indias, of spice, and mine,
   Be where thou leftst them, or lie here with me.
Ask for those Kings whom thou saw'st yesterday,
And thou shalt hear: 'All here in one bed lay.'   20

She is all States, and all Princes I,
      Nothing else is:
Princes do but play us; compar'd to this,
All honour's mimic, all wealth alchemy.
          Thou, sun, art half as happy as we,   25
          In that the world's contracted thus;
   Thine age asks ease, and since thy duties be
   To warm the world, that's done in warming us.
Shine here to us, and thou art everywhere;
This bed thy centre is, these walls, thy sphere.   30

In 1633–1719. H40 omits.
Text: Title The Sun Rising *1633–1719.*
Sun Rising *II.* Sun-Rising *DC.* To the Sun
Lec, C57; HK2, Cy. Ad Solem *H49, D, SP;*
S96; S. Ad Solem. A Song *Dob; A25.* Ad
Solem. To the Sun. Song. *Lut, O'F.* Song
ad Solem *S962. No title Wed; P, D17, B.*
Sun Rising *added in L74 in another hand.*
  6 sour(e) *or* sowre] slow *Cy, P, D17, B*
   (corrected from soore*).* soare *A25.*

7 will] doth *II; L74.*

17 Indias, of spice, and mine, *Ed.*
the'India's of spice and Myne *1633;*
Gr; Gar. the Indias of spice and mine
Ed (1956). There is no MS support for the
article except in S and S962.

19 whom(e)] which *II; III; A25, P, D17,*

S; *S962.*

21] She is all Princes and all states; I *Dob;*
S962 (comma after states). She is all
Princes and States: I *S96.* She is all
Princes and States, *(word deleted)* I *S.*
She is all States all Princes I *HK2.*

General note. It is probable that the idea of this poem was suggested to Donne
by Ovid, *Amores,* I. xiii; but, if it was, Donne has made many startlingly
original departures.

Ovid upbraids Aurora, asking her why he and his mistress should be disturbed in their embraces just because she wanted to get away from her old and
decrepit husband Tithonus. Ovid instances the ill-effects the dawn brings:
sailors could have navigated better by the stars; people on journeys had now to
rise, however tired; soldiers had to begin to fight again; men had to start tilling
the fields with heavy mattocks; oxen had once again to submit to the yoke;
schoolboys had to wake up, and go to the master who might cut their hands
with the cane; sureties had to appear in court, and perhaps pay over great sums;
lawyers had to take up new cases; women to begin their new weaving. All this,
however, the poet could put up with; but not that girls should have to leave the
bed of love. If Aurora had an attractive husband she wouldn't be up so early to
spoil their fun. And Ovid rounds off his poem neatly: Aurora had heard, and
blushed, but day came no later than usual.

It is really only in stanza 1 that Donne keeps close to Ovid. The rest of the
poem, with its bold hyperboles, its transvaluation of worldly values, and its
patronizing indication to the sun that his sphere is the lovers' bedroom, is
Donne's own brilliant invention. Even in stanza 1, however, Donne's originality is evident. The sun is contemptuously apostrophized as an old busybody.
He is *told* to chide the late schoolboys (and Donne adds the 'sour prentices'), to
get the court-huntsmen moving (another fresh touch), to activate the antlike
farm-labourers. Donne thus makes the contrast between other lives and those
of the lovers sharper and deeper than had Ovid.

Professor Wolfgang Clemen offers a highly interesting detailed comparison
between Donne's poem, Lodge's 'My Phillis hath the morning sun . . .',
1593, and Sidney's Madrigal 'Why dost thou haste away, / O Titan fair, the
giver of the day?', *c.* 1598 (see Charles S. Singleton (ed.), *Art, Science, and*
History in the Renaissance, Baltimore, 1968, pp. 423–33).

The sardonic belittling of mundane activities matches that in *The Canoniza-*
tion. As for the declaration of the inferiority of the sun to the beloved, this goes
back at least as far as Petrarch, but W. von Koppenfels (op. cit., pp. 65–6)
draws a close contrast with Sidney's 'Why dost thou haste away, / O Titan
fair, the giver of the day?'. Professor H. M. Richmond ('Donne and Ronsard',
N&Q 203 (1958), pp. 534–5, and *The School of Love,* Princeton, 1964, p. 232)

cites a similarly contemptuous apostrophe to the sun by Ronsard in Sonnet 100 of the *Amours de Cassandre*:

> Va te cacher, vieil pastoureau champestre,
> Tu n'es pas digne au Ciel d'estre un flambeau,
> Mais un bouvier qui meine les boeufs paistre.
> (*Oeuvres complètes*, ed. G. Cohen, Paris, 1950, vol. I, p. 42)

7] Professor Praz suggested long ago that this was a reference to James I's addiction to hunting, which made his attendants rise earlier than they would have wished. A French agent wrote of James *c*. 1584, long before he came to the English throne: 'He prefers hunting to all other amusements, and will be six hours together on horseback.'

8 *country ants*] farm-labourers.
offices] tasks.

9 *Love, all alike*] love, which is unchanging.

10 *the rags of time*] The meaning is probably: 'the mere tattered clothing of time'; or, alternatively, 'the shreds into which time is torn up and sub-divided'. John Hayward (in the Nonesuch Donne) refers to a sermon in which Donne, speaking of God's mercy, says: 'The names of first or last derogate from it, for first and last are but rags of time, and his mercy hath no relation to time, no limitation in time, it is not first nor last, but eternal, everlasting' (*Sermons*, VI. 170).

15–23] It is noteworthy that the thought of ll. 15–23 strongly resembles that of parts of stanzas 2 and 3 of *The Anniversary*.

17 *both Indias, of spice, and mine*] There is no MS support for an article before 'Indias' except in *S* and *S962*. The punctuation printed here is found in several MSS, e.g. *H49*, *L74*, *S96*, *DC*. The two 'Indias' are the East Indies and the West Indies respectively. Cf. a letter from Donne to Sir Robert Ker, *c*. 1624: 'Your way into *Spain* was Eastward, and that is the way to the land of Perfumes and Spices; their way hither is Westward, and that is the way to the land of Gold, and of Mynes' (Nonesuch Donne, pp. 481–2).

19–20, 21–2, 23–4] On a close reading these three passages seem to involve some contradiction. In ll. 19–20 the lovers are both 'Kings' ('rulers'), whereas in ll. 21–2 male dominance has asserted itself. Yet in l. 23 the beloved has become a ruler once more!

21] 'She is all the states there are, and I am all the princes there are'.

24 *alchemy*] mere counterfeit.

27–8] Condescendingly considerate!

30] 'This bed is the centre of your orbit, and these walls the outer shell within which your orbit is described.'

Break of Day

'Tis true, 'tis day,—what though it be?
Oh, wilt thou therefore rise from me?
Why should we rise? Because 'tis light?
Did we lie down because 'twas night?
Love, which in despite of darkness brought us hither,   5
Should in despite of light hold us together.

Light hath no tongue, but is all eye;
If it could speak as well as spy,
This is the worst that it could say,
That, being well, I fain would stay,   10
And that I love my heart and honour so,
That I would not from him, which hath them, go.

Must business thee from hence remove?
Oh, that's the worst disease of love;
The poor, the foul, the false, love can   15
Admit, but not the busied man.
He that hath business, and makes love, doth do
Such wrong, as if a married man should woo.

In 1633–1719. Cy omits. First printed in William Corkine's 'Second Book of Ayres', 1612.
Text: Title Break of Day *1633–1719; II; DC.* Sonnet III; *S962.* A Song *A25.*

2 Oh, *Ed.* Oh! *S.* O *1633 and some MSS; Gr; Gar.*
   O wilt thou therefore *1633–1719; DC; Dob; A25; S962 (therefore inserted).* Wilt thou therefore *II; L74; Wed; S96; HK2, P.* O wilt thou *I; H40; S (Oh!).* And will you therefore *Lut, O'F; B.* Will you therefore *D17.*
3 rise? *so punctuated in some MSS.* rise, *1633–1719.*
5 Love, which in despite *1650–4; I; H40; DC; S; S962.* Love, that in despite *II; L74; Wed.* Love, which in spite *1633–9; 1669–1719; III; HK2, A25, P, D17, B; Gr; Ed (1956); Gar.*

6 hold *II; L74; Wed; S96; HK2; Ed (1956).* keep *1633–1719; I; H40; DC; Dob, Lut, O'F; A25, P, D17, B, S; S962; Gr; Gar.*
7–12 *om. SP.*
9 is *II; L74; Wed; III; HK2, P, S; S962; Ed (1956).* were *1633–1719; H49, D, Lec, C57; H40; DC; A25, D17, B; Gr; Gar.*
11 love *II; L74; Wed; III; A25 (possibly corrected from lov'd, but possibly vice versa), P, D17, B; Ed (1956).* lov'd *1633–1719; H49, D, Lec, C57; H40; DC; HK2, S; S962.*
12 which hath *II; L74, Wed.* that hath *III; HK2, A25, P, D17, B; Ed (1956).* which had *H49, D, Lec, C57; H40; DC; S962.* that had *1633–1719; S; Gr; Gar.*
15 foul] fool *Lec, C57; H40.*
17 that *TC, N; L74, Wed; Lut, O'F;*

HK2, A25, P, D17, B; S962. which
1633–1719; I; H40; DC; S96, Dob; S;
Gr; Ed (1956); Gar. om. A18.
18 if . . . should II; L74; Wed; Lut, O'F;

HK2, P, D17, B; Ed (1956). when . . .
doth 1633; I; H40; DC; S96, Dob; A25,
S; S962; 1669–1719; Gr; Gar. when
. . . should 1635–54.

General note. Exceptionally for Donne, the poem is put into the mouth of the woman. E. K. Chambers pointed out (*Early English Lyrics*, 1907) that popular love-songs often took this form. As Grierson says, this particular poem is clearly descended from the popular *aube*, a lyric dialogue of lovers parting at dawn. The *aube* was originally Provençal.

The poem was first printed in William Corkine's *Second Book of Ayres*, 1612. For the attractively lively setting see Helen Gardner (*ESS*, p. 243). The text there diverges sharply from those in *1633*, and also almost all MSS, except *B*. (For further information see Appendix XII, p. 341.)

2 *Oh,*] *S*'s reading 'Oh!' brings out best that the word is not vocative but emotionally exclamatory. Yet the exclamation mark seems to break the run of the line too sharply.

3 *rise?*] This punctuation makes the line more lively, and avoids what might be monotony of structure if ll. 3 and 4 were punctuated alike.

5 *Love, which in despite*] The weight of MS authority favours 'despite' against 'spite' and 'which' against 'that'. 'Despite' also gives a slightly stronger force to 'which'. Yet it makes the line less regular, and it is arguable that 'spite' is a strong word, and that 'despite' could have been caught from l. 6.

6 *hold*] I still prefer the physically stronger and more unusual 'hold', and it seems sufficiently supported to warrant reading it against the balance of MS authority.

9 *is*] If, as I believe, it is better to adopt the Group II readings for ll. 11 and 12, then the present is preferable here.

11 *love*] seems better than 'lov'd', which might misleadingly suggest that the love was a thing of the past. The present tense also gives greater vividness.

12 *which hath*] MS authority strongly favours 'which'; and the present tense seems better, for the same reasons as for 'love' in l. 11.

13–18] Grierson quotes: 'It is a good definition of ill-love, that St Chrysostom gives, that it is *Animae vacantis passio*, a passion of an empty soul, of an idle mind. For fill a man with business, and he hath no room for such love' (*Sermons*, IV. 121). This is one of a multitude of cases where we find thoughts and images used in the *Songs and Sonets* surviving in Donne's religious writings.

17 *that*] MS evidence is evenly divided, and, as I have generally followed Group II, there seems no good reason for departing from it here.

18 *if . . . should*] The Group II version seems superior because (1) it avoids repeating 'doth', and (2) it makes the ending of the poem sharper. *1635–54* fall between two stools here.

The Canonization

For God's sake hold your tongue, and let me love,
  Or chide my palsy, or my gout,
My five gray hairs, or ruin'd fortune flout,
    With wealth your state, your mind with arts improve,
      Take you a course, get you a place,   5
      Observe his Honour, or his Grace,
And the King's real, or his stampèd face
  Contémplate; what you will, approve,
      So you will let me love.

Alas, alas, who's injured by my love?   10
  What merchant's ships have my sighs drown'd?
Who says my tears have overflow'd his ground?
    When did my colds a forward spring remove?
      When did those heats which my veins fill
      Add one man to the plaguy bill?   15
Soldiers find wars, and lawyers find out still
  Litigious men, which quarrels move,
      Though she and I do love.

Call us what you will, we are made such by love;
  Call her one, me another fly,   20
We are tapers too, and at our own cost die,
  And we in us find the Eagle and the Dove.

In 1633–1719. L74; A25 omit. S962 contains two disparate texts which I shall call S962A and S962B.

Text: Title The Canonization *1633–39; I; II; DC; Lut, O'F; HK2, Cy, P.* Canonization *Wed; S; 1650–1719.* Canonizatio *S96, Dob; S962A. No title H40; D17, B; S962B.*

3 five] true *1635–54.* fine *III; Cy, P; S962A.*
  fortune] fortunes *D17; S962A; 1669–1719.*

4 your mind with art(e)s] your mind with art(e) *H40; P; S962A.* with artes

your myndes *Wed; Dob* (minds); *.with* arte your minde *Cy.* with arts your minde *S962B.* with minds your art *HK2.*

6 Honour . . . Grace] *caps in 1719.*

7 And *MSS; Gar.* Or *1633–1719; Gr; Ed (1956).*

14 those *II; Wed; Dob, HK2, Cy, P, D17, S; S962A.* the *1633–1719; I; H40; DC; S96, Lut, O'F; B; S962B; Gr; Ed (1956); Gar.*

15 man *MSS (excl. Lec, C57); Ed (1956); Gar.* more *1633–1719; Lec, C57; Gr.*

The Phoenix riddle hath more wit
  By us; we two being one, are it.
So, to one neutral thing both sexes fit,   25
  We die, and rise the same, and prove
    Mysterious by this love.

We can die by it, if not live by love,
  And if unfit for tomb or hearse
Our legend be, it will be fit for verse;   30
  And if no piece of chronicle we prove,
    We'll build in sonnets pretty rooms;
    As well a well-wrought urn becomes
The greatest ashes, as half-acre tombs,
  And by these hymns, all shall approve   35
    Us *canoniz'd* for Love:

And thus invoke us: 'You, whom reverend love
  Made one another's hermitage;
You, to whom love was peace, that now is rage;
  Who did the whole world's soul extract, and drove   40
    Into the glasses of your eyes
    (So made such mirrors, and such spies,
That they did all to you epitomize)
  Countries, towns, courts: beg from above
    A pattern of your love!'   45

24 two] *om. III*
punctuation: it. *1633–69; I; Wed; Dob;
D17; Gr; Ed (1956).* it: *O'F; 1719.* it;
TCD, N; Chambers. it, *Lut; B; Gar.* it
*H40; TCC (seemingly), A18; DC; S96;
HK2 (seemingly), Cy, P, S; S962A;
S962B.*
25 So, *1633–39; S96; Chambers; Gar.* So
*other MSS; 1650–1719; Gr; Ed (1956).
P omits.*
fit, *H49, D, SP, Lec; Gr; Ed (1956).* fit;
Wed; Dob. fit. *1633–1719; C57; Lut,
O'F; B, S; Chambers; Gar.* fit *H40; II;
DC; S96; HK2, Cy, P, D17; S962A,
S962B.*

26 We die, *H49, Lec; TCC, N; Wed; S96,
O'F; S.* We die *1633–1719; other MSS
incl. H40; TCD, A18; HK2, D17;
S962A; Gr; Ed (1956); Gar.*
28–36] *B omits.*
29 tomb(e) *II; Lut, O'F; HK2, Cy, P,
D17, S; 1669–1719.* tomb(e)s *1633–
54; I; H40; Wed; DC; S96, Dob;
S962A, S962B; Gr; Ed (1956); Gar.*
or *H40; II; Wed; III; HK2, Cy, P, D17,
S; S962A; 1669–1719; Gar.* and
1633–54; I; DC; S962B; Gr; Ed (1956).
30 legend *II; Wed; III; HK2, Cy, P, D17,
S; S962A; 1635–1719; Gr.* legends
1633; I; H40; DC; S962B.

35 these hymn(e)s] those hymn(e)s *DC;*
S96, Lut, O'F; Cy; 1635–1719. this
hymne *Dob (with* those hymnes *in*
margin as alternative or correction);
S962A (Himne).
37–45] *TCD* omits. *(possibly on a missing*
sheet).
40 extract *MSS; Gar.* contract *1633–*

1719; *Gr; Ed (1956).*
drove] draw(e) *I; DC; HK2, Cy, P, B;*
S962B. have *H40.*
42–3] *brackets Gr.*
45 your *H40; II; III; HK2, Cy, P, D17,*
B; S962A, S962B; 1669; Gr. our
1633–54, 1719; I; Wed; DC; S (a
modern hand has inserted an initial y).

General note. Refusal to comply with interfering advice not to love had a long
history in lyric poetry stretching back to the Troubadours; but the vigour of
Donne's exasperation and the realism of the first two stanzas are typically
individual.

2 *Or . . . or*] Either . . . or.
2–3] The sense is: 'If you *must* speak, vent your malice on me in some other
way than by interfering with my love.'
4 *state*] probably primarily, 'status'.
5 *Take you a course*] Start a career.
place] post at Court.
6 *Honour . . . Grace*] Professor A. J. Smith rightly innovates among modern
editors by printing with capitals. *1719* prints capitals, and a few MSS, e.g.
C57, N, Dob, O'F, Cy, S, have a capital 'G' for 'Grace'.
6] The sense is: 'Pay court to some lesser or greater nobleman' (so climbing
the social ladder).
7] i.e. frequent the Court, or go in for money-making.
King's] almost certainly dating the poem after James I's accession in 1603.
8 *approve*] try.
9 *So*] The sense is: 'if only', or 'so long as'.
13] thereby damaging the farmers.
colds] probably 'chills of depression', when his love seemed unrequited.
14 *those*] This Group II reading, which is well supported, seems slightly
preferable, on the principle that the harder reading is to be preferred
(*difficilior lectio potior*), and also as giving a fuller sounding line.
15 *plaguy bill*] bill of mortality from the plague. 1603 and 1604 were both
plague years.
17 *which quarrels move*] who stir up quarrels.
19–27] Professor Guss (op. cit., pp. 72–3) draws our attention to an interesting combination in Guarini (Madrigal 37) of 'moth' (actually 'butterfly')
and phoenix images. Guarini claims that, though he dies like a butterfly in
the fire of his lady's eyes, the heat is fortunate for him, for although he will
die as a butterfly he will rise as a phoenix. Guarini was actually combining
the butterfly image found in Petrarch (*Canz.* 141) with the phoenix image
also found in Petrarch (*Canz.* 135) (see note on l. 23, below). As Professor

Guss later points out (p. 161), however, the two images had already occurred together in pre-Petrarchan poetry, in a poem by the Sicilian poet Jacopo da Lentini.

20 *fly*] probably here a moth; but the word could at that time be used very generally for any winged insect. Donne uses the same image in *Elegy VI*, ll. 17–19:

> . . . so, the taper's beamy eye
> Amorously twinkling beckons the giddy fly,
> Yet burns his wings; . . .

A. B. Chambers (*JEGP* 65, 1966) argues that the reference is to the taper-fly 'which burns itself to death by approaching a flame' and 'was considered hermaphroditic and resurrectable'. This would certainly lead naturally on to the phoenix image.

21 *We are*] The slur helps to indicate that the emphasis is to be placed not on 'we' but on 'tapers too'.
tapers] wax candles.

21] The sense is possibly: 'Each of us is a candle as well as a moth, and each of us is therefore burnt by the other, but the one who kills does so at his or her own cost' (for the candles are always diminishing). I owe this suggestion to Grierson in discussion. If the explanation is right, there may also be a reference here to the popular belief that the act of love diminishes length of life (cf. *Farewell to Love*, ll. 24–5). 'Die' was commonly used in Elizabethan slang to refer to sexual detumescence.

22 *the Eagle and the Dove*] i.e. each finds in the other superlative strength and gentleness; or, alternatively, the beloved finds strength in the lover, and the lover gentleness in the beloved.

23 *Phoenix*] The phoenix image was used in Sicilian poetry, and later by Petrarch (*Canz.* 135) and by many Petrarchans. Petrarch made the bird image his desire for Laura. The Petrarchans exploited the bird in many and various ways. Donne had plenty of precedent in the English sonneteers. Daniel hopes that his verse, phoenix-like, will renew his Delia's life, Giles Fletcher wishes to rise again like the phoenix from the fire of his love, Sidney refers to Stella as a phoenix, and so on. L. C. John (*The Elizabethan Sonnet Sequences*, New York, 1938, p. 117) notes that 'almost the only sonnet allusions to a specific bird are those to the phoenix'. Donne's brilliant originality lies in using the bird to mean *both* the lovers, and making it hermaphroditic.

23–7] On this punctuation the meaning will be: 'The riddle of the phoenix makes more sense because of us: we too, being one, *are* the phoenix. Thus, our two sexes, being made to fit together to form a sexually intermediate creature [having, however, both potency and fertility], we die, and then we rise again one and the same being as before, just as the identical phoenix rises again from its own ashes; and this love makes us a mystery worthy of reverence.'

24–5] For discussion of the punctuation of these lines, and justification of that here adopted, see Appendix VII, p. 328.

26 *die*] See note on l. 21 for use of the term in Elizabethan slang.

punctuation] The comma after 'die', found in a number of MSS, is useful. It focuses on the event of 'dying', before attention shifts to resurrection; and it also helps to make clear that 'the same' only modifies 'rise' and not also 'die'.

27] Henry Green (*Shakespeare and the Emblem Writers*, London, 1870, pp. 384–5) points out that the phoenix was primarily the symbol of holy mysteries.

29 *tomb*] The singular is better here. Final 's' is notoriously easily added in MS transmission. It is also, admittedly, easily dropped; but here we need to take account of 'legend' (l. 30), which must be right, because of 'it' later in the line. Now the strongest MS authority for 'tombs' is that of Group I, *H40* and *DC*; but these all read 'legends' in l. 30. Moreover, there is no more reason to multiply tombs than to multiply hearses. So, since MS authority by no means compels us to do this, we shall do well to discard the asymmetricality.

hearse] Not the modern carriage or car for bearing the coffin, but a temple-shaped structure used in royal and noble funerals, decorated with banners, heraldic devices, and lighted candles, and on which, as *OED* 2c tells us, it was customary for friends to pin short poems or epitaphs.

29–30] Though the two lines may seem to involve some contradiction (since elegies or epitaphs were frequently in verse), the sense is probably that even if the story of the two love-martyrs will not really make one of the Lives of the Saints, it will, at any rate, be a worthy subject for poetry.

30 *legend*] probably here primarily 'story' (*OED* 3) as recited in an elegy or epitaph; though, in view of the rest of the stanza, the word also obliquely connotes 'story of the life of a saint' (*OED* 1).

31] The meaning is: 'If we do not make history'; since the lovers' importance is not as political or worldly figures.

32 *sonnets pretty rooms*] James Reeves (*Selected Poems of John Donne*, London, 1952) pointed out a clever conceit here. Donne is using 'sonnets' loosely for love poems, and *stanza* in Italian means a room.

33 *well-wrought urn*] Professor Horst Meller has pointed out that some sixteenth-century editions of Petrarch showed the poet and Laura facing each other on a funeral urn surmounted by a rising Phoenix (see *TLS*, 22 April 1965).

becomes] 'suits' or 'befits'.

35 *approve*] 'prove' or 'confirm'.

37, 45] I have added the quotation marks.

39 *rage*] probably meaning 'violent sexual passion', 'lust' (*OED* 6b), possibly

241

     – partly at least – because not a 'mutual flame' (cf. *Love's Deity*, l. 17 and Note).

40 *extract*] Grierson considered 'contract' here 'doubtless correct', despite the MSS, which he thought confused in other respects at this point, Group I reading 'drawe', and *TCC*, *A18* and *N* dropping 'soul'. However, I feel sure that Professor Gardner is right here in following the MSS, and in holding that 'contract' would spoil what she convincingly suggests to be an alchemical metaphor here, namely, that of the extract of the world's soul, obtained by sublimation and distillation, being driven into the 'glasses' or vessels in which it is stored. She suggests that the 'glasses' then become mirrors, in which the lovers can see an epitome of the whole world.
     drove] must be right, for the rhyme.

42–3 parentheses] Though not impossible that 'soul' is the object of 'drove', the construction would be very awkward. Far more probably the object is 'Countries, towns, courts', the various kinds of scene of which the visible world consists. I have therefore adopted the parentheses supplied by Grierson.

44–5 *beg from above / A pattern of your love*] The sense is: 'ask God to give us a pattern of your love, so that others may love as you did'. They are now saints (cf. l. 36), and, as Grierson suggested to me, it is perhaps worth mentioning that this request conforms to the Roman Catholic doctrine that men pray to saints to pray for them.

The Curse

Whoever guesses, thinks, or dreams he knows
Who is my mistress, wither by this curse;
   His only, and only his purse
   May some dull heart to love dispose,
And she yield then to all that are his foes;   5
  May he be scorn'd by one, whom all else scorn,
  Forswear to others, what to her he hath sworn,
  With fear of missing, shame of getting, torn:

Madness his sorrow, gout his cramps, may he
Make, by but thinking who hath made him such: 10
   And may he feel no touch
   Of conscience, but of fame, and be
Anguish'd, not that 'twas sin, but that 'twas she:
  In early and long scarceness may he rot,
  For land which had been his, if he had not   15
  Himself incestuously an heir begot:

May he dream treason, and believe that he
Went to perform it, and confess, and die,
   And no recórd tell why:
   His sons, which none of his may be,   20
Inherit nothing but his infamy:
  Or may he so long parasites have fed,
  That he would fain be theirs, whom he hath bred,
  And at the last be circumcis'd for bread:

The venom of all stepdames, gamesters' gall,   25
What tyrants, and their subjects, interwish,
   What plants, mines, beasts, fowl, fish
   Can cóntribute; all ill which all
Prophets, or poets, spake; And all which shall
  Be annex'd in schedules unto this by me,   30
  Fall on that man; for if it be a she,
  Nature beforehand hath out-cursèd me.

In 1633–1719. S96; Cy omit.   A Curse *A25.* Curse *Wed; S.* Dirae *P. No*
Text: Title The Curse *1633–1719; I; H40;*   *title HK2.*
II; L74; DC; Dob, Lut, O'F; D17, B; S962.   9 gout *(or* gowte) his cramp(e)s *I; H40;*

II; *L74; Wed; DC; Dob; HK2, A25, B;
1669; Gar.* gout his cramp(e) *1633–54,
1719; Lut, O'F; P; S962; Gr; Ed (1956).*
gowts his crampe *S.* gowts his cramps
D17.

12 of fame *1633–1719; I (excl. SP); H40;
TCD, N; Wed; DC; Dob, Lut, O'F;
A25, D17, B.* of shame *SP (altered from
fame); TCC A18; L74 (altered from
? fame), P, S.* but fame, *S962.* of flame
HK2.

14–16 In early . . . begot *(followed by colon
or full stop) 1633; I; H40; DC; Dob; B;
S962.*

Or may he for her vertue reverence
One, that hates him onlie for im-
potence,
And equall traytours be she and his
sence. *(or:).*
II; *L74; Wed; Lut, O'F; HK2* (her
sence), *A25* (Her that hates), *P,* (her
that hates) . . . (and equally be she

traitors), *D17, S; 1635–1719. Lut, O'F
give 1633 version in margin as that* 'in
some copyes'.

18 Went to performe *II; L74; S962.*
Me(a)nt to performe *1633–1719; I;
H40; Wed; DC; Dob; HK2, A25, P,
D17, B, S; Gr; Ed (1956); Gar.* Ment to
enact *Lut (with* performe *in margin),
O'F.*

27 mynes *or* mines *H40; II; L74; Wed;
Dob, Lut, O'F; HK2, A25, P, D17, B,
S; S962.* myne *1633–1719; I; DC.*

29 spake *1633–1719; I; DC; Lut; D17.*
spoke *II; L74; Wed; Dob* (spoake);
HK2, A25. speak(e) *H40; O'F; P, B, S;
S962.*

31 it be] thou beest *Dob (with* it be *in
margin as alternative or correction).*

32 beforehand] already *Lut, O'F (gives
beforehand below as alternative or correction);* before *HK2;* aforehand *S962.*

General note. 'Curses' were a recognized form in Classical poetry. The most
celebrated instance is perhaps the *Dirae*, a poem in hexameters long attributed
to Virgil, but probably by another poet. That poem curses soldiers who had
dispossessed the poet of his farm. It is possible, however, that the curse-poem is
at least as old as Archilochus, the seventh-century Greek poet, who wrote a
poem cursing the father of the woman he loved for forbidding her to marry
him. Tradition has it that the poem resulted in both father and daughter
hanging themselves! The *Ibis*, doubtfully attributed to Ovid, belongs to the
same general class. That poem, however, was certainly a direct imitation of the
work of a Greek poet, Callimachus (born *c.* 310 BC).

In point of breakneck swiftness this poem is unrivalled among the *Songs and
Sonets.* The colons (rather than full stops) at the end of stanzas 2 and 3 in *1633,*
and, still more, the semicolon at the end of stanza 1 in *1633* testify to early
realization of the momentum of the poem. I followed Grierson in my 1956
edition (as here) in making all three colons, and Professor Gardner does the
same.

3–4] The meaning could possibly be: 'May the only purse he possesses, and
nothing but that purse, induce some frigid creature to love him!' ('His
only purse', so that he may have nothing left when the woman has finished
with him; and 'only his purse', so that the woman will not care a rap for
him when the money is gone.) F. L. Lucas, however, pointed out to me a
difficulty, viz. that the word order does not accord with this interpretation,

since, e.g. 'Heaven may strike him!' is not good English for 'May heaven strike him!' Mr Lucas's objection suggested to me another possibility, namely, that the subject of 'dispose' is 'some dull heart', and that the verb is a neuter verb used in a sense then current but now obsolete, 'to bargain', 'to agree on terms'. The meaning could then be 'May some frigid creature agree to love just the remains of his money (not him)'.

6–8] 'May he be scorned by some woman who is scorned by all other men, and may he have to deny on oath to others that he has said the things he has said to her, being torn between the fear of failing to win her, and the shame of doing so.'

9–10] 'May he turn his sorrow into madness, and his cramps into gout, by merely remembering who it is that has given him them.'

11–13] 'And may he feel no twinge of conscience at having seduced her, but only of remorse at his loss of reputation, and may he be racked by the thought, not that he has committed a sin, but that *she* was the woman he made love to.'

12 *of fame*] 'of reputation'. There is fair MS authority for 'shame'; but 'fame' is the subtler reading, and *difficilior lectio potior*. It is also better supported by the MSS, and is the reading of all the early editions.

14 *scarceness*] poverty.

14–16] Professor Gardner suggests (*ESS*, pp. 164–5) that Marston may be alluding to the *H40*, Group I version of these lines in his Tenth Satire, added in the second edition of *The Scourge of Villainy* in 1599. This seems to me to open the fascinating possibility that Donne's tirade was prompted by the thought that someone might penetrate the secret that he was wooing Ann, or was even already her lover, when the poem was written.

14–16] The alternative version has plenty of MS support. Professor Gardner indicates external reasons for thinking it the earlier of the two. It is certainly the less striking. If Donne altered it, we may wonder whether it was simply because he thought of something better, or whether there were more specific reasons. Professor Gardner suggests that Donne invented the property situation, and that Marston took it over in his Tenth Satire published in 1599 (A. H. Bullen (ed.), *Works*, London, 1887, vol. iii, p. 368). If her suggestion is right, *The Curse* would, of course, pre-date Marston's satire. I am not, however, wholly convinced that the case is 'a little too neat for real life'. Real life's repertoire of strange and comically neat sequences seems inexhaustible.

15–16] 'For land which he would have inherited if his adulterous connection with a near kinswoman had not interposed an heir between himself and the estate.'

18 *Went*] Despite the apparently massive authority of the MSS and early editions for 'Meant', I believe 'Went' is the better reading. It would indicate that the man dreamed that he had actually passed from treasonous intention to some overt act (cf. the similar distinction made in ll. 55–6 of

A Valediction: of my name, in the window). Treasonable intent, without any overt act, was not punishable by death, nor is it now. A number of the MSS favouring the other reading spell the word 'Ment', which could easily be a mistake for 'Went' in transmission.

19] i.e. so that he may not recover his reputation posthumously.

22–3] 'Or may he feed parasites for so long that he drains himself dry, and would wish to sponge on them in his turn.'

24] A hard line, perhaps meaning: 'And in the end turn Jew so as to keep alive' (alluding to mutual assistance within the Jewish community). The line might owe something to Genesis 34:22–3.

29 *And all*] I preserve the capital 'A' here as almost certainly intended to imitate the form of a legal document.

A Valediction: of the book

I'll tell thee now, dear love, what thou shalt do
  To anger destiny, as she doth us;
  How I shall stay, though she eloign me thus,
And how posterity shall know it too;
    How thine may out-endure   5
    Sibyl's glory, and obscure
    Her who from Pindar could allure,
  And her, through whose help Lucan is not lame,
And her, whose book (they say) Homer did find, and name.

Study our manuscripts, those myriads   10
  Of letters, which have past 'twixt thee and me,
  Thence write our Annals, and in them will be,
To all whom love's subliming fire invades,
    Rule and example found;
    There, the faith of any ground   15
    No schísmatic will dare to wound,
  That sees, how Love this grace to us affords,
To make, to keep, to use, to be, these his Recórds.

This book, as long-liv'd as the elements,
  Or as the world's form, this all-gravèd tome   20
  In cypher write, or new-made idiom;
We for Love's clergy only are instruments.

In 1633–1719. L74; S96; A25 omit.

Text: Title A Valediction: of the book *Gr.* A Valediction: of the Book *Gar.* A Valediction: of the book *Gr.* A Valediction of the Book *TC, N; DC.* A Valediction of this Book *A18.* A Valediction of the book *Dob; B* (yᵉ); *S962.* Valediction of the book *H49, SP, Lec.* Valediction: 3. of the Book *Lut, O'F (has full stop for colon).* The Book *Cy, P.* Valediction to his book *1633.* Valediction to his Book *1635–1719. No title H40; Wed, HK2, S.* A Valediction of a book left in a window *D17.*

20 tome] tomb(e) *Lec, C57; TCC, A18, N; Wed; DC; Cy, P, D17, S.*

21 cypher] cyphers *D17.*

write *H40; Wed; HK2, P, D17, S; Gar.* writ(t)(e) *H49, Lec, C57; II; DC; Dob, Lut, O'F; Cy, B; S962; Gr; Ed (1956).* writes *SP.* writtes *D.*

idiom; *1633–1719; D, SP; Wed; Ed (1956); Gar.* idiom, *H49, Lec; H40; DC; Gr.* idiom. *C57. no stop other MSS.* idiomes *HK2.*

22 only are] are only *A18; Lut, O'F.* , only are *Lec, C57.*

instruments. *Lec; Wed; B; Gar.* instruments, *1633–69; H49, C57; Ed (1956).* instruments; *D, SP. no stop other MSS.* instruments; *Gr. Lut, O'F put whole line in parentheses. om. P.*

When this book is made thus,
   Should again the ravenous
   Vandals and Goths inúndate us,   25
  Learning were safe; in this our Universe
Schools might learn sciences, spheres music, angels verse.

Here Love's divines (since all divinity
   Is love or wonder) may find all they seek,
   Whether abstract spiritual love they like,   30
Their souls exhal'd with what they do not see,
     Or, loth so to amuse
     Faith's infirmity, they choose
     Something which they may see and use;
  For, though mind be the heaven, where love doth sit, 35
Beauty a convenient type may be to figure it.

Here, more than in their books, may lawyers find
   Both by what titles mistresses are ours,
   And how prerogative those states devours,
Transferr'd from Love himself, to womankind;   40
     Who, though from heart, and eyes,
     They exact great subsidies,
     Forsake him who on them relies,
  And for the cause, honour, or conscience, give—
Chimeras, vain as they, or their prerogative.   45

Here statesmen (or of them, they which can read)
   May of their occupation find the grounds:
   Love and their art alike it deadly wounds,
If to consider what 'tis, one proceed;
     In both they do excel   50
     Who the present govern well,
     Whose weakness none doth, or dares, tell;
  In this thy book, such will their nothing see,
As in the Bible some can find out alchemy.

Thus vent thy thoughts; abroad I'll study thee,   55
   As he removes far off, that great heights takes;
   How great love is, presence best trial makes,
But absence tries how long this love will be;

> To take a latitude,
> Sun, or stars, are fitliest view'd   60
>   At their brightest, but to conclude
> Of longitudes, what other way have we,
> But to mark when, and where, the dark eclipses be?

25 Vandals and Goths inúndate *I; H40; II* (in-undate *N*); *Wed; DC; HK2, Cy, B.* Vandals and Goths invade *Dob, Lut, O'F; P, S; 1669, 1719.* Vandals or Goths invade *D17.* Vandals and the Goths invade *1633–54.* Goths and Vandals inundate *S962.*

39 those *H49, D, SP; H40; II; Wed; DC; Dob, Lut, O'F; Cy, P, D17, B; S962; Gar.* these *1633–1719; Lec, C57; HK2, S; Gr; Ed (1956).*

states] rites *II; DC.*

53 their nothing *D, SP, Lec, C57; II, Wed; Dob, Lut, O'F; B; S962; 1635–54.* their nothings *DC.* there nothing *H49; H40; Cy, S.* there noth-ings *D17.* they nothing *HK2.* there something *1633; P; 1669–1719.*

56 great heights] great height *S.* shadows *Lut, O'F.*

60 fitliest] fittest *II; DC; HK2, S.* fit(t)ly *Lut, O'F (b.c.); Cy, P.*

General note. Perhaps the most elaborate poem in the collection. Professor Guss (op. cit., pp. 144–5) interestingly suggests that a philosophical basis for the poem may have been provided by Guido Casoni da Serravalle's *Della magia d'amore*, Venice, 1592, which attempts to prove that 'Love is a metaphysician, physicist, astrologer, musicologist, arithmetician, grammarian, dialectician, rhetorician, poet, historian, lawyer', and master of virtually all other arts, sciences and crafts.

With regard to the love relationship expressed in the poem, it has clearly already existed for a long time. 'Myriads of letters' have passed between the lovers, and a pride in mutual love is manifest. Yet the poet does not seem to have complete confidence that the beloved's love for him will last (stanzas 5 and 7).

3 *eloign me*] The sense is: 'takes me far away' (Old French: *esloignier*, Fr. *éloigner*; *1633* spells 'Esloygne').

6 *Sibyl's glory*] The MSS and early editions generally have no apostrophe; and therefore leave uncertain whether 'Sibyl' is singular or plural. *Cy* and *1719*, however, make it singular. There is no positive evidence from early editions and MSS that it is plural. I therefore take it provisionally as singular, in which case it almost certainly refers to the Cumaean Sibyl, whose prophecies to Aeneas play such a vital part in *Aeneid* VI. If 'Sibyls' be taken as plural the reference would, of course, be to all the ancient Greek and Roman prophetesses called by that name, the most ancient of all being Herophile who prophesied about the Trojan War.

7] Corinna the Theban (*fl.* 500 B C), who was said to have instructed Pindar in poetry, and to have subsequently defeated him five times at Thebes (see Aelian, *Var. Hist.* XIII. 25, and Pausanias, *Hel. Per.* IX. 22).

8] Lucan's wife, Polla Argentaria, was reputed to have assisted him in correcting Books I–III of the *Pharsalia*. Apollinaris Sidonius (*Epist.* 2, 10, 6) lists her among wives who helped and inspired their husbands, saying that she often completed a verse for Lucan.

9] Towards the end of that vast digest of Pagan and Christian works, the *Myriobiblion* by Photius (twice Patriarch of Constantinople in the ninth century AD) there is an abstract of a so-called 'New History' by Ptolemy Hephaistion of Alexandria, a mine of suspect information. Photius summarizes Ptolemy in one place as stating that a certain Helena, daughter of Musaeus, wrote on the Trojan War, and that Homer took his subject from her work. In another place, however, Photius reports Ptolemy as offering the following account:

> Phantasia, a woman of Memphis, daughter of Nikarchos, composed the story of the Trojan War and of the adventures of Odysseus before Homer did, and she is said to have left the books at Memphis. Homer came there and received the copies from Phanites the priest-scribe, and followed them in composing [or, possibly, 'composed under their inspiration'].
>
> (*Myriobiblion*, CXC)

In neither case is Homer represented as simply giving a title to the work of someone else, or, necessarily, as seriously plagiarizing. The *Myriobiblion* was first printed at Augsburg in 1601, and translated into Latin in 1606.

13 *subliming fire*] 'purifying fire'; the chemical process of sublimation consists in converting a solid into vapour by heat, and then reconverting it into a solid by cooling; the sublimate is purer than the original solid.

15–16] 'No schismatic will dare to attack the truth of any fundamental doctrine expressed there.'

17 *that sees*] who sees.
   grace] The sense is: 'privilege' (*OED* II. 8b).

18 *Recórds*] As Professor Gardner points out, for the first three verbs 'Records' = 'archives', for the fourth 'witnesses' (see *OED* I. 3d, which quotes Acts 5:37 in Tyndale's version of the Bible: 'We are his recordes as concerning these thynges').

19–20 *elements . . . form*] i.e. the original matter and the form of the world.

20 *all-gravèd*] entirely engraved (so as to last).
   all-gravèd tome] there may be play here on 'grave' and on 'tome' and 'tomb'.

21 *write*] Professor Gardner commendably reads 'write'. She calls it a 'conjectural emendation', but she omits to note in her critical apparatus that 'write' is the reading of the good MS *H40*, and also of *P*, *D17* and *S*. It now turns out to be also the reading of *Wed*.

22 punctuation] Sense requires a heavier stop than *1633*'s comma at the end of the line.

22–3] The meaning is: 'We are exclusively documents and witnesses for Love's clergy.' Only they will be able to read the cypher or invented language.

23–7] i.e. the invaders would not understand the book, and it would thus survive as a compendium of all arts and sciences, so that culture would be saved.

25 *inúndate*] 'invade and overwhelm'. Grierson cites ample support for 'inundate' in Donne's own usage, e.g. 'the inundation of the Goths in Italy' (E. M. Simpson (ed.), *Essays in Divinity*, Oxford, 1952, p. 61).

26 *Universe*] possibly 'world of knowledge' and so 'encyclopaedia'; though Professor Gardner's suggestion 'University' is also possible.

27 *angels verse*] i.e. so as to sing the best hymns to God.

28–36] cf. *The Ecstasy*, ll. 69–72.

31 *exhal'd with*] drawn out by.

32 *amuse*] tantalize.

36 *type*] emblem.

　figure] symbolize.

37] To bring out the sense I have added commas after 'Here' and 'books', and removed a comma after 'find'.

37–45] A paraphrase might run: 'Here [in this book made of our letters] lawyers may find, better than in their legal treatises, the nature of our titles to our mistresses, and also how these estates of ours [in our mistresses] are eaten up by the prerogative [to exact feudal dues over and above those which were customary] which belongs of right to the lord, Love, but has been transferred to womankind. Women, although they claim large payments from the hearts and eyes of men, do not perform their part of the feudal bargain, but let down the men who rely on them, and give as excuse for doing so, "honour" or "conscience", which are mere figments of the imagination, as empty as they themselves and their prerogative are.'

39 *states*] legal estates.

43 *Forsake him*] Let him down.

46–54] Again, a paraphrase could be: 'Here statesmen (or rather, those statesmen who can read) will be able to discover the principles of their profession. Both love and politics are unable to stand scrutiny without collapsing under it. In both spheres of activity the most successful practitioners are the opportunists, who either take other people in, or make them afraid to expose them. In this book of yours, such people will see the emptiness of their art, just as some people learn alchemy from the Bible [or discover alchemy in the Bible].' The sense of ll. 53–4 is: 'Your book deals with genuine deep love, but will nevertheless teach what sham love is, just as the Bible can teach the humbug science of alchemy.'

53 *nothing*] then pronounced 'nō-thing'.

55 *vent*] probably 'make known'.

　abroad I'll study thee] 'While I'm abroad I'll read the Annals you have written.' Cf. l. 12.

56 *removes far off*] moves away to a good distance.
   takes] surveys.

57–8] Presence is the best test how great love is: but absence tests its endurance.

59–61] As Grierson points out, 'the latitude of any spot may always be found by measuring the distance from the zenith, of a star whose altitude, i.e. distance from the equator, is known'. There seems to me, however, almost certainly a further point here in 'at their brightest' beyond merely the contrast with 'dark eclipses', mentioned by Grierson: namely, that it was at least a common belief that stars were brightest when highest in the sky, i.e. nearest the zenith, and therefore when their distance from the zenith was easiest to measure.

59–63] The comparison is a highly fanciful one, resting almost entirely on a verbal basis, as Grierson thought. Yet I believe that the conceit is rather more precise than Grierson suggested when he said that here ' "longitude" means literally "length", "latitude", "breadth" '. Mr Leo Salingar has drawn my attention to *OED* sense 2 for 'longitude': 'Length (of time, etc.); long continuance. Now *rare*', citing Lancelot Andrewes (1626): 'The longitude, or continuance of the joy' (*Sermons*, 1661 edn, p. 15). There was also a more precise sense of 'latitude', which fits well here (*OED* sense 2: 'Extent . . . Now *rare*'). Donne may well, therefore, be punning with some subtlety, as we might expect.

61–3] Grierson writes:

> If the time at which an instantaneous phenomenon, such as an eclipse of the moon, begins at Greenwich (or whatever be the first meridian) is known, and the time of its beginning at whatever place a ship is, be then noted, the difference gives the longitude. The eclipses of the moons of Saturn have been used for the purpose. The method is not, however, a practically useful one. Owing to the penumbra it is difficult to observe the exact moment at which an eclipse of the moon begins. In certain phases of Saturn her satellites are not visible.

A Valediction: of weeping

Let me pour forth
My tears before thy face, whilst I stay here,
For thy face coins them, and thy stamp they bear,
And by this mintage they are something worth,
  For thus they be   5
  Pregnant of thee;
Fruits of much grief they are, emblems of more,
When a tear falls, that thou falls which it bore,
So thou and I are nothing then, when on a diverse shore.

On a round ball   10
A workman that hath copies by, can lay
An Europe, Afric, and an Asia,
And quickly make that, which was nothing, *All*;
  So doth each tear
  Which thee doth wear,   15
A globe, yea world, by that impression grow,
Till thy tears mix'd with mine do overflow
This world, by waters sent from thee, my heaven, dissolvèd so.

O more than Moon,
Draw not up seas to drown me in thy sphere,   20
Weep me not dead, in thine arms, but forbear
To teach the sea, what it may do too soon;
  Let not the wind
  Example find
To do me more harm than it purposeth;   25
Since thou and I sigh one another's breath,
Whoe'er sighs most, is cruellest, and hastes the other's death.

In 1633–1719. Wed; A25 omit.

Text: Title A Valediction: of weeping *Gr.*
A Valediction of weeping *1633–1719.*
Valediction of weeping *II; DC.* A Vale-
diction of tears *S96, Dob; Cy, S; S962.*
Valediction 2. of Tears *Lut, O'F.* A Vale-
diction *H40; I; L74; B. No title HK2, P,*
D17.

8 falls *I; H40; II; L74; DC; HK2, D17, S;*
 Ed (1956); Gar. falst *1633–1719; S96,*
 Lut; Cy, P (fal'st); *S962; Gr.* fall'st
 Dob; B. fallst *O'F.*

18 *punctuation*] *variously punctuated in MSS*
 and editions (see note).

Note on the title. Not = 'A farewell to weeping', but 'A farewell: on weeping'.

A Valediction: of weeping

General note. The most tempestuous of the four Valedictions, matching *The Expiration* in intensity of emotional charge; but also an ingeniously 'conceited' poem. Tear and sigh, conceits and hyperboles swarm in poems in the Petrarchan tradition. Donne's brilliant play here, as in some of the other lyrics, mingles sharply focused sensation of the small with a strong awareness of the world of continents and Ptolemaic spheres.

2 *whilst I stay here*] while I am still with you.

3] probably referring to two processes: (1) the causing of the poet's tears by the sight of the face of his lady, from whom he is soon to part (coining); and (2) the reflection of her face in his tears (stamping).

6 *Pregnant of*] filled with.

8 *that*] not a conjunction, but a demonstrative adjective qualifying 'thou'.
   falls] the third person singular; and the reading best supported by the MSS.

7–9] The sense of these lines is therefore probably: 'My tears are the result of much grief [at the thought of parting from you], and they are emblems of more grief to come [the grief of being absent from you]; when one of my tears falls, that particular "thou" which the tear carried in it also falls, and both my tear and your image perish; and this is emblematic of what will happen when we are parted; you, like your image in the tear, will be nothing then, and I, like my tear, will be nothing too.' In the Petrarchan tradition Donne is here, as elsewhere, referring to the absence of lovers as a sort of death.

9 *when on a diverse shore*] 'when we are in different countries with the sea between us'.

10 *round ball*] globe.

10–13] The image is of an artificer pasting a map on a globe. He will need more than one piece of mapped paper ('copy') to cover a sphere, and this may account for the plural 'copies'. Cf. a letter from Donne to Sir Robert Carre in Spain (1624): 'But the difference of our situation is in North and South; and you know, that though the labour of any ordinary Artificer in that Trade, will bring East and West together, (for if a flat map be but pasted upon a round Globe, the farthest East, and the farthest West meet, and are all one) yet all this brings not North and South a scruple of a degree the nearer' (*A Collection of Letters made by Tobie Mathew Kt*, London, 1660, p. 306; Nonesuch Donne, p. 482). Cf. also *Sermons*, VI. 59.

12 *Asia*] trisyllabic, and rhyming with 'lay'.

13 *nothing*] possibly, as Professor A. J. Smith suggests, because the globe was a big O.

14–15 *each tear / Which thee doth wear*] i.e. each of the poet's tears.

15] which bears your impression.

16 *A globe, yea world*] 'A globe, or rather, more than that, a real world.'

18 *This world*] Another crux. Does it mean (1) the real world, or (2) the poet, or (3) a tear of the poet's, or (4) a tear of his beloved's? I am inclined to

think that (3) is probably the answer. It offers the most ingenious conceit, and fits well with l. 16.

18   punctuation] The present edition prints this punctuation for the first time. The punctuation in the MSS varies importantly. *H40* and Group I MSS have commas after 'world' and 'thee'. *L74* and one Group II MS, *N*, and *DC*, also punctuate thus. This would give the meaning that the beloved (the poet's 'heaven') would destroy herself by her weeping. Group III MSS, however, punctuate very differently. *Dob* has commas after 'waters', 'thee' and 'heaven'; *S96* has a comma after 'world', no comma after 'waters', but a semicolon after 'heaven'. *Lut* and *O'F* have commas after 'world' and 'waters', and place 'my heaven' in parentheses. It is clear enough that in all cases the Group III MSS make 'dissolvèd' qualify 'this world', not 'my heaven'. Of the other three Group II MSS, *TCC* and *TCD* have a comma after 'world', and *A18* has a semicolon. None has any other commas. *1633* adopts the Group I punctuation, and Grierson and Professor Gardner follow, without, however, mentioning these MS variations. The Group III pattern seems to give better sense to 'so', the meaning being that 'this world' is, ironically enough, destroyed by the poet's 'heaven'. The lack of any copula before 'my heaven' makes the Group I meaning somewhat awkward. More important, the Group III meaning connects this stanza to the third. The beloved is destroying 'this world', and may destroy *him* by her weeping. There is no mention elsewhere that she would also be destroying herself. The Group I meaning would therefore be isolated from the rest of the poem. Fortunately, there is enough MS evidence to justify emending the *1633* punctuation.

14–18] On the interpretation of 'This world' here adopted, and with this punctuation of l. 18, the sense would be: 'In the same way each tear of mine by bearing your image grows into a world, but when you weep also, your tears mix with mine and overflow this world, which is thus dissolved by waters sent from you, my heaven.'

18   *my heaven*] Donne is probably comparing the beloved to the crystalline or watery heaven in the Ptolemaic astronomy.

19   *more than Moon*] probably (1), as Professor Gardner suggests, because the moon is only mistress of the tides, whereas the lady can draw seas up into her sphere; and probably also (2) because her sphere is the Crystalline (Ninth) Sphere, whereas the moon's is only the First.

19–21] 'Weep me not dead' seems to be a clear plea explaining the more arcane 'Draw not up seas to drown me in thy sphere'. If so, then those seas must be taken to mean floods of the woman's tears, not of the poet's. 'Weep me not dead' probably plays on (1) 'Don't weep for me as if I were dead' and (2) 'Don't kill me by weeping'.

21   *in thine arms*] i.e. probably (1) in the last place where I should feel dead; (2) in the place where I am safe from the dangers of the world; (3) in the place where you have me, not where you have lost me.

26] Professor Guss (op. cit., p. 73) cites a possible analogue in Guarini's Madrigal 69 where the lady's eyes seem to rescue her lover from death by telling him that her own heart is not so dear to her as his, and that if he dies it will not really be he that dies but she. Donne, however, also takes a hint from Guarini's word 'respiro' ('I breathe'), and possibly further complicates the conceit by thinking of 'breath' = *anima* = 'soul'.

26–7] cf. *Song*, 'Sweetest love', ll. 25–32.

27 *cruellest*] trisyllabic.

Song

Sweetest love, I do not go
   For weariness of thee,
Nor in hope the world can show
   A fitter love for me;
     But since that I   5
Must die at last, 'tis best
To use myself in jest,
   Thus by feign'd deaths to die.

Yesternight the Sun went hence,
   And yet is here today;   10
He hath no desire nor sense,
   Nor half so short a way:
     Then fear not me,
But believe that I shall make
Speedier journeys, since I take   15
   More wings and spurs than he.

Oh how feeble is man's power,
   That if good fortune fall,
Cannot add another hour,
   Nor a lost hour recall!   20
     But come bad chance,
And we join to it our strength,
And we teach it art and length,
   Itself o'er us to advance.

In 1633–1719. L74; Cy omit.

Text: Title Song *1633–1719 and some MSS. No title other MSS. Layout: As here in 1633–1719; III; P, S; S962; Gr; Gar. First four lines of each stanza written as two long lines in I; H40; II; Wed; DC; HK2; A25, D17. Sixth and seventh lines of each stanza as one long line in I; H40; II; Wed; DC; HK2. B has all three long lines in stanzas 1 and 4 only.*

  6–8 Must . . . to die] At the last must part, 'tis best, / Thus to use my self in jest / By fained deaths to die *Lut, O'F; 1635–54.* Must die at last, 'tis best / Thus to use my self in jest / By feigned death to die *1669–1719.*

  8 deaths] death *H40; S96; HK2, P, D17, S.*

  15 journeys, since I] returne, since I do *S96, Dob; S962.* journeys and do *D17.*

  22 join] add *Lut, O'F; A25, D17.*

  24 o'er *(variously spelt in edns and MSS)*] on *D, SP, Lec, C57 (H49 reads* ore (= o'er)). or *HK2, D17, S.*

Song

When thou sigh'st, thou sigh'st not wind,   25
 But sigh'st my soul away;
When thou weep'st, unkindly kind,
 My life's blood doth decay.
  It cannot be
That thou lov'st me, as thou say'st,   30
If in thine my life thou waste;
 Thou art the best of me.

Let not thy divining heart
 Forethink me any ill;
Destiny may take thy part,   35
 And may thy fears fulfil;
  But think that we
Are but turn'd aside to sleep;
They who one another keep
 Alive, ne'er parted be.   40

25–32 *lines om.* TCD, N.
28 life's blood] life blood *Wed; Lut, O'F;*
 HK2, A25, P, D17, B, S; S962.

32 Thou] That *Dob, Lut, O'F; B;*
 1635–1719; Hayward.
32] Thou art not fond of me *S96.*

General note. One of the tenderest poems in the collection, seemingly the fruit of a perfectly satisfying relationship which knew the experience of 'turning aside to sleep'. Moreover, as in *A Valediction: forbidding mourning*, there is a confident and comforting belief in love's survival of the physical separation of the lovers. Indeed, here the poet goes further, and hyperbolically denies that the lovers will really be 'parted' at all. What danger there is lies in sighing and weeping, when there is no basic justification for doing so.

 This is one of six poems grouped in *DC*, and three grouped in *II*, as 'Songs which were made to certaine Aires that were made before'. Two MS settings of the Song have been discovered, one in Tenbury Wells MS 1018 at f44ᵛ, and one in BL Add. 10337, at f55ᵛ. The settings seem rather inferior, and their text is corrupt. It seems very doubtful whether Donne wrote the words for these 'Aires'. (See Appendix XII, pp. 341–3.)

5–8] The parting of lovers was, of course, in the Petrarchan tradition, a metaphorical death.
7–8] to accustom myself to death by playing at it.
8 *deaths*] 'death' could well be the better reading. A terminal 's' can easily
 creep in in MS transmission. The more extravagant 'deaths', on the other
 hand, is quite in order, and more strongly supported.

23 *art*] skill.
   length] possibly a metaphor from archery or gunnery (cf. the use in cricket), meaning here, roughly, 'how to hit us'; on the other hand, possibly simply 'extension', and so, 'how to draw itself out'.
24] The sense is: 'to get the advantage of us', 'to get the better of us' (see *OED* 10).
27 *unkindly*] possibly both 'unnatural' and 'cruel'.
   kind] probably playing on (1) sort of person, and (2) kind person.
32 *Thou*] Probably the right reading. John Hayward objected that it made nonsense; but the strength of his objection is attenuated if we substitute the semicolon for *1633*'s comma which he adopted.
33 *divining*] prophetic (with the sense of foreboding and uncanny guessing).

A Valediction: forbidding mourning

As virtuous men pass mildly away,
    And whisper to their souls, to go,
Whilst some of their sad friends do say:
    'The breath goes now', and some say: 'No':

So let us melt, and make no noise,   5
    No tear-floods, nor sigh-tempests move;
'Twere profanation of our joys
    To tell the laity our love.

Moving of the earth brings harms and fears;
    Men reckon what it did and meant: 10
But trepidation of the spheres,
    Though greater far, is innocent.

Dull súblunary lovers' love
    (Whose soul is sense) cannot admit
Absence, because it doth remove   15
    Those things which elemented it.

But we, by a love so much refin'd
    That our selves know not what it is,
Inter-assurèd of the mind,
    Care less, eyes, lips, and hands to miss.   20

Our two souls therefore, which are one,
    Though I must go, endure not yet
A breach, but an expansion,
    Like gold to airy thinness beat.

If they be two, they are two so   25
    As stiff twin compasses are two:
Thy soul, the fix'd foot, makes no show
    To move, but doth, if the other do;

And though it in the centre sit,
    Yet whilst the other far doth roam,   30
It leans, and hearkens after it,
    And grows erect, as that comes home.

Such wilt thou be to me, who must,
　Like the other foot, obliquely run:
Thy firmness makes my circle just,　　　　　　35
　And makes me end where I begun.

In 1633–1719. HK2 omits.

Text: Title A Valediction: forbidding
mourning *1633–1719; I; H40; Cy.*
Valediction forbidding mourning *II; DC.*
Valediction *Wed.* A Valediction: upon
the parting from his Mistress *III (Lut, O'F
add* Valediction. 1.*); S962.* Upon parting
from his Mistress *S.* Valediction against
mourning *A25.* An Elegy *P.* To his Love
upon his departure from her *D17. No title
L74 (Elegy added in seemingly later hand).*

3 Whilst *1633–1719; III; Cy, D17;
　S962.* And *I; H40; II; L74; Wed; DC;
　A25, P, B, S.*

8 our *1633–1719; I; H40; Wed; DC;
　Dob; A25, S.* of our *II; L74; S96, Lut,
　O'F; Cy, P, B; S962.* of loue *D17.*

9 Moving(e) of th'(e) earth brings
　*1633–1719; I; H40; II; L74; Cy, P, B,
　S.* Moving(e)s of th'earth bringe *Wed;
　DC; A25.* Moving(e)s of th'earth
　cause *Dob, Lut, O'F; D17.* Movings of
　earth cause *S96.* Movinge of earth
　cause *S962.*

11 trepidation . . . sphear(e)s *1633–
　1719; II; L74; Wed; DC; Lut, O'F;
　A25, Cy, P, B; S962.* trepidations . . .
　spheares *I; H40; S96, Dob; S.* trepi-
　dations . . . spheare *D17.*

12 is *1633–1719; H49, D, SP, Lec; H40;
　II; L74; Wed; DC; Lut, O'F; A25, Cy,
　P, B.* are *C57 (corrected from* is*); S96,
　Dob; D17, S; S962.*

15 because it doth] because that doth *DC;
　A25.* for that it doth *S; S962.*

20 lips, and hands *almost all MSS;
　1669–1719.* lips, hands *1633–54.*
　hand, and lips *S96.*

21 therefore, which are one] then, which
　are but one *III (some without comma);
　S962.* therefore, which are but one *S.*

22 go] part *III; S; S962.*

24 Like] As *Wed; DC; III; A25, D17, S;
　S962.*

28 but] yet *III; D17; S962.*

30 whilst *III; S; S962.* while *D17.* when
　1633–1719; rest of MSS and edns.

32 as that *1633–1719; DC; S96, Lut, O'F;
　Dob (in margin); A25, D17, S; S962; Gr;
　Ed (1956).* as it(t) or yt *I; H40; II; L74;
　Wed; Dob (in text); Cy, B; Gar.* when it
　P.

35 makes] drawes *D17 (also other MSS
　not collated for this edition, e.g. JC; BL
　Sloane 1792; Bodleian Eng. Poet e 37;
　and a seventeenth-century commonplace
　book belonging to Sir John Sparrow); Hay-
　ward.*

General note. This poem is quoted (though with some variations from the earlier
and more authoritative texts) in Walton's *Life of Donne*, fourth edn, 1675.
(Chambers points out that it was not printed in the first three editions of the
Life.) Walton says that the lines were given by Donne to his wife when he left
her to go with Sir Robert Drury to France in 1611. Walton adds: 'And I beg
leave to tell, that I have heard some Criticks, learned, both in Languages and
Poetry, say, that none of the Greek or Latin Poets did ever equal them.'

Doubt has, however, been cast on Walton's account. Professor Gardner, for
instance, holds stanza 2 to be no argument to use to a wife, who has no need to
hide her grief at her husband's absence (*ESS*, p. xxix). I do not find the point
very persuasive. There are, surely, marriages and marriages, and the pride in a

love above the common run can be felt within the marriage bond as well as outside it? We do not need, on the other hand, to accept Walton's dating or particulars. The poem could easily belong to the period of Donne's courtship of his wife, or to some earlier time during his marriage than 1611. It is, however, in any case, as Grierson said (II, p. 40), very similar in tone to the song 'Sweetest love', and, with it, at least among the most tender of Donne's love-poems. If it stems from a specific love-relationship at all, I would bank on its being that with Ann.

The poem comes fairly close to being a Platonic poem. Yet stanza 4 does not assert a wholly Platonic position. The lovers are not said not to care at all about missing 'eyes, lips, and hands', but only to care less than 'dull súblunary lovers' do. They have not 'grown all mind', like the hypothetical listener in *The Ecstasy*, l. 23. Moreover, the highly language-conscious Donne could hardly fail in writing l. 32 to have in mind the sense of 'erect' which would apply to the male sexual organ, and he could well, in a typically original way, have meant to suggest, secondarily and covertly, that it is the woman's clitoris which stiffens as the male partner returns home.

6 *tear-floods . . . sigh-tempests*] commonplaces of Petrarchan hyperbole.
   move] stir up.
7 *profanation*] The primary sense in English is quite certainly religious = 'desecration of something sacred'. 'By extension' (*OED*): 'the degradation or vulgarization of anything worthy of being held in reverence or respect'. *OED* cites this passage from Donne as an instance of the extended meaning. There is, however, certainly more to it than this. By this word and the word 'laity' in l. 8, I think Donne almost certainly wishes to allude to love as a mystery or cult, with adepts or initiates such as himself and his wife (to whom the poem was probably written). This idea certainly occurs in a number of places in Donne, for instance in: 'We for Love's clergy only are instruments' in *A Valediction: of the book* (l. 22) (see Notes on that poem).
9 *Moving of the earth*] an earthquake.
   brings] causes.
10] Not such an easy line as it might look. I think the meaning is: 'People calculate the damage it has done, and try to estimate its significance.' (An alternative interpretation is that it means; 'people narrate, etc.': but this older use of 'reckon' was fast dying out at the end of the sixteenth century. *OED* gives no instance after 1586.) Despite the scientific explanations of earthquakes given by Aristotle and others, and supported by later medieval theologians (e.g. the Cardinal d'Ailly, in *Concordia astronomicae veritatis cum Theologia*, Paris, 1483), earthquakes were still generally regarded as evidence of the wrath of God.
11] At the date when the poem was written there were three current senses of the word 'trepidation': (1) was 'tremulous agitation' (applying to

persons); (2) was 'tremor' (applying to things); (3) was the astronomical sense, which *OED* describes as follows: 'A libration of the eighth (or ninth) sphere, added to the system of Ptolemy by the Arab astronomer Thabet ben Korrah, *c.* 950, in order to account for certain phenomena, especially precession, really due to motion of the earth's axis.' This libration (oscillation) would communicate itself to all the smaller spheres. It was harmless ('innocent' in l. 12 meaning 'harmless'), in the sense that no harmful effect or portentous significance had ever been attributed to it.

13 *súblunary*] 'earthly', and therefore inferior, and moreover, subject to change like everything below the moon in medieval cosmology: but the literal meaning of 'sublunary' also suggests, as Dr T. R. Henn pointed out (in *The Apple and the Spectroscope*, London, 1951, p. 22), that such lovers are subject to ebb and flow like the tides. Although an accurate detailed account of the forces governing the tides was not given before Newton, correlation between the phases of the moon and the tides had often been made even in ancient times (e.g. by Strabo, Posidonius, Pliny) and it continued to be made in medieval times (see Dante) and in the Renaissance (e.g. by Kepler, whose work Donne knew).

14 *(Whose soul is sense)*] This may mean: 'Whose whole essence is sensuality'; or possibly, as Dr Henn suggested to me, 'Whose souls depend on the properties of sensation'.
admit] we would now say, perhaps, 'stand'.

16 *elemented it*] 'were the elements of which it [sublunary love] was made'. 'Composed it' would be too loose a translation. 'Elemented it' is stronger; it indicates that the love was through and through 'sublunary', i.e. that the ultimate entities of which it was composed were 'sublunary'. Donne distinguishes the two concepts in a sermon (VIII. 333): 'Elemented and composed of heresies' (i.e. such that all the parts and even the least parts – the elements – were heresies).

17–28] For the problems of the duality and/or unity of the true lovers' souls, and their ignorance or knowledge of their motivation, cf. the not wholly parallel lines 29–48 of *The Ecstasy*.

19 *Inter-assurèd of the mind*] The sense is: 'mutually confident of the fidelity of each other's minds'; but probably 'inter-assurèd' also contains a reference to a solemn legal assurance, or transference of title.

22 *endure not yet*] nevertheless do not suffer.

23 *expansion*] to be pronounced as four syllables.

24] Alluding, of course, to the beating of gold into leaf. Dr Henn suggested to me that there may be a further allusion here: to the airy thinness of the bodies assumed by angels (cf. *Air and Angels*). Mr Ingram calls my attention also to the fact that one ounce of gold, beaten out to the present standard thickness of English gold leaf (1/250,000 in.), would cover an area of 250 sq. ft.

beat] spelt 'bett' in some MSS, and, no doubt, in any case, pronounced so as to rhyme with 'yet'.

25] As Grierson pointed out (II, p. 41), a simile based on compasses occurs in Omar Khayyám. He prints translations furnished by a Captain Harris, of which a prose version by J. H. McCarthy (1898) reads as follows:

> Oh my soul, you and I are like a compass. We form but one body, having two points. Truly one point moves from the other point, and makes the round of the circle; but the day draws near when the two points must re-unite.

One cannot say whether Donne knew of the Omar Khayyám, which is, in any case, not very close in its tenor to Donne's image. There were, in any case, other more accessible sources, which could have sparked it off. Professor Praz long ago (*Secentismo e Marinismo in Inghilterra*, Florence, 1925, p. 109, n.) drew attention to the image in one of the madrigals of Guarini (1537–1612) (no. XCVI, *Rime*, Venice, 1598):

> Con voi sempre son io
> Agitato ma fermo:
> E se il Meno ne involo; il Più ne lasso.
> Son simile al Compasso,
> Chè un piede in voi quasi mio centro io fermo;
> L'altro patisce di Fortuna i giri,
> Ma non può far che intorno a voi non giri.

Professor Don Cameron Allen, *MLN* 71 (1956), pp. 256–7, thinks Donne may have borrowed the image from Guarini; but he also cites two analogues supplied to him by Professor Georges Poulet, one from Monin's *Le Phoenix*, Paris, 1585, and one from Père Mersenne's *Quaestiones in Genesim*, Paris, 1623, in which God is compared to the fixed foot of a pair of compasses, and creatures to the moving foot, which cannot produce anything perfect without being joined to God.

Another interesting angle on this part of the poem is provided by Mr W. A. Murray, in his article 'Donne's gold-leaf and his compasses', *MLN* 73 (1958), pp. 329–30, where he points out that the chemical symbol for gold, found in the medical and alchemical texts of Paracelsus (1493–1541), was a point surrounded by a circle; which might well have played a part in causing the transition in Donne's poem from the image of stanza 6 to that of stanzas 7–9. Mr Murray also quotes a passage from Paracelsus' *Paragranum*, in which Paracelsus writes of the fixed foot of the compasses controlling the circle, while the moving foot describes a wide periphery, and compares them to the relationship between the size of man and that of the heavens. It is known that Donne was acquainted with some of the work of Paracelsus; but I should be surprised if he did not also know

Guarini's poetry, and the image in that madrigal is very close in spirit to that of Donne.

Donne could well have often been glancing at the emblem of the compasses inscribing a circle on a tablet, which was used by Christophe Plantin, the sixteenth-century Belgian printer. As Miss Doris Powers points out, Donne had at least two volumes with the Plantin device in his library (*RES*, n.s. 9 (1958), pp. 173–5).

31 *hearkens*] probably intended to suggest the forward-leaning posture of a listener.

32 *that*] the roaming foot. The reading 'it', adopted by Professor Gardner, has rather stronger MS support, and reads less awkwardly; but it also tends to needless ambiguity, and makes for a plethora of 'it's. 'It' could, in any case, be a corruption of 'yt' = 'that' (cf. *Air and Angels*, l. 24).

32, 36] What do these lines refer to? There are several views current: (1) That they both refer to the completion of the circle; (2) that they both refer to the closing of the compasses; (3) that l. 32 refers to the closing of the compasses, while l. 36 refers to the completion of the circle. I feel fairly convinced that l. 36, at any rate, refers to the completion of the circle, and that view (2) is therefore wrong. It would seem strange to say that the 'firmness' of the fixed foot makes the moving foot end up next to the fixed foot when the compasses are closed. Furthermore, there is evidence from phraseology in Donne's use elsewhere of the image of a pair of compasses or the description of a circle, that l. 36 refers to the completion of the circle. Mr Josef Lederer has, for another purpose, collected cases of Donne's use of the simile of a pair of compasses (see Mr Lederer's interesting article 'John Donne and the emblematic practice', *RES*, July 1946). In one of the passages he quotes (from *Fifty Sermons*, London, 1649, I. 3) Donne writes:

> The Body of Man was the first point that the foot of God's Compasse was upon: First he created the Body of *Adam*: then he carries his Compasse round, and shuts up where he began, he ends with the Body of Man againe in the glorification thereof in the Resurrection.

Here Donne actually uses a phrase 'shuts up where he began', which, even more strongly than 'makes me end where I begun', would in itself suggest the closing of the compasses; and yet, in this passage from the sermon, it clearly refers to the completion of the circle, not to the closing of the compasses. Mr Adrian Cohen has drawn my attention to another case of similar phraseology referring clearly to the completion of a circle, viz. ll. 275–6 of *The First Anniversary*:

> So, of the Starres that boast that they do runne
> In Circle still, none ends where he begun.

All this seems to point to l. 36 referring to the completion of the circle.

As to views (1) and (3), after some hesitation I incline to view (3). I think l. 32 more probably refers to the closing of the compasses, first, because the fixed leg does not strictly 'grow erect' (i.e. grow erect in all planes) at any time during the description of the circle; and secondly, because the expression 'comes home' seems clearly intended to contrast with 'far doth roam', and this latter phrase seems more naturally to refer to the distance between the feet than to the distance along the circumference from the starting point of the description of a circle.

I feel bound to add that if view (3) is correct, as seems probable, then, despite the fact that the circle was for Donne (as for so many medieval and Renaissance writers) the symbol of perfection, and despite also the fact that drawing circles, rather than being closed, is the special function of compasses, the ending of the poem is to me not wholly satisfying, since the completion of the circle is somewhat of an anticlimax as a symbol of home-coming after the symbol of the closing of the compasses.

34 *obliquely run*] i.e. the describing arm follows a curved path, not a straight line.

35 *makes*] *D17*'s reading 'draws' is also that of some other MSS not collated for this edition, e.g. British Library Sloane 1792, *JC*, and a seventeenth-century commonplace book belonging to Sir John Sparrow. 'Draws' was first printed by Hayward in the Nonesuch Donne. At first sight it is more attractive than 'makes', but it has its own disadvantages. First, it might be said, the fixed foot does not *draw* the circle. Secondly, the phrase 'to draw just' is rather unsatisfactory. On the other hand, 'draws' is less tame than 'makes', and also avoids the repetition; and, further, it suggests in a lively way the process of drawing. Moreover, it is only a stretch complimentary to the woman to say that if it causes the circle to be drawn perfectly, it in a sense 'draws' it. Finally, it involves a valuable suggestion of the attractive force which the woman exerts on the man. (Cf. the primary tractive meaning of 'draw', which is also, perhaps, present here in a reference to the centripetal force controlling the moving foot of the compasses.) On balance, therefore, despite the overwhelming weight of textual authority against it, it seems to me the better of two not altogether satisfactory words. After much hesitation, however, I have decided not to print 'draws', since not only is the amount of evidence for it slight, but Sloane MS 1792 is not an impressive MS, nor, on the whole, are the two twin MSS *D17* and *JC*.

The Funeral

Whoever comes to shroud me, do not harm
      Nor question much
That subtle wreath of hair, which crowns my arm;
The mystery, the sign, you must not touch,
      For 'tis my outward Soul,   5
Viceroy to that, which then to heaven being gone,
      Will leave this to control,
And keep these limbs, her provinces, from dissolution.

For if the sinew-threads my brain lets fall
      Through every part,   10
Can tie those parts, and make me one of all;
These hairs which upward grew, and strength and art
      Have from a better brain,
Can better do it; except she meant that I
      By this should know my pain,   15
As prisoners then are manacled, when they're condemn'd to die.

Whate'er she meant by it, bury it with me,
      For since I am
Love's martyr, it might breed idolatry,
If into others' hands these relics came;   20
      As 'twas humility
To afford to it all that a Soul can do,
      So, 'tis some bravery,
That since you would save none of me, I bury some of you.

In 1633–1719. H40; *Wed; HK2, A25, D17 omit.*
Text: Title The Funeral *1633–1719; MSS.*
3 That] This *DC.*
4 sign, *so punctuated in some carefully punctuated MSS, e.g.* TCD, N; *Dob.*
6 then to *MSS.* unto *1633–1719.*
9 sinew-threds *DC.* sinew threds *S.* sinewy thread *(variously spelt) rest of MSS and edns collated.*

12 These *H49, D, SP; II; L74; DC; S96, Dob; Cy, B; S962.* Those *1633–1719; Lec, C57; Lut, O'F; P.* The *S.*
17 with me *almost all MSS; 1635–1719.* by me *1633; Cy (corrected to* with me).
24 save *H49; II; L74; DC; Lut (with* or have *in margin); Cy, P, B.* have *1633–1719; D, SP, Lec, C57; S96, Dob, O'F; S962.* om. *S.*

The Funeral

General note. As noted in the Introduction, many of the *Songs and Sonets* of the second period are shot through with religious references and suggestions. Some of the references are, however, specifically Catholic, as in this poem and *The Relic*, where the same kind of object, a wreath of hair round one of the poet's bones, or, as here, 'crowning' his arm, forms the centre of the poem. In both poems the hair clearly evokes the poet's loving reverence, though in this poem it also arouses other attitudes. In both cases, however, the hair *and* the part of the poet's body are referred to as 'relics'; but, whether by the time the poet wrote the poems he had become a whole-hearted Protestant, or was secretly still inclined to Catholicism but in a world dominantly hostile to it, he is careful to make it clear that to regard these objects as relics would be 'idolatry' (*The Funeral*, l. 19) or 'mis-devotion' (*The Relic*, l. 13). It is hard to estimate what weight to attach to these anti-Catholic strokes. What is, however, clear is that in this poem the woman has herself 'crowned' the poet's arm with the hair, and that the poem speculates on the possible significance of it. It is first seen, hyperbolically, as preservative and vitalizing, but then (ll. 14–16) as a possible sign of the woman's intention to kill him through his love for her. The poet then orders whoever comes to shroud him to bury his hair with his body, and he plainly asserts that his death was caused by martyrdom to love, and gives this as a reason for burying the hair with his body, since both his arm (seemingly) and the hair might otherwise come into the hands of people (Lovers? Catholics? – which? – it seems like a Galtonian picture) who would regard them as relics. Lines 21–4 then seem to sum up the positive and negative attitudes to the hair, and to the woman. Though the poet's attitudes are ambivalent, it is important, I think, to be clear that nothing in the first part of the poem negates the assertion in ll. 18–20 that he was 'love's martyr'.

For the controversy concerning the possible connection between this poem and Magdalen Herbert see Appendix VIII, p. 330.

1   *shroud*] i.e. in preparation of his body for burial.
2   *question much*] ask much about.
3   *subtle*] perhaps 'finely wrought', but also, possibly, 'of mysterious import'.
3]   cf. *The Relic*, l. 6.
8   *dissolution*] to be pronounced as five syllables.
9   *sinew-threads*] Despite the massive support from the MSS and early editions for 'sinewy thread', I have decided to adopt the more 'difficult' reading of *DC* and *S*. 'Threads' suggests more readily the graphic picture of the descending sinews and filaments of the nervous system ('sinews' bore both meanings at the time). 'Thread', though not incorrect as a collective, does not have this effect. Moreover, 's' is notoriously easily dropped (though, admittedly, also easily added) by scribes in transmission. 'Threads' has also the advantage of matching the plural 'hairs' (l. 12). Donne uses the plural 'sinews' as 'sent forth' from the 'Brain' (*Sermons*, I. 192).

9–11] The common conception of the working of the motor and sensory nervous systems is indicated in a passage in John Woolton's *Treatise of the Immortality of the Soul*, 1576: 'The animal, or lively spirit, which hath his seat in the brain, is distributed by the sinews into every part, giving unto the same power of moving and feeling' (fol. 75ʳ).

11   *and make me one of all*] and co-ordinate all parts into the single being which is myself.

12   *upward*] The sense is: 'towards heaven and a purer condition', as Professor Smith suggests.

14   *except*] unless perhaps . . .

19   *idolatry*] cf. *The Relic*, stanza 2.

22   *To afford to it all that a Soul can do*] A difficult line, probably meaning: 'To confer on it all that a soul can confer', viz. its viceroyalty: alternatively, 'to credit it with all the powers of a soul' (cf. in either case, stanza 1).

23] The sense is: 'So, by way of compensation, it is a touch of bravado'.

23–4] Here we have a typically vigorous reaction against that form of Petrarchism which would accept Love's martyrdom without hitting back.

24   *save*] by returning his passion.

Love's Deity

I long to talk with some old lover's ghost,
　　Who died before the God of Love was born:
I cannot think that he who then lov'd most
　　Sunk so low as to love one which did scorn.
But since this god produc'd a destiny,　　　　　　　　5
And that vice-nature, custom, lets it be:
　　I must love her, that loves not me.

Sure, they which made him god, meant not so much;
　　Nor he, in his young godhead, practis'd it:
But when an even flame two hearts did touch,　　　　10
　　His office was indulgently to fit
Actives to passives. Correspondency
Only his subject was; it cannot be
　　Love, till I love her that loves me.

But every modern god will now extend　　　　　　　15
　　His vast prerogative, as far as Jove.
To rage, to lust, to write to, to commend,
　　All is the purlieu of the God of Love.
Oh! were we waken'd by this tyranny
To ungod this child again, it could not be　　　　　20
　　That I should love who loves not me.

Rebel and atheist too, why murmur I,
　　As though I felt the worst that Love could do?
Love might make me leave loving, or might try
　　A deeper plague, to make her love me too,　　　25
Which, since she loves before, I am loth to see;
Falsehood is worse than hate; and that must be,
　　If she whom I love, should love me.

In 1633–1719 and all MSS here collated.
TCC omits stanza 3, Wed stanza 4.
Text: Title Love's Deity *(variously spelt)*
1633–1719 and most MSS (? L74 inserted
later). Elegye P.
　8 which] that *H40 (corrected from* which*);*
　　L74; III; S962.

10 flame] desire *Cy, P. om. HK2.*
14 till . . . me] if I loue [her] who loues
　　not mee *Lut, O'F (which cancels* her*).* till
　　. . . not me *S962.*
21 That I should loue, who *I; H40 (no*
　　comma); II (TCC, A18 no comma); L74;
　　Wed; DC (no comma); HK2 (no comma),

A25, Cy (no comma), P (no comma), D17 (no comma); Gar. That I should loue her, who *S96, Dob.* That I should loue [her] who *Lut, O'F (cancels* That *not* her *as recorded in Gar).* yet I should loue her who *S962.* That I should Loue, that *S.* I should love her, who

loves not me(e) *1633–1719; B; Gr; Ed (1956).*

23 could] can *Lec (also C57 before correction); D17.*

24 might make *almost all MSS.* may make *1633–1719; C57, Lec.*

General note. The first three stanzas are vigorously rebellious against the God of Love. At the start of stanza 4 the poet seems to renegue on that attitude. Yet the final stanza actually envisages still worse courses of action by Love: stopping the poet from loving, or making the woman return his love. The idea of the lover having his love stopped is one on which Petrarch was somewhat ambivalent, whereas he always longed to have his love returned; and in these two attitudes many Petrarchans followed him. Donne here with much force rejects the idea of ceasing to love; but also rejects the idea of his love being returned. The attitude expressed in stanza 4 is, indeed, therefore, radically opposed to that expressed in the first three. The poet now says he wants to love, and *not* to be loved in return. Yet Donne is not reconciled to the ways of the God of Love; and in this respect he is as rebellious as ever.

3 *he who then lov'd most*] even the man who loved more than anyone else did.
5 *produc'd a destiny*] ordained a fate for lovers.
6 *vice-nature*] 'second nature'; but probably there is also a derogatory play on the word 'vice'.
8 *meant not so much*] possibly: 'did not mean to give him so much power'; alternatively: 'did not mean it to have this effect'.
9 *in his young godhead*] i.e. during the early part of his period of godhead.
10 *even*] of the same degree.
11–12] His function was obligingly to pair off the passive lovers with their corresponding active lovers (i.e., presumably, the women with the men).
13–14 *it . . . me*] i.e. nothing could be love unless it was mutual.
15 *modern*] probably 'common or garden' (see *OED* 4 *obs.*).
will] wants to.
17] i.e. all the expedients of lovers where mutual love does not, yet at least, exist.
18 *purlieu*] Henry II and John had incorporated land, not previously crown land, into royal forests, claiming to do so under their prerogative. Pressure on Henry III forced him to disafforest much of this land under the *Carta de foresta* (1217), and to grant wide rights of ranging over, cultivating and taking game from the disafforested tracts, which were known as 'purlieus'. Attempts were made by later monarchs, including the Stuarts, to regain rights over the 'purlieus'.
21] The MS support for this reading is overwhelming, but the line is perhaps not as pleasing as that printed in *1633*.

24] cf. the *1633* reading of *Twickenham Garden*, ll. 14–15.

24–8] The poet's reason for rejecting the return of his love (that the woman would be false) is, if genuine, clearly contrary to the attitude expressed in *Twickenham Garden*, ll. 26–7.

26 *loves before*] has a lover already.

27 *that must be*] that is what it would necessarily be.

28 *should*] were to.

Twickenham Garden

Blasted with sighs, and surrounded with tears,
 Hither I come to seek the spring,
 And at mine eyes, and at mine ears,
Receive such balms as else cure everything;
 But oh, self-traitor, I do bring   5
The spider love, which transubstantiates all,
 And can convert manna to gall;
And that this place may thoroughly be thought
 True Paradise, I have the serpent brought.

'Twere wholesomer for me, that winter did   10
 Benight the glory of this place,
 And that a grave frost did forbid
These trees to laugh, and mock me to my face;
 But that I may not this disgrace
Endure, nor leave this garden, Love, let me   15
 Some senseless piece of this place be;
Make me a mandrake, so I may groan here,
 Or a stone fountain weeping out my year.

Hither with crystal vials, lovers, come,
 And take my tears, which are love's wine,   20
 And try your mistress' tears at home,
For all are false, that taste not just like mine;
 Alas, hearts do not in eyes shine,
Nor can you more judge woman's thoughts by tears,
 Than by her shadow, what she wears.   25
O pérverse sex, where none is true but she
 Who's therefore true, because her truth kills me.

In 1633–1719 and all MSS here collated.
Text: Title Twickenham Garden Ed
(1956). Twicknam Garden 1633–1719;
(variously spelt) II; DC; III; P, S; S962. In a
Garden B. No title other MSS collated except
L74 where Twittnam Garden added in later
hand.
 2 come 1633–1719; I; H40; DC; III; Cy,
  P, S; S962; Gr; Ed (1956); Gar. came II;

L74; Wed; HK2, A25, D17, B.
4 balm(e)s . . . cure 1633; I; H40; Wed;
 DC; A25, D17; S962; Gr; Ed (1956);
 Gar. balmes . . . cures L74; TCD, N.
 balme . . . cures TCC, A18; III; HK2,
 Cy, P, B, S; 1635–1719.
8 may 1633–1719; I; H40; L74; DC; III;
 Cy, P; S962. might II; Wed; HK2,
 A25, D17, B, S.

12 grave] gray *III; Cy, D17; S962.* gray
grave *S.*
did] would *II; L74; HK2, A25, Cy, P.*
15 nor leave this garden *II; L74; Wed; III;
HK2, A25, Cy, P, D17, S; 1635–1719;
Ed (1956); Gar.* leave this garden *B
(which reads* and no more *for* Endure
nor*). nor yet leave loving *1633; DC;
Chambers; Gr. om. I; H40 (which have
endure at the end of l. 14 and* Love let
me *at the start of l. 16); S962 (which has
let me at start of l. 16).*
16 piece] part(e) *II; L74; HK2, Cy, P, S.*

17 gro(a)ne *H49, D, SP; H40; DC; TCC,
A18, N; TCD (altered from* groane *to*
growe, *and then back again to* groane);
Gr. grow(e) *1633–1719; Lec, C57;
L74; Wed; III; HK2, A25, Cy, P, D17,
B, S; S962; Gar.*
18 my *1633; I; H40; Wed; DC; B, S; S962;
1669–1719.* the *II; L74; III; HK2,
A25, Cy, P, D17; 1635–54.*
24 woman's *H49, D, SP; H40; TC, N;
L74; Wed; A25, B; S962; 1719; Gr.*
women's *1633–69; Lec; A18; DC; III;
HK2, Cy, P, D17, S.* women *C57.*

General note. Twickenham Park was the residence of Donne's friend, the Countess of Bedford, from 1608 to 1618. For further details concerning the connection of the poem with Lady Bedford see Appendix X, pp. 336–8.

The contrast between spring and the sadness of the unsatisfied lover was a recurring theme of Petrarchism originating in Petrarch's own attractive sonnet (*Canz*. 310), which was actually written after Laura's death, but much of which could well have been said during her life. Surrey's English adaptation of that sonnet, 'The soote season, that bud and bloom forth brings', is well known; but W. von Koppenfels (op. cit., p. 77) cites further English examples by Watson, Linche and Turberville. Donne's detailed inventions surpass any of those of his English predecessors, and are utterly different from and even superior to those in Petrarch's own fine sonnet.

1 *surrounded with tears*] 'flooded with tears'. This sense of 'surrounded' (*OED* 1), deriving from late Latin *superundare*, became obsolete soon after Donne's time. He uses the word in this sense many times in the sermons, a particularly striking case being where he writes that David 'surrounded his bed with tears' (*Sermons*, VIII. 196).
1–9] A miraculous subsumption and transformation of Petrarchan properties and hyperboles: sighs, tears, balms, Paradise, with a number of original touches: 'self-traitor', 'spider love', 'transubstantiates', and the conversion of 'manna to gall', instead of the commonplace 'honey to gall'. K. E. Faas (*Schein u. Sein in der frühelisabethanischen Lyrik u. Prosa (1550–1590)*, unpublished dissertation, University of Munich, 1965, p. 15) relevantly points out that in Elizabethan literature and emblem lore the spider was considered to suck poison from the same flowers from which the bee sucked honey – in Donne the bee, which would explain the appearance of the spider here, has not been brought in, because the 'honey' has been replaced by 'manna' (see W. von Koppenfels, op. cit., p. 79).
6–7] Alluding, as Chambers pointed out, to the popular belief that spiders were full of poison. Donne speaks several times in the sermons of spiders as

poisonous, e.g. at *Sermons*, I. 293, where he calls a spider 'a blister of Poyson'.

6 *transubstantiates all*] 'changes everything into another substance'. There may also be an ironical allusion to the Roman Catholic doctrine of transubstantiation.

9 *the serpent*] the great tempter, mentioned possibly because the speaker knows that what he wants is sinful.

10 *'Twere wholesomer for me*] It would make me less miserable.
that] if.

12 *grave*] probably intended as a play on (1) heavy, (2) austere. This play is achieved in modern English by 'severe'.

14 *disgrace*] probably 'affront' (*OED* 1c).

15 *nor leave this garden*] The Group I; *H40* reading

> But that I may not this disgrace endure,
> Love, let me, some senseless piece of this place be.

is clearly wrong in point of rhyme and metre. *1633*'s reading for l. 15, 'Indure, nor yet leave loving, / Love let mee' is evidently not, however, an invention by the *1633* editor, as Professor Gardner surmised it might be. Grierson rightly pointed out that it was older than *1633*, since it was the reading of the MS from which the Dutch poet Constantin Huyghens translated. We do not know what MS that was; but we now find the same reading in *DC*. As Grierson conceded, however, 'nor leave this garden' makes better sense.

16 *senseless*] insensible.

17 *mandrake*] Mandrakes have forked roots, and were popularly supposed to groan when uprooted. Presumably, however, Donne wishes to be able to groan more than once, and *in situ*, so he is probably referring to a mandrake as something insensible which groans; that is, *if* the reading 'groan' is to be accepted. (For further information on the mandrake see F. L. Lucas's excellent note in *The Works of John Webster*, London, 1927, vol. I, pp. 227–8.)
groan] for my reasons for preferring 'groan' to *1633*'s 'grow' see Appendix IX, pp. 334–5.

17–18] If Donne were a mandrake or a stone fountain his groaning or weeping would be inconspicuous, for a mandrake *has* to groan, and a fountain *has* to weep. He would also himself be insensitive to the intolerable present situation.

18] Petrarch often feels turned to stone by Laura's unresponsiveness. In one place (*Canz.* 243, ll. 13–14) he writes of himself as an insensible stone, and of Laura as 'Paradise'. The occurrence of 'Paradise' and 'stone' in Donne's poem might have sprung from some subconscious reminiscence of Petrarch's sonnet. As for the weeping fountain, Grierson, in his note on the line in *Metaphysical Lyrics and Poems of the Seventeenth Century: Donne to*

Butler, Oxford, 1921, quotes a parallel from Petrarch, *Canz*. 23, ll. 115 ff.

19 *crystal vials*] lachrymatories or tear-vessels. Many archaeologists, even in the nineteenth century, still took the small phials of glass or alabaster often found in Roman tombs to be lachrymatories. They were probably for holding scent.

19 ff.] An original and typically ingenious and ironical turn, with a barbed shaft at the female sex in general.

21 *try*] test.

26–27] This may mean: 'O perverse sex, no member of which is faithful except the one who is quite certainly faithful, because her faithfulness [to another] kills me.' Alternatively: 'O perverse sex . . . except the one who is faithful just in order that her faithfulness [to another] shall be mortal to me.' Whichever way the lines are to be taken, they are in the spirit of the courtly love tradition of the Troubadours.

The Blossom

Little think'st thou, poor flower,
  Whom I have watch'd six or seven days,
And seen thy birth, and seen what every hour
Gave to thy growth, thee to this height to raise,
And now dost laugh and triumph on this bough,   5
    Little think'st thou
That it will freeze anon, and that I shall
Tomorrow find thee fall'n, or not at all.

Little think'st thou, poor heart,
  That labour'st yet to nestle thee,   10
And think'st by hovering here to get a part
In a forbidden or forbidding tree,
And hop'st her stiffness by long siege to bow,
    Little think'st thou
That thou tomorrow, ere that Sun doth wake,   15
Must with this sun and me a journey take.

But thou which lov'st to be
  Subtle to plague thyself, wilt say:
'Alas! if you must go, what's that to me?
Here lies my business, and here I will stay: 20
You go to friends, whose loves and means present
    Various content
To your eyes, ears, and tongue, and every part.
If then your body go, what need you a heart?'

In 1633–1719. H40; L74; Wed; HK2, Cy,
P omit.
Text: Title The Blossom 1633–1719; all
MSS but A25. No title A25.
10 labour'st or labourest or labo(u)r(e)st
  D, SP; II; DC; III; A25, D17, B, S;
  1635–1719. labo(u)rs 1633; H49, Lec,
  C57; S962 (seemingly).
15 that Sun] the Sun III.

21 loves II; DC; S96, Dob; A25, D17, B,
  S; S962. love 1633–1719; I; Lut, O'F;
  Gr; Ed (1956); Gar.
23 tongue almost all MSS. Om. S. tast
  1633–1719.
24 need you a I; TCD, N; DC, III (O'F
  b.c.); A25 (y'a), B, S; S962. need your
  1633–1719. need you have a D17.
  need you TCC (a deleted), A18.

Well then, stay here; but know, 25
When thou hast stay'd and done thy most,
A naked thinking heart, that makes no show,
Is, to a woman, but a kind of ghost;
How shall she know my heart; or, having none,
Know thee for one? 30
Practice may make her know some other part;
But take my word, she doth not know a heart.

Meet me at London, then,
Twenty days hence, and thou shalt see
Me fresher, and more fat, by being with men, 35
Than if I had stay'd still with her and thee.
For God's sake, if you can, be you so too:
I would give you
There, to another friend, whom we shall find
As glad to have my body, as my mind. 40

---

38 would *H49, D, SP; II; DC; III (O'F b.c.); A25, D17, B, S; S962.* will *1633–1719; Lec, C57.*

General note. Addresses by the lover to his heart are commonplaces in the Petrarchan tradition. Among this poem's original features are the invention of the convincing details. Striking too are the frank expression of sexual desire, and the impudence of the sexual reference in l. 31. This sexuality distances the poem from Petrarchan poetry in its chaster forms. The poem has also a high degree of formal beauty, and the naturalness of the tone in which the heart is addressed, and in which it replies, is miraculously combined with the complex stanza form.

For the controversy concerning the possible connection between this poem and Magdalen Herbert see Appendix VIII, pp. 330–3.

1–24] The parallelism of the first two stanzas suggests that for the poet's heart to be taken away from the lady will be tantamount to the chill of death. Yet the heart bounces up in very lively repartee. Its reply is, however, criticized by the poet's reference to the heart as 'subtle to plague' itself, and in the rest of the poem the lover has the upper hand, and ends cock-a-hoop with the prospect of giving his heart to a woman who will welcome his sex as happily as his intellect. What apparently started as a Petrarchan lament therefore ends as an anti-Petrarchan triumph; unless of course, even the ending is an indirect form of courting.

2 *I have watch'd*] We must slur 'I have', not pronounce 'watched' as

disyllabic; otherwise we would have an extra foot, out of keeping with the other stanzas.

7–8] Dr Werner von Koppenfels interestingly draws our attention to the Petrarchan use of the frost-death of flowers and plants as a metaphor for the effect of the lady's coldness, and refers us to Luigi Tansillo's 'Qual arbor, che nascendo . . .', *Canzoniere*, ed. E. Percopò, Naples, 1926, p. 81 (Koppenfels, op. cit., p. 118).

9 *heart*] Throughout the poem there is play on 'heart' as (1) the soul or mind, as seat of the affections and will, and (2) the physical heart.

12 *forbidden or forbidding*]. 'forbidden' suggesting that the relationship Donne desires is illicit; 'forbidding' implying that the woman is trying to repel his advances towards a physical relationship.

15 *that Sun*] i.e. his lady. Cf. *A Nocturnal upon St Lucy's Day*, ll. 37–9. Normally in the Petrarchan tradition, and often in Donne, the woman as Sun would be considered superior to the ordinary sun; but here Donne is probably reversing that, and even parodying Petrarchism.

16 *this sun*] i.e. the ordinary sun, whose warmth, contrasting with the chill of l. 7, possibly hints at the more hopeful direction the poem is to take.

17–18] But you, who love to refine on your self-torture, . . .

17–40] Dialogues between self and heart, and separations between self and heart (as in *The Legacy*), were commonplaces in Petrarchan poetry. It is Donne's detailed invention that is brilliant.

21 *loves*] The plural has somewhat stronger MS support, and suggests more vividly the plurality and variety of his London friends.

22 *content*] satisfaction.

26 *done thy most*] i.e. to please his mistress.

27 *A naked thinking heart*] probably meaning a heart which merely feels about its mistress, without being able to show her attentions (because of the absence of the rest of the body or of the body as a whole).

35 *more fat*] better fed (*OED* 2), and so, we might say, 'in better fettle'.
   men] people (not necessarily males).

38 *would*] should like to.

The Primrose

Upon this primrose hill
   Where, if Heav'n would distil
A shower of rain, each several drop might go
To his own primrose, and grow manna so;
And where their form, and their infinity   5
   Make a terrestrial galaxy,
   As the small stars do in the sky:
I walk to find a true love; and I see
That 'tis not a mere woman that is she,
But must or more or less than woman be.   10

   Yet know I not, which flower
   I wish; a six, or four;
For should my true-love less than woman be,
She were scarce anything; and then, should she
Be more than woman, she would get above   15
   All thought of sex, and think to move
   My heart to study her, not to love;
Both these were monsters; since there must reside
Falsehood in woman, I could more abide
She were by art, than Nature, falsified.   20

   Live, Primrose, then, and thrive
   With thy true number, five;
And women, whom this flower doth represent,
With this mysterious number be content;
Ten is the farthest number; if half ten   25
   Belong unto each woman, then
   Each woman may take half us men;
Or, if this will not serve their turn, since all
Numbers are odd, or even, and they fall
First into this five, women may take us all.   30

In 1633–1719. H40; L74; Wed; HK2, A25, Cy, P, D17 *omit.*
Text: Title The Primrose *1633; MSS.* The Primrose, being at Mountgomery Castle, upon the hill, on which it is situate *1635–1719.*
17 study her, not to *I; II; DC; Dob, O'F; S; S962; 1635–39; Gar.* study her, and

not to *1633, 1719; S96* (study her:
. . .); *Gr; Ed (1956)*. study her, not
Lut. study her and not to *B; 1650–69*.

26 Belong(e) *almost all MSS; Gr*. Belongs
1633–1719; C57.

30 this five, *1633; I; II; DC; S96, Dob; B,
S; S962; Ed (1956)*. this, five, *Gr; Gar*.
five, *Lut, O'F; 1635–1719; Chambers*.
women] they *DC*.

Note on the title. Mo(u)ntgomery Castle was the seat of the Herbert family. Aubrey (*Brief Lives*, ed. A. Clark, London, 1898, vol. I, p. 308) writes: 'Southwards, without the castle, is *Prim-rose hill*: vide Donne's Poems, p. 53'; and he quotes the first stanza of this poem, noting against l. 1: 'In the parke'.

General note. The general drift of the poem, with its delightfully fanciful conceits, is that the most satisfactory relationship between man and woman involves both sex and mind. In ll. 25–7 Donne seems to be teasing women with the idea that they are only up to satisfying half of a man's desires or needs, and so only deserve half of each man; but he ends by conceding humorously that if that is not enough for them they can have the whole of each man.

For the controversy concerning the possible connection between this poem and Magdalen Herbert see Appendix VIII, pp. 330–3.

2–4 *Where . . . grow manna so*] i.e. where there are so many primroses that if Heaven should let fall a shower of rain upon it, each single drop would be able to find its home in a primrose, and so turn into vital food. (I owe this interpretation to discussion with Grierson.)

4 *his*] its.

5–7] Professor C. M. Coffin has suggested (*John Donne and the New Philosophy*, New York, 1937, ll. 151–4) that these lines make it almost certain that the poem post-dates Galileo's *Siderius Nuncius*, 1610, where telescopic evidence for the view that the Galaxy consisted of an immense number of small stars was first announced. As Professor Coffin rightly states, however, such a *theory* of the Galaxy had been held by various writers since ancient times.

6 *galaxy*] Milky Way.

8 *a true love*] playing on the two senses (1) a beloved, (2) a primrose with an irregular number of petals (i.e. more or less than five), considered as a symbol of faithful love, see note on l. 12 below). I think Grierson does not represent the precise situation when he says (II, p. 48) that Donne is seeking for a primrose to symbolize his love, but 'fears to find either more or less'. Donne is not at first looking for a five-petalled primrose, he is looking for a six or four, since those oddities were considered symbols of faithful love. He only renounces sixes and fours later, when he has realized what creatures would correspond to them.

12   *a six, or four*] a six-petalled, or four-petalled primrose. With regard to the six-petalled primrose, Chambers quotes from Browne's *Britannia's Pastorals* a passage in which such a primrose is described as being used as a 'true-love', i.e. as a symbol of faithful love. A four-leafed *clover* has for centuries been regarded as auspicious to lovers.

19–20 *I could . . . falsified*] The sense is probably: 'I would far rather have her made false artificially, than that she should be false by nature'. 'Art' may refer to deliberate interference, such as seduction. It is just conceivable that Donne is here casting a wistful glance at the possibility that he might be the seducer. Alternatively, the falsification may simply be, as Professor Gardner suggests, the woman's painting of her face. Alternatively the sense might be, as Professor D. L. Peterson suggests (op. cit., p. 302), that it is better that women should be false through affectation than that nature should have created them other than they are.

24   *mysterious*] potent in occult thinking. Mentioning the number 'five' in connection with the Pentateuch (E. M. Simpson (ed.), *Essays in Divinity*, Oxford, 1952, p. 10), Donne shows some indulgence for the 'harmless recreation and entertainment' of Cabalistic speculations.

25   *Ten is the farthest number*] i.e. the number at the upper extreme of the scale 1–10, and so, in the decimal system, any larger number can only be expressed by using some smaller number, i.e. any digit in the range 1–9. In *Essays in Divinity*, p. 59, Donne refers to ten and seven as 'the two greatest numbers', saying of ten: 'for *ten* cannot be exceeded, but that to express any further Numbre you must take a part of it again', . . .

25–7] The poet has already (ll. 23–4) taken the normal five-petalled primrose to represent woman. So, if ten be taken to correspond to the whole of each man, then, each woman counting for five, each woman can have half of each man. This seems more likely, I think, than Professor Legouis's view that the meaning is that each woman may take half all existent males; though that view cannot be ruled out.

28–30] The sense may be: 'Or, if they are not satisfied with that, then, since all numbers are odd or even [and therefore any number or numbers chosen to represent a man are either odd or even], and since the numbers which symbolize or represent the odd and even [two and three, the number one not being either odd or even] are contained in this number five [since they add up to it], then women may each take all of a man.' (I owe much to Grierson's note here, though as a whole my interpretation differs from his.) Professor Legouis took the meaning to be that each woman could have all the men in the world.

30   *this five*] Grierson found difficulty here, and punctuated 'this, five', taking the two words as in apposition; but the phrase 'this five' seems to be more satisfactory as it stands. It seems to represent just that play of almost childish fancy, in which Donne is indulging in much of this poem. Children playing dominoes often say such things as 'there's that double six

again' or 'I don't like this double five'. The demonstrative adjective expresses a sort of intimacy, and the usage is perhaps a case of incipient animism.

The Relic

When my grave is broke up again
Some second guest to entertain
(For graves have learn'd that woman-head,
To be to more than one a bed),
    And he that digs it spies   5
A bracelet of bright hair about the bone,
    Will he not let us alone,
And think that there a loving couple lies,
Who hop'd that this device might be some way
To make their souls, at the last busy day,   10
Meet at this grave, and make a little stay?

If this fall in a time, or land,
    Where mis-devotion doth command,
    Then he that digs us up will bring
    Us to the Bishop, and the King,   15
    To make us relics; then
Thou shalt be a Mary Magdalen, and I
    A something else thereby;
All women shall adore us, and some men;
And, since at such times miracles are sought,   20
I would have that age by this paper taught
What miracles we harmless lovers wrought.

First, we lov'd well and faithfully,
    Yet knew not what we lov'd, nor why;
    Difference of sex we never knew,   25
    No more than our guardian angels do;
    Coming and going, we
Perchance might kiss, but not betwixt those meals;
    Our hands ne'er touch'd the seals
Which nature, injur'd by late law, sets free: 30
These miracles we did; but now, alas,
All measure, and all language, I should pass,
Should I tell what a miracle she was.

In *1633–1719*. H40; L74; Wed; HK2, Cy,
P omit.

Text: Title The Relique *1633–1719; MSS
except A25. No title A25.*

9 Who hop'd . . . some *Ed.* Who
thought . . . some *1633–1719; Gr; Ed
(1956); Gar.* Wch. thought . . . some
II; DC. Who hop'd . . . a *I; III; D17,
B, S; S962.*

14 Then he that digs us *1633–1719; II;
DC.* He that doth dig it *I; III; B, S;
S962.* He which doth dig us *D17.* He
which doth dig it *A25.*

17 Thou shalt be *1633–1719; II; DC.*
You shall be (*or* shalbe) *I; III; A25,
D17, B, S; S962.*

20 times *II; DC; III; D17, B, S; S962; Gar.*

time *1633–1719; I; A25; Gr; Ed (1956).*

21 I would have that age *1633–1719; I;
III; A25, D17, B, S; S962; Gr.* I would
that age were *II; DC; Gar.*

25–6 we never knew, / No more than
our *S96, Dob; B (no comma); S962; Ed
(1956).* we never knew, / No more
than *1635–1719; Lut, O'F.* no more
we knew, / Than our *1633; II (TCC,
A18 read* know*); DC (reads* know*); Gr;
Gar.* we never knew, / More than our
I (SP, Lec no comma); A25, D17, S.

28 betwixt *I; III; A25, D17, B, S; S962.*
between *1633–1719; II; DC.*

29 the *1633–1719; I; III; A25, D17, B, S;
S962.* those *II; DC.*

General note. Fundamentally this poem is a glorification of Platonic love, to
which it finally ascribes a deeply religious character. The poem starts with a
gibe at women in general, but already in stanza 1 shows concern for the particular love between the poet and the woman, which Donne expresses in the
movingly wistful fiction of the 'device'. In stanza 2 Donne's satirical strain
again asserts itself, this time directed against what he considers the abuses of
Roman Catholicism, and the credulity which feeds them, especially that of
women. At the end of stanza 2, however, Donne brilliantly turns the imagined
future situation to his purpose by offering to the imagined believers, thirsting
for a miracle, the miracle of the Platonic love between him and the woman,
which he describes in stanza 3, rising to the afflatus of the final lines, in which
the wonder is said to be the woman herself. It might be possible to interpret
this hyperbolical praise of the woman as cynical. Such a view may be hard to
refute conclusively. Yet I personally would find it hard to swallow. Donne is,
indeed, fond of reversals; but this particular reversal would run so strongly
against the prevailing spirit of the poem that the ending would be unclear; and
unclarity is not typical of Donne.

For the controversy concerning the possible connection between this poem
and Magdalen Herbert see Appendix VIII, p. 330.

1–2] Common by Donne's time where burial-ground was crowded.

3 *woman-head*] 'womanly nature', with a possible undertone derived from
the similarity of form to 'maidenhead'.

6] cf. *The Funeral*, l. 3.
bright] probably golden, as in Renaissance paintings of Mary Magdalen.

9 *hop'd*] the emotional content makes this reading more attractive than
'thought' (*II, DC, 1633–1719*).

some] this reading is rhythmically more satisfying than 'a', and also alliter-
ates happily with 'souls' (l. 10).

10 *last busy day*] the Resurrection.

12 *this*] i.e. the digging-up of the body.
fall] happen.

13 *mis-devotion*] 'false idolatry'. In view of what follows it is probable that
Donne is here covertly attacking Roman Catholicism. The use of relics had
been abandoned in all the Reformed churches.

15 *the Bishop, and the King*] This is a somewhat strange phrase; if the reference
is meant to be to Roman Catholic practice, it appears to be, technically at
least, mistaken. The King never had any power in the Roman Church dis-
cipline to recognize relics, i.e. to recognize any physical object as a relic.
Kings, on the other hand, had from time to time assisted in the translation
of relics, i.e. their transference to a shrine where they could be venerated.
Edward I, for example, assisted in the translation of the remains of St
Hugh of Lincoln. Bishops, however, from early Christian times, had
recognized relics, and this practice was specifically enjoined by the Council
of Trent at about the middle of the sixteenth century. (For further details
see *The Catholic Encyclopaedia*, Ibrola, NY, 1907–14, Articles 'Relics',
'Beatification' and 'Canonization'.) On the other hand, a Council of Metz
in 813 required that the sanction of either the prince or the bishop, and the
permission of a sacred synod should be obtained for the *translation* of relics
(see the article 'Relics' in J. Hastings (ed.), *The Encyclopaedia of Religion
and Ethics*, 13 vols, Edinburgh, 1908–26).

18 *A something else*] This phrase is capable of two interpretations. It may mean
simply (1) 'some other relic', or it may (2) have a very bold sense, namely,
that people in that age of 'mis-devotion' will take Donne's bone for one of
Christ's. Mr R. C. Cook, with whom I discussed this line, rightly suggested to me that the very possibility of interpretation (1) is itself some
support to interpretation (2), since it would afford a cover against any
imputation of blasphemy. In any case, as Mr Cook also urged, Donne is
only attributing such a thought to an age of 'mis-devotion'. Interpretation
(2) is a teasing possibility, and I am inclined to think it is the right one,
since interpretation (1) is so tame. F. L. Lucas told me that he had
independently hit upon the idea of Christ as the only possible one. He
suggested to me that support for it could be found in Luther's pronouncement that Christ and the Magdalen were lovers. This occurs in an extraordinary passage in Luther's *Table Talk* (Weimar edn, vol. II, p. 107), in
which he alleges that Christ was three times an adulterer, once with the
woman at the well, once with Mary Magdalen, and once with the woman
taken in adultery. Professor Gardner (*ESS*, p. 222) writes of 'the story of
Luther's remark', calling it 'a hoary *canard*'. It is unclear whether she is
denying that Luther ever made the allegations attributed to him in his
Table Talk, even in his cups. If so, one would need to know the evidence

for doing so. She also maintains that 'however sunk in "mis-devotion" an age was, it would surely be aware that the grave of Christ contained no relics other than his grave-clothes'. With respect, this is by no means evident: the scope of 'mis-devotion' is surely astonishing? Professor Christopher Ricks has made the interesting point that 'a Jesus Christ' and 'a something else' are metrically equivalent (see A. J. Smith (ed.), *John Donne: The Complete English Poems*, Harmondsworth, 1971, p. 397).

thereby] i.e. through the action of the Bishop and the King. (I owe this point to Mr J. Russell.)

19 *adore*] Again, it may be worth pointing out that in strict Roman Catholic practice relics are not adored but venerated. No doubt, though, actual practice has often enough deviated from pure doctrine.

and some men] possibly a cynical distinction, constituting a hit at the credulity of women: or possibly, simply, as F. L. Lucas suggested to me, a reference to the greater interest of women in love romances.

20] That God 'fittingly honours relics by working miracles in their presence' is categorically stated by St Thomas Aquinas (*Summa Theologica*, III. 9. 25. 6). They came to be particularly expected at the time of consecration.

21 *this paper*] i.e. the poem.

22 *harmless*] probably 'free from guilt', 'innocent' (*OED* 3).

24 *what*] i.e. what in each other. Cf. *The Ecstasy*, l. 32.

25–6] *1633* and all MSS here collated, except *Lut*, *O'F*, contain 'our'. On the other hand, 'Than our guardian angels do' (*1633, II, DC*) has always seemed to me rhythmically weak; while 'More than our' (*I, A25, D17, S*) cannot bear the weight of the antecedent clause. 'Any more' (which has no support in early editions or MSS) or 'No more' (which does have MS support) seems required. Hence I have adopted the reading of *S96, Dob, B* and *S962*. This reading also receives some support from the fact that all the remaining printed editions 1635–1719 read:

> Difference or sex we never knew,
> No more than guardian angels do.

Since all the MSS, however, contain the word 'our', the reading adopted seems preferable to that of the printed editions 1635–1719. I suspected their omission of the word 'our' of being merely an editorial attempt to make the metre quite regular, until I found that this is also the reading of *Lut* and *O'F*.

27 *Coming and going*] Grierson points out that this was one of the uses of kissing sanctioned in the Bible. He also points out that Erasmus, writing in 1499, seems to regard the kiss of salutation and the kiss of parting as specially English.

28 *meals*] the kiss being the food of the soul.

29–30 *Our hands . . . free*] A paraphrase might run: 'We never attempted that physical union which Nature allows to all, but which upstart human laws have subjected to restraint.' The passage is, as Grierson pointed out to me, a close imitation of Ovid, *Metamorphoses*, x. 329 ff. (cf. also Grierson, *Criticism and Creation*, London, 1949, p. 104). The lines in Ovid are as follows:

> Felices quibus ista licent! Humana malignas
> Cura dedit leges et quod natura remittit
> Invida jura negant.

These lines are rendered by Golding, the Elizabethan translator, as follows:

> . . . In happy case they are
> That may do so without offence; but man's malicious care
> Hath made a bridle for itself, and spiteful laws restrain
> The things that nature setteth free . . .

Myrrha is defending to herself her unlawful passion for her own father, and in these lines she is envying the animals, who are not bound by human laws against incest. The verbal similarity of Donne's l. 30 to the last clause in the passage from Golding is striking. There are other passages in Donne's own work which are closely parallel, e.g. ll. 191–203 of *The Progress of the Soul*. The last three lines of that passage are as follows:

> Men, till they took laws which made freedom less,
> Their daughters, and their sisters did ingress;
> Till now unlawful, therefore ill, 'twas not.

30 *betwixt*] makes for a brighter line.
31 *but now, alas*] Probably an apology that he could not restrain the praises of his lady within the limitations of good sense and language.
32–3] 'I should exceed all bounds and even the resources of language itself, were I to say what a miracle she herself was!'

The Undertaking

OR

Platonic Love

I have done one braver thing
    Than all the Worthies did,
Yet a braver thence doth spring,
    Which is, to keep that hid.

It were but madness now to impart   5
    The skill of specular stone,
When he which can have learn'd the art,
    To cut it, can find none.

So, if I now should utter this,
    Others (because no more   10
Such stuff to work upon there is)
    Would love but as before.

But he who loveliness within
    Hath found, all outward loathes,
For he who colour loves, and skin,   15
    Loves but her oldest clothes.

If, as I have, you also do
    Virtue attir'd in woman see,
And dare love that, and say so too,
    And forget the He and She;   20

In 1633–1719. L74; Wed; S96; A25, Cy; S962 omit.

Text: Title The Undertaking *1635–1719.* Platonic Love *II; DC. No title 1633; I; H40; Lut, O'F; HK2, P, D17, B, S. In Dob* The Undertaking *added in a later hand.*

  3 Yet *MSS; Gar.* And yet *1633–1719; Gr; Ed (1956).*
    doth] did *D17.*

  7–8 art, / To cut it, *C57; Ed (1956).* art, / To cut it, *1633–54.* art / To cut it, *many MSS; 1669–1719; Gr; Gar.*

  16 her *Dob, Lut, O'F (b.c.);* B. their *1633–1719; I; H40; II; HK2, P, D17, S; Gr; Ed (1956); Gar.*

  18 attir'd] *om. Lut, O'F; 1635–1719.* woman] women *Dob, O'F; HK2, P, S.*

And if this love, though placèd so,
    From profane men you hide,
Which will no faith on this bestow,
    Or, if they do, deride:

Then you have done a braver thing   25
    Than all the Worthies did;
And a braver thence will spring,
    Which is, to keep that hid.

25 you have *1633–1719; I; H40; TCD,*   have you *TCC, A18; Dob, Lut, O'F;*
N; DC; HK2, P, S; Gr. you'have *Gar.*   *D17, B.*

Note on the title. I have preserved both the title first printed in *1635* and that in Group II MSS and *DC*, in the belief that both contribute to an understanding of the poem.

General note. The only open, general panegyric on Platonic love in the whole collection. Donne is not simply claiming that he has compassed the superior achievement of Platonic love for a woman, and, still more splendidly, kept it secret. He is recommending others to do the same.

1 *braver*] finer, more splendid.
2 *all the Worthies*] Lists of the Nine Worthies varied somewhat, but they were most usually understood to be three Gentiles (Hector, Alexander and Julius Caesar); three Jews (Joshua, David and Judas Maccabaeus); and three Christians (Arthur, Charlemagne and Godfrey of Bouillon). The general structure of the list is neatly put by Dryden in *The Flower and the Leaf*:

> Nine Worthies were they called, of different rites,
> Three Jews, three Pagans, and three Christian knights.

As Professor G. Blakemore Evans points out (*MLR* 57 (1962), pp. 60–3), none of the Worthies was especially notable for spiritual love. Professor Evans also emphasizes the importance for the poem that in fourteenth- and fifteenth-century pageants there was a tradition of 'boasting Worthies', and he stresses that Donne himself is 'making his boast' in the poem. It is perhaps worth adding that Donne is utterly turning the tables on the Worthies by claiming, with typical ingenuity, not only to have done something finer than anything they had done, but, by keeping secret about it, to have done something quite beyond them, i.e. not to have *boasted* (which, however, in reality, he has nevertheless done!).
6 *The skill of specular stone*] A difficult phrase, which has caused trouble to commentators. 'Specular stone' most probably means *selenite*, a translucent or transparent form of gypsum (Ca (SO_4). 2 H_2O). It is often foliated, and

can be split into sheets. Cleavable slabs up to 5 ft long have been found. (For further details see Dana's *System of Mineralogy*, C. Pazache, H. Berman and C. Frondel, seventh edn rev., New York and London, 1951.) Evidently, in ancient times, considerable use was made of 'specular stone' for glazing. 'The skill of specular stone' might, therefore, be thought to mean 'the craft of splitting selenite into sheets to prepare it for glazing'; but the matter is more complex. Splitting selenite into sheets is apparently so easy that it would hardly deserve to be called a craft or 'skill'. It is, in fact, virtually certain that Donne did not realize what 'specular stone' really was, i.e. selenite. It seems likely that selenite was used for glazing in some parts of Europe, and also in certain parts of South America, e.g. Bolivia, until early in the nineteenth century. Yet Donne apparently thought that 'specular stone' was not merely not used, but no longer to be found. It is practically certain that he derived this misinformation from Guido Panciroli's *Rerum Memorabilium iam olim deperditarum: et contra recens atque ingeniose inventarum, Libri 2*. OED, Professor Richard M. Ringler and Professor Gardner all refer us to this work in relation to 'specular stone'. It specifically states that 'specular stones are not found today' ('Speculares hodie non reperiuntur'). Panciroli's book (to which Donne refers in *Ignatius His Conclave*) was first written in Italian, but published in a Latin translation at Hamburg in 1599. Andrea Baccius, in contrast with Panciroli, tells us in his *De gemmis et lapidibus pretiosis* (also originally written in Italian, but published in a Latin translation at Frankfurt in 1603) that *lapis specularis* was prepared for glazing at the time in Thuringia and Saxony (ch. XXIII). Professor Ringler, in his sagacious note (*MLR* 60 (1965), pp. 333–9), has offered a convincing explanation of how Panciroli came to make the mistake which almost certainly misled Donne into thinking that 'specular stone' was no longer to be found, and also that it was not selenite but phengites, a hard, translucent kind of marble. (For further discussion of the crux see Appendix XI, pp. 339–40.)

5–8] The meaning of the lines, whatever the identity of 'specular stone', is, of course: 'It would be absurd to teach anybody now how to cut specular stone, since whoever might learn how to cut it would not be able to find any to cut.'

7–8] The punctuation in C57 brings out most clearly that 'the art' is that of *cutting* 'specular stone'. If Donne understood 'specular stone' to be a hard stone, as seems to have been the case (see Appendix XI, pp. 339–40), then cutting it could well have deserved to be called an 'art'.

9–12] 'In the same way, if I should tell anyone about this Platonic love of mine, since there is no woman left who can be loved in just this way, it would make no difference to other people's ways of loving; they would go on loving in the same way as they did before.'

16 *her*] the better reading. 'their' would most naturally refer to 'colour' and

'skin', yielding nonsense. If it were taken to refer to 'women', there would be no antecedent, and it would also strain the syntax, and make the stanza needlessly obscure. 'Her' refers back to 'loveliness', and the sense is clear.

20] i.e. and forget sex.

21–2] 'And if you hide this love, which you have set upon the Platonic idea of virtue, from the common run of people, who cannot understand such mysteries'.

23] 'who will not believe this to be true'.

25] with the implication, of course, that this is what Donne himself has done.

text] Professor Gardner maintains that *1633* ought to have inserted an elision mark between 'you' and 'have'; but that would tend to take the accent off 'you' (where it surely ought to be?) and put it on 'Then', where it certainly should not be. If it be argued that even with the elision mark the accent would still be on 'you', then we may ask why the elision mark should be inserted at all.

A Fever

Oh do not die, for I shall hate
    All women so, when thou art gone,
That thee I shall not celebrate,
    When I remember, thou wast one.

But yet thou canst not die, I know;   5
    To leave this world behind, is death;
But when thou from this world wilt go,
    The whole world vapours with thy breath.

Or if, when thou, the world's soul, goest,
    It stay, 'tis but thy carcase then;   10
The fairest woman, but thy ghost,
    But corrupt worms, the worthiest men.

O wrangling schools, that search what fire
    Shall burn this world, had none the wit
Unto this knowledge to aspire,   15
    That this her fever might be it?

And yet she cannot waste by this,
    Nor long bear this tortúring wrong,
For much corruption needful is,
    To fuel such a fever long.   20

These burning fits but meteors be,
    Whose matter in thee is soon spent:
Thy beauty, and all parts which are thee,
    Are unchangeable firmament.

In 1633–1719. A25 omits.

Text: Title A Fever *1633–1719; I; H40;*
S96; Dob; S962. Fever *II; Wed; DC; S.* The
Fever *Lut, O'F; Cy, P. No title HK2, D17.*
Of a fever *added in L74 in another hand.*

 7 wilt] dost *Lut.* wo(u)ldst *HK2, Cy, S.*
10 It] That *D17.*
14 had] have *L74; Cy.*
16 might] must *TCC, A18.*
18 torturing] tormenting *HK2, D17, S;*
S962; O'F (corrected from torturing*).*

19 For much] For more *Lut, O'F; HK2;*
   1635–1719. Far more *Cy; P.*
22 is soon *1633–54; I; H40; II; Wed; DC;*
   S96, Dob; B; Gr; Ed (1956); Gar. soon is
   L74; Lut, O'F; HK2, Cy, P, D17, S;
   S962; 1669–1719.
23 parts which are thee] parts which are
   in thee *S96, O'F.* parts that are in thee
   Dob. parts in thee *Lut.*

> Yet 'twas of my mind, seizing thee,   25
>   Though it in thee cannot perséver:
> For I had rather owner be
> Of thee one hour, than all else ever.

General note. A brilliantly inventive, logical exploitation by Donne of the Petrarchan situation of the beloved's illness and threatened death. Professor Guss (op. cit., pp. 88–90) draws interesting contrasts between this poem and treatments of their ladies' illness by Tasso (Sonnet 26) and Guarini (Madrigal 56), and rightly emphasizes both the logical and richly fanciful character of Donne's poem, and the coherence of its hyperboles. As to the tone of the poem, after its emotional start it seems to me to be pyrotechnically witty, over a basis of serious concern. This is also, if I understand him rightly, the view of W. von Koppenfels (op. cit., pp. 119–20).

1–4] The first four words ring out as a painful *cri de coeur*; but Donne does not sentimentalize. He switches, I believe, to an anti-solemn irrelevance, which, we may suppose, the woman could be taken to understand and accept as such.

  3 *celebrate*] almost certainly (1) 'sing your praises', rather than (2) 'solemnize your funeral', which would be tasteless.

5–8] The sense is: 'But yet actually I know that you can't die; for death consists in leaving this world behind; but you can't leave this world behind, because when you depart, the world will evaporate in your last breath.' Mario Praz ('Donne's relation to the poetry of his time', in T. Spencer (ed.), *A Garland for John Donne*, Cambridge, Mass., 1931, p. 66) first drew attention to some precedent in Petrarch for this hyperbolical assertion (*Canz.* 338). Yet Donne goes much further than Petrarch, who, apostrophizing Death, accuses it of leaving the world, without its sun, dark and cold, but not of destroying the world totally. The same is true of the further poems in the *Canzoniere* cited by Professor Gardner (*ESS*, p. 187). None of them refers to the destruction of the world. *Canz.* 268 asserts that by Laura's death the world has lost all that was fine in it (ll. 20–2). *Canz.* 326 accuses Death, not of destroying the world, but of extinguishing the flower and light of beauty and despoiling human life. *Canz.* 352, addressing Laura's spirit, declares that with her departure Love and Graciousness left the world, and the sun fell from the sky. Yet the world clearly survived, though God knows how.

  9 *the world's soul*] Donne exploits this conceit elsewhere, e.g. in a verse-letter to Lady Bedford 'To have written then . . .', where he calls her 'the world's best part' (i.e. soul); and, of course, most elaborately in the two *Anniversaries*, writing of Elizabeth Drury in *The Second Anniversary*, ll. 71–2, as one

> Who could not lack, whate'er this world could give,
> Because she was the form that made it live.

11–12] 'The most beautiful woman will be merely a ghost of you, and the finest men nothing but corrupt worms.'

13–14 *O wrangling schools . . . world*] The Stoics taught that the physical world would, at the end of each cycle of existence, be destroyed by a general conflagration. What fire would give rise to this was disputed. Most Stoics thought it would be primary fire or ether; but Cleanthes thought it would be the sun. (See Zeller, *Stoics, Epicureans and Sceptics*, tr. Reichel, London, 1892, pp. 161–9.) In the Early Christian era the reference in 2 Peter 3:7 to the final fire which would destroy the world gave rise to further disputes about its origin and nature, and these were continued and elaborated by the Scholastics, and went on until Donne's own time. On the latest phases of the dispute see D. C. Allen, 'Three notes on Donne's poetry', *MLN* 65 (1950), pp. 104–6.

21–2] 'These feverish fits are merely the heat of transitory foreign bodies, which will soon lose their substance in you.'

22 *is soon spent*] perhaps semantically the weightier reading, though giving a less regular line.

24] i.e. are as unchangeable as the sphere of the fixed stars. Galileo, in *Siderius Nuncius*, 1610, reported *inter alia* sighting through his telescope many hitherto unknown stars, and the appearance and disappearance of stars previously regarded as fixed. Professor C. M. Coffin (*John Donne and the New Philosophy*, New York, 1937, pp. 123–4) considers Donne's reference to the firmament as 'unchangeable' to be evidence that the poem predates Galileo's book; but Donne could easily be using Ptolemaic conceptions as poetic material (as he does elsewhere, e.g. in *Air and Angels*), and he could, in any case, have regarded Galileo's discoveries as consistent with the fixity of the firmament, or even not have known of their relevance, or stubbornly repudiated them.

25] The sense is: 'Yet it had the same idea as I have, in seizing you.' There is a legal quibble here. 'To seize' meant also to take corporeal possession of something as owner. This gives added significance to the word 'owner' in l. 27.

25–8] An expression of aspiration to male possession, but, at the same time, a fantastic compliment to the woman. The equilibrium is fairly typical of Donne in his lyrics of genuine love, though here it takes an unusual form.

26 *perséver*] persist.

28 *than all else ever*] i.e. than owner in perpetuity of everything else in the world.

The Dissolution

She's dead; and all which die
　　To their first elements resolve;
And we were mutual elements to us,
　　And made of one another.
　　My body then doth hers involve,　　　　　　　5
And those things whereof I consist, hereby
In me abundant grow, and burdenous,
　　And nourish not, but smother.
　　My fire of passion, sighs of air,
Water of tears, and earthy sad despair,　　　　10
　　　　(Which my materials be,
But near worn out by love's security),
She, to my loss, doth by her death repair;
　　And I might live long wretched so,
But that my fire doth with my fuel grow.　　　　15
　　　　Now, as those active kings
　　Whose foreign conquest treasure brings,
Receive more, and spend more, and soonest break:
This—which I am amaz'd that I can speak—
　　　　This death, hath with my store　　　　20
　　　　My use increas'd.
And so my soul, more earnestly releas'd,
Will outstrip hers; as bullets flown before
A latter bullet may o'ertake, the powder being more.

In 1633–1719. Among MSS collated for this edition only II; DC; Lut, O'F; S962 include. Text: Title The Dissolution *1633–1719; MSS.*

10 earthy *Lut, O'F; 1635–1719.* earthly *1633; II; DC; S962; Gr; Ed (1956); Gar.*

11–12 (Which . . . security) *Ed.* (Which . . . be) . . . security) *Lut, O'F.* (Which . . . be) *II; S962.* (Which . . . security *unclosed DC.* Which . . .

security *no parentheses 1633–50; Gr; Gar.* (But . . . security) *1669, 1719; Ed (1956).*

12 near *MSS* (near(e) *or* neare); *1635–1719;* Gr. ne'r *1633.*

13 by *1633–1719; II; DC; S962.* with *Lut, O'F.*

19 —which . . . speak—*Ed.* (which . . . speak) *1633–1719; MSS.*

General note. This poem occurs in the same few MSS as *A Nocturnal*, and the theme is also fairly similar, though less elaborately treated. For possible personal reference of both poems see Appendix X, pp. 336–8.

The complex conceit in this poem depends for its effect on the element of fire (= passion) being thought of as consuming the other elements (ll. 15–21). The death of the beloved released her elements into the lover's body; and that over-burdened him, and made his life wretched. It could have been a long torment. Fortunately for him, however, his passion (fire) grew stronger after the beloved's death, and consumed the baser elements (with their sighs, tears and despair) more rapidly, creating eventually such an explosive situation that when the poet would die his soul would follow that of his beloved so swiftly that it would overtake hers.

The conceit is highly ingenious; but the emotion behind the poem, which bursts out typically in the first two words (cf. 'Oh do not die': *A Fever*, l. 1), shows through all the complexity, both in the despondent phase up to l. 14, and after the astonished transition to joyous optimism.

Donne must have known well enough the expressions of longing for the dead Laura in the *In Morte* series by Petrarch. He would also be aware of the use of conceits on the elements in the Petrarchan tradition, e.g. in some of the English sonneteers. His complex poem rings just as authentic as Petrarch's poems (e.g. *Canz.* 278 and 298), and his development of the conceit is far more continuous and meaningful than any earlier comparable case I have encountered, except the fine use of the elements in Shakespeare's Sonnets 44 and 45, which may well have been earlier, but which we cannot be sure that Donne knew.

5 *involve*] include.

6 *those things whereof I consist*] i.e. my elements.

   hereby] i.e. by her death.

7] because of the sudden dumping of crude elements in my body after her dis-solution.

8] because they are not organized, but in a crude state.

9–12] The sense is: 'My four elements, which had almost ceased to exist in me in their crude state, because of the security I felt in reciprocated love'. Donne gives to each of the four elements a psychological character – in the case of three of them a dominantly sad one. 'Earth' was, however, tradi-tionally associated with melancholy and despair.

10 *earthy*] Although 'earthly' in the obsolete sense 'earthy' (see *OED* 3) may properly be preserved in a text in seventeenth-century spelling and punctuation, the reading 'earthy' is probably more appropriate in a modern recension, to emphasize the element 'earth'. It is, however, possible that in the seventeenth century 'earthly' could be used, and that Donne used it here, to play on the two senses (1) 'earthy', (2) 'earthly' (as opposed to 'heavenly').

12 *security*] could mean either (1) 'well-founded confidence' (*OED* 2) or (2) 'culpable lack of anxiety' (*OED* 3). I prefer (1). A sense of guilt does not seem to cohere with the rest of the poem.

13 *repair*] here 'replenish'.
14 *wretched*] i.e. because smothered with crude elements.
15] A paraphrase might run: 'If it were not for the fact that my element of fire is replenished at the same time as my fuel elements are'. The element of fire (passion) is, of course, increased through being thwarted by the loss of his lady.
18 *break*] become insolvent.
19 *speak*] speak of.
20 *store*] stock of elements.
21 *use*] expenditure.
22 *earnestly*] The sense is: 'ardently', 'eagerly'; because of his fire of passion consuming the rest of his body more rapidly than in the case of normal dissolution.
23 *flown*] i.e. shot into the air.
24 *the powder being more*] when the explosive charge is greater.

A Nocturnal upon St Lucy's Day;
being the shortest day

'Tis the year's midnight, and it is the day's,
Lucy's, who scarce seven hours herself unmasks;
   The sun is spent, and now his flasks
   Send forth light squibs, no constant rays;
      The world's whole sap is sunk;   5
The general balm the hydroptic earth hath drunk,
Whither, as to the bed's-feet, life is shrunk,
Dead and interr'd; yet all these seem to laugh,
Compar'd with me, who am their epitaph.

Study me then, you who shall lovers be   10
At the next world, that is, at the next Spring:
   For I am every dead thing,
   In whom love wrought new alchemy.
      For his art did express
A quintessence even from nothingness,   15
From dull privations, and lean emptiness:
He ruin'd me, and I am re-begot
Of absence, darkness, death; things which are not.

All others, from all things, draw all that's good,
Life, soul, form, spirit, whence they being have;   20
   I, by Love's limbeck, am the grave
   Of all that's nothing. Oft a flood
      Have we two wept, and so
Drown'd the whole world, us two; oft did we grow
To be two Chaoses, when we did show   25
Care to aught else; and often absences
Withdrew our souls, and made us carcases.

In 1633–1719 and II; DC; Lut, O'F. om. all
other MSS here collated.
Text: Title from 1633–1719; MSS.
  2 scarce seaven houres herself *1633–*
    1719; II; Lut, O'F. scarce her selfe
    seauen houres *DC.*

4 no] not *Lut, O'F.*
12 every] a very *Lut, O'F (altered from*
    every).
16 emptinesse: *1719; Gr.* emptinesse
    1633–54. emptinesse, *1669.*

But I am by her death (which word wrongs her),
Of the first nothing the Elixir grown;
   Were I a man, that I were one   30
   I needs must know; I should prefer,
      If I were any beast,
Some ends, some means; yea plants, yea stones, detest,
And love; all, all, some properties invest;
If I an ordinary nothing were,   35
As shadow, a light and body must be here.

But I am none; nor will my Sun renew.
You lovers, for whose sake the lesser sun
   At this time to the Goat is run
   To fetch new lust, and give it you,   40
      Enjoy your summer all:
Since she enjoys her long night's festival,
Let me prepare towards her, and let me call
This hour her Vigil, and her Eve, since this
Both the year's, and the day's, deep midnight is.   45

Note on the title. St Lucy's Day, 13 December, is taken here by Donne to be 'the shortest day in the year', according to the old Julian Calendar, used in England until 1752; and that was the popular belief. The real Winter Solstice, however, was 12 December; and the shortest day, which varied, was never, according to Professor Garrod, on the authority of Professor Plaskett, 13 December in any year during Donne's lifetime. Dr Robert Arnold has made to me the attractive suggestion that it is perhaps relevant to the poem that St Lucy was the patron saint of the blind, so that images of darkness would especially belong to her province.

General note. There is controversy as to whom the poem refers to. Grierson suggested that it was perhaps written about Lucy, Countess of Bedford, when she was seriously ill and nearly died in 1612. Another idea has been that it may have been about Donne's wife, who was very ill in 1611, and who died in 1617. For discussion of the various possibilities see Appendix X, pp. 336–8.

   This powerful expression of the desolation of bereavement has precedent in some of the poems Petrarch wrote after Laura's death. W. von Koppenfels (op. cit., pp. 122–3) draws our attention to *Canz.* 275, 306, 310, 332, 352, 363. It seems to me especially close to *Canz.* 332. It would have been natural for Donne to look at his Petrarch when evolving this poem. Yet the bold and argumentative insistence on the limit of non-existence to which death has reduced him, and the possibly ironic reference (cf. *Twickenham Garden,* ll. 19–22) in the final stanza to the lovers who still have earthly enjoyment before them, diverge from Petrarch, and are characteristically Donne.

For a challenging and controversial close reading of the poem see Richard Sleight's article in *Mandrake* 69. II (1953).

3 *flasks*] powder-horns. Professor Gardner rightly says that Donne means the stars, which were thought to store up light from the sun. She refers us to *Paradise Lost*, VII. 354–69.

4 *squibs*] Dr T. R. Henn pointed out to me that this term was used for the half-charges on which military recruits were practised.

6 *the hydroptic earth*] clearly the subject of this clause.

general balm] possibly the general aromatic fragrance of nature, which subsides with the fall of the sap the earth has 'drunk', rather than specifically the resin and volatile oils of the genus *Balsamodendron*. Yet possibly there is a play on the aromatic ointment made from these, and used for soothing pain and healing wounds (1563: T. Gale: 'The Balm wherewith green and fresh wounds are speedily cured', *OED* 5). Another possibility is that 'balm' is here used in the Paracelsian sense of 'preservative vital essence'. I am, however, strongly tempted by a possibility suggested to me by Mr Ingram, that the 'general balm' may itself *be* the sap (which is, in any case, what the earth has 'drunk'). Some writers of the time thought that 'balm' was the sap of certain plants; so why should not 'general balm' mean the sap of all plants? All four meanings mentioned may be involved in this possibly complex term.

hydroptic] dropsical, and therefore insatiably thirsty; cf. a letter from Donne to Sir Henry Goodyer, September 1608: 'An hydroptique immoderate desire of humane learning and languages' (Nonesuch Donne, p. 456).

7 *bed's-feet*] Probably the foot of the bed, rather than the four feet of a four-poster bedstead, or the depths of a flower-bed. The image is probably that of a dying man whose life has ebbed away to his feet, and so to the foot of the bed. Some cases of death can plausibly be conceived in that way. Dr Robert Arnold rightly points out, however, that we have then here a rather abrupt transition from the death of plant life to that of human life, the former sinking downwards, the latter shrinking laterally.

12 *every*] 'a very', the reading of *Lut, O'F, 1635–1719*, has some intrinsic attraction; yet not only is the MS support for *1633*'s 'every' overwhelming, but it coheres well with l. 21–2.

12–18] A hard passage. Possibly the sense is: 'For I am made of everything dead, and Love transmuted me by a new chemical process: for he managed to extract ['express' = 'squeeze out'] a quintessence even from nothingness, from melancholy absences and starvation [? of desires]. He completely destroyed me, and then begot me again out of absence, darkness and death, things which don't exist.'

301

15 *quíntessence*] the 'fifth essence' of ancient and medieval philosophy, supposed to be the stuff of which the heavenly bodies were composed, and to be actually latent in all things. The extraction of it by distillation and other methods was one of the great objects of alchemy.

16 *emptiness:*] The *1719* punctuation, followed by Grierson, is preferable to the absence of a stop, and even to a comma, since to take l. 16 with l. 17 (given, moreover, the 'from' in l. 15) would require forced construction of 'From' in l. 16.

17 *ruin'd*] probably 'destroyed' (*OED* 2. *obs.*).

19–22] 'Everyone else but me draws everything good out of other things. They acquire from them, life, soul, form and spirit, which are what give them their being. I, however, through the trick of Love's chemistry, am simply the burial-ground of everything that doesn't exist.'

21 *limbeck*] alembic, a primitive form of retort.

24 *us two*] i.e. we were the whole world (cf. perhaps *The Good-morrow*, ll. 10–14).

24–5 *grow / To be*] The sense is: 'come to be' (*OED* 11); though the vastness of 'Chaoses' is perhaps also implied in 'grow'.

25–6 *when. . . . else*] The meaning is probably: 'when either of us made the other jealous by showing an inclination for someone or something else'.

28–9] Continuing the allusions to cosmic events such as the Creation and the Flood, made in the latter part of the preceding stanza, Donne now says that an even more immense and extraordinary thing has taken place in him, through the death of his lady, than anything that occurred to them both while she was alive. He has become the quintessence ('Elixir' here = 'quintessence') of the *first* Nothing, which subsisted before the Creation of the world, which Donne, like Augustine, thought of as the actualizing of Ideas in the mind of God (see *Essays in Divinity*, p. 29).

31–3 *I should prefer . . . means*] 'If I were a lower animal of some sort I should at least have preferences as to objectives and as to the means of attaining them.'

33 *yea stones, detest*] Grierson quotes a passage from a sermon in which Donne says that stones may have life (*Sermons*, IX. 147). Cf. the later systematic philosophy of Leibniz's *Monadology*.

34 *all, all, some properties invest*] absolutely everything is endowed with *some* properties.

35] He is the quintessence of the first Nothing, which, unlike an 'ordinary' nothing, does not imply the existence of anything else.

36 *As*] Such as.

36] i.e. as he is the quintessence of the first Nothing, neither light nor body exist, and therefore shadows cannot be cast.

37 *none*] not an ordinary nothing.

my Sun] i.e. his dead lady, whose beams will never shine on him again on earth.

38 *the lesser sun*] i.e. the sun.

39 *the Goat*] This can be taken to mean either the Tropic of Capricorn or the zodiacal sign of Capricorn. It does not much matter which; for the sun enters the sign of Capricorn about 22 December (or 12 December in the old Julian Calendar); and at roughly the same time it shines perpendicularly over the Tropic of Capricorn, the farthest limit of its journey into the Southern Hemisphere (cf. *The Progress of the Soul*, ll. 336–7, and *The First Anniversary*, ll. 263–7).

40] the goat being notoriously the most lustful of animals.

42 *she*] i.e. his dead beloved.

her long night's festival] probably both (1) the long sleep of death, cf. Catullus'

> nobis cum semel occidit brevis lux,
> nox est perpetua una dormienda.
>
> (*Carmina*, V)

and (2) her resurrection, cf. Donne's sermon on 1 Corinthians 15:26, *The last Enemy that shall be destroyed, is Death*: 'This is a Text of the Resurrection, and it is not Easter yet; but it is Easter Eve; all Lent is but the Vigill, the Eve of Easter: to so long a Festivall as never shall end, the Resurrection, wee may well begin the Eve betimes' (*Sermons*, IV. 45).

43 *Let me prepare towards her*] The probable meaning is primarily: 'Let me prepare myself devotionally [as would an intending Easter communicant] as a participant [or even? 'ministrant'] in the celebration of her festival.' This would also naturally imply that he wishes to share in her death and resurrection. I am grateful to Mr Ingram for help in arriving at this possible explanation.

44 *Vigil*] service used on the night before a holiday or festival; but there is possibly also here a reference to a devotional watch over a dead body.

42–5] The hour is especially appropriate to his loss and grief, and also to her eternal festival, for it is the deepest midnight there is – the midnight of the longest night of the year.

APPENDIX I

'THE INDIFFERENT', l. 16

Professor Mark Roberts, in his review of Professor Gardner's edition of *The Elegies and the Songs and Sonnets* in *Essays in Criticism*,[1] has already pointed out her omission of any reference to the Group I and *H40* readings in this line. There, *1633*, followed by the other early editions, reads:

> Rob mee, but binde me not, and let me goe.

Grierson and Professor Gardner follow that reading. It is, indeed, supported by all the Group II and Group III MSS, and also by *DC*, *P* and *S*, as well as by the miscellany *S962*. On the other hand, Group I MSS and some others (such as *D17* and *B*) read 'Racke' or 'Rack' or 'Wracke', while *H40* reads 'Reach'. It could, indeed, be argued that 'Reach me', taken in the then current but now obsolete sense 'seize me', 'lay hold of me' (see *OED* 4) would make somewhat better sense than either 'Rack me' or 'Rob me'. The poet would be asking his mistress for an intense but not protracted or faithful relationship. 'Rack' does, admittedly, yield the reasonable sense 'torture', but it does not offer as good an image as seizing, since binding might well be thought of as *preceding* torture (which it often does). As to 'Rob', though its image is more satisfactory in point of temporal sequence than that of 'Rack', it has a vagueness, and also a mercenary train of associations which does not seem to be supported elsewhere in the poem.

We next need to consider the textual position. *1633* does not read with Group I here, while elsewhere in the poem it does read with Group I, against Groups II and III and *DC*. This would suggest that the *1633* editor actually rejected the Group I reading at this point. If he did so, his reason can only, in our present state of knowledge, be a matter of speculation. It seems at least possible, however, that the *1633* editor, not satisfied with the sense of 'Rack', turned to the Group II or other MS (from which he took the title), and, thinking its reading made better sense, adopted it. He may well not have known of *H40*'s reading. The common ancestor of *H40* and Group I could have read either 'Reach' or 'Rack' in one or other of their various current spellings. It could, for instance, have read 'Reche' (a current spelling of

[1] *EC* 14 (July 1966), pp. 309–29, at pp. 312–13.

304

'Reach'), and could easily have been misread in the line of transmission to Group I as 'Racke'. Alternatively, the common ancestor could have read 'Racke', which some copyist in the line of transmission to *H40* might have misread as 'Reche'. Textually, then, Group I and *H40* seem to have equal claims; but *H40* seems semantically superior. 'Reach', therefore, at least deserves mention as an alternative to 'Rob'.

APPENDIX II

This is a fuller account of the problem of the meaning of the passage than it would have been proportional to give in the Notes.

Grierson (II, p. 53) explains the whole stanza, as emended by him, as follows:

> Donne's argument then is this: 'Why of all animals have we alone this feeling of depression and remorse after the act of love? Is it a device of nature to restrain us from an act which shortens the life of the individual' (he here refers to a prevalent belief as to the deleterious effect of the act of love), 'needed because that other curse which Adam brought upon man, the curse of mortality,
>
> > . . . Of being short,
> > And only for a minute made to be,
> > Eagers [i.e. whets or provokes] desire to raise posterity?'

My own view is that, apart from the fact that if possible one should keep the old reading, Grierson's emendation is open to a strong objection, namely that it does not seem like Donne to pad in l. 29 in such a very awkward way.

John Hayward, in the Nonesuch Donne (pp. 766–7), also suggested an emendation, which consists in transposing the comma in l. 30 from after 'eager' to after 'desires', so that the line would read:

> Eager desires, to raise posterity.

Hayward objected to Grierson's emendation and explanation (1) that it would destroy a rhythm characteristic of Donne (I do not accept that point); (2) that he could not agree that 'That other curse of being short, / And only for a minute made to be', refers to the curse of mortality brought upon man by Adam. (That is a crucial point which I shall deal with below.) Hayward thought these lines (28–9) refer to the short ecstasy of physical union. His third objection to Grierson's view was (3) that it is hard to see why, if the curse of mortality stimulates desire to raise posterity, Nature should decree that man should despise that very reasonable desire. (My own answer to this would be that Donne would not be saying, on Grierson's view, that Nature has perhaps

306

decreed that man should despise that desire, but only that Nature has perhaps decreed that man should despise the *sport* of sexuality.)

On the basis of his own view that ll. 28–9 refer to the short ecstasy of physical union, Hayward explained the stanza as follows:

> Unlike the beasts, man feels sad after the act of love. Why is this? Nature decreed that it should be so, and would have man despise the sport of raising posterity since the act itself is short and the desires that promote it are made eager by nature for a moment only; moreover, it is said that each such act diminishes the length of life a day.

Hayward's emendation and explanation do at least try to avoid the awkward padding in l. 29 which vitiated Grierson's text and explanation; but they are open in turn to several objections: (1) that if good sense can be given to the reading of the old editions, it should clearly be preferred; (2) that ll. 29–30, as emended by Hayward, seem less characteristic of Donne than as emended by Grierson; (3) that there is no question in the poem of man despising 'the sport of raising posterity'; (4) that Donne is not suggesting in ll. 28–30 features of the 'sport' in virtue of which man ought to despise it, but either reasons for Nature's decree or reasons why man (or the 'curse, of being short', or the act of love) 'desires to raise posterity'; (5) that Hayward puts the point about diminution of life at the end, almost as an afterthought, and his explanation thus fails to bring out that this is actually the reason Donne attributes to Nature for making her decree.

Ever since I first considered the knotty problem set by this passage, I had thought that a good sense might be given to the old reading. I myself at first adopted a modified form of Grierson's view about the meaning of 'that other curse', viz. that it referred to humanity's living for a short while and only for an extremely brief period at a high pitch of life. On this interpretation I thought the sense of the old reading might be: 'since humanity's other curse, of living only for a short while, and only for an extremely brief period at a high pitch of life, makes men long to have children'. My own objection to this reading and explanation was that it seemed to involve rather too vigorous construction of the word 'desires', perhaps too vigorous even for Donne's work.

After reading, however, the brilliant note by Dr George Williamson ('Donne's *Farewell to Love*', *MP* (1939), pp. 301–3), I came round to the view that Hayward was probably right, against Grierson, in maintaining that 'That other curse' was the brevity of sexual play. Dr Williamson accepted Hayward's view on this point, but he made an ingenious addition, viz. the view that 'to raise posterity' has nothing to do with humanity's begetting of children, but refers to the fact that the act of love itself, because of its shortness and only momentary sharpness, wishes to repeat itself (i.e. 'raise posterity' *to itself*). Dr Williamson suggested that the meaning of the whole stanza is:

If it be not that (since each such act, they say, diminishes the length of life a day) wise Nature decreed this, as if she would that man should despise the sport [not that she does]; because that other curse of being short, and but momentarily eager, desires to raise posterity [i.e. desires to increase and multiply, for only by multiplying itself can the curse of shortness and momentary ardour escape its limitations].

Dr Williamson also explained that this other curse of love provides the reason for the necessity of Nature's decree, not the reason for despising the sport. The decree itself is what provides a reason for despising the sport, since the mere brevity of the experience is not sufficient to discourage people from indulging in it. In fact the brevity has the opposite effect, and that is why Nature needs to provide the safeguard of 'sorrowing dullness'. The fundamental reason, however, why Nature makes her decree, is suggested in the parenthesis. It is because Nature is concerned to preserve human life, and so wishes to discourage excessive sexuality. Of course Nature is interested in multiplying life as well as preserving it, a fact which is allowed for in the 'as if' mood of Donne's reasoning about her, but which is not in issue in the poem. Nature achieves both objects by subjecting man to the two curses of love, which hinder each other: the curse of brevity demands continual repetition, the curse of a dull aftermath produces eternal dissatisfaction. So the only solution for a man concerned for his own happiness is to renounce love. And that brings out the significance of the title of the poem. A similar explanation was offered by Mr A. M. Coon in *TLS*, 12 August 1939.

This ingenious emendation and explanation has attractive features. In particular, the reserved subtlety of l. 30, as so explained, seems truly worthy of Donne at his best. The interpretation is, however, open to certain objections, as we shall see.

Ten years later Dr Leslie Hotson attempted an explanation of the original text. He took 'that other curse' to refer to the curse of mortality, and suggested that 'Because' (l. 28) is here used to refer to the future, with the force 'in order that' (see E. A. Abbott, *A Shakespearian Grammar* (1869), §117), the sense being 'in order that man should desire to raise posterity'. He was, however, unable to cite an *exact* parallel for this use of 'Because'. His explanation also seems to me to miss the point that the primary reason for Nature's decree was that the act of love diminishes the length of human life.

Shortly afterwards, Miss Helen Gardner (as she then was) wrote a note in *TLS*, 10 June 1949, rejecting Dr Hotson's explanation, and also attacking Dr Williamson's interpretation on the grounds (1) that it is improbable that Donne would use the phrase 'raise posterity' in that metaphorical way in a poem concerned with the very act by which posterity is raised in the ordinary sense; (2) that 'that other curse' is not the subject of 'desires', which is indeed not a verb here at all. Of these objections (1) seems to me by far the stronger. It seems to me very doubtful that 'desires' is not a verb, and, in any case, that is one of the points at issue. Miss Gardner also put forward her own explanation, which involves the insertion of a comma after 'minute' in l. 29. She took 'made to be eager' as a transitive verb with 'desires' as its object. She held that the comma after 'eager' in the original text is necessary to make us take 'eager' with 'to be' and not with 'desires'; and that the past tense 'made' is used because it was this accentuation of our desires which Nature's decree remedied. Her paraphrase is as follows:

> Possibly Nature decreed this after-sorrow to prevent man from destroying himself by repeated indulgence, because that other curse of brevity in enjoyment sharpened or made more acute the natural desires to propagate.

Professor Gardner holds to this interpretation in *ESS*, p. 214. That explanation has some attractive features. It takes 'posterity' in the ordinary sense; and it brings out clearly that the reason for Nature's decree was to protect human life from self-destruction through excessive sexual intercourse. On the other hand, it is an emended text, though the emendation does, in point of fact, have the support of the miscellany *S962*, on which, however, I do not suppose Professor Gardner would have wished (or would wish now) to place much weight. The explanation does also seem to me open to more serious objections: (1) that the clause 'of being short, / And only for a minute' does seem a very awkward customer. Had it been 'of being short, / Yea, only for a minute' or 'of being short, / Indeed but for a minute' or something of that kind, it would have avoided being so desperately lame. In contrast 'of being short, / And only for a minute made to be / Eager' makes substantial sense. Professor Gardner (*ESS*, p. 214) defends 'being short, / And only for a minute' as a repetition similar to that in ll. 47–8 of *The Autumnal*:

> . . . may still
> My love descend, and journey down the hill.

but the cases are not really similar. 'Being short', in this context, seems to require to be followed by something like 'indeed', as urged above; whereas the lines from *The Autumnal* are far from lame as they stand. A further objection (2) is that it seems unnatural to say that the brevity of the sexual act sharpens desire *to raise posterity*. Wanting to have more sexual intercourse is, as we all very well know, far from being the same thing as to wanting procreate children. Professor Gardner defends herself against this kind of objection by quoting l. 110 of *The First Anniversary*:

> We kill our selves to propagate our kind.

and stating that in that line 'to propagate our kind' is equivalent to 'by indulgence in love'. Now, if one examines the passage of *The First Anniversary* from which Professor Gardner has quoted, I suggest that one finds that in l. 110 'to propagate our kind' means what it plainly says, i.e. 'to produce offspring', and is not simply equivalent to 'by indulgence in love'. 'We kill our selves' does, indeed, involve the idea that sexual intercourse shortens life; but that is quite a different matter, and not the point at issue. Similarly in l. 30 of *Farewell to Love* I suggest that 'to raise posterity' means plainly what it says, i.e. 'to procreate children'; and I am surprised that Professor Gardner who, in her earlier *TLS* article, held it impossible that Donne would use the phrase 'to raise posterity' in the metaphorical way Dr Williamson had suggested, should after sixteen years be so strongly inclined to regard 'to propagate our kind' as not having its plain sense, but being equivalent to 'by indulgence in love'. I still maintain, moreover, that it seems unnatural to say that the brevity of the sexual act sharpens desire *to raise posterity*.

F. L. Lucas drew my attention to some possible objections to Dr Williamson's explanation, and he also provided me with an attractive explanation of his own, involving Grierson's emendation, which he considered 'more convincing than most conjectures are'. Lucas took the shortness referred to in l. 28 to be that of coitus. On the other hand, he objected to the phrase 'desires to raise posterity' in the original text being taken to mean 'wishes to repeat itself', on the ground that the subject of 'desires' is not the *act*, but the *curse*. He also found Dr Williamson's interpretation of 'to raise posterity' forced. His own explanation (from 'Unless wise Nature . . .') was as follows:

> One can only suppose that Nature so ordained (copulation being, as it is, harmful) because she wanted men not to think *too* much of the act of love; for, on the other hand, the brevity of coitus increases physical desire, so that the race may be perpetuated.

The idea is that Nature has provided both a stimulus and a deterrent to coitus: (1) She has made coitus *brief*, so that men should wish to repeat it often, and so be fruitful and multiply. (If human coitus took a couple of months, as it does with some creatures, clearly the birth-rate would be considerably decreased.) But (2) lest men should make love *too* much, she added the melancholy reaction afterwards. Lucas would have preferred to add to Grierson's emendation a comma after 'desire', the sense being: 'heightens sexual desire, in order to perpetuate the race', rather than 'heightens the desire to perpetuate the race'. (I see that here Lucas was making the same important distinction which I have just been urging against Professor Gardner.)

The objections made by Miss Gardner and Lucas to Dr Williamson's interpretation seem to me strong enough to make it extremely unlikely to be correct. As to Lucas's own interpretation, it seems to me, despite three drawbacks, to be, on the whole the most satisfactory of those considered in this note. The three drawbacks are: (1) that it involves an emended text: (2) that it does not meet the objection that I made against Grierson's interpretation, namely, that it makes l. 29 into a very awkward form of padding. Lucas calls the whole sexual process referred to 'the coitus', but one seems to want, on his kind of interpretation, to reserve l. 29 to refer to the coitus itself, and to take l. 28 to refer to the whole sexual play within which coitus falls – on the original reading this distinction could easily be made; (3) that the phrase 'to raise posterity' seems to stand in an isolation not typical of Donne's syntax. On the other hand, Lucas's interpretation makes excellent sense; and it succeeds in combining the interpretation of ll. 28–9 as referring to sexuality and not life, with the interpretation of 'to raise posterity' in its natural sense. It also avoids my second objection to Professor Gardner's interpretation. These are no mean advantages.

Yet I now believe that it may, after all, be possible to make good sense of the original *1635–1719* texts:

> Because that other curse of being short,
>   And only for a minute made to be
> Eager, desires to raise posterity.

If we take 'short' to mean 'short-lived' (and that would appear to be within the general scope of *OED* II. 5 and 5b) and to apply to human life (which was how Grierson took it), then the sense of the three lines in the original text can, I believe, be:

> since humanity's other curse, of being short-lived and only for a very brief space of time at a high pitch of life (including sexuality), demands procreation of children.

This would involve taking 'desires' as meaning 'demands', which would be in accordance with *OED* sense 3, '*trans.* Of things: To require, need, demand'. It is possible that the sense may come out even more clearly if we adopt the punctuation of manuscript *S96*:

> Because that other curse, of being short
>   And only for a minute made to be
> Eager, desires to raise posterity.

APPENDIX III

This line has given trouble to editors and commentators.

1633 reads:

> So shall I live thy stay, not triumph bee;

1635 altered this to:

> So shall I live thy Stage, not triumph be;

and the rest of the early editions followed. Grierson was not happy with the *1633* reading, and adopted *1635*'s 'Stage', inserting, however, commas after 'I' and 'live'. He did this 'to make quite clear that "live" is the adjective, not the verb'. He thought *1633*'s 'stay' defensible, but that *1633* was 'somewhat at sea about this poem', and he mentions a misprint in l. 5 and some variations introduced into the text while the edition was printing. His note continues:

> All the MSS. I have consulted support 'stage'; and this gives the best meaning: 'Alive, I shall continue to be the stage on which your victories are daily set forth; dead, I shall be but your triumph, a thing achieved once, never to be repeated'.[1]

Actually, Grierson's *apparatus criticus* cites *JC* (admittedly an inferior MS) as reading 'stay', and the Group I MSS *D*, *H49* as reading 'staye'. Moreover, in point of fact, *O'F*, which he cites as reading 'stage', looks as if it originally read 'stay', and was corrected to read 'stage'.

Professor Gardner adopts 'Stage', but deletes Grierson's comma after 'I', and takes 'live' as a verb, cognate with 'be'. She interprets the line thus:

> If he lives he will be the stage on which she can perpetually display her power over him instead of triumphing once and for all. The culmination of a Roman Triumph was the slaughter of the captives.[2]

[1] *Gr*, II, p. 51.
[2] *ESS*, p. 163.

312

Professor Gardner's critical apparatus reads as follows:

> I live,] I live *1633*: I, live, *Gr.*
> Stage Σ¹: stay *1633*, *H49*, *JC*.

Her apparatus is, of course, selective only, and particular MSS are chosen to represent the various groups.² Here, however, a fuller view of the MSS shows the following varieties of reading:

> So shall I live thy staye, not triumph be
> *H49, D; Lut (but possibly it reads 'stage').*
> So shall I live thy stay, not triumph be
> *SP; O'F (seemingly, before correction); D 17 (without comma).*
> So shall I live thy stage, not triumph be
> *O'F (after correction); P (without comma); B; S962.*
> So shall thy Stage, not triumph be
> *Cy.*

and, most important of all:

> So shall I live thy stage, and triumph be
> *H40.*

Professor Gardner does not note this reading of *H40*. The reason is, no doubt, that she does not consider *The Prohibition* to form part of the collection of Donne's poems strewn through *H40*, but takes it to be part of the miscellany found both in *H40* and in *RP31*. That miscellany she designates with the siglum *H40**.³ I am not convinced that *The Prohibition* belongs to the miscellany. It is, indeed, to be found both in *H40* and *RP31*, but the text of the poem in *H40* differs from that in *RP31*. I therefore submit that this poem was probably among the extra poems available to the copyist of *H40*, and should be considered as part of *H40*, not of *H40**. Now, *H40* Professor Gardner deems to offer 'the best version of the "Group I text" ' of the *Songs and Sonets*. However this may be, my own view is that the reading quoted above as that of *H40* offers an important hint towards establishing the best text of the line we are now considering. I shall attempt to justify this opinion presently. Meanwhile, however, it is worth drawing attention to the spelling of 'staye' in *H49, D*, and possibly *Lut*. Plainly 'staye' and 'stage' could easily be mistaken for each other, either in Secretary or in Chancery hand. Moreover, MS support for 'stay(e)' is at least as strong as that for 'stage'.⁴

¹ Denoting 'all MSS except those specifically excepted'.
² For the *Songs and Sonets C57*, *H49* and *H40* represent Group I texts; *TCD* (plus *TCC* where it differs or importantly confirms) and *L74* represent Group II texts. *Dob*, *O'F* and *S96* represent Group III texts. *HK2*; *Cy*, *P*; *A25*, *JC*; *B* and *S* are cited as readings under her general umbrella 'V'.
³ *ESS*, pp. lxv–lxvi.
⁴ It is unfortunate that a number of MSS omit the poem, e.g. *Lec*, *C57*; *L74*; *Wed*, *A25* and *S*; and that Group II; *DC*; *Dob* and *S96* omit stanza 3.

'Stay' also makes much better sense in the total context of the poem than 'stage'. Stanza 1 warns the beloved not to love her lover, because the excess of joy that would give him would kill him, and so frustrate her love for him. Stanza 2 warns her not to hate him, for that would kill him too, and so she would lose the glory of her triumph, which would involve his being a living trophy of her success. She must therefore neither love nor hate him, since both will kill him. Stanza 3 attempts to solve the problem set by the first two. Whereas, however, 'triumph' in l. 22 is totally relevant to stanza 2, 'Stage' would have no relevance whatever to stanza 1, for there is no question there of the mistress wishing for 'victories' over her lover, or 'displaying her power' over him. She is there imagined as *loving* him, and this love would be frustrated by his death. Contrariwise, if he were to remain alive, he would be a 'stay' for her. Again, in stanza 2, she would lose by his death, which would be the result of hating him or triumphing *too much* in her victory. What she would lose would be the 'style of conqueror', including, no doubt, the glory of the lover's being led alive in the triumphal procession. Stanza 3 would solve the problem either in the way described in ll. 19–20, or in that indicated in l. 21, the result being that she will have him alive *both* as her 'stay' (support) (as stanza 1 supposes she would wish) *and* as her 'triumph' (as stanza 2 supposes her wish to be).

It is perhaps worth adding that 'not' in l. 22 could have been caught, early in transmission, from 'not' in l. 21.

APPENDIX IV

'THE DREAM', ll. 19–20

In *1633* the lines read:

> I must confesse, it could not chuse but bee
> Prophane, to thinke thee any thing but thee.

and *1635–1719* followed, and so did Grierson. The extant MSS, however, read 'I doe confesse', and Professor Gardner emends *1633* accordingly. It would be interesting to know where the *1633* editor got 'must' from; but on the present MS evidence it is certainly right to read 'do'. For the remainder of the two lines Professor Gardner follows *1633*. The readings of the MSS collated for this edition, and the readings of the early editions are as follows:

19 I *HK2, A25, Cy, P, B, S; S962.* it *1633–1719, and the rest of the MSS.*
20 Profane *or* Prophane *1633–1719; Lut*[1]; *HK2, A25, Cy, P, B, S; S962.*
   Profanes *or* Profanenes *or* Prophannes *or* Prophanenes(s)(e) *I; II; L74; DC; S96, Dob.* (*O'F possibly corrected twice, from* Profane *to* Profanesse *and back again*).

Professor Gardner writes:

> I reject 'Prophaness', in spite of its high manuscript authority, because I can find no parallel in Donne's lyric verse for a line with an extra syllable attached to its first foot with no possibility of an elision. 'Prophaness' gives a hopelessly unmetrical line and ruins the splendid run of the stanza up to its climax. I cannot believe that Donne wrote it, and prefer the charge of inconsistency to that of being deaf to the music of Donne's verse.[2]

Now, actually there seem to be a number of lines in the *Songs and Sonets* with an extra syllable attached to the first foot with no possibility of an elision. If any one of the following lines is of such a kind, Professor Gardner's generalization is invalid:[3]

---

[1] Professor Gardner says that Group III reads 'Prophaness'. This is not so. One Group III MS, *Lut*, reads 'Prophane'. So, ultimately, does *O'F*.
[2] *ESS*, p. 210.
[3] I indicate in each case what would seem a reasonable scansion.

Whŏ e'r rĭgg'd/faĭre shĭp/tŏ lĭe/ĭn hărbŏrs,
                    (*Confined Love*, l. 15)

Bў beĭng/tŏ theé/thĕn whát/tŏ me/thŏu wást;
                    (*The Prohibition*, l. 5)

Ăs vĭrtŭ/oŭs mén/páss míld/lў awáy,
                    (*A Valediction; forbidding mourning*, l. 1)

Ŏn mán heă/vĕns ĭnfl/ŭénce wórkes/nŏt só
                    (*The Ecstasy*, l. 57)

Ănd bŭrde/nŏus cór/pŭlénce/mў lóve/hăd grówne,
                    (*Love's Diet*, l. 2)

These are not the only cases, but they should suffice. It is possibly worth adding the line from *The Dream* with scansion marks to indicate the possible parallels:

Prŏfáneness,/tŏ thínke/theé án/ў thíng/bŭt theé.

It might be objected against some of the examples I have given that the first foot is really an iambus, and the second an anapaest. If that mode of scansion were adopted for my examples, however, precisely the same kind of scansion would apply to the line from *The Dream*. Therefore, I suggest, Professor Gardner's generalization does not hold. There remains, however, the aesthetic issue. Is the line with 'Profaneness' really 'hopelessly unmetrical'? If any one of my examples is a true parallel, it will also be 'hopelessly unmetrical', yet Professor Gardner has printed all those other lines without demur. My own view is that none of them is 'hopelessly unmetrical', and I find myself in good company in thinking that the reading of Groups I and II in l. 20 of *The Dream* is rhythmically quite acceptable. Mr J. C. Maxwell, in his review of Professor Gardner's edition,[1] found nothing objectionable in the reading 'Profaness', and Professor Mark Roberts not only thought that there were insufficient grounds for rejecting that reading, but also reported that Mr F. W. Bateson had told him in a letter that he actually preferred the reading 'on prosodic grounds'.[2] There is, however, a point against 'Profaneness' (in any of its spellings) which Professor Gardner does not mention, namely, that the ending could easily have been caught from 'confess(e)' in the preceding line. I do not think, nevertheless, that that objection has enough weight by itself to overcome the strong MS evidence for 'Profaneness'.

It is worth while now to consider the evidence for reading 'I' rather than 'it' in l. 19. It is important to note that the MS readings suggest that two versions were substantially current before the publication of *1633*:

> I doe confesse, I could not chuse but bee
> Prophane, to thinke thee any thing but thee.

[1] *MLR* 61 (1966), p. 276.
[2] *EC* 17 (1967), p. 277.

and

> I do confesse, it could not chuse but bee
> Prophaness, to think thee any thing but thee.

We have no reason to believe that, with the exception of *Lut* (and *O'F* after seemingly two corrections), there was any MS support for the *1633* version adopted by Grierson and by Professor Gardner. Of the two versions for which there is substantial MS support I would suppose that the version 'I . . . Prophane' is the earlier, and I would guess that Professor Empson[1] was quite possibly right in suggesting that Donne altered the lines when revising his poem, so as not to confess that he might be profane. If Professor Gardner is right in thinking that Group I MSS descend from a revised text of 1614, just before Donne's ordination, Professor Empson's suggestion would seem to have a fair degree of probability. Which version, then, should a modern editor print? I think one should perhaps print the more vital version 'I . . . Prophane', while making it clear that there was another version with substantial support in the MSS. I am not in favour of printing the version of *1633* which has so little MS support.

---

[1] *Crit.Q.* 8 (1966), p. 268.

APPENDIX V

'AIR AND ANGELS', ll. 24, 26–8

The argument in the main part of this note will proceed on the assumption that the correct reading in l. 24 is 'it'; but, in my view, that assumption can by no means be regarded as certainly correct. It is quite possible that the correct reading may be 'yt' = 'that'. I shall postpone discussion of the meaning of ll. 24 and 26–8 on that reading till the end of this note. It is, however, worth mentioning it at this stage, since it may be interesting for readers to bear that alternative reading in mind when considering the arguments and counter-arguments about the lines on the basis of the reading 'it'. The further variant 'yet(t)' is also possible, though the most likely meaning on that reading would presumably be that the air of the face and wings of the angel could be expected to become purer at some stage. This does not seem a very attractive meaning. I know of no theological authority for such an idea; and I do not see that it would contribute to the poem. I believe it would only introduce needless confusion.

24 *it*] It is a vexed point whether 'it' refers back to 'Angel' (l. 23) or to 'air' (l. 24). The main arguments against the view that 'it' refers back to 'Angel' are (1) that that would be bad syntax, since the pronoun would naturally refer to the last noun before it; (2) that it would be bad angelology, since in the Bible angels were always referred to as male: and that it would be contrary to Donne's own usage, since he accepts the biblical practice; (3) that Donne is referring in the poem to the Thomist doctrine that angels manifest themselves to men by taking on bodies of *specially condensed* air; and that to switch attention from that point to an utterly different one, viz. the difference in purity between incorporeal angels and the bodies they take on, would be to cloud the sense of the poem. (These arguments were originally put forward with great force in an unpublished note on the poem by Mr Hugh Sykes Davies, and I am indebted to him for the loan of his brilliant piece. His arguments have since been published, in 'Text or context', *REL* 6 (1965), pp. 93–107, with a reply by Professor Gardner at pp. 108–10.)

In my view, the most substantial of these arguments is (2). As to (1), Donne's practice in matters of syntax is flexible: there are other cases in his work in which the pronoun 'it' is not used to refer to the last noun before it.

Moreover, if 'it' referred back to 'air', what kind of air would it be referring to? It could not be to uncondensed air, for that was not the kind of air in which angels were supposed to be bodily manifested. Nor could it be to condensed air, for then Donne would be saying that condensed air is not as pure as condensed air, which is absurd.

As to (3), I for one should not be willing to concede that attention is concentrated in the poem on the point of Thomist doctrine that the air of the bodies assumed by angels is *condensed*. There is, therefore, in my view, no question of *switching* attention *from* that point. It would seem to me, on the contrary, that if at all, it is only in this one line (l. 24) that that specific point is referred to, and that the reference is merely parenthetical. The poem as a whole, in so far as it lives up to its title, seems to me to be concerned with air and angels, not with two kinds of air, one rarefied and one condensed. I find no evidence of the specific doctrine elsewhere in the poem at all. Again, the relevant passage from St Thomas Aquinas (*Summa Theol.*, I, li. 2), quoted by Grierson, does not say that the condensed air of an angel's body is less *pure* than rarefied air: it simply says that it is thicker. Now honey, for example, can be just as 'pure' whether it is thick or thin. There is, therefore, at least one sense of 'pure' in which condensed air would be as pure as rarefied air. It is admittedly possible that Donne means here by 'pure', *clear*, not *free from impurities*. Yet I see no reason to suppose that that is what he does mean. Moreover, the adjective 'pure' could properly be applied in Donne's time to the physical state of an angel before taking on an airy body. Grierson, in his note (II, p. 21) quotes a passage from Tasso, in which Gabriel is said to take on a body of air:

> La sua forma invisibil d'aria cinse,
> Ed al senso mortal la sottopose: . . .

Now, Fairfax translates these lines as follows:

> In form of airy members fair imbared,
> His spirits pure were subject to our sight.

Here the term 'pure' clearly refers to the incorporeal state of the angel. May it not be, then, that even if 'it' refers to 'Angel', Donne is not parting company with Thomist doctrine, but simply referring to that part of it which teaches that angels, which are pure spirits, take on bodies of air which are not as pure as their spirits are, but are pure compared with other bodies, e.g. bodies composed of more than one element?

If this point is valid, the only outstanding objection to the view that 'it' refers to 'Angel' is that of the sex of angels (argument 2). I do find this quite a strong objection: and I believe it worth serious consideration. Donne does sometimes refer to angels as male. Yet he most often refers to them without indication of sex. I am indebted to Mr Robin Wilson for urging me to reconsider the evidence against argument (2), and for collecting for me a considerable number of instances of Donne's use of the term 'angel'. He rightly lays stress on ll. 25–6 of *The Relic*:

> Difference of sex we never knew,
> No more than our guardian angels do; . . .

This *could* indeed be interpreted as meaning that all guardian angels were male: but taking the passage within Donne's system of usage I believe the correct interpretation to be that Donne thought of angels as sexless, or, more strictly, as beings to whom *per se*, in virtue of their incorporeality, the attribute of sex was wholly irrelevant. That angels were *per se* incorporeal was the considered view of such authorities as Dionysius the Areopagite and St Thomas Aquinas. There does seem, moreover, to be an additional objection to the view that 'it' refers to air, namely this: Suppose that the last three lines of the poem are suggesting that men's love corresponds to the angel, and women's love to the air of the angel's body, then to interpret 'it' in l. 24 to refer to 'air' would result in a line which makes a great deal of fuss about a supposed difference in 'purity' between rare and condensed air, which would have no relevance to the last three lines, and might well cause great confusion to a reader. Clearly, though, this objection would have no force at all unless the last three lines do suggest that men's love corresponds to the angel, and women's love to the air of the angel's body. It will therefore be proper to postpone final judgement on this objection till ll. 26–8 have been considered.

To sum up I should say: (*a*) that logical syntax strongly favours the view that 'it' refers to 'Angel'; (*b*) that in correct usage rarefied air would not be 'purer' than condensed air; (*c*) (i) that there is support elsewhere in Donne for the view that he concurred with high theological authority in holding that angels were *per se* incorporeal, and (ii) that it would naturally follow that in his view they had *per se* no sex. The upshot is that I think there is in any case a preponderance of support for the view that 'it' refers back to 'Angel'. On the other hand, I do still find Mr Sykes Davies's objection (2) quite strong, and I am not wholly convinced that it is possible to refute it conclusively. What one needs in order to do that is to produce a passage in which Donne explicitly refers to an angel as 'it', and such a passage I have so far been unable to find.

26–8] I should argue for the view that these lines imply that men's love is purer than women's, as follows: (1) If the phrase 'Just such disparity' (in l. 26) refers *back*, it would be most natural to take it to refer to the 'disparity' between the angel and its body, which has been the subject of the immediately preceding three lines taken as a whole, rather than to refer to the 'disparity' between rarefied and condensed air, which, if referred to at all in the poem, is at most the subject of a parenthetical reference in l. 24 only, which is separated by a whole line from the phrase 'Just such disparity' in l. 26. If this point is valid, then it is obvious that l. 27 would most probably refer to the disparity between the angel and air in respect of purity; and not to the disparity between rare and condensed air. It might be contended (though, in my opinion, not very convincingly) that the words 'Just such disparity' in l. 26 do not refer back at all, but only forward; and that therefore argument (1) carries no weight. While not accepting the premises of this objection, I should go on to make an independent point:

(2) Even if we were to take 'it' in l. 24 to refer to 'air', the main point of ll. 23–5 would still be that the woman's love can be the *sphere* of Donne's (the element in which it works, or the sphere which it controls: both meanings are possible). The meaning of ll. 23–5 in that case would be: 'So the solution will have to be that just as an angel takes on a face and wings of air (not rarefied air, but pure air all the same), so my love must assume your *love* as its body, or, to vary the metaphor, my love must take your love as its sphere, just as an angel exerts control over a sphere' (*or*, if we take 'sphere' to mean *element*: 'so my love must assume your love as the body or element in which it can act'). That is, however we take 'sphere', the relationships will be these: 'The poet's love must be to his lady's love as the angel is to the body that it takes on.'

Now, the next step in my argument would be that whatever else there is reason to suppose the last three lines of the poem to be doing, there is certainly no reason to suppose that they are contradicting the three previous lines or blurring the comparison already made in them. Lines 26–8 are pointing to a perennial distinction between women's love and men's. If this perennial distinction were a wholly different one from the difference between Donne's love and his lady's, which has been indicated in ll. 23–5, then that comparison would be blurred. It would scarcely be a caricature to say that what would be happening would be that Donne would be saying: 'My love must be to your love as an angel is to the body it assumes; and, as a matter of fact, women's love perennially differs from men's love in the same way in which pure air differs from the body of an angel'; which would be, I suggest, a complete *non sequitur*.

In contrast, there would be no hitch at all if we were to interpret the points made in the last six lines of the poem as being these: 'My love must be to your love as the angel is to the body it assumes; and, as a matter of fact, the *perennial* distinction between women's love and men's is that women's is like the aerial body whereas men's is like the angel itself.' I would insist here on the word 'ever' in the last line, which would seem to me only to have point if the last three lines are an appeal to a generalization within which Donne's own case falls.

(3) Finally, I would also urge that to interpret the last three lines as referring to a distinction between the purity of an angel before it takes on a body, and the purity of that body, fits better the general sense of the poem. Donne's love, the man's love, is to take a body (l. 10). It fails at first to find a satisfactory body; then it finds one. It did not have a body to begin with, or the search would be pointless. The original state of the man's love is therefore bodiless, and this fits the comparison with the angel, for the angel is also originally bodiless. St Thomas Aquinas clearly maintained this (see e.g. the Opusculum *De Substantiis*

Separatis (Mandonnet (ed.), *Opuscula Omnia*, Paris, 1927, pp. 70–144)). If, then, the last three lines of the poem are referring to the natural bodiless character of angels, they would be emphasizing a fundamental point in Thomist angelology; and an important point in the comparison between Donne's originally bodiless love and the originally bodiless angel; and they would also be performing a very proper function in harking back to the first stanza.

These, then, are my reasons for believing that the last three lines of the poem imply that men's love is purer than women's. This is not necessarily a cynical touch on Donne's part, though. Women's love is also called 'pure' by implication. I should rather regard the statement as a gentle piece of badinage.

24] We may now return to l. 24, and attempt, as promised, a decision on the last objection to the view that 'it' refers back to 'air'. If my view of ll. 26–8 is correct, then it would seem disproportionate for Donne to mention in l. 24 a difference between the purity of condensed and rarefied air, in view of what would then be its irrelevance to ll. 26–8. Could one meet this objection in any way? Could one give some point to l. 24 which would not make it a disproportionate fuss? I think one *might* be able to. Lines 23–4 say that the face and wings of the angel are made of *air*: this is part of the main point Donne wishes to make. However, with the live mind he had, he might then have seen that someone might make the niggling objection that this air is not ordinary pure air, but something less pure, and therefore not a fit image for women's love; and so he might have wished to knock the bottom out of this objection once for all by conceding that the air of the angel's body was not as pure as ordinary air, while maintaining that it was pure all the same. That would *perhaps* be a *possible* interpretation were this the only objection to the view that 'it' refers back to 'air'. But, in any case, I am not convinced that it is in fact the true interpretation, since the total case against 'it' referring back to 'air' seems to me fairly strong.

It remains to consider what the situation will be if we adopt in l. 24 'yt', the reading of the most reliable Group I manuscripts, and take 'yt' as 'that', of which it was a common spelling at the time. 'Not pure as that' could then refer back *either* to 'Angel' *or* to 'air'. If it were taken to refer back to 'Angel', then the reference would no longer be open to Mr Sykes Davies's objection from the sex of angels. If it were taken to refer to 'air', the position would be the same as on Mr Sykes Davies's interpretation of 'it'; and the line would be open to the objection I urged that it would seem to yield an impossible meaning whether we take the air referred to to be uncondensed or condensed (see p. 319). In any case, I would also maintain, as before (see pp. 319–21) that, even if the reference in l. 24 were to a difference in 'purity' between condensed and uncondensed air, that reference would be merely parenthetical, and would not affect the implication in ll. 26–8 that men's love is purer than women's.

APPENDIX VI

'THE ECSTASY': A NOTE ON INTERPRETATION

Controversy about interpretation of this poem centres on two main issues: (1) whether the poem is, as Pierre Legouis thought,[1] a poem of seduction, or, as Grierson believed,[2] though with some qualification, a justification of the interdependence of soul and body in human love between the sexes, or, as Ezra Pound held, an expression of 'Platonism believed';[3] (2) whether the last part of the poem (ll. 49–76) suggests, as is believed by many critics including Pierre Legouis and also, more recently, Professor Robert Ellrodt,[4] that the lovers, after their spiritual union in the ecstasy, should in future (or, more extremely, almost at once) have sexual intercourse, rather than content themselves with spiritual union; or whether, as Professor Gardner believes, 'the only plea made in these lines is that the lovers' souls should return from their ecstatic communion to reanimate their bodies'.[5]

I intend first to sketch a possible interpretation of the poem, and then relate it to the main issues.

Now, the first three stanzas seem to establish at least two facts: first, that the two lovers were already 'one another's best'; and secondly, *pace* Professor Gardner,[6] that they have not already had sexual intercourse. Surely stanza 3 *must* imply that their physical relationship has not yet got very far? The next two stanzas (ll. 13–20) appear to suggest that the two souls are trying to win each other ('armies' and 'victory' seem to suggest some form of battle, whilst 'negotiate' evokes the idea of diplomatic activity or some form of parley between the leaders of opposing forces). On the other hand, 'advance their state' is a more neutral phrase, which involves the notion of improving their position without necessarily doing so through conflict, and this may point to union rather than winning; which would fit well with the idea of a single soul flowing from the 'interinanimation' of two souls (ll. 41–4). The true interpretation of ll. 13–20 might, indeed, be that the first idea of each soul was

[1] *Donne the Craftsman*, Paris, 1928, pp. 68–9.
[2] II, p. xlvii.
[3] *An ABC of Reading*, London, 1934, p. 126.
[4] See *Les Poètes Métaphysiques Anglais*, part 2, Paris, 1960, pp. 401–10.
[5] *ESS*, p. 260.
[6] *ESS*, p. 262.

to win the other, but that this was to be superseded by the inspired alternative of uniting. In ll. 21–4 a hypothetical listener appears, a thorough Platonist in belief and action, 'grown all mind' by 'good love'. And this man, by listening to the unanimous speech of the ecstatic souls might become 'far purer', through some process of metaphorical *heating* ('concoction' involves heating; and looks forward to 'allay' (l. 56), whose fusion with more valuable metal is also produced by heat).

The rest of the poem (ll. 29–76) is, of course, the single speech of the two ecstatic souls. They say (ll. 29–32) that their ecstasy has enabled them to see clearly what they love in each other, and that it was not sex that caused their love, and, indeed, that they had not known its cause before at all. They now realize (ll. 33–44) that what happens when people really fall in love is that, whereas their separate souls were made up of a mixture of qualities which they were not aware of, love mingles the two souls so that each complements the other's deficiencies, and as a united soul they have become stronger, richer, and greater than they were before. So far the general outline of the argument seems fairly clear, and quite plausible. In ll. 45–8, on the other hand, it appears to me to become sophistical. It is, in any case, not quite plain why the new united soul, even though 'abler' than either soul was before, should know what it is made of. It may be that love has given it that knowledge, but this is far from explicit in the poem, and it is not even clear that it is implicit. But a more serious matter is that, since the two separate souls have already undergone change, there seems to be no good ground for asserting, as l. 48 does, that because the 'atomies' from which the new soul has grown are souls, no change can invade them. Yet, if the argument *is* defective here, the particular damage is only local.

Whether the further tenor of the argument (from l. 49 onwards) is sound remains to be considered. Let us look at it fairly closely. The two souls sense a desire to return to their bodies; and they argue for doing so. The first argument (ll. 51–2) is that the bodies belong to them, and that as souls they are related to their bodies as celestial intelligences are related to the 'spheres' which they control. This is quite a cogent argument. The souls would be guilty of some kind of dereliction of duty if they abrogated their function of controlling their bodies. The analogy with celestial intelligences might, however, be questioned. The next point made is that the souls ought to be grateful to their bodies for having originally brought them together, and for having put their senses at the souls' disposal (ll. 53–5). This is not so strong as an argument for *returning* to their bodies, though the premiss is true enough, and the idea is a pleasant one. More substantial is the point (l. 56) that their bodies are not simply contemptible appendages which they can now cast off, but substances which give them an additional benefit, just as gold or silver coins are made harder by an 'allay'. This would be a very good argument for returning to bodies if the premiss were true; but it is a mere assertion here, and there is no indication earlier in the poem that their bodies have had any such effect. On the contrary, it has been insisted that the souls have become far more closely united since they escaped from their bodies. The rhetoric of the image, with its suggestion of fusion by heat, may be powerful; but to an alert reader, I would urge, the premiss ought to appear suspect.

Next (in ll. 57–60) Donne attempts to establish an analogy between the idea that the planets and stars influence (perhaps can only influence) people by first affecting the air, and the idea that souls may have free access to and influence on each other by working through the intermediary of bodies. It can readily be seen that the perfect analogy would, in fact, be that souls *do* (not merely *may*) have free access to and influence upon each other by working through the inter-mediary of bodies, or even that they can only do so in that way. Yet Donne can-not say either of those things, because it would seem to contradict what he has been saying in earlier stanzas of the 'Dialogue of One'. So all he claims is that souls *may* communicate and influence each other through their bodies. This claim is fair enough; but it does not seem a very strong argument for 'going to bodies', since the souls have already shown that they can communicate with and influence each other without recourse to their bodies. Donne, however, makes his lovers persist. They (and he, of course) offer a further argument (ll. 61–8): Just as blood 'labours' (? like a woman in childbirth) to beget spirits as like souls as it can make them (because such almost immaterial fingers are required to tie that extremely elusive knot which holds soul and body together and makes a human being), so, on their side, souls must come down from the purely spiritual to feelings and powers within the range of the senses; otherwise human love cannot freely pass between a man and a woman. This time the lovers say 'must'. The apparent parallel between the upward effort of the blood and the downward obligation of the souls is ingenious, and appeals to a sense for symmetricality. The nub of the argument, however, is that if the souls do not 'descend' from pure spiritual love, then that great and valuable thing, human love, will not have freedom of action. Now, this is the best justification offered so far. Once we admit that human love is great and valuable and involves both soul and body, then pure spiritual love *must* be insufficient. And the lovers, and the poem, do seem to be asking us to make the required admission.

The last eight lines (ll. 69–76) appear to offer yet another argument for returning to bodies, namely that otherwise people who do not yet fully believe in the real union of love, but need some outward sign to convince them, may come to believe. Donne does sometimes (e.g. in *The Canonization*) write of the love between him and a woman as being a pattern for others to follow; and therefore it is quite possible that here also the exemplary character of true love is a serious consideration in favour of going to bodies. However this may be, the lovers now shift their attention (ll. 73–6) to considering the possibility (adumbrated in ll. 21 ff.) that some lover has heard their 'Dialogue of One'. What, however, does 'such as we' mean? Does it imply that the lover is as yet 'Platonic'? If it is the same sort of lover as was described in ll. 21 ff., then it must imply this; and it would surely be confusing if he were a different kind of lover? This carries a further implication: that the lovers themselves are also as yet Platonic, at least in the sense that they have not yet had sexual intercourse (and, indeed, only in that sense now, since they are abjuring satisfaction with pure spiritual union). 'Such as we', however, also has the additional implication that the hypothetical listener is, like them, *spiritually* united to his beloved. What he is being told, then, is that 'going to bodies' will have very little effect on the quality of the love of people already united by spiritual love; the implication being that lovers already spiritually united need not fear 'going to bodies'.

Now, on the hypothesis that this interpretation of the argument is valid, what is the true position on the two main issues that have divided critics? Is the poem a poem of seduction, as Pierre Legouis thought? Surely, we cannot answer either way with justified confidence? The poem could be used, and may, indeed, have been used, as such. On the other hand, it could equally well not be. As to Grierson's view that, on the whole, the poem seems to justify the interdependence of soul and body in human love between the sexes, that would seem undoubtedly right. On the other hand, I do not feel satisfied with Grierson's qualifying observations:

> There hangs about the poem just a suspicion of the conventional and unreal Platonism of the seventeenth century. In attempting to state and vindicate the relation of soul and body he falls perhaps inevitably into the appearance, at any rate, of the dualism which he is trying to transcend. He places them over against each other as separate entities and the lower bulks unduly.
>
> (II, p. xlvii)

This is, as one would expect of Grierson, sensitive and intelligent writing; but it appears to involve some confusion. Since the poem seems largely concerned to emphasize that physical relations between a man and a woman will not substantially derogate from an already existent spiritual union, it is surely natural that there should be marked insistence on the importance of the body. Since the lovers become spiritually united in the ecstasy (which also bulks large in the poem, justifies the title, and even makes it hard to argue convincingly for the role of the bodies), there is no need for any further stress on the spiritual element in human love. As to the 'dualism', is Donne really trying to 'transcend' it in this poem? Certainly not in the sense that he is trying to make the body 'disappear from sight', as Grierson suggests Donne does in *The Anniversary*. In *The Ecstasy* Donne is rather suggesting that the lovers' bodies are important for full human love, and that those lovers whose souls are already united have nothing to fear from 'going to bodies'; and for this idea the poem needs to keep clearly in view the distinction between souls and bodies. 'Transcend' is, indeed, a misnomer, not only if taken in in the sense that Grierson indicates, but in any sense, since it suggests that the distinction vital for the poem is intended by the poet either to vanish or to cease to be meaningful. And what of Ezra Pound's view that in the poem we have 'Platonism believed'? That lapidary assertion by itself is ambiguous, and it is necessary to add some more of the passage from which it comes:

> Platonism believed. The decadence of trying to make pretty speeches and of hunting for something to say temporarily checked. Absolute belief in the existence of an extra-corporal soul, and of its incarnation. Donne stating a thesis in precise even technical terms.

Though the passage is not clear in all its details, the additional words do at least clear up the ambiguity of the laconic words. Pound does not mean that Donne is asserting in the poem that spiritual union is enough for human lovers; but that he believes in an immaterial soul, and that in a human being this is simply embodied – and is not for instance simply a 'form', or an epiphenomenon, of the body, or itself material. Pound's remark 'Platonism believed', so understood, is a perfectly true statement about the poem; and, moreover, interestingly enough, in no way inconsistent either with Grierson's view or even with that of Legouis.

As to the second 'issue': whether the last part of the poem (ll. 49–76) suggests that the lovers, after their spiritual union in the ecstasy, should in future (perhaps even in the immediate future) have sexual intercourse; or whether, as Professor Gardner believes, against most critical opinion, 'the only plea made in these lines is that the lovers' souls should return from their ecstatic communion to reanimate their bodies', my own view, on the interpretation I have suggested, is that all that is explicitly stated is a plea that the souls should return to their bodies. To that extent Professor Gardner appears to me to be right. The further question, however, is whether the drift of the poem would suggest to a properly responding reader that 'going to bodies' includes within its connotation sexual union as an element – not necessarily immediate sexual union, but sexual union at some time. My own opinion is that it does. It would seem extraordinary, in a poem about the nature of human love which urges souls for the sake of full human love to return to their bodies, that this plea should omit to imply the one physical act widely regarded as of supreme importance in manifesting and cementing the union of lovers.

APPENDIX VII

'THE CANONIZATION', ll. 23–7 (PUNCTUATION)

1633 prints ll. 23–7 thus:

> The Phoenix ridle hath more wit
> By us, we two being one, are it.
> So, to one neutrall thing both sexes fit.
> Wee dye and rise the same, and prove
> Mysterious by this love.

Chambers altered the stop after 'it' to a semicolon, thus connecting l. 25 with ll. 23–4. Norton, in the American Grolier Club edition, did the same, and also removed the comma after 'So' in l. 25, thus making 'So' an adverb of degree. Grierson thought that l. 25 '*must* go with what follows', and he restored *1633*'s full stop after 'it', and emended the full stop after 'fit' to a comma. He also deleted *1633*'s comma after 'So', but for a different reason from Norton's. Grierson took 'So' to be a subordinate conjunction of effect, and paraphrased ll. 25 ff. as follows: 'Both sexes fit *so* entirely into one neutral thing that we die and rise the same . . .'. Professor Gardner went into reverse. She restored *1633*'s full stop after 'fit', but emended its full stop after 'it' to a comma, taking l. 25 to be 'an elucidation and expansion of the two preceding lines', and ll. 26–7 as adding 'the further resemblance of miraculous resurrections'. She also restored the comma after 'So', evidently taking 'So' as an illative conjunction.

Let us first look at the textual evidence, and then at the matter of meaning.

We need to remember, in this case as in many others, the principle that the *presence* in MSS of particular marks of punctuation is more significant than their *absence*. Now, it is a striking fact that all the Group I MSS, and a few others (including *Wed* and *Dob*, which show more than usual care about punctuation) have a full stop after 'it' in l. 24. Moreover, three other MSS (*O'F*, *TCD*, *N*) have here stops heavier than a comma; and only one of these MSS (*O'F*) has a heavier stop after 'fit' in l. 25. This all points towards the greater break being after 'it', and not after 'fit'. Furthermore, even if we were to take more seriously than we ought to, the absence of any stop after 'it' in the ten MSS indicated, that would scarcely support an argument for the greater break being after 'fit', since

328

none of those MSS, except *S*, has a stop after 'fit' either. As far as MS evidence goes, indeed, the case of Chambers, Norton and Professor Gardner for connecting l. 25 with ll. 23–4 rather than with l. 26–7 would be extremely slender. It would rest on *Lut* (it, . . . fit.), *O'F* (it: . . . fit.), and *S* (it [*no stop*] . . . fit.). It is clear from Professor Gardner's statements about those MSS in her Textual Introduction and elsewhere in her edition, that she at least would hardly feel much confidence in a case which had to rely on them.

Let us now look into the question of meaning. The really important question is: What good meaning can be attached to a text punctuated in a way conforming to the predominance of MS authority, that is, making the greater break after 'it', and not after 'fit'? Now, it seems to me that one perfectly possible meaning would be that offered by Grierson. That, however, does involve deleting *1633*'s comma after 'So'. This would not be a very serious matter, since the editor of *1633* could have misunderstood the line, and among the MSS I have collated, only *S96* has a comma there. Yet the presence of the comma is of some importance, and its absence in the other MSS may not be particularly significant. Moreover, all the early editions printed the comma. If we do retain the comma, I think another meaning is certainly possible. This would depend on taking 'fit' in the sense 'made to fit' (*OED* a3), a sense current at the time, though now obsolete. The meaning of the lines would then be: 'The riddle of the Phoenix makes more sense because of us: we two, being one, *are* the Phoenix. Thus, our two sexes, being made to fit together to form a sexually intermediate creature, we die, and then we rise again one and the same being; . . .'. This sense of 'fit' was normally applied to a manufactured article; but I see no reason why Donne should not have exploited it metaphorically here.

Besides being textually better supported, the punctuation 'it./ . . . fit,' has the slight advantage that it avoids the needless separation of the two characteristics, sexual neutrality and the power of self-resurrection, which might make l. 26 seem rather more distinct from the drift of l. 25 than it in fact is. There is, on balance, not much to choose between the sense on Professor Gardner's punctuation and the sense on Grierson's or on that adopted here; but the weight of textual authority is certainly against Professor Gardner's punctuation.

APPENDIX VIII

'THE FUNERAL', 'THE BLOSSOM', 'THE PRIMROSE', AND
'THE RELIC': PERSONAL REFERENCE IN THESE POEMS

Grierson thought (II, pp. xxiv and 47) all these poems were probably written to Magdalen Herbert, mother of Edward, Lord Herbert of Cherbury, and of George Herbert. She was the youngest daughter of Sir Richard Newport, married Richard Herbert in 1581, but was widowed in 1596. She was remarried in 1608 to Sir John Danvers. Grierson's 'clue' was the title of *The Primrose*, as it appeared in *1635*, and in all the subsequent early editions: *The Primrose, being at Mountgomery Castle, upon the hill, on which it is situate.* Montgomery Castle was the residence of the Herbert family, and Magdalen Herbert lived there until 1599, when she moved to Oxford, where she lived for over a year, while her eldest son Edward (later Lord Herbert of Cherbury) was finishing his studies. Grierson was also impressed by the fact that these four poems, together with *The Damp*, occur together in many manuscripts. Grierson hesitated to connect *The Damp* with Mrs Herbert, but believed that the four were 'addressed to Mrs Herbert in the earlier days of Donne's intimacy with her in Oxford or London'. Grierson attached weight, moreover, to the mention of the Magdalen in *The Relic*.

Professor Gardner has examined the relevant evidence with considerable care (*ESS*, pp. 251–8). She believes that Donne may have met Mrs Herbert in Oxford in 1599; but that his close friendship with her began in 1607. With regard to Grierson's view, Professor Gardner is not impressed with the argument from the occurrence of the poems together in many manuscripts. She does not believe it possible to argue from physical connection of poems among Donne's papers to the conclusion that they must have been composed at the same time and addressed to the same person. As to *The Primrose*, she takes seriously the title setting it on the hill of Montgomery Castle, but prefers to connect the poem with Edward Herbert rather than his mother, on the ground that he lived there, on and off, throughout his life, whereas Mrs Herbert left Wales in 1599. Professor Gardner further argues that the poem is not addressed to any woman, and that the speaker has no particular woman in mind; 'he is looking for "a true love"'. She considers the poem 'undramatic and speculative, divorced from any love-affair real or imagined'; and continues:

I would suggest that its ironic and cynical tone makes it an admirable cooling-card to such high-flown poems of Herbert's as the three called 'Platonic Love'; and that it was for the benefit of the master of Montgomery Castle rather than for that of his mother, that Donne argued in this curiously frigid poem for the superiority of a 'mere woman' to those rare 'monsters' who were 'more or less then woman'.

(ESS, p. 256)

She also notes that, according to the manuscript *H49*, Donne was on his way to visit Edward Herbert in Wales when he wrote *Good-friday* in 1613. Professor Gardner, 'on the principle of Occam's razor', thinks we ought not to postulate any other visit by Donne to Wales; and she also accepts Professor Coffin's suggestion[1] that the poem must be dated after 1610, when Galileo's *Siderius Nuncius* was published. She therefore dates *The Primrose* Spring 1613. Finally, with regard to *The Relic*, Professor Gardner agrees with Professor Garrod[2] in thinking that there is no need to assume that the lady in the poem who gave her lover a 'bracelet of bright hair' was herself called 'Magdalen' because the Bishop and King in a time of 'misdevotion' will declare this to be a relic of the saint who 'loved much' and who is always depicted in art with brilliant golden hair. Professor Gardner holds that the irony in the poem lies in the misunderstanding of the 'bracelet of bright hair': by the grave-diggers who will think it a device of a 'loving couple', and by the King and the Bishop who will think it a love-token given by the great penitent of Christian tradition in her unregenerate days; whereas the truth is that it is a symbol of a love for which no penance need be demanded, and which was itself a miracle. Professor Gardner's view is that we do not know what experience in life lies behind the poem, and she does not see that we ever can know; but she cannot think from what we know of Donne's relations with Mrs Herbert, 'that there is any strong reason for connecting this poem with her'.

What are we to say? I believe that her point that we cannot argue from physical connection of poems among Donne's papers that they must have been composed at the same time and addressed to the same person is entirely valid. On the other hand, I cannot see why it could not count as part of an argument for the poems being addressed to the same person if there were also other evidence. Her argument about Edward Herbert's long residence at Montgomery Castle does not seem to me very strong, since Magdalen Herbert lived there for a great part of the time during which she bore ten children to her first husband. Again, the poem is not, indeed, addressed to any woman, but I cannot see that one has good ground for saying categorically that the speaker has no particular woman in mind; and I find the statement that the poem is 'undramatic and speculative, divorced from any love-affair real or imagined' rather too sharp in its inference. Her suggestion as to the poem's suitability for

[1] C. M. Coffin, *John Donne and the New Philosophy*, New York, 1937, pp. 152 ff.
[2] H. W. Garrod, 'Donne and Mrs Herbert', *RES* 21 (1945), pp. 161–73.

Edward Herbert, on the other hand, cannot be ruled out; though I believe that one can spin a yarn which could also cohere with the facts and connect the poem with the mother rather than the son.

The Relic is a poem which looks back upon a long Platonic relationship. The other three poems are quite different. *The Funeral* and *The Blossom* both seem to express frustration at the thwarting of an advance. In *The Funeral* the poet conceives himself Petrarchanly as 'Love's martyr'. In *The Blossom* he had hoped by long courtship to convert a Platonic into a fully sexual relationship. In *The Primrose* he is, indeed, looking for a 'true-love', and talking in witty generalities. On the other hand, one cannot rule out the implication that he is obliquely referring to a woman who may want to 'get above all thought of sex', whereas what he wants is a woman (quite possibly *that* woman) who is a natural woman, and wishes to be loved sexually, not simply contemplated. Now, why should not all these four poems refer to the same woman – *The Relic*, after a long relationship which has remained Platonic and in the end has given the poet a special satisfaction; and the other three poems to the same woman at a very early stage, when she rebuffed an attempt by the poet to court her? The occurrence of the unusual reference to the hair twisted round the bone in both *The Funeral* and *The Relic* is striking, and we do not find it in any of the other lyrics; furthermore, it might well be a good stroke to connect the Platonic satisfaction expressed in *The Relic* with the dissatisfaction expressed at the rebuff in *The Funeral*. Yet another point is that it would be unlikely for Donne to use the name 'Magdalen' in *The Relic* without having in mind the woman whose friendship he so greatly valued. Indeed, what is there to exclude the woman involved in all four poems being Magdalen Herbert? Why should not the three earlier poems have been written at the time when Donne may have come to know her in Oxford in *c.* 1599, and *The Relic* some years later, after his own marriage, and when he had come to find great satisfaction in the relationship with Magdalen Herbert having remained Platonic? Furthermore, can Occam's razor exclude the possibility that Donne may have been invited to Wales by Edward Herbert at some time during his Oxford years, and that Donne should have written *The Primrose* then, and not in 1613? Professor Coffin argues that Donne certainly took the idea from Galileo. He bases this view on three points: (1) that Kepler, to whose work Donne was greatly indebted, does not mention the idea that the Galaxy consisted of small stars; (2) that Donne's reference is categorical; (3) that 'infinity' is much closer to Galileo's words 'innumerarum Stellarum . . . congeries' than, for instance, to the terms used by the Jesuit mathematician Christopher Clavius in his commentary on the *De Sphaera* of John of Sacrobosco (Rome, 1581), 'ex multitudine nimia stellarum exiguarum'. None of these arguments seem to me very strong. As to (1), indeed Donne evidently learnt much from Kepler; but it does not follow that he would need to have obtained *this* idea from Kepler, had Kepler had it; he could easily have obtained the idea from some earlier writer, such as Clavius. (Professor Coffin himself, indeed, grants[1] that a *theory* of the Galaxy as small stars had been held by various writers since ancient times.) With regard to (2), if Donne held such a theory to be true, he could quite legitimately use it poetically in a categorical form – a poet is surely not bound to write only in hypothetical terms in such a case? With regard to (3) I do not find the difference in the Latin phrases at all sharp. If I am right, there would seem to be no need for the poem to postdate the publication of Galileo's *Siderius Nuncius* in 1610. Finally, I must confess that the style and tone of *The Relic* have long struck me as quite different from that of the other three poems, which seem to me to belong to an earlier manner.

I am far from asserting categorically that this is the true account of personal reference in these four poems, but only suggesting that such an account has not been excluded by any argument so far advanced.

---

[1] Op. cit., pp. 152 ff.

APPENDIX IX

'TWICKENHAM GARDEN', l. 17 ('GROAN' OR 'GROW'?)

Grierson emended *1633*'s 'grow' to 'groane' on MS evidence, commenting:

> It is surely much more in Donne's style than the colourless and pointless 'growe' [*sic*]. It is, too, in closer touch with the next line. If 'growing' is all we are to have predicated of the mandrake, then it should be sufficient for the fountain to 'stand', or 'flow'. The chief difficulty in accepting the MS reading is that the mandrake is most often said to shriek, sometimes to howl, not to groan.

Nevertheless, he argues that the lover most often groans, and that in a metaphor where two objects are identified such a transference of attributes is quite permissible, and quotes *2 Henry VI*, III. ii. 310–11, in which the mandrake is actually said to 'groan':

> Would curses kill, as doth the mandrake's groan,
> I would invent as bitter searching terms . . .

He also adds ll. 53–4 of Donne's *Elegie upon . . . Prince Henry*:

> . . . though such a life wee have
> As but so many mandrakes on his grave.

with the comment: 'i.e. a life of groans'.

Professor Gardner restores the *1633* reading. Her note reads:

> I differ from Grierson in retaining the reading of *1633* which follows *C57* and *Lec* against the other Group I manuscripts and Group II. As a general rule I have abandoned *1633* on such occasions; but here *C57* and *Lec* have the support of Group III and *HK2*, &c. 'Groane', the reading of Groups I and II, could have arisen independently from the strong association of mandrakes with groans. But the mandrake was not held to groan when *in situ*; it only groaned when it was torn up; see Browne, *Pseudodoxia Epidemica*, book ii, chap. vi.

Professor George Williamson had already defended 'grow', as more closely associated with 'senseless' and 'mandrake', all three representing the 'vegetal' soul, which was below the 'sensible' soul, and entirely incapable of sensation.[1]

---

[1] 'Textual difficulties in Donne's poetry', *MP* 38 (1940), repr. in *Seventeenth Century Contexts*, London, 1960.

The crux is not an easy one. 'Groan' is a more exciting word, and links more clearly with l. 18. It is also emotionally more in tone with the rest of the poem. Yet 'grow' is not as pointless as Grierson thought. If 'grow' were accepted, 'so' should probably be taken to mean 'as long as', or 'if only'; whereas, with the reading 'groan' it would probably mean 'so that', though it could have the other meaning. The MS evidence, though numerically in favour of 'grow(e)', is qualitatively inconclusive. As Grierson said, the spellings 'grone' and 'growe' could easily be mistaken for each other. We must hope to settle the matter by other criteria. Professor Gardner's stricture about the occasions on which mandrakes were held to groan is countered by the Donne passage quoted by Grierson. Poets cannot be expected to observe the precise limits of scientific truth. In point of sense and power I believe 'groan' is to be preferred.

APPENDIX X

Grierson thought that *Twickenham Garden* and *A Nocturnal upon St Lucy's Day*
were both written to the Countess of Bedford. Twickenham Park was the
residence of Lady Bedford from 1608 to 1618. Lucy was her name; and the two
poems Grierson believed to be similar in thought, feeling and rhythm (II,
p. xxii).

If the *Nocturnal* was, indeed, written about Lady Bedford, that could have
been during an illness of hers in 1612, when she nearly died, or perhaps even in
1627, when she did actually die. The atmosphere of the poem resembles the
start of Donne's poem on the death of the Countess's brother, Lord Harrington (*Obsequies to the Lord Harrington*), especially to ll. 15 ff. Lord Harrington
died at his sister's house at Twickenham early in 1614.

J. B. Leishman, in *The Monarch of Wit* (1951), took a different view. He
wondered if the poem may have been written by Donne to his wife during
some grave illness, for instance in 1611. Leishman cites the resemblance (which
had struck me independently) between stanza 3 and *A Valediction: of weeping*,
and suggested that the *Nocturnal* is much more like the poems which were
certainly or probably written to Donne's wife than to 'the Platonic or Courtly
poems'. Yet can we properly use these epithets of *Twickenham Garden*, which
could be about Lady Bedford and a phase in their relationship?

Professor Gardner (*ESS*, p. 249) has accepted Grierson's connection of
Twickenham Garden and the *Nocturnal* with each other 'as works of art'; but she
holds that 'interpreted biographically they are poles apart':

> The first mourns the 'cruelty' of a mistress, whose 'truth' to another kills
> her lover; the second mourns the death of a mistress with whom her lover
> had been wholly united. In view of all we know of Donne's relations with
> the Countess of Bedford and the tone of his letters to her in prose and verse,
> it seems incredible that either poem should be thought to be concerned with
> Donne's actual feelings for his patroness.

Professor Gardner believes, on the other hand, that the poems may very well be
connected with Lady Bedford; and she suggests that *Twickenham Garden* was

possibly a poem Donne wrote for the Countess on a theme set by her, and perhaps in response to some verses of her own that she may have shown him in that very garden. That she did at some date show him such verses is attested by an undated letter from Donne to her.[1] The letter makes it clear that Lady Bedford's verses were very complimentary to Donne. He begs her to give them to him, promising not to show them to anyone or to believe them. Professor Gardner thinks the verses were probably written in reply to one of his verse-letters asking her favour; and urges that the actual subject of *Twickenham Garden* is so trite and conventional that it might well have been a subject proposed, or one on which the two of them competed.

This seems to me a perfectly possible explanation. On the other hand, I do not see that Professor Gardner's arguments exclude the possibility that the poem may have had for Donne a meaning of a more passionate kind. If there was at some time a passionate relationship between Donne and the Countess, even if it only went so far as exchanging love poems, that would have been the one thing that, for obvious reasons, each would have wished to conceal. If the concealment was successful, moreover, the mutual passion would not form part of 'all we know' of their relationship, and would certainly not appear in the tone of the letters in prose and verse written to her, which could readily be shown to other people. In any case, I hardly think we shall be justified in feeling confident that our knowledge of the relationship of Donne with the Countess definitely excludes moments of passion or jealousy in the course of a long friendship. As Grierson very wisely and memorably observed (II, p. xxiii), 'friendship between man and woman is love in some degree'.

As to the *Nocturnal* in relation to *Twickenham Garden*, I believe Professor Gardner is quite right in holding that 'as works of art they stand together'. They are both 'seasonal poems'; in both 'other lovers are appealed to'; and in both the idea that 'plants and stones' are able to 'detest and love' is used. Also the versification and slow pace of the two poems are similar. Those points would not, however, be enough to connect the *Nocturnal* with Lady Bedford, even if *Twickenham Garden* is connected with her, as seems extremely likely. The additional point made by Grierson was that the Countess's name was Lucy. Professor Gardner gives due weight to this factor, and suggests the possibility that the idea of writing a poem on St Lucy's Eve was 'a gesture of compliment to the Countess', adding, however:

> If so, the poem far transcends its original conception and has become the most profound expression of the sensation of utter and irremediable loss. The sombre and passionate intensity of both poems, their haunting slow rhythms, may more properly be ascribed to the date at which they were written than to some imagined crisis in Donne's relations with his patron. If they are connected with Lucy Bedford they must have been written after 1607 when Donne was approaching middle age and his verse was developing

---

[1] *Letters to Severall Persons of Honour*, 1651, pp. 67–8.

the intensity of his *Divine Poems*, which is different from the ecstatic intensity of his celebrations of love's mysteries.

Once again, it seems to me perfectly possible that the idea of writing the poem was the 'gesture of compliment' which Professor Gardner suggests; but it also seems to me possible that the idea sprang from some critical event, such as a serious illness of the Countess. Moreover, the 'passionate intensity' could surely derive from some real (if hidden) feelings, finding a shelter or disguise in a poem originating as a task or gesture? That could, furthermore, be as good an explanation of this particular form of 'intensity' as a change in his sensibility allied to the intensity of the *Divine Poems*. The *Nocturnal* is, after all, a love poem, and the intensity of a man's love for a woman does not, one hopes, necessarily cease at the age of thirty-six or even forty-six.

The *Nocturnal* could, on the other hand, refer to some illness of Donne's wife (for instance in 1611) or to her death in 1617; and I am personally quite attracted by these alternatives.

The controversy cannot be regarded as settled with respect to either poem, and it may never be settled. As far as the *Nocturnal* is concerned, the use of the word 'Lucy' is striking; but not conclusive for the poem being directly connected with Lucy Bedford. The poetical use of the festival of St Lucy in connection with the death of some other woman with whom Donne had had an extremely close relationship (notably and primarily his wife) could have been a combination which Donne felt to be particularly appropriate. Lucy Bedford was on friendly terms with Donne's family, and was godmother to Donne's daughter Lucy, who died in January 1627, actually before the Countess, who died in May 1627 at the age of forty-six.

The Dissolution remains to be considered. As Professor Gardner notes (*ESS*, p. 218), this poem is linked with the *Nocturnal* both in manuscript tradition and in theme. There is, however, no reason to connect the poem with Lady Bedford, and the physical closeness of the relationship implied in ll. 3–5 would suggest that this poem, at least, probably refers to the death (real or imagined) of Donne's wife, unless it has no biographical source at all, which I, for one, feel disinclined to admit.

APPENDIX XI

'THE UNDERTAKING', l. 6 ('SPECULAR STONE')

'Specular stone' is equivalent to the Latin *lapis specularis*. What was *lapis specularis*? Most translators of the term as used in Classical texts render it as 'talc' or 'mica'. Yet most probably the correct translation is 'selenite', a translucent or transparent form of gypsum. The Elder Pliny's *Natural History* is the chief Classical authority for *lapis specularis*. Modern scholars differ in their interpretations of his references to the mineral. K. C. Bailey,[1] for instance, considers that two passages suggest gypsum, but, on balance, interprets Pliny as referring to mica. H. Zeitler[2] maintains that Pliny definitely meant mica. On the other hand C. E. N. Bromehead argues most cogently[3] that of the seven localities mentioned by Pliny[4] as producing *lapis specularis* (Spain, Cyprus, Cappadocia, Sicily, North Africa, the region of Bologna, Arabia [probably meaning Arabia Petraca, i.e. Sinai]), all can produce gypsum or selenite, whereas, though two or three might produce mica, there is no evidence that any could produce crystals large enough for glazing. Yet *lapis specularis* was certainly used for glazing, not only in Classical times and during the early centuries of the Christian era, but also in Donne's own time (see ref. to Andrea Baccius on p. 291), and even well beyond.

Donne makes at least two other references to 'specular stone'. One occurs in a verse-letter to the Countess of Bedford at ll. 28–31:[5]

> You teach (though wee learne not) a thinge unknowne
> To our late times, the use of specular stone,
> Through which all things within without were shown.
> Of such were Temples; so, and of such you are.

---

[1] *The Elder Pliny's Chapters on Chemical Subjects,* Text, Translation and Notes, parts I and II, London, 1929 and 1932.

[2] *Mica: its history, production and utilisation,* London, 1913.

[3] 'The forgotten uses of selenite', *The Mineralogical Magazine* XXVI, 182 (September 1943).

[4] *NH* XXXVI, xlv.

[5] *Gr,* I, p. 219; W. Milgate (ed.), *Satires, Epigrams, and Verse Letters,* Oxford, 1967, p. 101.

The other is in a sermon delivered on 1 April 1627:

> The *heathens* served their Gods in Temples, *sub dio*, without roofs or cover-
> ings, in a fine openness; and, where they could, in Temples made of *Specular
> stone*, that was transparent as glasse, or crystall, so as they which walked
> without in the streets, might see all that was done within.
>
> *(Sermons*, VIII. 397)

It is clear from the first of these passages that Donne thought that specular
stone was no longer used; and from both passages that he believed that temples
had been made of it in ancient times. In *The Undertaking*, of course, he also
implies that the stone can no longer be found. As already noted in my Commentary, it appears quite likely that Donne was misled into thinking this by the
categorical statement to that effect by Panciroli. Professor Richard M. Ringler
suggested this in his valuable note in *MLR* 60 (1965), pp. 333–9, where he
quotes a passage from Panciroli in which it is also stated that Nero built the
Temple of Fortune with specular stone, which seems again quite untrue. Professor Ringler also indicates how Panciroli's own mistakes probably arose.
Pliny, after describing *lapis specularis*, mentioning the ease with which it could
be split into sheets as thin as required, indicating its areas of provenance, and
alluding to its flakiness, goes on to describe another stone, *phengites*, 'as hard as
marble', and translucent. He writes that Nero rebuilt the Temple of Fortune
with this stone, whose effect was that in daytime it was as light as day in the
temple, even when the doors were shut, but that it was different from that of
windows of specular stone, since the light was, as it were, contained inside, not
transmitted from outside. Professor Ringler noticed that sixteenth-century
texts of Pliny had perverted the meaning of this passage by the unwarranted
inclusion of the word '*haud*', which made the passage say that the *phengites*
produced an effect 'scarcely different' from that of specular stone. From this it
could readily be concluded that Pliny was saying that Nero rebuilt the Temple
of Fortune from a kind of specular stone. Professor Ringler suggests that this
was what Panciroli concluded, and he quotes a passage in which Panciroli
categorically states that Nero built the temple out of specular stone. In the same
passage, which Professor Gardner also quotes (*ESS*, p. 180), Panciroli states
that people inside could be seen quite clearly from outside, and also that
specular stone is no longer to be found. It seems certain that this passage was
the source of Donne's mistaken beliefs. That Donne knew Panciroli's book is
clear not only from *Ignatius his Conclave*, but also from the seventeenth item in
The Courtier's Library (ed. E. M. Simpson, 1930, p. 34).

If Panciroli was the source of the reference in *The Undertaking*, then, clearly,
the poem must be dated 1599 or later.

APPENDIX XII

MUSICAL SETTINGS OF SOME 'SONGS AND SONETS'

Mr John P. Cutts did a great deal of research in the 1950s on settings of lyrics in the seventeenth century.[1] Then in 1958, Professor Vincent Duckles gave a paper at the seventh International Congress of Musicologists at Cologne, 'The Lyrics of John Donne as set by his Contemporaries'.[2] Professor Duckles lists twenty-nine such settings, but only eight of these are settings of love-lyrics quite definitely by Donne. Seven of these settings were printed and discussed by M. Jean Jacquot in 1961.[3] The eighth (William Lawes's setting of *The Apparition*) is so incomplete in the manuscript in which it occurs[4] that M. Jacquot considered reconstruction hazardous.

In Group II manuscripts three of the *Songs and Sonets* are described as written 'to certaine Aires which were made before', and *DC* so describes six in all, including the same three. The six are *The Message*, 'Go and catch', *Confined Love*, *Community*, *The Bait* and 'Sweetest love'. If Donne did write all these poems to pre-existing airs, it is only *The Bait* for which such an air may be extant. This is a simple, not very striking tune, that may have been used for Marlowe's poem, for its successors in *England's Helicon* (1600) (Raleigh's and the anonymous poem which follows it) and also for Donne's poem; but we cannot be confident about any of these cases. The air was eventually printed in the purely instrumental part of William Corkine's *Second Book of Ayres* in

---

[1] See J. P. Cutts, 'A Bodleian Song-Book; Don. C57', *Music and Letters*, July 1953, pp. 193–211; 'Seventeenth Century Lyrics in Oxford Bodleian MS b.1', *Musica Disciplina*, 1956, pp. 142–209; and *A Selection of hitherto unknown Seventeenth Century Lyrics from a music MS*, Reading University School of Art Printing Press, 1956; 'Early Seventeenth Century Lyrics at St Michael's College', *Music and Letters*, July 1956, pp. 221–33.

[2] See *Bericht über den siebenten Internationalen Musikwissenschaftlichen Kongress Köln*, Kassel, 1959, pp. 91–3.

[3] In *Poèmes de Donne, Herbert et Crashaw mis en musique par leurs contemporains. Transcription et réalisation par André Souris d'après des recherches effectuées sur les sources par John Cutts. Introduction par Jean Jacquot*, 2 vols, Paris, 1961.

[4] Edinburgh University Library, Music MS Dc. 1. 69, pp. 13–14.

1612, as a piece for lyra viol, with the incipit 'Come live with me, and be my love'.[1]

A setting for *The Message* – with some variations of text – by Giovanni Coperario (John Cooper), *c.* 1575–*c.* 1626, exists in Tenbury Wells MS 1019, f 1ᵛ. Cooper went to Italy early in the seventeenth century, and Italianized his name there. In Italy Coperario learned to adopt a declamatory style with irregular rhythms. As two distinguished musicologists[2] have written, Coperario's songs 'foreshadow "recitative music"'. I cannot say that I am really happy about his setting of *The Message*. Donne's poem is, after all, not prose or free verse, but metrically pretty strict, despite the wonderful spontaneity of the rhythmical play over the metrical structure. Coperario went too far towards irregularity, and created something which, though clever, is, I feel too complex and heavy-handed, and too dictatorial to the poem.[3]

There is an anonymous setting for 'Go and catch' in British Library Egerton MS 2013, f 58ᵛ which is scored for song and lute. There are occasional textual variations, e.g. 'tymes' for 'yeares' (l. 3). I should be sorry to think that Donne had been inspired to write his poem by this mediocre air; and, indeed, I find it incredible.[4]

For *Confined Love* and *Community* no contemporary setting has yet appeared. On the other hand, for 'Sweetest love' a setting exists in two versions: (1) a plain setting for voice and bass in Tenbury Wells MS 1018, f 44ᵛ, and (2) a setting with an ornamented voice part in British Library, Add. MS 10337, f 55ᵛ. In both cases M. Jacquot prints a lute part supplied by M. André Souris. The poem starts in both MSS 'Dearest love', and the text is pretty corrupt, partly because the composer has changed words to fit his tune. Musically, the setting is a cut above that for 'Go and catch', and has its moments; but it is metrically impossible that Donne wrote his poem to this tune, and I personally do not find the tune of much interest.[5]

M. Jacquot prints settings of two of Donne's love-lyrics not among the six described in *DC* as written 'to certaine Aires which were made before', *The Expiration* and *Break of Day*.

There are two extant settings of *The Expiration*, one by Alfonso Ferrabosco,

---

[1] A transcription of the tune by Dr F. W. Sternfeld, who also fitted Donne's words to the tune, is printed by Professor Gardner (*ESS*, p. 239).

[2] *The English Lute-Songs*, ser. I, vol. 17 (Coperario), transcribed and edited by Gerald Hendrie and Thurston Dart, 1959, p. ii.

[3] Besides the printing in Jacquot, op. cit., pp. 6–7, and in *The English Lute-Songs*, the setting of the first stanza is printed by Professor Gardner (*ESS*, p. 241). For further details about the setting, and a more favourable assessment, see the interesting chapter '"Not, Siren-like, to tempt": Donne and the composers', by Professor Brian Morris, in A. J. Smith (ed.), *John Donne: Essays in Celebration*, London, 1972, pp. 219–51.

[4] For the setting see Jacquot, op. cit., pp. 4–5; Gardner, *ESS*, pp. 240–1; and for a detailed analysis, Morris, art. cit., p. 225.

[5] For the setting see Jacquot, op. cit., pp. 1–3; Gardner, *ESS*, pp. 239–40; and for a critique, Morris, art. cit., pp. 226–7.

printed in his *Ayres* (1609), and the other anonymous, to be found in Bodleian Library MS Mus. Sch. F. 575, f 8ᵛ.[1] The appearance of the poem in Ferrabosco's *Ayres* was the first appearance of a poem by Donne in print. The text has some variants from that in early editions of Donne. The variants come from certain manuscripts. Ferrabosco's setting is fairly expressive of a possible, though highly disputable, interpretation of the poem, in terms of what Professor Brian Morris has convincingly called 'a light-hearted witty velleity, masking the pain of verbalising it, and offering appropriately dignified stances for the lovers'. Like him I believe the poem deserves to be taken more seriously, and with a discriminating response to the thoughts and feelings. On the other hand I am not so enthusiastic as Professor Morris about the anonymous setting, which, though admittedly superior in some respects to Ferrabosco's, especially in following the turns of thought and feelings more closely, is, in my opinion, not highly charged enough if we take the poem as a fiercely passionate one, which appears to me to be the right view of it.

It remains to speak of *Break of Day*. This was printed in William Corkine's *Second Book of Ayres* (1612),[2] set for voice and bass viol. (A lute part has been written by A. S. Daws in his edition of the *Second Book of Ayres* in vol. 13, 2nd ser., of *The English School of Lutenist Song Writers*, ed. E. H. Fellowes, who himself proposes a performance with lute.) The text of the poem varies considerably from *1633*. The setting is pleasant in a quite straightforward way. It is possibly questionable whether the major key altogether suits the sentiments of the song. It would, on the other hand, be rather too demanding to require that a setting should suit all the shifts of feeling in all the stanzas of a formally stanzaic song. Admittedly, this setting does not do so; but I do not find that a very serious defect.

As a matter of musicology it is important that scholars have brought to light these settings of these few love-lyrics by Donne; but their quality makes them, I feel, of historical, rather than intrinsic, interest. None of the settings comes anywhere near the high standard of the two settings of Donne's *Hymn to God the Father*, by John Hilton (d. 1657), extant in British Library Egerton MS 2013, and by Pelham Humfrey in *Harmonia Sacra*, 1688.[3]

---

[1] For the settings see Jacquot, op. cit., pp. 8–11, and Gardner, *ESS*, pp. 241–3; and for a detailed critique, Morris, art. cit., pp. 232–6. Ferrabosco's setting also appears in E. H. Fellowes (ed.), *The English School of Lutenist Song Writers*, 2nd ser., vol. 16, London, 1927.

[2] For the setting see Jacquot, op. cit., pp. 15–17, and, for the first stanza, Gardner, *ESS*, p. 243, as well as the edition by A. S. Daws cited in this paragraph. For some detailed comment see Morris, art. cit., pp. 230–1.

[3] Pelham Humfrey, *Complete Solo Devotional Songs*, ed. P. Dennison, London, 1974, no. 4.

APPENDIX XIII

Not only in those poems which are concerned to persuade, but also in those which simply express feelings, thoughts and attitudes, Donne shows himself an accomplished rhetorician. He had, of course, received a training in formal rhetoric, not only at University, but also at the Inns of Court. Indeed, rhetoric had recently been moved from the more advanced part of the arts courses at Oxford and Cambridge to the course for the BA Degree.[1] There is considerable use of rhetorical figures in the *Songs and Sonets*, and it is more than possible that the vigour, ingenuity, wit, and clarity of line that so many of us admire in Donne's love poems owe a substantial debt to the rhetorical training he had undergone. The fact that training in formal rhetoric is no longer part of the normal training for students has had the result of covering Donne's devices up to some extent. It has made them less obvious, save to deliberate inspection. I believe, however, that it is well worth looking closely at Donne's use of rhetorical devices in the love-lyrics. To do so can well add appreciably to one's awareness of Donne's art as a love poet. In this belief, and at the risk of appearing pedantic, I propose to set out in this Appendix a list of some (by no means all) of the rhetorical figures to be found in these poems, with at least one quotation for each, together with some further references. Among these figures there will be found some to which I have already drawn attention in non-technical terms in pp. 29–47 of the Introduction. In some cases I shall add one or two brief observations, but these are to be taken only as desultory points and not as any attempt at a full discussion of Donne's use of the figures in these poems. A whole book could be written on the similes and metaphors alone. Indeed such books have already been written.[2]

Before starting on the list it is probably advisable to say something general about figures and their classification. Theorists of rhetoric have classified figures in various ways, some of which are inconsistent with others. For my present purpose I am adopting, first of all, Cicero's distinction (*De Oratore*

[1] See M. H. Curtis, *Oxford and Cambridge in Transition, 1588–1642*, Oxford, 1959, p. 94.
[2] e.g. M. A. Rugoff, *Donne's Imagery*, New York, 1939; M. Hasan, *Donne's Imagery*, Aligarh, India, 1958.

III. 201) between *figures of thought* (*figurae sententiarum*) and *figures of speech* (*figurae verborum*). Figures of thought, such as *prosopopoeia* (the introduction of an imaginary or absent speaker), still hold even if the words used are changed; whereas figures of speech vanish if one changes the words. Then I am accepting a fourfold classification of figures of speech into (1) *figures of diction*, consisting of changes of letters or syllables within words (e.g. *syncope*, as in *virûm* for *virorum*); (2) *figures of construction*, in which normal grammar is departed from (e.g. *grammatical syllepsis*, as in 'Each drop fell in the silence, and I heard *them* distinctly'); (3) other figures, such as repetition in various forms, where the words keep their ordinary senses; (4) *tropes*, where words take on meanings different from their ordinary senses. I shall deal almost entirely with figures of speech, and only slightly with figures of thought, some of which I have, however, already discussed, though not in a technical way. Among figures of speech, (3) and (4) are the most interesting for my purpose, and I shall concentrate on them. The classification I have adopted is open to some philosophical objections, but it is serviceable enough for present requirements.

Similes One initial difficulty must be mentioned. Into which class do *similes* fall? Aristotle called a simile 'a kind of metaphor' (*Rhet.* III. 4). Yet the words in a simile may well all be used in their ordinary senses; and a simile cannot therefore be classified as a trope. I am going to regard similes as falling either into the class of figures of thought or into class (3) of figures of speech. I am not greatly exercised by the problem, since what I really want to do is simply to say a few things about Donne's similes in these poems. As indicated earlier, there are more metaphors than similes in the *Songs and Sonets* (on a rough count about double the number). On the other hand, the similes occupy more lines – over 250 of the 1600 lines of the corpus, against slightly over 200 lines for the metaphors (not counting dead or moribund metaphors or the personifications (e.g. of Love) which, if we accepted *OED*, would count as metaphors). The statistical position need not surprise us, since similes are most often longer than metaphors. The similes are almost always particularly uncommon and striking, both in their references and in the words used to express them. They are often far-fetched, but well worth the fetching, e.g. in *Love's Exchange* (ll. 24–8) the military simile:

> Small towns, which stand stiff, till great shot
> Enforce them, by war's law condition not.
> Such in love's warfare is my case;
> I may not article for grace,
> Having put Love at last to show this face.

Where the comparison made is more readily accessible the diction most often takes on a certain added (compensatory?) sophistication, as in *Love's Growth*, ll. 1–4:

> I scarce believe my love to be so pure
> As I had thought it was,
> Because it doth endure
> Vicissitude, and season, as the grass;

The following fairly full list of the similes in the *Songs and Sonets* may prove handy:

Woman's Constancy, l. 8; *The Undertaking*, ll. 1–2, 5–12; *The Triple Fool*, ll. 6–9; *Air and Angels*, ll. 1–4, 23–5, 26–8; *Break of Day*, ll. 17–18; *The Anniversary*, ll. 13–15; *A Valediction: of my name, in the window*, ll. 4, 5–6, 13–16, 19–22, 33–42, 65–6; *Twickenham Garden*, ll. 24–5; *A Valediction: of the book*, ll. 5–9, 19–21, 37–40, 53–4, 55–6, 57–63; *Community*, ll. 15, 19; *Love's Growth*, ll. 1–4, 13–14, 15–18, 19–20, 21–4 (two similes), 25–8; *Love's Exchange*, ll. 15–16, 24–8; *Confined Love*, ll. 8–14 (three similes), 15–18; *The Dream*, ll. 13–20 (two similes), 27–9; *A Valediction: of weeping*, ll. 10–18; *Love's Alchemy*, ll. 7–12, 18–22; *The Flea*, ll. 26–7; *A Nocturnal*, ll. 7, 35–6; *The Broken Heart*, ll. 5–8 (implicit), 15, 24, 29–32; *A Valediction: forbidding mourning*, ll. 1–8, 9–12, 21–4, 25–36; *The Ecstasy*, ll. 1, 13–16, 18, 33–6, 37–44, 57–60, 61–8; *The Will*, ll. 48–51; *The Funeral, ll. 14–16; The Primrose*, ll. 5–7; *The Damp*, ll. 13–15; *The Dissolution*, ll. 16–21; *A Jet Ring Sent*, ll. 1, 2; *The Paradox*, ll. 13–14, 15–16; *Farewell to Love*, ll. 4–6, 11–15, 21–3, 36–8; *A Lecture upon the Shadow*, ll. 3–11; [*Picture and Dream*] ll. 4–5.

I now want to mention just a few *figures of thought* used in these poems:

Antithesis (words in contiguous clauses or sentences expressing an opposition or contrast of ideas):

> How great love is, presence best trial makes,
> But absence tries how long this love will be;
> (*A Valediction: of the book*, ll. 57–8)

I believe that this figure is best classified as a figure of thought. Donne uses it a great deal in these poems. He is as alive to clear contrasts as he is to unusual resemblances. The following are only a few of the many cases of use:

The Apparition, ll. 16–17; *The Curse*, ll. 8, 9–13; *A Valediction: forbidding mourning*, ll. 9–12, 13–20; *The Broken Heart*, ll. 3–4, 19–20, 29–32; *Love's Diet*, l. 18; 'Sweetest love', stanzas 3 and 5; *The Legacy*, stanza 2; *A Fever*, stanza 2; *The Anniversary*, stanza 2, ll. 21–2; *A Valediction: of the book*, ll. 59–63; *Community*, stanza 1; *The Dream*, stanza 2; *The Primrose*, ll. 13–17.

Epiphonema (a general reflection summing up or arising out of a passage which has gone before):

> That love hath not attain'd the high'st degree,
> Which is still diligent lest others see.
> (*A Lecture upon the Shadow*, ll. 12–13)

This is also much used in the *Songs and Sonets*. It forms part of their intellectual grasp. Other cases:

A Lecture upon the Shadow, ll. 25–6; *The Relic*, ll. 31–3; *The Good-morrow*, ll. 19–21; *The Sun Rising*, ll. 29–30; 'Sweetest love', ll. 29–30; *Air and Angels*, ll. 26–8; *Break of Day*, ll. 17–18; *A Valediction: of my name*, stanza XI; *Twickenham Garden*, ll. 26–7; *Community*, ll. 22–4; *The Flea*, ll. 26–7; *Love's Deity*, ll. 27–8.

Epiphrasis (a moral comment crowning a sentence which one could well have considered to have already finished). A solitary, but very effective instance: *The Curse*, ll. 30–1.

I vividly remember Grierson as an old man laughing with wonderment at this preposterous turn of Donne's.

Paradox (statement or command which in terms appears self-contradictory, but *may*, however, covertly be sound):

> If thou love me, take heed of loving me.
>
> (*The Prohibition*, l. 8)

> If thou hate me, take heed of hating me.
>
> (ibid., l. 16)

This figure was evidently dear to Donne, who delighted in paradoxes, both in prose and verse. They obviously appealed to his intellectual agility and ingenuity. Other examples from these poems are:

'Go and catch', l. 11; *Woman's Constancy*, ll. 12–13; *The Paradox*, ll. 19–20; *The Canonization*, ll. 23–4; *Lovers' Infiniteness*, ll. 28–9; *The Computation*, ll. 9–10; *A Valediction: of my name*, l. 12; *The Legacy*, l. 10.

Rhetorical Questions must also be reckoned among figures of thought. There are many instances in the poems, e.g.

> Are sun, moon, or stars by law forbidden
> To smile where they list, or lend away their light?
> Are birds divorc'd, or are they chidden
> If they leave their mate, or lie abroad a-night?
>
> (*Confined Love*, ll. 8–11)

also e.g. ibid., ll. 15–18; *The Good-morrow*, ll. 1–4, 17–18; *Woman's Constancy*, ll. 1–13; *The Sun Rising*, ll. 1–4, 11–12; *The Indifferent*, ll. 10–13; *The Canonization*, ll. 10–15; *Break of Day*, ll. 1–4, 13; *The Anniversary*, ll. 25–6; *A Valediction: of the book*, ll. 59–63; *Community*, ll. 23–4; *Love's Alchemy*, ll. 13–17; *The Flea*, ll. 19–22; *The Broken Heart*, ll. 5–8, 17–18; *The Ecstasy*, ll. 49–50; *Love's Deity*, ll. 22–3; *The Blossom*, ll. 21–4; *The Relic*, ll. 7–11;

A Jet Ring Sent, ll. 3–4, 6–7; *The Computation,* l. 10; *The Paradox,* ll. 5–6; *Farewell to Love,* ll. 21–3, leaving virtually no questions in the poems which are not rhetorical questions.

Let us now consider a few of the tropes used in these poems.

Metaphor, in contrast with simile, is a *trope.* In general, as is perhaps natural, the metaphors in the *Songs and Sonets* are often not so far-fetched as the similes, though there are a number that are as far-fetched as one could wish, e.g. the alchemical 'concoction' in *The Ecstasy,* l. 27, and the theologico-astronomical 'intelligences' and 'sphere' in l. 52 of the same poem. Sometimes the surprise and force of a metaphor lie rather in the use of a familiar image in an unusual context, e.g. 'epitaph' in l. 9 of *A Nocturnal* or 'rags' for the pieces of the shattered heart in *The Broken Heart,* l. 31, or for 'hours, days, months' in *The Sun Rising,* l. 10. Donne's alert ingenuity comes out particularly sharply when, in the *élan* of uttering a *hyperbole,* he creates a metaphor within a metaphor, as in the 'vain bubble's shadow' of *Love's Alchemy,* l. 14, or 'the Elixir' of 'the first nothing' in *A Nocturnal,* l. 29. In these two cases, incidentally, we have equally successful examples of familiar and far-fetched images. Similar energy and adroitness are shown in pushing further the comparatively ordinary metaphor of 'treason' in love, by adding the legal refinement of 'overt act', in *A Valediction: of my name, in the window,* ll. 55–6. Again it may be found useful to have a list of at least a fair number of the lines in which metaphors occur:

The Good-morrow, ll. 11, 16, 17; 'Go and catch', ll. 6, 13, 20; *The Undertaking,* ll. 15, 18; *The Sun Rising,* ll. 5, 8, 10, 13, 15, 20, 21, 24; *Air and Angels,* ll. 13, 14, 15, 17, 18; *Break of Day,* l. 7; *The Anniversary,* ll. 9, 10, 13–14, 18, 23–4, 26; *A Valediction: of my name,* ll. 23–4, 28–30, 31–2, 46, 55–6; *Twickenham Garden,* ll. 6, 9, 12, 20; *A Valediction: of the book,* ll. 13, 42; *Community,* ll. 22, 24; *Love's Growth,* l. 7; *Love's Exchange,* ll. 8, 10–11, 12, 38–42; *A Valediction: of weeping,* ll. 3–4; *Love's Alchemy,* ll. 1–2, 14, 24; *A Valediction: forbidding mourning,* l. 6; *The Ecstasy,* ll. 5, 7–8, 9, 11–12, 17, 27, 52, 56, 63, 64, 68, 72; *Love's Deity,* ll. 10, 16, 18; *Love's Diet,* ll. 1–2, 5, 11, 13, 14, 15, 19, 22–4, 25–30.

Hyperbole (words which exaggerate by making something seem either excessively large or great or excessively small or mean) is a figure which, at least since Aristotle, has been recognized as dynamic, and characteristic of young men. Aristotle even goes so far as to say that it is unbecoming for older people to use hyperboles. The eighteenth-century rhetorical theorist Du Marsais (*Des Tropes,* Paris, 1730) is less interferingly restrictive, simply stating that young people use hyperbole more than people advanced in age. The Donne of the *Songs and Sonets* makes considerable use of both magnifying and diminishing hyperbole, especially the former. Good instances occur in *The Dream:*

> Thou art so true [or 'truth'], that thoughts of thee suffice
> To make dreams truths, and fables histories;
>
> (ll. 7–8)

On either of the two possible readings in l. 7 this is, indeed, hyperbolical praise of the beloved; and the hyperbole is carried still further in the following stanza. A striking instance of diminishing hyperbole is the final couplet of *A Lecture upon the Shadow*:

> Love is a growing, or full constant light;
> And his first minute, after noon, is night.

while *A Nocturnal* is crammed with diminishing hyperboles, which find their climax in its fourth stanza, taken with the first line of the fifth and final stanza:

> But I am by her death (which word wrongs her),
> Of the first nothing the Elixir grown;
>> Were I a man, that I were one
>> I needs must know; I should prefer,
>>> If I were any beast,
> Some ends, some means; yea plants, yea stones, detest,
> And love; all, all, some properties invest;
> If I an ordinary nothing were,
> As shadow, a light and body must be here.

> But I am none; nor will my sun renew.

Other instances of hyperbole:

Twickenham Garden, ll. 1, 4, 6, 19–22; *A Valediction: of the book*, ll. 5–9, 24–7; *A Valediction: of my name*, ll. 1–4, 5–6; *Love's Exchange*, ll. 29–35; *A Nocturnal, passim; The Bait*, ll. 13–16; *A Fever*, ll. 5–16, 27–8; *The Goodmorrow*, ll. 5–7, 10–11, 14; *The Anniversary*, ll. 6–10, 23–6; *A Valediction: of weeping*, ll. 10–18, 19–22; *The Sun Rising*, ll. 15–16, 17–20, 21–2, 27–30; *The Canonization*, ll. 37–45; *Confined Love*, ll. 19–21; *Love's Alchemy*, ll. 23–4; *The Curse*, ll. 31–2; *The Broken Heart*, ll. 29–32; *The Will*, ll. 46–54; *The Computation*, whole poem; *The Paradox*, ll. 17–20.[1]

Irony commonly appears in the lists of tropes. It is, however, sometimes defined so narrowly that many of the instances of what would normally be considered *irony* would be excluded. For example, according to such a narrow definition as 'Irony is the figure by which one wishes to make people understand the contrary of what one says' we should have to exclude such lines as those in which Donne tauntingly asks the young women in *The Indifferent* (ll. 10–13):

> Will no other choice content you [than being true]?
> Will it not serve your turn to do as did your mothers?

---

[1] A number of these instances are noted, and discussed, by Professor B. W. Vickers in his article 'The "Songs and Sonets" and the Rhetoric of Hyperbole' in A. J. Smith (ed.), *John Donne: Essays in Celebration*, London, 1972, pp. 132–74.

> Have you old vices spent, and now would find out others?
> Or doth a fear, that men are true, torment you?

Yet Donne is surely being ironical in posing these questions? It is better, I believe, to think of rhetorical irony more broadly, as what Puttenham[1] in one place called 'a merry scoff', and in another 'the dry mock'. The attitude behind irony is one of superiority, either superiority over someone else, or a critical superiority over oneself. The ironical words may or may not actually be intended to make people understand the contrary of what is said. The 'irony' of the narrow definition is only one form of irony. More broadly, irony can be considered as raillery from a position of assumed superiority. There is a fair deal of irony, taken in this broad sense, in the *Songs and Sonets*. So construed, the questions in *Woman's Constancy*, ll. 1–13, would be instances of irony, and other instances would be:

The Sun Rising, stanza 2; *Love's Usury*, ll. 23–4; *The Canonization*, stanzas 1 and 2; *The Triple Fool*, ll. 17–22; *A Fever*, ll. 13–16; *Break of Day*, last stanza; *Community*, ll. 19–24; *Love's Exchange*, ll. 8–14; *Confined Love*, ll. 15–21; *Love's Alchemy*, ll. 13–22; *The Will*, *passim*; *The Relic*, ll. 1–2.

Irony is, however, too complex a topic to discuss satisfactorily in a short space.

Personification (the representation of a thing or abstraction as a person). There is fair use of personification in the *Songs and Sonets*, most particularly of the personification 'Love'. *OED* describes personification as a species of metaphor. Yet a case could be made for regarding it rather as a form of *metonymy*, for it is not, for instance, in virtue of a comparison between the god of love and love that the personification is used, but rather because the god of love *causes* (or is thought of as causing) love. Now, one form of metonymy is that of naming the cause for the effect. Personifications of love occur in:

Love's Usury, whole poem; *Twickenham Garden*, l. 15; *A Valediction: of the book*, ll. 17–18, 28, 40; *Love's Exchange*, whole poem; *A Nocturnal*, stanzas 2 and 3; *The Broken Heart*, stanza 2; *Love's Deity*, whole poem; *The Will*, *passim*; *The Paradox*, ll. 7–8. There are also other personifications, e.g. of Nature in *Community*, l. 7, and *Farewell to Love*, ll. 24–30; and of the quaint 'giants' *Disdain* and *Constancy*, and the 'enchantress' *Honour* and 'witch' *Secretness* in *The Damp*.

Metonymy As for this figure, it has been variously defined. In the widest sense it includes all changes of name, and therefore all the tropes, but in its more restricted senses it does not include metaphor, which requires a real or supposed similarity as its basis. Many kinds of restriction have been suggested. One reasonable suggestion is that it covers only cases where a word designating a reality A is substituted for a word designating a reality B, *and* the relation, either actual or imagined, between A and B, is of one of the following kinds:

---

[1] In *The Arte of English Poesie*, 1589.

(1) A is the cause or effect of B; (2) A contains B; (3) A is the place where B is or was made; (4) A is the sign of B; (5) A is an abstract 'reality' and B the corresponding concrete reality; (6) A is a part of the body regarded as the seat of a certain emotion or emotions B; (7) A is the master of a house and B is the house. An enormous amount of work has been done on metonymy, and the situation must now be regarded as pretty fluid.[1]

In these poems of Donne the only kinds of metonymy that have struck me (and they have not struck me very forcibly) are (1), (5) and (6); though 'paper' in *The Relic*, l. 21, could be a good example of (2). The personifications of Love may suffice as examples of (1). The following are perhaps examples of (5):

'beauty' (*The Good-morrow*, l. 6); 'loveliness' (*The Undertaking*, l. 13); 'abundance' (*The Indifferent*, l. 2); 'loneness' (ibid., l. 3), 'variety' (ibid., l. 20); 'vexations' (*The Triple Fool*, l. 9); 'weariness' ('Sweetest love', l. 2); 'corruption' (*A Fever*, l. 19); 'admiration' (*Air and Angels*, l. 17); 'nothingness' (*A Nocturnal*, l. 15); 'privations' (ibid., l. 16), 'emptiness' (ibid., l. 16); 'good' and 'ill' (*Community, passim*); 'fashion' (*A Jet Ring Sent*, l. 8); 'mis-devotion' (*The Relic*, l. 13); 'minstrelsy' (*Love's Alchemy*, l. 22); 'idolatry' (*Love's Exchange*, l. 30); 'truth' (*Twickenham Garden*, l. 27).

Of (6) many of the mentions of 'heart' are probably examples, e.g. *The Message*, ll. 9, 17; *Lovers' Infiniteness*, ll. 14, 21, 27, 29, 32.

Donne was, indeed, pretty certainly well aware of the figure of metonymy, and of the closely allied *synecdoche*, which gives a particular sense to a word properly used more generally or vice versa, or which uses plural for singular or vice versa, or species for genus or vice versa, or a determinate number for an indeterminate one. Yet Donne's use of metonymy and of synecdoche, at least in these poems, does not seem particularly noteworthy, in contrast, for instance, with his use of simile, metaphor and hyperbole, and also, as I hope will be clear from what will be said later in this Appendix, with his use of non-tropical figures of speech. The reason why can probably only be a matter of speculation; but I wonder whether it was perhaps because the limits of metonymy and synecdoche were fairly strictly circumscribed by Classical precedent,[2] whereas there was an open field for imagination in the realms of simile, metaphor and hyperbole. As for non-tropical figures, what is interesting is the use Donne

[1] Readers wishing to follow up this point may find the following useful: H. Lausberg, *Handbuch der literarischen Rhetorik*, 2 vols, Munich, 1960; A. Preminger, F. V. Warnke and O. B. Hardison (eds), *An Encyclopaedia of Poetry and Poetics*, Princeton, 1965; G. Genette, *Figures*, Paris, 1966; A. Henry, *Métonymie et Métaphore*, Paris, 1971; M. Le Guern, *Sémantique de la Métaphore et de la Métonymie*, Paris, 1973; H. Morier, *Dictionnaire de Poétique et de Rhétorique*, Paris, 1965 (2nd edn 1975).

[2] We find Du Marsais writing, in 1730, that one would make a fool of oneself by speaking of a fleet 'of a hundred masts', instead of using the sanctioned phrase 'of a hundred sail' (op. cit., pp. 96–7).

makes of the considerable number of figures which had been developed in the course of rhetorical practice; in particular, which ones he was especially prone to use, and which he used less frequently.

Synecdoche is, in fact, rare in the *Songs and Sonets*. 'Bread' for 'the means of subsistence' (*The Curse*, l. 24) may be an instance of what is now considered an 'expansive synecdoche', here a subclass for a whole class, as in the lines of Voltaire on Louis XIV's refusals of help to certain literary men:

> Je l'ai vu refuser, poliment inhumain,
> Une place à Racine, à Crébillon *du pain*.[1]

'Sense' (in general) for 'sense of sight' (*The Paradox*, l. 12) may be an instance of the 'restrictive synecdoche'. Yet the only instances of synecdoche that seem substantially present in these poems are the uses of determinate for indeterminate numbers, e.g. 'twenty' in *The Indifferent*, l. 15 (but probably not 'twenty' in *Love's Usury*, l. 3); 'ten thousand' in 'Go and catch', l. 12; 'hundred' in *The Broken Heart*, l. 30; 'thousand' in *Confined Love*, l. 20. I do not believe that 'the whole world, us two' in:

> . . . Oft a flood
> Have we two wept, and so
> Drown'd the whole world, us two . . .
>
> > (*A Nocturnal*, ll. 22–4)

should be considered a synecdoche. There the two lovers are identified with the whole world by a metaphor, whose whole point is that they are *not* part of the world. The same is true of ll. 14–16 of *A Valediction: of weeping*. With regard to ll. 10–11 of *The Good-morrow*:

> For love, all love of other sights controls,
> And makes one little room, an everywhere.

my view is that the 'little room', by the end of the lines, has, indeed, *become* an 'everywhere', so that the word 'everywhere' is not standing to the room as a whole to a part, and therefore there is no synecdoche, but, once again, a hyperbolical metaphor.

It is about time I passed to non-tropical figures of speech; but before doing so I should perhaps mention that there is one miniature case of *allegory* in stanza 1 of *The Blossom*, and that there are several instances of *euphemism*, sometimes tinged with irony, as in *The Relic*, ll. 1–2:

> When my grave is broke up again
> Some second guest to entertain. . . .

[1] Quoted by Pierre Fontanier, *Les Figures du Discours*, Paris, 1968, p. 93.

sometimes not, as in 'seals' in l. 29 of the same poem. Other instances of euphemism are:

'thing' (*Farewell to Love*, l. 14); 'friend' (*The Blossom*, l. 39); 'some other part' (ibid., l. 31); 'more' (*The Apparition*, l. 9); 'do' (*The Dream*, l. 10); (*Love's Growth*, l. 14).

That Donne was steeped in rhetoric is perhaps even clearer from his use of non-tropical figures of speech and other rhetorical devices. The following are among such figures and devices used in the *Songs and Sonets*. I shall give one or two quotations illustrating each, and some further references:

Alliteration (in the sense of repetition of consonants, particularly at the start of words or when the accent falls on the syllable beginning with the consonant concerned):

> A bracelet of bright hair about the bone . . .
> *(The Relic*, l. 6)

> Being double dead, going, and bidding go,
> *(The Expiration*, l. 12)

also e.g. *The Good-morrow*, ll. 1–4, 12–14; *The Undertaking*, ll. 6, 13–16; *The Sun Rising*, ll. 7–8; *Love's Usury*, ll. 14–16; 'Sweetest love', ll. 33–6; *The Legacy*, ll. 15–16, 18; *A Fever*, ll. 21–4; *The Paradox*, ll. 13–14; *The Relic*, ll. 11, 20, 24.

Anadiplosis (repetition, at the start of a clause or sentence or verse, of the last word of the preceding verse, clause, or sentence):

> I may not article for grace,
> Having put Love at last to show this face:
>
> This face, by which he could command
> And change the idolatry of any land . . .
> *(Love's Exchange*, ll. 27–30)

also e.g. *Lovers' Infiniteness*, ll. 12–13; *A Valediction: of my name, in the window*, l. 42; *Witchcraft by a Picture*, l. 10; *The Ecstasy*, l. 51; *The Expiration*, ll. 6–7.

Anaphora (repeating a word or words at the start of two or more verses, phrases, clauses, or sentences). Donne uses the figure a great deal. It helps to give the verse drive, and also shape:

> Let sea-discoverers to new worlds have gone,
> Let maps to others, worlds on worlds have shown,
> Let us possess our world; each hath one, and is one.
> *(The Good-morrow*, ll. 12–14)

also e.g. *The Canonization*, ll. 13, 14, 19, 20, 37–9; *The Message*, ll. 1, 9; *The Bait*, stanzas 1 and 2; *The Indifferent*, ll. 1–9, 10–13; *A Valediction: of the book*, ll. 3–5, 7–9, 28, 37, 46; *Community*, ll. 7, 13, 16, 20–1; 'Sweetest love', ll. 25–7; *The Legacy*, ll. 19–20; *The Anniversary*, ll. 1–2; *A Valediction: of my name*, ll. 7–9; *Love's Exchange*, ll. 29, 31; *Love's Diet*, ll. 13–16; *Confined Love*, ll. 8, 10; *The Dream*, ll. 15, 17; *The Sun Rising*, l. 24.

Antanaclasis (repeating a word changing its sense): Donne makes little use of this figure in these poems:

> My rags of heart can like, wish, and adore,
> But after one such love, can love no more.
>> (*The Broken Heart*, ll. 31–2)

also e.g. *The Curse*, l. 3; probably *The Good-morrow*, ll. 13–14; *Community*, ll. 13–14; *A Nocturnal*, l. 19; possibly *The Broken Heart*, l. 32.

Antimetabole (repeating two or more words in inverse order – rather stricter than *chiasmus*):

> Such life is like the light which bideth yet
> When the light's life is set,
>> (*The Paradox*, ll. 13–14)

also possibly *The Ecstasy*, ll. 51–2. Donne uses chiasmus somewhat more.

Aposiopesis (a sudden interruption in the course of speaking). Donne scarcely ever uses the device; though he does use the different devices of apostrophe, parenthesis and exclamation. The following is, however, a case of aposiopesis:

> This – which I am amaz'd that I can speak –
> This death, hath with my store
> My use increas'd.
>> (*The Dissolution*, ll. 19–21)

Apostrophe (the speaker turns, in the course of speaking, to address a person or thing):

> Study me then, you who shall lovers be
> At the next world, that is, at the next Spring:
>> (*A Nocturnal*, ll. 10–11)

also e.g. *A Nocturnal*, ll. 38–41; *The Broken Heart*, stanza 3; *The Primrose*, ll. 21, 23; *The Will*, ll. 7, 16, 25, 34, 43, 52; *The Funeral*, l. 24; *Twickenham Garden*, ll. 19–22.

Asyndeton (heaping of words, phrases, or clauses on one another without conjunctions); Donne uses this figure very frequently. It is rightly recognized by a number of theorists of rhetoric as forceful and energetic:

> The venom of all stepdames, gamesters' gall,
> What tyrants, and their subjects, interwish,
> What plants, mines, beasts, fowl, fish
> Can contribute; all ill which all
> Prophets, or poets, spake . . .
>
> (*The Curse*, ll. 25–9)

also e.g. *Love's Deity*, l. 17; *Love's Usury*, ll. 5–8; *A Nocturnal*, ll. 18, 20; *The Sun Rising*, ll. 5–8; *The Canonization*, ll. 4–6; *Break of Day*, l. 15; *A Jet Ring Sent*, l. 2; *The Dream*, l. 26; *Love's Alchemy*, l. 4; *Love's Diet*, l. 29.

Auxesis (a sequence of words, phrases, or clauses, in order of increasing importance). Donne does not use the figure very frequently in these poems:

> Our ease, our thrift, our honour, and our day [life],
> Shall we for this vain bubble's shadow pay?
>
> (*Love's Alchemy*, ll. 13–14)

also e.g. *A Valediction: of the book*, ll. 15–18; possibly *The Flea*, ll. 16–18; and *A Nocturnal*, ll. 30–7 (though this case could simply or also be regarded as one of *tapinosis*).

Chiasmus (order of words in the first of two parallel clauses inverted in the second):

> The fairest woman, but thy ghost,
> But corrupt worms, the worthiest men.
>
> (*A Fever*, ll. 11–12)

also e.g. *The Prohibition*, l. 5; *The Good-morrow*, l. 15; *Twickenham Garden*, ll. 26–7; *The Will*, ll. 12–13; *A Jet Ring Sent*, ll. 1–2; *Love's Diet*, l. 17; *The Indifferent*, l. 14; *The Sun Rising*, l. 21.

Epanalepsis (repeating at the end of a line, phrase, clause or sentence, the word which started it). Donne is clearly aware of the figure, and uses it a few times:

> He thinks that else none can, nor will agree
> That any loves but he:
>
> (*The Paradox*, ll. 3–4)

also e.g. *The Dream*, ll. 17, 23; *The Primrose*, l. 25; *The Ecstasy*, ll. 19–20; *The Legacy*, l. 5; *The Indifferent*, l. 27; *A Jet Ring Sent*, ll. 1–2.

Epanorthosis (correcting a word or phrase by a more accurate or stronger one):

> Oh stay, three lives in one flea spare,
> Where we almost, nay more than married are . . .
>
> *(The Flea*, ll. 10–11)

This figure occurs, though infrequently, in the *Songs and Sonets*: e.g. *A Valediction: of weeping*, l. 16; possibly *The Expiration*, l. 11.

Epistrophe (repeating, at the end of a subsequent line, clause, or sentence, a word ending a previous line, clause or sentence). This is quite frequently used in these poems. It gives, naturally enough, an effect of deliberate insistence:

> Let us possess our world; each hath one, and is one.
>
> *(The Good-morrow*, l. 14)

also e.g. *The Sun Rising*, ll. 28–9; *The Indifferent*, l. 8; *Love's Usury*, ll. 21, 23; *The Canonization*, ll. 9–10, 18–19, 27–8, 36–7 (note also the endings of 1 and 45, whether an example or not); *Lovers' Infiniteness*, ll. 11–12; *The Anniversary*, ll. 22–3; *A Valediction: of my name*, ll. 23–5; *Community*, ll. 1–2; *The Ecstasy*, ll. 53–6; *The Dream*, ll. 20–1.

Epizeuxis (immediate repetition of a word). There are not many instances of this, but we have:

> . . . all, all, some properties invest; . . .
>
> *(A Nocturnal*, l. 34)

also e.g. *The Expiration*, ll. 1, 6–7; *The Dream*, l. 21; *Community*, ll. 2, 12.

Exclamatio (Ekphonesis) (an exclamatory word or phrase). Donne uses this figure a good deal in these poems, especially in phrases containing the word 'oh', e.g.:

> Send home my long-stray'd eyes to me,
> Which, oh too long, have dwelt on thee; . . .
>
> *(The Message*, ll. 1–2)

also e.g. *The Legacy*, l. 24; *The Flea*, ll. 9, 10; *A Jet Ring Sent*, ll. 6, 12; *Love's Deity*, ll. 22–3; *The Broken Heart*, ll. 9–10; *The Relic*, l. 31; *The Ecstasy*, ll. 49–50; *A Lecture upon the Shadow*, l. 24; *Witchcraft by a Picture*, ll. 5–7; *Love's Alchemy*, l. 6.

Oxymoron (a phrase containing two at least apparently contradictory words). Donne uses it very little in these poems, despite his love of paradox. We have:

> . . . unkindly kind, . . .
>
> *('Sweetest love'*, l. 27)

. . . sweet salt . . .

(*Witchcraft by a Picture*, l. 8, and *The Anniversary*, l. 16)

also e.g. *The Ecstasy*, l. 74; and possibly *The Sun Rising*, l. 15.

Parembole (the insertion of relevant material parenthetically into the course of speaking). This is used frequently in the *Songs and Sonets*, e.g.:

> When I died last (and, dear, I die
> As often as from thee I go), . . .
>
> (*The Legacy*, ll. 1–2)

also e.g. *The Undertaking*, ll. 10–11; *A Valediction: of my name*, l. 14; *The Dream*, l. 14; *A Valediction: forbidding mourning*, l. 14; *The Ecstasy*, ll. 15–16, 25–6; *The Dissolution*, l. 12; *Farewell to Love*, ll. 12, 24–5; *The Anniversary*, ll. 14, 18.

Parison (a sequence of phrases, clauses, or sentences, of similar structure). The figure occurs very frequently in these poems, as indeed also in Euphuistic writing. It gives the impression of tight intellectual control, and lends itself to displays of wit. A good instance is:

> Go and catch a falling star,
> 　　Get with child a mandrake root,
> Tell me where all past years are,
> 　　Or who cleft the Devil's foot,
> Teach me to hear mermaids singing,
> 　　Or to keep off envy's stinging . . .
>
> ('Go and catch', ll. 1–6)

also e.g. *The Blossom*, stanzas 1 and 2; *The Sun Rising*, ll. 5–8; *The Will*, ll. 48–51; *Love's Alchemy*, ll. 3–5; *The Dream*, ll. 15–18, 29; *The Canonization*, ll. 11–15; *The Curse*, l. 8; *The Ecstasy*, ll. 31–2; *Community*, ll. 20–1; *The Legacy*, ll. 6, 19–20; *Air and Angels*, l. 3; 'Sweetest love', ll. 22–3; *Lovers' Infiniteness*, ll. 3–4.

Paronomasia (the use of words similar in sound but different in meaning, in some phrase, line, clause or sentence). This figure is used quite often in these poems, with varying effects:

> So, in forgetting, thou rememb'rest right,
> 　　And, unawares, to me shalt write.
> 　　　　(*A Valediction: of my name*, ll. 59–60)

also e.g. *The Blossom*, l. 12; *The Canon. tion*, l. 28; *The Paradox*, ll. 13–14; *A Fever*, ll. 21–2; *The Anniversary*, l. 19; *The ˙rse*, ll. 3, 23–4; *Love's Exchange*, l. 7; 'Sweetest love', l. 27; *Love's Deity*, l. 24.

Periphrasis (substitution of an explanatory phrase for a word). I mention this figure only to indicate that it is virtually absent from these poems; which are marked by condensation rather than rarefaction!

Ploce (repeating a word in the same phrase, line, clause, or sentence, for play or emphasis). This is very frequently used, e.g.:

> If they be two, they are two so
> As stiff twin compasses are two. . . .
> (*A Valediction: forbidding mourning*, ll. 25–6)

also e.g. ibid., ll. 35–6; *The Dream*, ll. 10, 15–18, 20, 21, 23; *Woman's Constancy*, ll. 12–13; *The Will*, ll. 7–8, 16, 25, 34–5, 52; *Negative Love*, ll. 13–15; *A Nocturnal*, l. 19; *The Anniversary*, ll. 21–4; 'Sweetest love', ll. 25–6; *Community*, ll. 1–2, 12; *Love's Growth*, l. 14; *Love's Exchange*, ll. 17–18, 19–20; *Love's Alchemy*, l. 16; *The Flea*, ll. 1, 3, 13, 18; *The Curse*, ll. 3, 13; *A Nocturnal*, ll. 11, 30, 33, 34, 43; *The Broken Heart*, l. 25; *The Ecstasy*, ll. 26, 54–6, 59; *Air and Angels*, ll. 24–5.

Polyptoton (using words from the same root in fairly swift succession, or repeating the same word after a short interval in a different case or inflexion). This figure is frequent in these poems. Like *ploce*, it gives the effect of insistence, e.g.:

> We see by this it was not sex;
> We see we saw not what did move . . .
> (*The Ecstasy*, ll. 31–2)

also e.g. ibid., l. 35; *The Sun Rising*, l. 28; *Twickenham Garden*, ll. 26–7; *The Legacy*, l. 1; *Love's Exchange*, ll. 6–7; *The Anniversary*, l. 9; *The Dream*, l. 15; *The Curse*, ll. 6, 10; *The Will*, l. 47; *Witchcraft by a Picture*, l. 10; *The Prohibition*, ll. 8, 16; *Love's Deity*, ll. 3–4, 7, 14, 21.

Tapinosis (a belittling figure, working either gradually or suddenly). There are a few quite striking examples in the *Songs and Sonets*, e.g.:

> Hope not for mind in women; at their best
> Sweetest and wit, they are but Mummy, possess'd.
> (*Love's Alchemy*, ll. 23–4)

also e.g. possibly *A Valediction: of the book*, ll. 37–45, 46; *Love's Usury*, ll. 5–8; *Break of Day*, ll. 13–18; *Love's Exchange*, ll. 22–8; possibly *A Nocturnal*, stanza 1, ll. 30–6 (but cf. *Auxesis*). Possibly, it might be better to classify both auxesis and tapinosis as figures of thought rather than figures of speech.

It must be emphasized that the list of figures here given is not a complete list of rhetorical figures, but only a list of some of the more important ones; and also that the primary purpose of the list is to show in some detail Donne's evident familiarity with rhetorical processes.

SELECT BIBLIOGRAPHY

Fuller information will be found in Sir Geoffrey Keynes's *Bibliography of Dr John Donne*, 4th edn, Oxford, 1973; and also in the bibliography in T. Spencer and M. Van Doren, *Studies in Metaphysical Poetry*, Cambridge, Mass., 1939, and L. E. Berry (ed.), *A Bibliography of Studies in Metaphysical Poetry, 1939–1960*, Madison, 1964. *The Year's Work in English Studies* reviews leading current work. See also J. R. Roberts (ed.), *Essential Articles for the Study of John Donne's Poetry*, Hamden, Conn., 1975.

I *Some modern editions of Donne's poems (and a concordance)*

The Poems of John Donne, ed. H. J. C. Grierson, 2 vols, Oxford, 1912. (The great modern edition, in old spelling and punctuation, with *apparatus criticus*, critical and textual introductions, and commentary.)

The Poems of John Donne, ed. H. J. C. Grierson, Oxford, 1929. (A plain text, in old spelling and punctuation, with introduction, and sparse textual apparatus.)

Complete Poetry and Selected Prose, ed. John Hayward, London, 1929. (The Nonesuch Donne. Text all in old spelling and punctuation; based on original study of the old editions and many manuscripts; a few explanatory notes. Excellent selection of the prose.)

The Complete Poems of John Donne, ed. R. E. Bennett, Chicago, 1942. (A plain text in modern spelling and punctuation, embodying original study of manuscripts.)

Selected Poems, ed. John Hayward, London, 1950. (A plain text in old spelling and punctuation, with brief introduction, and a few notes.)

The Divine Poems, ed. Helen Gardner, Oxford, 1952; 2nd edn rev. 1978. (An outstanding *editio major*, with revised text in old spelling and punctuation, critical and textual introductions, full *apparatus criticus*, and thorough explanatory notes.)

Poèmes Choisis, ed. and trans. Pierre Legouis, Paris, n.d. [1955]. (A well-chosen selection, scrupulously translated, briefly annotated, and with a full introduction.)

The Songs and Sonets of John Donne, ed. Theodore Redpath, London, 1956. (Text in modern spelling and punctuation, with some revision from manuscripts, introduction, fairly full explanatory notes facing the poems, and select bibliography.)

Selected Poems of John Donne, ed. and trans. J. Fuzier and Y. Denis, Paris, 1962. (A fine selection, excellently edited and translated).

The Anniversaries, ed. F. Manley, Baltimore, 1963. (Text in old spelling and punctuation) critical apparatus, and full commentary.)

The Elegies and the Songs and Sonnets, ed. Helen Gardner, Oxford, 1965. (Carefully revised text in old spelling and punctuation, selective textual apparatus, critical and textual introductions, and commentary: a standard edition.)

Satires, Epigrams, and Verse letters, ed. W. Milgate, Oxford, 1967. (Carefully revised text in old spelling and punctuation, with full *apparatus criticus*, critical and textual introductions, and commentary: a standard edition.)

The Complete Poetry of John Donne, ed. J. T. Shawcross, New York, 1968. (Text in old spelling and punctuation, short introduction, brief glosses at foot of text and a few longer notes at back, highly selective critical apparatus at back, useful select bibliography.)

John Donne: The Complete English Poems, ed. A. J. Smith, Harmondsworth, 1971. (Text in modern spelling, with occasionally modernized punctuation; fairly full, useful notes, with frequent reference to variant textual readings; table of biographical dates, and select bibliography.)

The Epithalamions, Anniversaries, and Epicedes, ed. W. Milgate, Oxford, 1978. (Carefully revised text in old spelling and punctuation, with full *apparatus criticus*, introductions and commentary.)

A Concordance to the English Poems of John Donne, ed. H. C. Combs and Z. R. Sullens, Chicago, 1940; repr. New York, 1970.

This is perhaps also the best place to include a book to which so many of us owe so much: *Metaphysical Lyrics and Poems of the Seventeenth Century: Donne to Butler*, selected and ed. H. J. C. Grierson, Oxford, 1921. (Essay included.)

II *A few modern editions of prose work*

Sermons: Selected Passages with an Essay and Notes, ed. L. Pearsall Smith, Oxford, 1919.

Sermons, ed. G. R. Potter and E. M. Simpson, 10 vols, Berkeley and Los Angeles, 1953–62.

Paradoxes and Problems or *Juvenilia*, ed. G. Keynes, London, 1923.

Paradoxes and Problems, ed. H. Peters, Oxford, 1980.

Deaths Duell, ed. G. Keynes, London, 1973.

Essays in Divinity, ed. E. M. Simpson, Oxford, 1952.

Biathanatos, ed. J. W. Hebel, New York, 1980. (Reprinted in facsimile from the first edition.)

Pseudo-Martyr, ed. F. J. Sypher, New York, 1974. (Facsimile with introduction; otherwise not reprinted since 1610.)

Ignatius His Conclave, ed. T. S. Healy, Oxford, 1969. (Also in the Nonesuch Donne, see below.)

Letters, ed. M. T. Hester, New York, 1977. (Facsimile of *Letters to Severall Persons of Honour*, with introduction. The Nonesuch Donne contains a fair selection of letters.)

Complete Poetry and Selected Prose, ed. John Hayward, London, 1929 (the Nonesuch Donne).

Selected Prose (chosen by E. M. Simpson), ed. Helen Gardner and T. Healy, Oxford, 1967.

On all aspects of the prose works the reader should consult E. M. Simpson, *A Study of the Prose Works of John Donne*, Oxford, 1924; 2nd edn 1948. The modern edition of the Letters on which I. A. Shapiro has long been working, is now being completed by Robert Sorlien, of West Kingston, Rhode Island, USA.

III *Biography*

R. C. Bald, *Donne and the Drurys*, Cambridge, 1959.

R. C. Bald, *John Donne: A Life*, Oxford, 1970. (Now the standard life.)

M. Clive, *Jack and the Doctor*, London, 1966.

E. Gosse, *The Life and Letters of John Donne*, 2 vols, London, 1899.

E. Le Comte, *Grace to a Witty Sinner*, London, 1965.

Izaak Walton, 'Life of Dr John Donne', in Walton's *Lives*, ed. G. Saintsbury, Oxford, 1927.

John Carey's challenging and controversial bio-critical study, *John Donne: Life, Mind and Art*, London, 1981, came into my hands too late for me to take account of it. There have been many articles on points about Donne's life. For these see the bibliographical reference books cited above.

IV *Some critical studies*

BOOKS ON DONNE'S POETRY AND THOUGHT

N. J. C. Andreasen, *John Donne: Conservative Revolutionary*, Princeton, 1967.

D. Cathcart, *Doubting Conscience: Donne and the Poetry of Moral Argument*, Ann Arbor, 1975.

C. M. Coffin, *John Donne and the New Philosophy*, New York, 1937.

H. Faerber, *Das Paradoxe in der Dichtung von John Donne*, Zurich, 1951.

H. I'A. Fausset, *John Donne*, London, 1924.

P. A. Fiore (ed.), *Just So Much Honor: Essays Commemorating the 400th Anniversary of the Birth of John Donne*, University Park, Pa., 1972.

Select bibliography

H.-H. Freitag, *John Donne: zentrale Motive u. Themen in seiner Liebeslyrik*, Bonn, 1975.

H. Gardner (ed.), *Twentieth-Century Views: John Donne*, Englewood Cliffs, 1962.

R. Granqvist, *The Reputation of John Donne, 1779–1873*, Uppsala, 1975.

D. L. Guss, *John Donne, Petrarchist*, Detroit, 1966.

E. Hardy, *John Donne: a Spirit in Conflict*, London, 1942.

M. Hasan, *Donne's Imagery*, Aligarh, India, 1958.

R. E. Hughes, *The Progress of the Soul. The Interior Career of John Donne*, London, 1969.

C. Hunt, *Donne's Poetry: Essays in Literary Analysis*, New Haven, 1954.

M. Jha, *The Phoenix Riddle*, New Delhi, 1972.

J. F. Kermode, *John Donne*, London, 1957.

J. F. Kermode (ed.), *Discussions of Donne*, Boston, 1962.

W. von Koppenfels, *Das Petrarkistische Element in der Dichtung von John Donne*, Munich, 1967.

P. Legouis, *Donne the Craftsman*, Paris, 1928.

J. B. Leishman, *The Monarch of Wit*, London, 1951.

D. Louthan, *The Poetry of John Donne*, New York, 1951.

J. Lovelock (ed.), *A Casebook on the Songs and Sonets*, London, 1973.

W. F. Melton, *The Rhetoric of Donne's Verse*, Baltimore, 1906 (photocopy, Ann Arbor, 1967).

M. Praz, *La Poesia Metafisica inglese del Seicento: John Donne*, Rome, 1945.

M. Praz, *Studi sul concettismo: John Donne*, Florence, 1946.

M. Praz, *John Donne*, Turin, 1958.

M. P. Ramsay, *Les Doctrines Médiévales chez Donne*, Paris, 1917; rev. edn 1924.

M. Roston, *The Soul of Wit: A Study of John Donne*, Oxford, 1974.

M. A. Rugoff, *Donne's Imagery*, New York, 1939; repr. 1961.

J. W. Sanders, *John Donne's Poetry*, Cambridge, 1971.

I. Simon, *Some Principles of Donne Criticism*, Brussels, 1952.

A. J. Smith, *John Donne: The Songs and Sonets*, London, 1964.

A. J. Smith (ed.), *John Donne: Essays in Celebration*, London, 1972.

A. J. Smith (ed.), *John Donne: The Critical Heritage*, London, 1975.

T. Spencer (ed.), *A Garland for John Donne*, Cambridge, Mass., 1932.

E. Spörri-Sigel, *Liebe u. Tod in John Donnes Dichtung* (unpublished doctoral dissertation, University of Zürich, 1949).

A. Stein, *John Donne's Lyrics*, Minneapolis, 1962.

L. Unger, *Donne's Poetry and Modern Criticism*, Chicago, 1950.

J. Winny, *A Preface to Donne*, London, 1970.

BOOKS ON DONNE AND OTHER ENGLISH POETS

A. Alvarez, *The School of Donne*, London, 1961.

J. Bennett, *Four Metaphysical Poets*, Cambridge, 1934; expanded and revised as *Five Metaphysical Poets*, Cambridge, 1963.

Select bibliography

J.-J. Denonain, *Thèmes et formes de la poésie métaphysique*, Alger, 1956.

V. Deubel, *Tradierte Bauformen u. Lyrische Struktur: die Veränderung elisabethanischer Gedichtschemata bei John Donne*, Stuttgart, 1971.

J. E. Duncan, *The Revival of Metaphysical Poetry*, Minneapolis, 1959.

R. Ellrodt, *L'Inspiration Personnelle et l'Esprit du Temps chez Les Poètes Métaphysiques Anglais*, 2 vols, Paris, 1960.

J. B. Leishman, *The Metaphysical Poets*, Oxford, 1934.

L. L. Martz, *The Poetry of Meditation*, New Haven, 1954.

L. L. Martz, *The Wit of Love*, Notre Dame, 1969.

D. L. Peterson, *The English Lyric from Wyatt to Donne*, Princeton, 1967.

M. Praz, *Secentismo e Marinismo in Inghilterra: John Donne, Richard Crashaw*, Florence, 1925.

H. M. Richmond, *The School of Love*, Princeton, 1964.

V. K. Roy and R. C. Kapoor, *John Donne and Metaphysical Poetry*, Delhi, 1969.

T. Spencer and M. van Doren, *Studies in Metaphysical Poetry*, New York, 1939.

H. C. White, *The Metaphysical Poets*, New York, 1936.

G. Williamson, *The Donne Tradition*, Cambridge, Mass., 1930.

G. Williamson, *Seventeenth Century Contexts*, London, 1960.

G. Williamson, *A Reader's Guide to the Metaphysical Poets*, London, 1968.

V *Essays and periodical articles*

Note: I have omitted, for reasons of space, all but a handful of articles on particular poems. A few are referred to in my Commentary. For others see J. R. Roberts (ed.), *Essential Articles for the Study of John Donne's Poetry*, Hamden, Conn., 1975; and other bibliographical material mentioned on p. 359. I have also omitted articles concerned specifically with Donne's work other than the *Songs and Sonets*.

CRITICAL ESSAYS AND ARTICLES

D. C. Allen, 'Donne's knowledge of Renaissance medicine', *JEGP* 42 (1943).

R. M. Alden, 'The lyrical conceits of "The Metaphysical Poets"', *SP* 17 (1920).

J. Bennett, 'The love poetry of John Donne – a reply to Mr C. S. Lewis', in *Seventeenth Century Studies presented to Sir Herbert Grierson*, Oxford, 1938.

J.-M. Benoit, 'La geométrie des poètes métaphysiques', *Critique* 27 (August–September 1971).

L. I. Bredvold, 'The naturalism of Donne in relation to some Renaissance traditions', *JEGP* 22 (1923).

G. Bullough, 'Donne the man of law', in P. A. Fiore (ed.), *Just So Much Honor*, University Park, Pa., 1972.

J. Carey, 'John Donne', *Time and Tide*, 4–10 April 1963.

Select bibliography

W. Clemen, 'Donne and the Elizabethans', in C. S. Singleton (ed.), *Art, Science, and History in the Renaissance*, Baltimore, 1968.

R. G. Cox, 'The poems of John Donne', in B. Ford (ed.), *Pelican Guide to English Literature*, Harmondsworth, 1956.

J. E. V. Crofts, 'John Donne', *ES* 22 (1937).

E. Crankshaw, 'Hermetic elements in Donne's poetic vision', in A. J. Smith (ed.), *John Donne: Essays in Celebration*, London, 1972.

P. Cruttwell, 'The love poetry of John Donne', in M. Bradbury and D. Palmer (eds), *Metaphysical Poetry*, Stratford-upon-Avon, 1970.

H. S. Davies, 'Text or context?', *REL* 6 (1965).

F. A. Doggett, 'Donne's Platonism', *Sew. R.* 42 (1934).

J. B. Douds, 'Donne's technique of dissonance', *PMLA* 52 (1937).

E. E. Duncan-Jones, 'Donne's praise of autumnal beauty: Greek sources', *MLR* 56 (1961).

T. S. Eliot, 'The metaphysical poets' (1921), included in *Selected Essays*, 3rd edn, London, 1951.

R. Ellrodt, 'Chronologie des poèmes de Donne', *Et. Angl.* 13 (1960).

W. Empson, 'Donne and the rhetorical tradition', *Ken. R.*, 11 (1949).

W. Empson, 'Rescuing Donne', in P. A. Fiore (ed.), *Just So Much Honor*, University Park, Pa., 1972.

H. Fluchère, 'Fragment d'un "Donne": Réflexions sur *Songs and Sonets*', *RLC*, January–June, 1976.

A. L. French, 'Dr Gardner's dating of the *Songs and Sonets*', *EC* 17 (1967).

H. Gardner, 'The argument about *The Ecstasy*' in H. Davies and H. Gardner (eds), *Elizabethan and Jacobean Studies presented to F. P. Wilson*, Oxford, 1959.

D. L. Guss, 'Donne and the Greek anthology', *N&Q* 208 (1963).

D. L. Guss, 'Donne's conceit and Petrarchan wit', *PMLA* 78 (1963).

R. W. Hamilton, 'John Donne's Petrarchan poems', *Renaissance and Modern Studies* 23 (1979).

D. W. Harding, 'Coherence of theme in Donne's poetry', *Ken. R.*, Summer 1951.

B. Hardy, 'Thinking and feeling in the *Songs and Sonnets*', in A. J. Smith (ed.), *John Donne: Essays in Celebration*, London, 1972.

J. Hollander, 'Donne and the limits of lyric', A. J. Smith (ed.), *John Donne: Essays in Celebration*, London, 1972.

M. Y. Hughes, 'The lineage of "The Extasie"', *MLR* 27 (1932).

M. Y. Hughes, 'Kidnapping Donne', *University of California Essays in Criticism*, 2nd ser., Berkeley, 1934.

M. Y. Hughes, 'Some of Donne's "Ecstasies"', *PMLA* 75 (1960).

W. R. Keast, 'Johnson's criticism of the metaphysical poets', *ELH* 17 (1950).

L. C. Knights, 'On the social background of metaphysical poetry', *Scrutiny* 13 (1945).

L. C. Knights, 'All or nothing: a theme in John Donne', in R. Gill (ed.), *William Empson: The Man and his Work*, London, 1974.

K. M. Lea, 'Conceits', *MLR* 20 (1925).

F. R. Leavis, 'The line of wit', in *Revaluation*, London, 1936.

E. Le Comte, 'Jack Donne: from rake to husband', in P. A. Fiore (ed.), *Just So Much Honor*, University Park, Pa., 1972.

J. Lederer, 'John Donne and the emblematic practice', *RES* 22 (1946).

P. Legouis, 'John Donne', *TLS*, 21 February 1937.

P. Legouis, 'L'État présent des controverses sur la poésie de Donne', *Et. Angl.* 5 (1952).

P. Legouis, 'Donne, l'amour et les critiques', *Et. Angl.* 10 (1957).

P. Legouis, 'Donne through French eyes', in *Aspects du XVIIᵉ Siècle*, Paris, 1973.

C. S. Lewis, 'Donne and love-poetry in the seventeenth Century', in *Seventeenth Century Studies presented to Sir Herbert Grierson*, Oxford, 1938.

R. E. MacFarland, 'Figures of repetition in John Donne's poetry', *Style* 11 (1977).

J. A. Mazzeo, 'A critique of some modern theories of metaphysical poetry', *MP* 50 (1952).

J. A. Mazzeo, 'Metaphysical poetry and the poetic of correspondence', *JHI* 14 (1953).

J. A. Mazzeo, 'Universal analogy and the culture of the Renaissance', *JHI* 15 (1954).

J. A. Mazzeo, 'Notes on John Donne's alchemical imagery', *Isis*, June 1957.

J. Miles, 'Ifs, ands, buts for the reader of Donne', in P. A. Fiore (ed.), *Just So Much Honor*, University Park, Pa., 1972.

J. Miles, Chapters on Donne in *Poetry and Change*, Berkeley and London, 1974.

J. F. Moloney, 'Donne's metrical practice', *PMLA* 65 (1950).

B. Moran, 'Some notes on Donne's attitude to the problem of body and soul', *Litera* (Istanbul), 1953.

B. Morris, 'Not Siren-like, to tempt', in A. J. Smith (ed.), *John Donne: Essays in Celebration*, London, 1972.

W. A. Murray, 'Donne and Paracelsus', *RES* 25 (1949).

L. Nathansen, 'The context of Dryden's criticism of Donne's and Cowley's love-poetry', *N&Q* (1957).

D. Novarr, '"The Extasie". Donne's address on the states of union', in P. A. Fiore (ed.), *Just So Much Honor*, University Park, Pa., 1972.

R. Nye, 'The body is his book: the poetry of John Donne', *Crit. Q.* 14 (1972).

J. E. Parish, 'Donne as a Petrarchan', *N&Q* (1957).

G. R. Potter, 'Donne's "Extasie", contra Legouis', *PQ* 15 (1936).

M. Praz, 'Donne's relation to the poetry of his time', in *A Garland for John Donne*, Cambridge, Mass., 1931; repr. in *The Flaming Heart*, New York, 1958.

K. Raine, 'John Donne and the baroque doubt', *Horizon*, June 1945.

H. M. Richmond, 'Donne and Ronsard', *N&Q* (1958).

R. Sharrock, 'Wit, passion and ideal love: reflections on the cycle of Donne's reputation', in P. A. Fiore (ed.), *Just So Much Honor*, University Park, Pa., 1972.

Select bibliography

A. J. Smith, 'Donne in his time: a reading of "The Extasie"', *RLMC* 10 (1957).

A. J. Smith, 'The metaphysic of love', *RES*, n.s. 9 (1958).

A. J. Smith, 'Donne's reputation' and 'The dismissal of love', both in *John Donne: Essays in Celebration*, London, 1972.

T. Spencer, 'The poetry of Sir Philip Sidney', *ELH* 12 (1945).

A. Stein, 'Meter and meaning in Donne's verse', *Sew. R.* 52 (1944).

A. Stein, 'Donne's prosody', *PMLA* 59 (1944).

A. Stein, 'Donne's obscurity and the Elizabethan tradition', *ELH* 13 (1946).

A. Stein, 'Structures of sound in Donne's verse', *Ken. R.*, Winter and Spring 1951.

W. Sypher, 'The metaphysical and the baroque', *Part. R.* 11 (1944).

K. Tillotson, 'Donne's poetry in the nineteenth century', in *Elizabethan and Jacobean Studies presented to F. P. Wilson*, Oxford, 1959.

E. M. W. Tillyard, 'A note on Donne's "Extasie"', *RES* 19 (1943).

B. W. Vickers, 'The "Songs and Sonnets" and the rhetoric of hyperbole', in A. J. Smith (ed.), *John Donne: Essays in Celebration*, London, 1972.

F. J. Warnke, 'Metaphysical poetry and the European context', in M. Bradbury and D. Palmer (eds), *Metaphysical Poetry*, Stratford-upon-Avon, 1970.

G. Watson, 'Hobbes and the metaphysical conceit', *JHI* (1955).

E. L. Wiggins, 'Logic in the poetry of John Donne', *SP* 42 (1945).

Y. Winters, 'The sixteenth century lyric in England', *Poetry* 53–4 (1939).

SOME ARTICLES AND ESSAYS MAINLY ON TEXTUAL PROBLEMS

These are listed chronologically so that the reader may more easily follow the controversies.

G. Williamson, 'Textual difficulties in the interpretation of Donne's poetry', *MP* 38 (1940).

C. M. Armitage, 'Donne's poems in the Huntington MS 198: new light on "The Funeral"', *SP* 63 (1966).

P. Legouis, Review of Helen Gardner's edition of *The Elegies and the Songs and Sonnets*, *RES*, n.s. 17 (1966).

M. Roberts, 'If it were Donne when 'tis done . . .', *EC* 16 (1966).

A. MacColl, 'The new edition of Donne's love poems, I', *EC* 17 (1967).

M. Roberts, 'The new edition of Donne's love poems, II', *EC* 17 (1967).

W. Empson, 'Donne in the new edition', *Crit. Q.* 8 (1966).

H. Gardner, 'John Donne', *Crit. Q.* 8 (1966).

W. P. H. Merchant, 'John Donne', *Crit. Q.* 8 (1966).

W. P. H. Merchant, 'Ill Donne: well Donne. Scholarship and para-scholarship', *TLS*, 6 April 1967.

H. Gardner, (a reply), *TLS*, 24 August 1967.

M. Roberts, (a reply to H. Gardner), *TLS*, 7 September 1967.

W. Empson, 'Rescuing Donne', in P. A. Fiore (ed.), *Just So Much Honor*, University Park, Pa, 1972.

T. Redpath, 'Some textual problems in Donne's "Songs and Sonets"', *ES* (1979).

VI *The English and Continental background to Donne's love-lyrics*

For readers interested in exploring European lyric poetry up to Donne's time, either for its own sake, or in comparison and contrast with Donne's work, the following suggestions may be of use. The field is vast, and one needs, perforce, to pick and choose. Besides Classical love poetry (Catullus, Ovid, Propertius, and the Greek Anthology), the work of the Provençal love poets, of the poets of the *dolce stil nuovo*, Dante, Petrarch, the Italian *quattrocentisti* Petrarchans (Cariteo, Tebaldeo, and Serafino) and later Petrarchans (including Bembo, Giovanni della Casa, and Gaspara Stampa), anti-Petrarchans (like Burchiello and later, Berni), the pastoralist Sannazaro, the poems of Michelangelo, the work of Ariosto, Tasso, Guarini and also of Marino (who post-dated Donne's lyrics), may all suggest interesting comparisons and contrasts, and in many cases make worthwhile reading on their own account. Among the French, Marot, Scève, Du Bellay, Ronsard, Desportes, Sponde and Malherbe may prove most fruitfully comparable. As for the Spanish love poets, Boscán and Garcilaso are very different from Donne, and so are even the 'wittier' Lope de Vega, Góngora and Quevedo; but they may all stimulate critical thoughts, besides providing what is even more important – enjoyable, though often tough, reading. In the case of England, medieval lyrics are not very relevant to Donne, but clearly Wyatt, Surrey, Sidney, Spenser, Gascoigne, the sonneteers of the 1590s, and the lyrics in the various anthologies from Tottel (1557) to *England's Helicon* (1600) will be especially worth attention if illuminating comparison is sought. So also will Shakespeare with whom I have, however, deliberately avoided any detailed comparison in this already long book. Rhetorical and poetic theorists, both ancient (Cicero, Quintilian, and the *Rhetorica ad Herennium*) and sixteenth century (e.g. Rainolde, Wilson and Puttenham), have a bearing on Donne's lyrics. The Italian philosophers of love also need to be taken into account, especially Ficino, Bembo, Speroni, Equicola, Leone Ebreo, Varchi, Tullia d'Aragona, and Betussi. Castiglione's *Cortegiano* is, of course, of capital importance in this field. Some glances into Scholastic philosophy, and into the science and law of Donne's time have also thrown light on his lyrics, and may yet throw more.

The following list of miscellaneous secondary works and anthologies may help to open up lines of interest:

D. Alonso, *Poesia española. Ensayo de métodos y límites estilísticos*, Madrid, 1950.

D. Alonso, *Estudios y ensayos gongorinos*, Madrid, 1955.

D. Alonso, *La poesia del Petrarca ed il Petrarchismo*, Florence, 1959.

D. Alonso, 'Poesia correlativa inglesa en los siglos XVI y XVII', *Filologia Moderna* 2 (1961).

V. Altolaguirre, *Garcilaso de la Vega*, Madrid, 1935.

J. W. H. Atkins, *English Literary Criticism: The Renascence*, London, 1947.

L. Baldacci, *Il Petrarchismo italiano nel Cinquecento*, Milan, 1957.

L. Baldacci (ed.), *Lirici del Cinquecento*, Florence, 1957.

B. Bauer-Formiconi, *Die Strambotti des Serafino dell'Aquila*, Munich, 1964.

J. M. Berdan, *Early Tudor Poetry*, New York, 1920.

T. G. Bergin, *Petrarch*, New York, 1970.

M. Bishop, *Petrarch and his World*, London, 1964.

R. R. Bolgar, *The Classical Heritage and its Beneficiaries*, Cambridge, 1954; repr. 1973.

P. Borghesi, *Petrarch and his Influence on English Literature*, Bologna, 1906.

C. P. Brand, *Torquato Tasso: A Study of the Poet and of his Contribution to English Literature*, Cambridge, 1965.

C. P. Brand, *Ariosto*, Edinburgh, 1974.

A. Cecchini, *Serafino Aquilano e l'influenza della lirica italiana sulla lirica inglese del Cinquecento*, Aquila, 1934.

D. L. Clark, *Rhetoric and Poetry in the Renaissance*, New York, 1922.

D. G. Coleman, *Maurice Scève*, Cambridge, 1975.

S. M. Cooper, *The Sonnets of Astrophel and Stella: A Stylistic Study*, The Hague, 1968.

W. G. Crane, *Wit and Rhetoric in the Renaissance*, New York, 1937; repr. Gloucester, Mass., 1964.

B. Croce, *Poesia popolare e poesia d'arte*, Bari, 1933.

M. Evans, *English Poetry in the Sixteenth Century*, London, 1955.

J. U. Fechner, *Der Antipetrarkismus*, Heidelberg, 1966.

G. G. Ferrero, 'Il petrarchismo del Bembo e le rime di Michelangelo' in *L'Erma* 6 (Turin, 1935).

L. W. Forster, *The Icy Fire*, Cambridge, 1969.

D. W. and V. R. Foster, *Luis de Góngora*, New York, 1973.

R. Freeman, *English Emblem Books*, London, 1948.

R. Fromilhague, *Malherbe; technique et création poétique*, Paris, 1954.

J. G. Fucilla, *Estudios sobre el petrarquismo en España*, Madrid, 1960.

E. Fusco, *La Lirica*, Milan, 1951.

G. Grabher, *La poesia minore dell'Ariosto*, Rome, 1947.

A. Graf, *Attraverso il Cinquecento*, Turin, 1888.

O. H. Green, *Courtly Love in Quevedo*, Colorado, 1952.

D. Guerri, *La corrente popolare nel Rinascimento*, Florence, 1931.

D. L. Guss, *John Donne, Petrarchist: Italianate Conceits and Love Theory in the Songs and Sonets* (with excellent bibliography of primary Italian works), Detroit, 1966.

A. C. Hamilton, *Sir Philip Sidney: a Study of his Life and Works*, Cambridge, 1977.

Select bibliography

H. Hauvette, *Les Poésies lyriques de Pétrarque*, Paris, 1931.

J. Jacquot (ed.), *Poèmes de Donne, Herbert et Crashaw mis en musique par leurs contemporains*, Paris, 1961.

L. C. John, *The Elizabethan Sonnet Sequences*, New York, 1938.

E. K. Kane, *Gongorism and the Golden Age*, Chapel Hill, 1928.

J. Lavaud, *Philippe Desportes*, Paris, 1936.

R. Lebègue, *Ronsard, l'homme et l'œuvre*, Paris, 1950.

R. Lebègue, *La poésie française de 1560 à 1630*, Paris, 1951.

S. Lee, *Elizabethan Sonnets*, 2 vols, Westminster, 1903.

Leone Ebreo, *Dialoghi d'amore*, ed. S. Caramella, Bari, 1929. English trans. as *The Philosophy of Love*, by F. Friedeberg-Seeley and J. H. Barnes, London, 1937.

J. W. Lever, *The Elizabethan Love Sonnet*, London, 1956.

C. S. Lewis, *The Allegory of Love*, Oxford, 1936; repr. London, 1953.

C. S. Lewis, *English Literature in the Sixteenth Century, Excluding Drama*, Oxford, 1954.

G. de Lisa, *Un rimatore cortegiano del Quattrocento* [Tebaldeo], Salerno, 1928.

V. Mariani, *La Poesia di Michelangelo*, Rome, 1940.

H. A. Mason, *Humanism and Poetry in the Early Tudor Period*, London, 1959.

G. Mazzoni, *Il petrarchismo e il bembismo dei lirici del Cinquecento*, Milan, 1894.

W. Mönch, *Das Sonett: Gestalt u. Geschichte*, Heidelberg, 1955.

O. de Mourgues, *Metaphysical, Baroque and Précieux Poetry*, Oxford, 1953.

K. Muir, *Life and Letters of Sir Thomas Wyatt*, Liverpool, 1963.

J.-A. Muñoz-Rojas, 'Un libro español en la biblioteca de Donne' [G. Gracian's *Josefina*], *Rev. de Filol. Esp.* 25 (1941).

E. Percopò (ed.), *Le Rime di Benedetto Gareth detto il Cariteo* (with introd.), Naples, 1892.

D. L. Peterson, *The English Lyric from Wyatt to Donne*, Princeton, 1967.

M. Piéri, *Pétrarque et Ronsard*, Marseilles, 1895.

H. Pyritz, *Paul Flemings Liebeslyrik – Zur Geschichte des Petrarkismus*, 1932; repr. Göttingen, 1963.

A. E. Quaglio, *Francesco Petrarca*, Milan, 1967.

A. Ronda, *Un poeta di corte della seconda metà del XV secolo* [Serafino Aquilano], Aquila, 1923.

V. Rossi, *Il Quattrocento*, Milan, 1933.

F. Ruchon and A. Boase, *La vie et l'œuvre de Jean de Sponde*, Geneva, 1949.

M. Santoro, *Pietro Bembo*, Naples, 1937.

V. Saulnier, *Du Bellay*, Paris, 1951.

S. Scheid, *Petrarkismus in Lope de Vegas Sonetten*, Wiesbaden, 1966.

G. G. Smith, *Elizabethan Critical Essays*, 2 vols, Oxford, 1904; repr. 1937.

P. M. Smith, *Clément Marot*, London, 1970.

B. T. Sozzi, *Petrarca*, Palermo, 1963.

G. Spagnoletti, *Il Petrarchismo*, Milan, 1959.

J. E. Stevens, *Music and Poetry in the Early Tudor Court*, London, 1961.

Select bibliography

P. Thomson, *Sir Thomas Wyatt and his Background*, London, 1964.

G. Toffanin, *Il Cinquecento*, Milan, 1935.

R. Tuve, *Elizabethan and Metaphysical Imagery*, Chicago, 1947.

J. Vianey, *Le Pétrarquisme en France au Seizième Siècle*, Montpellier, 1909.

B. W. Vickers. *Classical Rhetoric in Engish Poetry*, London, 1970.

M. Vinciguerra, *Interpretazione del Petrarchismo*, Turin, 1926.

A. Virgili, *Francesco Berni*, Florence, 1881.

G. Watson, *The English Petrarchans: A Critical Bibliography of the 'Canzoniere'*, London, 1967.

E. H. Wilkins, *Studies in the Life and Works of Petrarch*, Cambridge, Mass., 1955 (especially the short sketch of European Petrarchism in ch. 12).

G. Zonta (ed.), *Trattati d'amore del Cinquecento*, Bari, 1912.

INDEX OF TITLES

371

INDEX OF FIRST LINES

373